Hollywood Sports Movies and the American Dream

Hollywood Sports Movies and the American Dream

Grant Wiedenfeld

OXFORD
UNIVERSITY PRESS

OXFORD
UNIVERSITY PRESS

Oxford University Press is a department of the University of Oxford. It furthers
the University's objective of excellence in research, scholarship, and education
by publishing worldwide. Oxford is a registered trade mark of Oxford University
Press in the UK and certain other countries.

Published in the United States of America by Oxford University Press
198 Madison Avenue, New York, NY 10016, United States of America.

Library of Congress Cataloging-in-Publication Data
Names: Wiedenfeld, Grant, author.
Title: Hollywood sports movies and the American dream / Grant Wiedenfeld.
Description: New York : Oxford University Press, 2022. |
Includes bibliographical references and index.
Identifiers: LCCN 2021046213 (print) | LCCN 2021046214 (ebook) |
ISBN 9780197624920 (hardcover) | ISBN 9780197624937 (paperback) |
ISBN 9780197624951 (epub) | ISBN 9780197624968 | ISBN 9780197624944
Subjects: LCSH: Sports films—History and criticism. |
Motion pictures—United States—History—20th century. | Sports in motion pictures. |
Sports in popular culture. | Motion pictures—Political aspects—United States. |
Popular culture—United States—History—20th century. |
Sports—Social aspects—United States. | United States—Politics and government—20th century.
Classification: LCC PN1995.9.S67 W53 2022 (print) | LCC PN1995.9.S67 (ebook) |
DDC 791.43/655—dc23
LC record available at https://lccn.loc.gov/2021046213
LC ebook record available at https://lccn.loc.gov/2021046214

DOI: 10.1093/oso/9780197624920.001.0001

1 3 5 7 9 8 6 4 2

Paperback printed by Marquis, Canada
Hardback printed by Bridgeport National Bindery, Inc., United States of America

Contents

Acknowledgments

I would like to warmly acknowledge all the support that I have received in the course of this project. My interest in the subject began when I was a graduate student and lecturer at Yale University. Colleagues in the departments of Comparative Literature, Film & Media Studies, and English who gave special encouragement and read early drafts were Dudley Andrew, Haun Saussy, Francesco Casetti, Kathryn Lofton, Chloe Taft, Marika Knowles, Joshua Sperling, and Masha Shpolberg. At Sam Houston State University, Mass Communication Department Chair Jean Bodon, College of Arts and Media Dean Ronald Shields, and many colleagues have helped pull the oars. The editorial assistance of Sally Shafto, Dana Benelli, Prachi Vashisht, and Bobby Smiley was pivotal. I received useful feedback from Dominic Lash, Diana Lemberg, Kara Felt, Mathis Mayo, Jen Cooper, and several anonymous reviewers. To my family and friends who cheered me onward I am sincerely thankful.

A number of organizations have supported the development of this project. Sam Houston State University awarded the project an internal research grant. The *Rocky* chapter expands upon a paper presented at the SECAC conference (formerly Southeastern College Art Conference) and then developed into an article published in *Critical Studies in Media Communication*. Chapters on *Slap Shot*, *The Natural*, and *A League of Their Own* were developed from papers presented at the Society of Cinema and Media Studies' annual conference in panels organized by Michael Dwyer, David Melbye, and Gerald Sim, respectively. The chapters on *White Men Can't Jump* and on *Ali* derive from papers presented at the American Studies Association of Texas' annual conference, organized by Barbara Miles. One SCMS conference seminar on genre study, co-organized with Annie Berke, and another seminar on "Cinéma/idéologie/critique," organized by Daniel Fairfax and Elif Sendur, helped develop my thinking on those subjects.

Above all, my work builds upon the estimable writers cited and criticized in the pages that follow.

1

Introduction

America's Civic Screen

"The royal treatment I am getting makes me feel like the first Black president of the United States," declared Muhammad Ali on December 9, 1974.[1] Seven years after he was convicted for draft evasion, the U.S. political establishment was crowning Ali a national hero. In Zaire he had stunned the world by unexpectedly knocking out George Foreman and had thus regained the titles stripped from him years earlier. Now New York City was celebrating "Muhammad Ali Day" with an eight-hour motorcade and a medal presentation at City Hall.

The red carpet rolled all the way to the nation's capital. In the White House he joked with President Gerald Ford, a Republican: "You made a big mistake letting me come here, because now that I see it, I'm going to have to run for your job."

Ford, who had been a star athlete in college himself, replied in jest, "Sometimes, with the problems I have, I think you can have it."[2] Their good humor, captured in Figures 1.1 and 1.2, seems to laugh off the hostility of the 1960s.

Book and movie deals for Ali soon followed. Toni Morrison edited Ali's autobiography *The Greatest: My Own Story*, which quickly became a bestseller in 1975. (Before becoming the nation's premiere novelist, Morrison had shepherded a wave of Black culture and Black American authors through Random House.[3]) Columbia Pictures then launched a movie version that starred Ali himself in the title role, with up-and-coming Black filmmaker Bill Gunn adapting the screenplay. They had reason to expect success on par with Alex Haley's novel *Roots*—its adaptation into a television miniseries set ratings records in 1977.[4] As blaxploitation cinema gave way to mature expressions of African-American culture, Ali's comeback story promised to bridge many divides.[5]

At this moment sports movies were also becoming Hollywood's latest craze. Across the second half of the twentieth century, American sports culture flourished everywhere: television, illustrated magazines, youth programs, municipal stadium building, fitness fads, apparel and equipment manufacturing, and now the movies. The millions earned by football farce *The Longest Yard* (1974) signaled the genre's development from racing and Kung Fu movies to more conventional sports subjects. There could be no better testament to popular success than the condemnation of highbrow critic Andrew Sarris, who tried to argue "Why Sports Movies Don't Work" in 1980.[6] Despite his judgment, the sports genre would become a staple comparable to the western and the musical in their heyday.

Hollywood Sports Movies and the American Dream. Grant Wiedenfeld, Oxford University Press. © Oxford University Press 2022. DOI: 10.1093/oso/9780197624920.003.0001

Figures 1.1–1.2 Muhammad Ali and Gerald Ford pretend to glare at one another competitively before erupting in laughter during the heavyweight champion's 1974 visit to the White House. Courtesy, Gerald R. Ford Library.

Yet amid the commercial sports boom, Ali's boxing peak, and a national climate of reconciliation, it was Sylvester Stallone's *Rocky* that triumphed on the big screen. While the real champion's movie project stumbled and failed to draw a large audience, *Rocky* (1976) became a phenomenal blockbuster and won the Academy Award for Best Picture. The divergent outcomes thus pose an intriguing historical question: Why did *Rocky* flourish far beyond expectations while *The Greatest* flopped under roughly the same circumstances?

The first way to explain the disparity is artistic quality. With the freedom of fiction to embody dramatic archetypes, *Rocky* weaves together a love story and a boxing folk tale. Director John Avildsen surrounds young Stallone with a talented supporting cast and coaxes a certain charm from him. Bill Conti's phenomenal score and Garrett Brown's Steadicam top it off with a novel style. In contrast, Ali's biopic struggles to condense four hundred pages around a central thread. A life lived through changing political situations with multiple marriages cannot conform to dramatic convention. Nor can the heterogeneousness of Morrison's collage-style book and Gunn's indie films translate to a popular movie form, especially with a nonprofessional actor in the lead. George Benson's excellent song "The Greatest Love of All" is relegated to the opening and closing credits, not integrated into the score. The cinematography offers little more than the usual house style. It did not help that director Tom Gries passed away suddenly during the production and that Gunn was replaced.[7] Clearly, a gap in artistic quality exists between the two films.

Rocky is nonetheless no *Citizen Kane*, and Stallone no Brando. Initial critics perceived a small picture at risk of being oversold and were surprised when it won Best Picture over evidently more sophisticated films: *Taxi Driver*, *Network*, *All the President's Men*, and *Bound for Glory*. *Rocky*'s internal artistic qualities cannot alone explain its phenomenal success. In truth, Stallone's seemingly simple and uplifting story better captured the zeitgeist of 1970s America. We must therefore reconsider this context.

The rising conservative movement offers a second explanation. Many critics have perceived the aura of Ronald Reagan in Rocky Balboa, especially after the Republican president hailed Stallone's film *Rambo* in 1985.[8] From this point of view, *Rocky*'s hard body signals the backlash to feminism, his success story favors the Protestant work ethic over the welfare state, and his underdog character channels White ethnic resentment over minority advancement. Indeed, his adversary Apollo Creed is a character clearly based on Muhammad Ali. It is significant that *Rocky* pits a fictional white hero against a black villain while *The Greatest* features a real-life Black hero oppressed by a White establishment. Despite the official successes of Black and Latino athletes in the United States, Hollywood studios turned away from minority subjects by the late 1970s. The NAACP even threatened boycotts in 1982 if minority representation were not improved.[9] The fate of these two films could therefore be said to reflect the conservative backlash to the 1960s that was taking hold at the time. *The Greatest* was the last mainstream Black movie produced for a decade, while white stars featured prominently in the rising sports genre and in the general revival of Hollywood blockbusters led by *Jaws* (1975) and *Star Wars* (1977).[10] Although an African-American champion like Ali earned presidential respect, the nation's symbolic heroes still defaulted to European-American models.

While there is truth to this gloss, it struggles to account for subsequent developments. It is well known that 1990s Hollywood embraced Black subjects, minority stars, and liberal themes. Among sports movies, for instance, Wesley Snipes and Rosie Perez share the marquee with Woody Harrelson in *White Men Can't Jump* (1992); star athlete Michael Jordan had no trouble finding movie success with *Space Jam* (1996); and Denzel Washington took the lead in *He Got Game* (1998), *The Hurricane* (1999), and *Remember the Titans* (2000). Ali was chosen to be the nation's ultimate torchbearer at the 1996 Atlanta Olympic Games; the following year at the Academy Awards he again climbed onto the national stage to grand acclaim when Leon Gast's *When We Were Kings* (1996), which recounts Ali's 1974 fight against Foreman, won Best Documentary. Thus a conservative backlash account of the late 1970s would demand an account of liberal reversal by the 1990s. Historical understanding does not go deep enough if each electoral cycle marks a reversal.

The slow progress of anti-racism offers a third explanation for the disparity between *Rocky* and *The Greatest*. From this angle, the 1977 Ali biopic was ahead of its time for popular cinema despite the boxer's acceptance in other spheres of American culture. Meanwhile *Rocky* offered more social unity and artistry; the genre's white heroes simply reflected the conventions of the time, not any special racism. The fact that Apollo Creed becomes an ally in *Rocky III* (1982) and *Rocky IV* (1985), and that his son becomes the franchise hero with Ryan Coogler's reboot *Creed* (2015), supports this picture of incremental progress. Hollywood's upbeat stories reflect a confidence in such liberal growth.

Yet this story makes increasing diversity appear inevitable, as if racism and discrimination fall away like autumn leaves. It cannot easily explain why change happens in the 1990s rather than the 1970s, or why the process spans three decades. And if one dismisses diversity on screen as a mere illusion of progress, one abandons empirical observation entirely. Deterministic views of either progress or regress exclude the free will of artists and audiences alike.

Neither artistic quality, conservative backlash, nor gradual progress fully accounts for the different receptions of Ali and Rocky in late 1970s cinema and the changes in the decades that followed. To better understand this era of the United States requires study in greater depth.

Sports movies offer a particularly telling set of tarot cards, in a way comparable to the western. The Old West served as a mythic setting in the national imagination for much of the twentieth century. Robert Pippin elucidates how the Hollywood genre furnished allegories of political foundation.[11] For instance, *The Man Who Shot Liberty Valence* (1962) depicts the transition from the martial virtues of honor and glory to bourgeois, domestic virtues under the rule of law. The same themes course through sports movies in another way. Rather than a mythic setting, sports are a mythic activity embedded in quotidian settings.[12] Typified by a dramatic structure that parallels on- and off-field plots, Hollywood sports movies explore the ongoing tension between competitive and egalitarian values in American life. The modern sports genre emerges in the aftermath of the Vietnam War and the national conflict over civil rights. Tending to sentimental comedy more than epic, these inward-looking tales concern spiritual revival. Where the western looked back to origins, sports movies express the prophecy of the American dream for an evolving nation. Like Pippin's, the object of this study is the political mind of the United States as seen through the prism of genre films.[13]

A closer look at six sports movies will discover signs of democracy's subtle evolution in America. Chronologically arranged chapters examine in detail *Rocky* (1976), *Slap Shot* (1977), *The Natural* (1984), *White Men Can't Jump* (1992), *A League of Their Own* (1992), and *Ali* (2001). From these intuitively selected works emerge three themes that characterize the era generally. The virtue of community prevails over individual victory in every case, speaking to the importance of the people and their fundamental equality. This theme challenges accounts of a conservative era centered on individual success. However, a crisis of confidence in civic institutions raises a concern that has been widely overlooked. Multiculturalism, meanwhile, follows an ambivalent path—first taking hold in the representation of white minorities before circling back to women and African-American subjects. A concluding glimpse of the political controversy that surrounded Colin Kaepernick and the Black Lives Matter movement in the 2010s offers a point of comparison to the 1970s. Approaching Hollywood cinema with a focus on civic communities, institutions, and inclusion shines a new light on the meaning of the American dream.

Readers eager for that story to unfurl are advised to jump to the next chapter. What follows here is a discussion of popular culture's relationship to politics. More than a personal take on a few movies, this investigation will ground interpretation in a certain philosophical perspective. Centered on Hannah Arendt, my approach differs from prior studies of the subject that were oriented by the Frankfurt School. This introduction will underline the need for an alternative approach and contrast how each one frames the political significance of popular culture.

The Politics of Affirmation

These Hollywood movies have been studied before (*Rocky* extensively), but their democratic themes of equality and progress have been disregarded by previous scholars. Academic criticism is disciplined by interpretive method—that is to say, philosophical principles that guide judgment of an artwork's meaning. For this popular subject, the principle that affirmation spoils progress appears pivotal.

For instance, in his study *Sport and Film*, Seán Crosson writes that *The Jackie Robinson Story*, *The Blind Side*, *Rocky*, and *The Fighter* all share "the utopian sensibility that both sport and film, as popular forms of entertainment, invoke, a sensibility that may ultimately obscure and mislead audiences regarding the issues touched upon within the films themselves, including race and social class."[14] Echoing Frederic Jameson, Crosson asserts that the happy ending soothes all sociopolitical complications.[15]

Aaron Baker likewise criticizes 1990s Hollywood movies with Black stars that pretend to represent multicultural progress, like *White Men Can't Jump*: "Such films reaffirm the values of whiteness that still dominate American culture despite the commodification of blackness and present what Stuart Hall calls 'a difference that doesn't make a difference of any kind.'"[16] Baker argues that emphasis on individual performance and a transparent mode of representation flatten out the racial and economic difference that should be recognized. Black independent films present more of the difference he considers important, while Hollywood movies affirm a conservative tradition of White dominance.

Robin Wood lobs a similar criticism at Hollywood's early gay movies, *Making Love* (1982), *Victor/Victoria* (1982), or the running film *Personal Best* (1982), whose subject would seem to represent a significant historical step. "Certainly there are positive things to be said, and I shall say these first; ultimately, however, the constraints within which the films operate seem more illuminating than the superficial advances in frankness and liberalism. Apparently representing the only progressive trend in 1980s Hollywood cinema, the films in fact belong very much to their period and constitute no real anomaly, paradox, or problem."[17] Wood implies that a film must present a real paradox to make a significant difference because affirmation conserves the status quo.

I have cut across the differences among these critics to bring into view a school of thought centered on negation. Its basic features appear in Max Horkheimer and Theodor Adorno's chapter on "The Culture Industry: Enlightenment as Mass Deception" in their opus *Dialectic of Enlightenment* (1944). Their argument that the "culture industry" inhibits democracy by conforming the masses and that negation is necessary to counteract it has become widely influential.

Max Horkheimer became the director of the Institute for Social Research, from which the Frankfurt School of Critical Theory developed, in 1929. Its cadre included Walter Benjamin, Herbert Marcuse, and Adorno, all of whom emigrated during the Nazi regime. Horkheimer joined Adorno in Los Angeles during World War II, and there they composed *Dialectic*; they would later return to West Germany to lead the institute.[18] Their protégé Jürgen Habermas developed a model of the democratic public sphere rooted in the autonomy formed privately by arts and letters.[19] From that perspective the mass spectacle erodes reason and democracy. Comolli and Narboni's famous declaration that "every film is political" follows a similar approach to the political dimension of popular culture that has dominated criticism in film and media studies.[20] Although postmodern critics (such as Jameson) abandoned the older generation's elitist defense of high art, the principle of negation and the idea of the culture industry remain influential.

The very phrase *culture industry* paints popular entertainment as the manufacture of ersatz culture. Like a public relations arm for capitalism, its cant serves the lower aims of power and profit. "What parades as progress in the culture industry, as the incessantly new which it offers up, remains the disguise for an eternal sameness," Adorno writes. "Everywhere the changes mask a skeleton which has changed just as little as the profit motive itself since the time it first gained its predominance over culture."[21] Horkheimer and Adorno locate the fundamental political problem in a free-market economic system and an instrumental tendency of thought that together dominate the world. The epitome of capitalism's deceptive ideology is the rags-to-riches American dream of individual success. They decry its affirmative expression in Hollywood spectacle and promote resistance through unconventional alternatives and anticapitalist criticism. This school of thought contends that affirmation conserves or deepens inequality and that wholesale negation is necessary for change.

However, that ethic of negation and critique has come into question. Rita Felski locates a problem in "the hermeneutics of suspicion" and has led a drive for more positive approaches to literary criticism.[22] Joseph North also suggests that the critical distance sought through negation has created another version of academic scholarship's ivory tower.[23] Yet their attempts to develop a "postcritical" method based in the reading experience have been insufficient.[24] They recall an earlier countercurrent in film studies whose "post-theory" turn to historical style and cognitive science did not answer an underlying call to collective political engagement.[25]

On a more practical front, the entrenchment of contemporary partisan politics raises doubt that negation, conflict, difference, and resistance will alone drive democratic change. Both right and left apply these central themes of critical theory to their own agendas, indicating that negation may not dismantle capitalism so much as propagate skepticism. Panoramic resistance conserves the status quo through conflict, mirroring the inertia instilled by affirmation.

In my view, Horkheimer and Adorno overemphasize autonomous critical thought as the lynchpin to democratic politics while neglecting civic components. They do not acknowledge that affirmation of egalitarian principles, institutions, and actions are necessary for progress. I develop a competing idea of Hollywood movies as a "civic screen" that can foster democracy through solidarity, recognition, and norms.

My criticism springs from the political philosophy of Hannah Arendt, specifically *The Human Condition*. Her philosophy of public action challenges critical theory in ways that have not been sufficiently elaborated. Contrasts have been drawn before between Arendt and Adorno, whose divergent interpretations of the Nazi holocaust appear to track Durkheim's rivalry with Weber in sociology.[26] Arendt does not take up the question of art and democracy, so I extend her political philosophy through Jeffrey Alexander's Durkheimian idea of the civil sphere. Through detailed comparison, this chapter develops an approach to criticism that will inform the case studies that follow and that will be shown to complement critical theory in certain ways.

Autonomy, Art, and Negation

Horkheimer and Adorno claim that the culture industry erodes the autonomy of the individual, which they consider a "precondition" for democracy. Adorno states this point clearly when he writes that the culture industry "impedes the development of autonomous, independent individuals who judge and decide consciously for themselves. These, however, would be the precondition for a democratic society which needs adults who have come of age in order to sustain itself and develop."[27] Believing that good literature and art are necessary to form rational individuals, Horkheimer and Adorno warn that pop junk breeds a weak-minded mob. They argue that the industry "fetters consciousness" through generic formulae designed for economic ends.[28]

The pejorative label *culture industry* denies its object any of art's key qualities: individual expression, the intricacy of high art, the rebelliousness of low art, the artifice crucial to imagination's free play, the resistance they find in classical tragedy, or the responsibility of art to represent reality and the idea of the good life.[29] Through those qualities art develops rational persons and disrupts the economic system.[30] The commercial industry instead produces mindless "trash" that presents the illusion of culture.[31] In their view, the culture industry causes the spiritual death of art and accelerates capital's exploitation of the masses. Rather than enlightening the world, the industry's pseudo-art plunges it back into darkness.

Horkheimer and Adorno detail the industrial tendency toward instrumental thinking. In carving out a cognitive path of least resistance, mass entertainment turns consumers into drones. "The products of the culture industry are such that they can be alertly consumed even in a state of distraction."[32] Like a drip feeder, repetitive content follows a "recipe" that distracts the consumer while training their nerves like a worker bee.[33] Mass spectacle thus functions as a technical tutorial that coordinates the senses to quick stimuli and improves labor efficiency indirectly. Epitomized now by the action film, "the automated sequence of standardized tasks" conforms worker-consumers in thought and in behavior. "It must cost no effort and therefore moves strictly along the well-worn grooves of association. The spectator must need no thoughts of his own," they write. "Any logical connection presupposing mental capacity is scrupulously avoided."[34] The whole process cannot be described as brainwashing because it does not wash away any particular notions; repetitive patterns discourage the free play of the imagination like a cultural neurotoxin.[35] In this way the culture industry serves capital beyond selling products—it conforms the masses to the will of the ruling class through the power of entertainment. Improving the technical acumen of workers who conform to industry ideology amounts to what Foucault calls "biopower."[36] Deceived by the freedom of choice between, say, Marvel or DC comic-book movies, consumers forfeit their autonomy without being aware of it. No democracy can emerge from so many pawns.

The process is no conspiracy. No cynical masterminds are required because it is driven automatically by the profit motive and by a deep human instinct to control.

Modern industry tends to organize society around it like a Taylorist factory. Pop culture is also yoked by industry's economic interest to control and subdue the masses. Even innocent content creators are swept along by the tides of society's power centers. The path of least resistance alienates us from our better selves.

Moreover, Horkheimer and Adorno perceive the tendency to instrumental thought in all intellectual and social forms. The culture industry is merely one symptom of the general pull to hierarchical organization. It pulls at society, material production, and our own logic. With a grand anthropological scope, the first chapter of *Dialectic of Enlightenment* traces the origin of concepts themselves to primitive idols:

> Just as the first categories represented the organized tribe and its power over the individual, the entire logical order, with its chains of inference and dependence, the superordination and coordination of concepts, is founded on the corresponding conditions in social reality, that is, on the division of labor.[37]

Horkheimer and Adorno argue that intellectual forms are inherently social forms that consolidate power. The capitalist ideology that serves economic power is merely the latest species after nomadism and feudalism.

Hierarchy even exerts power through formulaic representation in language, drama, and images. Although we always feel in control of our words, discourse consists in patterns with their own momentum. Culture industry clichés and conventions also correspond to a hierarchical social order of owner and worker classes. The containers that limit thought become invisible; even the corporate mantra to "think outside of the box" creates yet another box that is more hidden. The subtle deception of these forms makes people less conscious of their threat. More foolishly convinced of their own individual freedom, the alienated masses become more easily manipulated.

Because Horkheimer and Adorno consider all forms to be inherently stupefying and oppressive, negating them becomes the only avenue to liberation and truth.

They explicate what negation entails through the ancient doctrine of iconoclasm: "The Jewish religion brooks no word which might bring solace to the despair of all mortality. It places all hope in the prohibition on invoking falsity as God, the finite as the infinite, the lie as truth."[38] This passage encapsulates the main thesis of their book—that enlightenment must surpass its own arrogant tendency to misrepresent truth by an endless process of negation. *Dialectic of Enlightenment* takes its title from Hegel, who labeled his theory of logic *dialectic* after the Greek word for dialogue. It characterizes reason as a debate that volleys back and forth, interminably growing through struggle. The negative movement is described as a kind of critical reflection:

> Determinate negation does not simply reject imperfect representations of the absolute, idols, by confronting them with the idea they are unable to match. Rather, dialectic discloses each image as script. It teaches us to read from its features

the admission of falseness which cancels its power and hands it over to truth. Language thereby becomes more than a mere system of signs.[39]

As with iconoclasm, dialectical thinking evidently involves contemplating a representation from afar and with a skeptical eye. Horkheimer and Adorno thus frame the pursuit of truth as an ongoing struggle between positive formulas and their negation.

Art is a primary avenue for negation alongside philosophy. Adorno belongs to the Romantic current of German Idealism that saw art as a stimulant for and expression of consciousness.[40] Based in the body's senses, poetry and the arts counter the abstractions of ideology with the struggle of feeling and experience. Because this current locates reason's development in the individual's unique realization of self, the arts take priority as a playful activity. The Frankfurt School emphasizes negation as the shield that preserves the free play of individual conscience and as critique's penetrating challenge to given appearances. From their point of view, the broader development of reason in society depends upon individual formation through the arts.

However, Robert Pippin demonstrates how Adorno's overemphasis on negation clouds his theory of art. Adorno wants to define art by the nonconceptual so that contemporary art expresses the impossibility of art itself, of instrumental thought's bid for knowledge, and of life under capitalism. But such self-negation leads to indeterminate strangeness and mysticism, forfeiting the artwork's characteristic purposiveness and self-conception. Pippin comments, "he is basically throwing the baby of esthetic determinacy out with the bathwater of a misguided version of hyperconceptualism." (158)[41] Pippin contends that mass culture art retains determinate form, in what Hegel called a sensible-affective modality, even if popular works have less ambition than elite art. This counterargument supports Pippin's criticism of the serious political meaning of certain Hollywood westerns and supports my inquiry in the sports genre.

In sum, autonomy of the self-conscious mind is the epochal issue for Horkheimer and Adorno. An endless process of dialectical negation is necessary to cannibalize the forms that dominate the individual and group, fueling a countermovement of individual freedom and equality.

Hannah Arendt agrees with Horkheimer and Adorno that instrumental thought and individual alienation are key problems of modernity, but she concentrates on a different cause—the dissolution of public freedom. Going further than Pippin's subtle correction, her philosophy puts forth action as an alternative to autonomy and suggests that an overemphasis on private, critical thought can inhibit democracy in another way.

La Vita Activa

Arendt's 1958 opus *The Human Condition* puts action and public freedom at the center of political life. Actions consist in meaningful words and deeds recognized by the public. "Action, the only activity that goes on directly between men without the intermediary of things or matter, corresponds to the human condition of plurality, to the fact that men, not Man, live on the earth and inhabit the world."[42] Actions go hand in glove with a public context. "Men in the plural, that is, men in so far as they live and move and act in this world, can experience meaningfulness only because they can talk with and make sense to each other and to themselves," she writes.[43] Arendt's philosophy emphasizes plurality, communication, and action, in sharp contrast to Horkheimer and Adorno's focus on the individual, autonomy, and contemplation. Her civic humanism breaks from their obsessive concern with control and opens an alternative perspective on the role popular movies can play in democracy.

Human equality and individuality appear in a new light for Arendt. "Plurality is the condition of human action because we are all the same, that is, human, in such a way that nobody is ever the same as anyone else who ever lived, lives, or will live," Arendt writes.[44] First, equality stems from the plural basis of human life. This sameness appears most evident in everyone's agency in interpreting words spoken to a group, or in the potential of everyone to speak to a democratic assembly. Whereas Horkheimer and Adorno situate democracy behind the horizon of individual self-consciousness (which tends to the restriction of participation to elites), through action Arendt envisions democracy as predicated upon the equal assembly of all.

Individuality also comes to be defined in relation to others, not through the isolation of autonomy. The unique difference of each person is set against plurality's background of sameness. Action realizes this relationship through the spontaneous initiation of one person. Arendt calls this quality of individual initiation *natality*, reflecting how birth alone renders each person unique. A person who speaks or acts among others also exhibits difference in their voice, body, and what is said or done. Note how the sense of having *courage* to act or the *virtue* acknowledged in one's character become less martial and sexual when considered through the lens of natality. In contrast to Adorno's Romantic view of unique being as a state of perfection that must be developed privately, Arendt's active individuality is realized by public gathering, initiative, and recognition.

One might object that recognizing action elevates the individual over the group and entails social hierarchy. In reply Arendt cites John Adams, who contrasts the virtue of emulation with the vice of social distinction: "Every individual is seen to be strongly actuated by a desire to be seen, heard, talked of, approved and respected by the people about him, and within his knowledge."[45] The founding father's description agrees with our contemporary concept of recognition. Adams's virtuous emulation neatly situates action in the main current of the national tradition and surprisingly indicates that individualisms oriented around dominance and autonomy diverge from the American dream. Action achieves unity within difference by situating an individual agent among peers who recognize their uniqueness and share the same potential to act.

To Cultivate Democracy

Arendt traces the modern decline of action to an erosion of two key distinctions: between public and private spheres and between animal needs and free aspects of human life. Classical philosophers distinguish three avenues of living: pleasure, contemplation, and action—known in Greek and Latin as *Bios apaulostikos* (*vita voluptuosa*, or life of enjoyment); *Bios theoretikos* (*vita contemplativa*, or life of the mind); and *Bios politicos* (*vita activa*, or life of affairs).[46] Action stands out as the most public pursuit, whereas pleasure and contemplation thrive in privacy.

Arendt reveres the ancient polis as the model for political life. The Greek word for "city," *polis*, is defined by civic affairs—a meaning made evident by its Latin equivalent, *civitas*. Her sense of the political broadens from state affairs to all public events and concerns. Communal assembly and relevant individual action take precedence over economic policy and global systems. Memory of great actions, and the dramatic imagination of possible action, have renewed political importance from this point of view.[47] Contemplation detracts from the more egalitarian public affairs and action that take place in the polis.

Furthermore, Arendt detects a decline in freedom in the shift away from civic life. The rise of the Christian church put a wider emphasis on other-worldly contemplation that distorted the distinction between public and private spheres. She states that "the enormous weight of contemplation in the traditional hierarchy has blurred the distinctions and articulations within the *vita activa* itself."[48] Her study aims to restore those distinctions of *la vita activa* among labor, work, and action. They pivot upon the classical distinction between animal needs and human freedom, with action defined against the body's need for nourishment, reproduction, refuge, and so on, that define labor. *Work* is a middle term that concerns the artifice of things that condition the world of a people, in contrast to the ephemerality of labor and action.

Arendt decries the dominance of economics in political affairs because it is rooted in private needs and instrumental thought. Utilitarian affairs confuse the distinction between labor and action, thereby diminishing public freedom. In ancient Greece *economics* referred to the management of household affairs—*oikos* means home—that consist of private needs. The wall of the estate from the public street symbolizes that barrier. It could be maintained for self-sufficient agricultural estates or small-scale merchants, but consolidation of ever-larger spheres eroded the old distinction between private and public spheres. Monarchy and industrialization favored consolidation and complemented the Christian focus on contemplation, effectively conspiring against democratic public life. Private contemplation and public utility constitute the deeper causes behind the scourges of alienation and instrumentality.

The repair and extension of democracy appear to depend upon three things for Arendt: the revival of public freedom, the subordination of political economics, and the decentering of contemplation.

Reviving public freedom involves a potential to gather and participate in civic life free from necessity. Orlando Patterson describes freedom as a tripartite chord composed of personal freedom, sovereignal freedom to control others, and civic freedom to participate in communal life and governance.[49] Whereas both liberal political philosophy and critical theory emphasize personal freedom (albeit in different ways), republican political philosophy puts more weight on civic freedom. When applied to the individual, personal freedom can be described as non-interference, while civic freedom involves a more modest condition of as non-domination.[50] Shared structures that order society, such as laws, norms, and commerce, may interfere with individual movement without necessarily dominating.[51] In fact, norms are vital to civic freedom. Participation in determining such rules, structures, and norms constitutes the civic component of freedom; hence civic freedom is mutually self-determined and relational in nature, complementing Arendt's theory of action.

Arendt notes the importance of public freedom to the United States' revolutionary thinkers. "The Americans knew that public freedom consisted in having a share in public business," writes Arendt, "and that the activities connected with this business by no means constituted a burden but gave those who discharged them in public a feeling of happiness they could acquire nowhere else."[52] She notes that American usage of the term "public happiness" in the revolutionary era compares to the French "public freedom."[53] That fact changes radically how we interpret Thomas Jefferson's phrase "Life, Liberty, and the pursuit of Happiness" in *The Declaration of Independence*. The modifier *public* would have been implicit for *happiness* at the time; its drift in meaning to a private pleasure has cloaked the famous phrase in ambiguity.[54] Jefferson may have derived his sense of the word from Montesquieu, who wrote, "The love of equality, in a democracy, limits ambition to the sole desire, to the sole happiness, of doing greater services to our country than the rest of our fellow-citizens."[55] The civil rights movement exemplifies this ethic in American history, just as the denial of full civic participation to minorities represents the nadir of public freedom.

The civic republican movement in political philosophy revives Montesquieu and Arendt's emphasis on integrity and public freedom.[56] Arendt's position is also sympathetic to labor protections and social welfare as means to preserve time for citizens outside of utilitarian needs. In brief, the importance of public freedom to democracy is rooted in free assembly, civic participation, and the integrity of institutions more than in personal freedom.

Reviving democracy also involves reigning in other emphases. Arendt demotes social science, especially political economics, because it disregards the distinctions of *la vita activa*. The concept of the *social* treats people as a uniform mass more animal than human, erasing the distinction between private and public as well as overlooking the unique difference of individuals and peoples.[57] Worse, modern economics focuses on social systems of necessity.

In the modern dynamic, systemic thinking dominates public life while freedom is relegated to the private realms of art and religion. Charles Taylor describes how "modern society, we might say, is Romantic in its private and imaginative life and utilitarian or instrumentalist in its public, effective life."[58] Liberal political philosophy exemplifies this dynamic in its emphases on personal freedom and on a neutral state that mediates among private actors. Arendt, Taylor, and communitarian philosophers they inspired seek to reconfigure the dynamic of private and public spheres by restoring the shared meaning and participation of civic life.[59]

Arendt even criticizes the obsession with scientific thinking and technology as a cause of many of the human problems its adherents seek to solve.[60] The scientific point of view steps outside the cosmos to contemplate it from a distance. Such a picture of society abstracts the observer from the plurality of people and abstracts them from the gathering where spontaneous action might take place. Arendt here illustrates how the basic premise of social science performs the instrumentality that she finds at the root of modernity's troubles. Tacitly she agrees that class society alienates humanity, but where Horkheimer and Adorno seek to restore the Romantic individual's holistic being in solitude, Arendt seeks the artifice of public freedom.[61] Social science cannot grasp at the freedom of action and natality because they depend upon chance, which is antithetical to instrumental thought.[62]

Moreover, the overemphasis on *la vita contemplativa* contributes to instrumental thinking and alienation. In addition to physical science, Arendt suggests that philosophy ought not to occupy the central plaza of public life. Influenced by Heraclitus, Arendt appears to challenge Aristotle and Plato's model of the philosopher-king (and the Egyptian model of priestly nobles they inherit). Action does not depend upon the private endeavor of theoretical contemplation. Without being anti-intellectual (her argument itself is patently philosophical) Arendt advocates for civic affairs and action.

La Vita Contemplativa

Horkheimer and Adorno's dialectic negation exemplifies *la vita contemplativa*, in my view, and poses challenges for democratic politics that they do not consider sufficiently. Although critical theory breaks out of classical philosophy's ivory tower through political engagement, its very name indicates a traditional orientation around *Bios theoretikos*.[63] And although a Hegelian might argue that critique goes beyond the privacy of the self, it does not have action's kind of publicness. Their insistence on critique and individual autonomy develops from a philosophical tradition centered on contemplation. That general tradition and their particular elaboration trigger two problems that this section will illustrate: a conservativism oriented around the white male warrior and a skepticism that favors anarchy.

The Prussian tradition of *Bildung* forms a conservative political background to Horkheimer and Adorno's thought. The tradition's guiding idea of stoic self-mastery as the best means of human development is rooted in classical models of discipline. Wilhelm von Humboldt, for instance, admires the ancients because they faced "harder struggles" which elicited "greater and more original energies."[64] He posits individual vigor and manifold diversity as the key ingredients for developing originality and autonomy. Hegel's influential philosophy also revolves around the rigor of *Bildung*. He elevates the struggle of formation to the absolute idea. Indeed, Hegel was commonly considered the state philosopher of "Restoration" Prussia for half a century before Marx and others recuperated his system. And the Romantic current to which early Marx belonged focuses on internal struggle, centered firmly on the individual.[65]

The conservatism of the *Bildung* ethos surfaces in Horkheimer and Adorno's defense of feudal patronage of the arts. They credit noble patrons with delaying the culture industry's emergence: "In Germany the incomplete permeation of life by democratic control had a paradoxical effect. Many areas were still exempt from the market mechanism which had been unleashed in Western countries," they recount. "This stiffened the backbone of art in its late phase against the verdict of supply and demand, heightening its resistance far beyond its actual degree of protection."[66] They favor the last vestige of nobility, high art, as a stronghold of critical resistance against "democratic control"—contradicting their own commitment to democracy.

Their emphasis on art with "backbone" maintains the formative tradition of a noble warrior class. In the same way that weightlifting and competition develop a resilient body, difficult arts develop a critical mind. Horkheimer and Adorno elevate literature without illustration, music with complex structures, and classical art because each poses cognitive challenges absent from movies, popular jazz, and magazine advertisements. Their elitism is self-evident.

Moreover, an ethos of dominance informs Horkheimer and Adorno's case for difficult art and the critical contemplation they advocate. The models of the ancient warrior and medieval knight inform the vision of radical autonomy that underlies critique. Hegel, whose direct influence we have shown already, demonstrates this conservative, masculinist heritage in his description of self-consciousness. In *The Phenomenology of the Spirit* he theorizes the fundamental relationship of unity with difference as the doubleness of self-consciousness: "Self-consciousness has before it another self-consciousness; it has come outside itself."[67] In this mirror, difference involves the ego's struggle for mastery. He describes the double action at play: "The relation of both self-consciousnesses is in this way so constituted that they prove themselves and each other through a life-and-death struggle," he writes evocatively. "And it is solely by risking life, that freedom is obtained."[68] Hegel employs a metaphor of combat to underline the dominance and risk involved in striving for absolute knowledge:

> The individual, who has not staked his life, may, no doubt, be recognized as a person; but he has not attained the truth of this recognition as an independent self-consciousness. In the same way each must aim at the death of the other, as it risks its own life thereby.[69]

For Hegel, the road to truth and pure self-consciousness must pass through this moment of figurative combat. Note that Hegel elevates contemplation above public recognition—a key difference from Arendt's philosophy of action.

Horkheimer and Adorno may criticize Hegel for elevating pure thought over experience, but their doctrine of negation never abandons the autonomy of the conscious mind.[70] Pippin also makes clear that they follow Hegel's philosophy of art in rejecting the softer esteem for beauty and nature that persisted up to Kant.[71] From Arendt's point of view, their reduction of art to critique abandons pleasure and action for pure contemplation.[72] That development ostensibly favors the objectivity of critique to the subjective quality of taste.[73] But one can also perceive the austere influences of Teutonic culture and Pietist, Protestant Christianity in the elevation of pure contemplation over pleasure.[74] Adorno undoubtedly epitomizes that austerity in his rejection of the culture industry.

Critical theory seems to fold the classical and liberalist traditions upon themselves like a self-loathing smart aleck. They criticize the liberal (bourgeois) ethic of competition, personal responsibility, self-reliance, and individual freedom that develops from the imperial Prussian tradition of *Bildung* and resurfaces in American culture. But they do not strongly promote alternatives such as solidarity, equality, and neighborly love. Critical theory instead elevates liberal individualism to a hyper-independent state of contemplation. It is clear that dialectic combat cannot abandon entirely the conservative traditions of autonomy and patriarchal dominance that form the basis of dialectic itself.

In addition, the racist heritage around *la vita contemplativa* also leaves its scent on critical theory. Europe's colonial order contrasted the white race's coldly contemplative minds from the hot, laboring bodies of non-whites. "The primacy of contemplation over activity rests on the conviction that no work of human hands can equal in beauty and truth the physical *cosmos*, which swings in itself in changeless eternity," explains Arendt.[75] "Politically speaking, if to die is the same as 'to cease to be among men,' experience of the eternal is a kind of death."[76] To contemplate such systemic totality demands stepping outside the movements of living into a death-like state of observation. European images of divinity, especially the crucifix, express this connection between whiteness, death, and contemplation.[77] The white knight's characteristic poise and deathly glare also showcase the conservative heritage of *la vita contemplativa*. Hegel's combat metaphor indicates how that tradition bleeds into Enlightenment critique.

We have seen how Horkheimer and Adorno describe the critical distance of determinate negation in a similar way to Arendt's description of contemplation. "Dialectic discloses each image as script" to one who observes representation critically, they write.[78] Physicality is excluded from critique itself.[79] That is not to say that critique itself is white supremacist; rather, contemplation was culturally situated in a racist context for centuries.[80] Not surprisingly, critique became the key to antiracism for both the color-blind mode of acknowledging prejudice and for critical race theory, its unblinded counterpart.[81] Although antiracism is rooted in critical self-consciousness, this mode of thought cannot ignore its own cultural heritage from Europe's colonial era.

Arendt's civic humanism is no panacea to racism, but by recognizing both words and deeds as admirable action she displaces the mind/body dualism that undergirds classical constructions of whiteness. *La vita activa* imagines a way to incorporate diversity that is not predicated on conflict or autonomy. Public recognition, a key component of multiculturalism, recovers its importance in Arendt's philosophy of action. Of course her philosophy is rooted in the same classical tradition; its conservatism surfaces instead around "great man history," for instance. A philosophy of action nonetheless offers some advantages for democratic politics over an exclusive focus on contemplation.

Skepticism's Inertia

Dialectic negation also involves a skeptical attitude that can have conservative effects in political affairs. Horkheimer and Adorno warn that affirmation conserves the status quo, but clearly skepticism can resist reform as much as it resists the establishment. Their discussion of Buddhism illustrates the absolute doubt at the heart of dialectic negation.

In the first chapter of *Dialectic of Enlightenment*, Horkheimer and Adorno criticize the doctrine of nothingness for paradoxically creating a mystical illusion of truth. Naming *nothingness* creates another idol that inhibits the process of negation: "The indiscriminate denial of anything positive, the stereotyped formula of nothingness as used by Buddhism, ignores the ban on calling the absolute by its name no less than its opposite, pantheism, or the latter's caricature, bourgeois skepticism."[82] They criticize Buddhism for not being skeptical enough, comparing its anti-idol idol—nothingness—to a mystical belief in nature's divinity. They make a similar criticism of Hegel for naming the *absolute* as the endgame of the dialectic, claiming that he thereby "succumbed to mythology."[83] For Horkheimer and Adorno the process of negation should have no end. Their iconoclasm is total.

Their criticisms of Buddhism's nothingness and Hegel's absolute demonstrate how the guise of demystification can also mystify anew. The book's title, *Dialectic of Enlightenment*, reflects this central theme. Horkheimer and Adorno theorize how the Enlightenment could have led to the monstrous events of the twentieth century. They primarily attack positive, ersatz truths with negation. But with Buddhism they attack nothingness for rejecting truth altogether because it abandons the struggle of negation. Their dialectic is not a cynical attitude that would permit the creation of new myths. Critical skepticism motors endlessly as a perfectionist quest for truth, never content to accept any one truth or the claim that no truth exists.

The endpoint of dialectic must be *la vita contemplativa*, cut free from necessity, action, or pleasure. In this respect, dialectic relates to Descartes's attempt to base truth upon the absolute doubt. Dialectic negation is effectively a manner of contemplation through interminable skepticism. It is not *total* doubt because it is driven by a quest for truth; *ultimate* doubt better describes its spectral faith in knowledge.

Dialectic's skeptical mindset creates three interrelated problems for democracy. First, it corresponds to anarchist resistance to all authority and institutions that are necessary for representative government. Resisting power must extend to all intellectual and social forms. Such total resistance gravitates toward a Romantic state of nature, illustrated in the contemporary United States by the libertarian fantasy of living off the grid. The anarchist tendency inhibits all collective action except destruction.[84]

Second, dialectic negation lacks the guidance necessary for reform. It mirrors a blind faith in intuition's grasp of truth, doubting things for no good reason.[85] With no limit to the objects of negation, the process can proceed by chance, by habit, or by individual intuition. If guided automatically by chance or habit, dialectic does not necessarily correct the modern scourge of instrumentality. Moreover, if the act of negation must happen everywhere, for its own sake, it becomes esthetic—purposiveness without a purpose.[86] So it may not restore the boundary between esthetics and politics that is another concern of Horkheimer and Adorno. Dialectic proceeding in every direction, spontaneously and reactively, could be considered egalitarian in a weak sense of equal possibility. However, a pure resistance to synthesis and compromise threatens to inhibit any constructive measure. Too, the idea that widespread criticism automatically moves toward truth and justice comes to resemble Adam Smith's invisible hand and liberalism's neutral state, despite setting out to dismantle that model of political economy. In these ways negation conserves the status quo.

Third, dialectic's ultimate skepticism poses a danger of instilling order through a kind of double negation.[87] This effect is seen in conspiracy theorists or, in a more sophisticated form, as counter-ideology.[88] The patina of rebellion can shield certain myths from negation (especially for many people not equipped with the higher education necessary for critical theory). The conservative populism that flourished in the 2010s illustrates how skepticism contributes to antidemocratic action and partisan entrenchment (from the Left's point of view, in any case).

This section has highlighted chauvinism, racism, and skepticism as antidemocratic qualities within the cultural tradition of *la vita contemplativa* that are pertinent to Horkheimer and Adorno's dialectic but not well remarked by them. Redoubling critique can address these problems but is no simple antidote. Furthermore, sharpening autonomy to an ever more acute species of contemplation merely relocates the deep modern problems of alienation and automatism. For these reasons *la vita activa* advocated by Arendt provides a useful and complementary alternative. Action restores a publicness with democratic access and recognition that critical contemplation lacks. The social basis of truth that Kant calls *sensus communis* (common or community sense) also comes to the fore with Arendt's principle of plurality, and provides a useful complement to the negative, private movement of dialectic.[89] Through these civic humanist alternatives the democratic importance of popular culture will become clear.

Having outlined the more abstract differences between the philosophies of Arendt and Adorno, the second part of the chapter will confront the more practical matters of the culture industry as a component of the economy and the civil sphere as a countervailing political force supported by popular culture.

The Economic System and the Culture Industry

Horkheimer and Adorno claim that the culture industry is an instrument for capitalism. "To impress the omnipotence of capital on the hearts of expropriated job candidates as the power of their true master is the purpose of all films, regardless of the plot selected by the production directors," they write.[90] While it is true that the liberal economic system fosters inequality, their deterministic focus on the economic system neglects the counterforce of the civil sphere.

Horkheimer and Adorno consider the media and entertainment sector as a unified whole—one subsystem within the total economic system. "Film, radio, and magazines form a system. Each branch of culture is unanimous within itself and all are unanimous together."[91] Beneath an apparent diversity, extended by new technologies, all media operate unanimously as commercial ventures. Because the wider marketplace integrates all producers and consumers, it forms one total system that fosters inequality.[92] "Free" exchange always favors the side with more assets—as any employee desiring a raise in wages can attest, and as studies have confirmed—resulting in unequal classes of owners and workers.[93] Given the dominance of capital and the dependence of high-tech media like cinema upon investment, it is reasonable to presume that mass entertainment would serve the interests of the owner class.

Many early twentieth-century critics defended mass culture because it offered access that had been antithetical to the fine arts.[94] Based on the idea that the arts form rational citizens and that education is a great equalizer, new technology carried a democratic hope despite its commercial character. Siegfried Kracauer and Frankfurt School critic Walter Benjamin, for instance, make strong arguments for cinema as a democratic art.

Writing in the 1940s, Horkheimer and Adorno adopt a more pessimistic attitude to new technology, to capitalism, and even to socialism. An older generation had seen state-led socialism as a rational bridle for the free market, but various catastrophes led to the despairing realization that capitalism was a pathological realization of Enlightenment reason.[95] Just as the factory increases profit through efficiency and regularity, rational thinking aims for universal concepts applied with logical efficiency. Convenient truths pave over the complexities and struggle of actual existence. In this way economics and popular reason conspire to paint a false picture of the world that hides oppression, inequality, and their own roles in generating those problems. Enlightenment thought is therefore predisposed to corruption by capitalist ideology. The refugees from fascist Germany did not find in the United States a promised land. In so-called liberal democracy, they perceived another instance of an oppressive system dominating human life on the level of thought and imagination. Having abandoned the socialist effort to control the market economy, they favor the development of autonomy via dialectic as a more fundamental bulwark to social control.

Horkheimer and Adorno describe a deceptive ideology, spawned systemically from the interest of capital's owner class, that takes form as "the religion of success." The American dream of individual riches, earned through hard work and good fortune, epitomizes this ideology.[96] Given that an unfair cut of the worker's rewards flows to the investor, this mythic doctrine reinforces the dominance of capital. Although a lucky few ascend, the working class never gains economic power to rival big investors. Presuming that politics follows economics, the inequality of exchange always results in an undemocratic state. The ideology of success is therefore deceptive because it promises wealth to all but effectively increases the wealth of a few. And it violates personal freedom by interfering with reason through the deceptive power of spectacle.

Movies enact a ritual of social dominance for the religion of success. In particular, Horkheimer and Adorno describe how star actors glamorize normative behavior for the masses. "The way in which the young girl accepts and performs the obligatory date, the tone of voice used on the telephone and in the most intimate situations," they continue, "bears witness to the attempt to turn oneself into an apparatus meeting the requirements of success, an apparatus which, even in its unconscious impulses, conforms to the model presented by the culture industry."[97] Promised an opportunity for wealth and power, and seduced by the image of the commoner who found success, viewers conform to the system apparently of their own volition. (Their example of the young girl also seems to make the sexist implication that pop culture emasculates the audience, and that difficult arts are more manly.) Any affirmation reinforces ideology's control. Even works with rebellious, anticapitalist themes conform to conventional modes of representation and therefore do not disrupt the system. The economy operates by the logic of profit, so that the universal motive of inequality permeates all activity, from the job site to the bedroom.

It is worth noting that Horkheimer and Adorno claim that all civic organizations are also subordinate to the dominant ideology. They amount to front organizations for capitalism. "All [people] find themselves enclosed from early on within a system of churches, clubs, professional associations, and other relationships which amount to the most sensitive instrument of social control," they write. "Anyone who wants to avoid ruin must take care not to weigh too little in the scales of this apparatus."[98] One must act right by these civic brokers of power to succeed, it seems. Without requiring direction from above, all institutions and subjects orient themselves around the power of capital through a cult of success.

However, their argument rests on the assumption that the economic sphere necessarily dominates other spheres. Horkheimer and Adorno, in fact, maintain the same priority for economics as the capitalists they oppose, albeit with different attitudes. Hannah Arendt traces this continuity from the Enlightenment's liberal economists to Marx: "Marx developed classical economics further by substituting group or class interests for individual and personal interests and by reducing these class interests to two major classes, capitalists and workers, so that he was left with one conflict, where classical economics had seen a multitude of contradictory conflicts."[99] That single class conflict and the totalizing reach of the market in modern life underlie critical theory and its picture of deceptive ideology in the culture industry. But negation does not develop an alternative as much as it motivates internal resistance. Dialectic therefore accommodates the modern dichotomy between private freedom and utilitarian public life that I described earlier.[100] Albert Camus famously made the point that collective affirmation must accompany negation to overcome solipsism.[101] Likewise, pure negation cannot build political power to upset undemocratic economic interests.

The Civil Sphere and Public Power

Jeffrey Alexander asserts the agency of the civil sphere over the economic system in his 2006 book. This section explicates how the civil sphere supports public freedom and action, and how Arendt's theory of public power supports Alexander's argument in turn. Together they establish the democratic virtues of popular culture, in contrast to the culture industry approach.

Alexander envisions multiple spheres—economic, civil, military, religious, and so on—within a field of mutual influence. He distinguishes the civil sphere as "a world of values and institutions that generates the capacity for social criticism and democratic integration at the same time."[102] Through public opinion, state agencies, and other organizations that compose the civil sphere spring forth forces that can overpower rival spheres and their forces. Alexander develops Durkheim's republican view of democracy as "a dynamic political force" that influences all social spheres.[103]

Solidarity is fundamental to composing the civil sphere, but it has inherently uncivil boundaries. "Societies are not governed by power alone and are not fueled only by the pursuit of self-interest. Feelings for others matter, and they are structured by the boundaries of solidarity," Alexander declares.[104] Feelings of solidarity hold all societies together, but that membership is also defined negatively against others excluded from the group. He describes fundamental "boundary processes" that differentiate *we* from *they* according to various qualities such as language, race, class, abstract beliefs, or historical experience. "The very introduction of particular criteria is uncivil," Alexander admits.[105] Inclusive solidarity entails the exclusion of some other.

For a civil sphere to emerge from an uncivil process of social differentiation requires democratic codes of conduct. Alexander articulates a list of democratic and counterdemocratic codes that he applies to social motives, relationships, and institutions. With regard to social relationships, for instance, a democratic code of open, trusting, critical, and honorable conduct opposes a counterdemocratic code of secret, suspicious, deferential, and self-interested discursive structures.[106] From this perspective, capitalism's self-interest and critical theory's hermeneutics of suspicion each work against democracy. Whereas skeptical and cynical conduct breeds uncivil forces, affirmative and generous structures of discourse foster solidarity positively and thereby reinforce the power potential of the civil sphere.

Arendt's alternative conception of power undergirds the idea of civic agency. In contrast to critical theory's focus on social forms, she locates the origin of power in people gathering. "While strength is the natural quality of an individual seen in isolation, power springs up between men when they act together and vanishes the moment they disperse," she writes.[107] Power is always potential. With this understanding Arendt distinguishes power from the material forces of animal needs and economic interest. The civil sphere therefore has the potential to overpower the economic system as well as the power to structure other spheres if enough people are motivated to gather. Critique can recognize given structures and their conditions, but negation is not necessarily sufficient to assemble anyone. Civic agency springs from power itself.

To outline the different forms that power takes, Arendt turns to Montesquieu. She describes a "moving principle" from which "structural forces of law and power spring."[108] In his theory of government, Montesquieu states that the principles of equality, honor, and fear produce democracy, monarchy, and despotism, respectively.[109] Alexander likewise describes "structures of feeling" that appear to translate such principles to authority on a personal level. Affirmation of these principles and structures conditions the world of a given people, including artwork and action that constitute culture in a continual feedback loop. Rather than understanding power as a necessarily hierarchical form of control, the civic humanist approach unfolds how meaning can shape a world in different ways.

Arendt's study of totalitarianism supports her view of power as people gathering. She shows how both Nazi and Bolshevik ideologies create a divisive atmosphere through mutual suspicion. Pervasive fear isolates all citizens and erodes solidarity in the nation-state, whose authority is given over to a secret police and internal party organizations.[110] Hence the real danger of the totalitarian regime lies in the dismantling of civil society and its institutions, not in its bureaucratic largesse or mass citizenry. In alienating all subjects, the totalitarian regime suppresses assembly, even in its abstract form of public opinion.

Public Opinion

The power of gathering in the civil sphere flows through public opinion. Civic power is not simply a mass of animal bodies. And *public opinion* is a bit of a misnomer, in this Durkheimian way of understanding it, because power is not limited to individual preferences. Publicness is general and conditions life continually, in the background and in the context of exceptional action.

Arendt explains that the world people inhabit is composed of public images or appearances that structure their ability to act. "Power is what keeps the public realm, the potential space of appearance between acting and speaking men, in existence," she writes.[111] Alexander likewise compares public opinion to the "sea where the civil sphere swims."[112] He describes it as a real, non-binding force that structures civil society.

Seen in this light, public opinion transcends the individual. Communication among people who gather can be thought of abstractly as one total opinion that influences everyone. Johannes Ehrat describes it this way: "Public opinion is the opinion of All. It is what *I* think that *All* think, it is what *you* think that *All* think, and it is what *all* think that *All* think."[113] In its positive aspect, what everyone else thinks are shared values that define solidarity and shared images that construct a world. *Everyone* or *All* conceives of people without limit and is therefore felt like divine power. Ehrat illustrates this force as the chorus in Ancient Greek drama. In that ritual, choral singers voice how the gods judge the action, mediating between spectators and the ultimate. Their transcendent power can concentrate upon the figure of the dramatic hero or charismatic leader. As a representative of the divine opinion of All, the figure becomes endowed with a charisma that exceeds their individual capacity.[114] In everyday life one rarely encounters power so concentrated, but it flows continually in the normative background that conditions any familiar world.

Public appearance even determines reality, according to a certain philosophical point of view. Charles Peirce defines real objects as those that "have an existence independent of your mind or mine or that of any number of persons."[115] Whatever all think that All think sublimates from individual opinion and thus becomes real.[116] James Carey echoes this view when he declares that "communication is a symbolic process whereby reality is produced, maintained, repaired, and transformed."[117] This definition of reality follows from Kant's idea that we cannot know things-in-themselves, only things as they appear to us, mediated by sensation and known in thought. His idea of *sensus communis*, a socially constructed basis for general knowledge, complements an understanding of reality as public opinion. Universality is normative and becomes absolute only in the final opinion to which it aspires.[118] In other words, even what appears to us as real and universal is grounded in public opinion.

Paradoxically, the reality of public opinion is contingent. Such contingency would seem to imply that reality can be false, but one cannot feel its contingency usually. Arendt makes the point that human existence is conditioned by earthly as well as man-made conditions. "Whatever enters the human world of its own accord or is drawn into it by human effort becomes part of the human condition. The impact of the world's reality upon human existence is felt and received as a conditioning force."[119] Human reality is contingent because it is conditioned by our own work, public deeds, and great words in addition to the necessary earthly conditions of labor. Popular culture partakes in the work of public opinion that constructs a world.

This understanding of civil society, public opinion, and reality supports the idea that affirmation is necessary to democracy. For democracy to be realized in a public sphere requires that the people have an affirmative conception of themselves as a public and trust in institutions and officials who represent them faithfully.[120] "The *normative legitimacy* and *political efficacy* of public opinion are essential to the concept of the public sphere in democratic theory," states Nancy Fraser.[121] Affirmation is necessary to legitimate civic institutions and to build the democratic power that flows through them. At the mass scale of modern life solidarity must be mediated by institutions, including media of amusement.

The civil sphere clearly involves ontology and metaphysics that differ from critical theory. It would take a tome to explore those implications in detail. Yet, from our perch, several issues stand out. To negate all images produced by mass media, as Horkheimer and Adorno demand, would destroy a common world that is a necessary condition for democracy—perhaps a more fundamental one than autonomy. And power cannot accumulate through resistance alone, which fractures any assembly into so many atoms. The civil sphere and Arendt's public conception of power both challenge and complement critical theory, affording a different approach to popular culture and its role in democracy, one that is more focused on meaning than on materials.

Civil Religion and the American Dream

Discussion of transcendent ideals and the American dream brings us to the issue of religion. To understand the political importance of popular movies, I believe it is useful to consider them as a kind of *secular ritual*—which may appear to be a contradiction in terms. Many Enlightenment thinkers denigrated religion as myth that deceived people from rational understanding. However, Durkheim's broader view of religion as a universal form of social organization invites an understanding of the civil sphere through religious terminology.

Civil religion names the common secular faith and practices of the nation-state. Coined by Rousseau, Robert Bellah revived the term to understand the sacred aspect of secular life in the United States.[122] Presidential inaugurations and state funerals exemplified civil religion for him, while the anthem and flag have become more common testaments to the sacred quality of national symbols and practices—especially controversy around their profanation. Those official symbols and practices could be said to represent the High Church side of American civil religion. Certain aspects of popular culture, especially expressions of the American dream in movies, constitute a Low Church side of the nation's secular faith. Civil religion therefore relates film to national politics in a way that is different from economics, I contend.

Sacred symbols and rituals represent the structures of feeling that bind society together. "A [civil] sphere relies on solidarity, on feelings for others whom we do not know," Jeffrey Alexander writes, "because of our putative commitment to a common secular faith."[123] Even banal objects like a state mailbox carry iconic importance to the nation in the background of the everyday, as Michael Billig reminds us.[124] Whereas a small tribe could be bound by kinship, social groups on a larger scale are held together in a way that is akin to a religious community.[125] Alexander outlines the

anthropological development from participatory tribal rites into cosmological ceremonies that legitimated elite rulers over larger populations.[126] But where the iconoclasts Horkheimer and Adorno stress negation to destroy that legitimacy, Alexander
highlights the shift from despotic religious authority to a secular and civil authority
that has democratic potential. Secular society still depends upon civic symbols, rituals, and dogma to represent the reciprocal feeling shared among strangers in the
group. That secular faith and its symbols then legitimize the state as a representative
of the people. In a republic, democracy therefore depends upon the integrity of civic
institutions and officials in representing the people justly, not upon the negation of all
authority over the autonomous individual.

Alexander asserts that ideals nourish and bind collective life: "People are oriented
not only to the here and now but to the ideal, to the transcendent."[127] He evidently
does not mean transcendent in an exclusively theological sense. The religious term
derives from Durkheim, who located the basis of the sacred in the unity of society
itself, epitomized by what he describes as collective effervescence. Durkheim's discussion of religion in sociological terms departs from an Enlightenment current
for whom *religion* connotes irrational superstition or other-worldly belief. From his
point of view the sacred and the profane structure all social groups, so such religious
language is fitting.[128] Sacredness seems to spring from the collective in the same way
that Arendt sees power as a potential latent in people gathering. Importantly, the
abstractions that structure feelings of solidarity differ from the material gratifications
and interests that take precedence in economic perspectives on social life.

The ideals of a civil religion are multiple and contested. For American civil religion, Philip Gorski discovers two competing currents: prophetic religion and civic
republicanism. The prophetic character speaks to ongoing evolution while the
republican character speaks to pragmatic rules. At their extremes these currents correspond to Christian nationalism and radical secularism, represented by the Bible
and the U.S. constitution, respectively. We have seen how modern culture organizes
these currents into private and public aspects of life, with prophetic belief situated in
a Romantic inner sphere and instrumental logic controlling common affairs. Arendt,
Horkheimer, and Adorno all challenge this modern dynamic. But Arendt's philosophy of action better complements Gorski, who advocates for the synthesis of the
two currents as "prophetic republicanism."[129] The prophetic elements of contingency
and aspiration are vital to action and public freedom without carrying religion's the-
ology or dominance into public affairs. Gorski's synthesis emphasizes a vital center of
shared but ecumenical faith.

The American dream is a central part of civil religion. It could be described as a
myth in the sense that it connotes a theme or scenario that expresses the nation's various tropes and ideals: migration, aspiration, democracy, justice, and so on. Cultural
historians and sociologists have distilled from its many expressions a general hope for
a better life.[130] When fleshed out, that belief associates with certain policies that rule
and guide civic life. The rags-to-riches tale championed by capitalists and condemned
by anticapitalists is simply one influential version of the myth.

A civic humanist interpretation of the American dream depicts an evolving project of democracy in the republic. The emphasis on the republic puts sacred importance on the representative institutions of government and other civic organizations—the agencies of Alexander's civil sphere. Arendt's philosophy of public freedom and action come to the fore with the word *democracy*, which suggests the communal assembly and the happiness of public recognition. By understanding individuality through initiative and relation to others, rather than autonomy, she lifts the American dream from the private domains of contemplation and economics.[131] Moreover, the idea of an evolving project reflects the uncertainty of dreams and their orientation to the future. The nation's original sin of racism, for example, was overcome through righteous conflict. Evolution entails social change through immigration and intermarriage as well as through laws whose reform is guided by foundational principles.[132] The American dream of evolving democracy establishes an aim that transcends material abundance and mere human flourishing.[133] The case studies that follow will discover this understanding of the American dream in a surprising set of movies.

Sacred Sport

Sports in the United States have deep connections to national policy and the American dream. In *Making the American Team*, Mark Dyerson shows that sports were organized in the postbellum era to build civic solidarity through wide participation and through a kind of popular folklore, and to evangelize the rule of law through a "gospel of fair play." Dyerson argues that sports generally had a stronger effect on the "sporting republic" of the United States than classroom or religious education.[134] One can also imagine how those different spheres cooperate, especially during the Progressive Era.

But fair competition is not, in principle, democratic—a point of misunderstanding since the postbellum era at least. In *The Spirit of Laws*, Montesquieu defines monarchy by the competition for honor according to universal rules.[135] Fair competition and meritocracy therefore conform to the motivating principle of monarchy, not to democratic equality or despotic fear. Although fair competition may afford equal opportunities, contests aim to generate unequal outcomes. At the scale of society, that inequality corresponds to a hierarchy of privilege. America's liberalist gospel of competition therefore belongs to an imperial heritage from Great Britain, in tension with a democratic tradition of equal participation. The subject of sports offers an allegorical field for observing that tension in the national imagination.

Since the 1940s sports have clearly grown more intertwined with national meaning. At that time "The Star-Spangled Banner" began to be performed at all public athletic events, and the ritual has not abated.[136] Civic stadium and facility construction for schools, boosted by patronage, has matured into a cycle in which different localities compete to grow bigger and faster. The expansion of athletic activity through exercise, teambuilding, and leisure has reinforced the importance of sports and opened new avenues for sacred practice in secular life. Other ceremonies, like the White House visit for champion athletes and the presidential interview before the Super Bowl, have deepened the place of sports in American civil religion. Controversy around these ceremonies, one of which we discuss in the conclusion, testifies to the importance of sports to the nation's political heart. This study's interest lies in the representation of sports in movies; the game is there subordinated to another civic ritual—drama.

Movies as Popular Drama

Popular movies participate in civil religion and express the American dream through drama.[137] The ancient ritual of drama developed in parallel with the enlargement of states into empires and tightly knit nation-states. The growing separation of actor and spectator mimics the state's growing scale and culminates in the fourth wall of modern drama, Alexander explains. He does not discuss cinema directly, but its screen obviously represents the limit of that separation while its recordings allow performance to cross borders with unprecedented ease.

Dramatic performance communicates social norms. Alexander says that the mass media "create the characters that people civil society and establish its communicative boundaries with noncivil domains."[138] The distinction between heroes and villains corresponds to the fundamental social boundary between *us* and *them*. Beyond characters, popular movies construct the world of civil society in other ways. Nonfiction constructs the actual world overtly while fiction constructs reality implicitly, as a general background of the plausible or by surpassing that limit in fantasy. Aristotle famously described poetry as more philosophical and serious than history for this reason.[139] But both fiction and nonfiction are normative in their construction of reality. For instance, behind the abstract ideas that drama communicates is the concrete feature of the language spoken by the characters. I call movies a "civic screen" because their dramatic representation structures a people's world.

The more public mediums of drama and oral poetry correspond to *la vita activa*, whereas the Frankfurt School prefers the private medium of literature.[140] In this way art may complement entertainment as private and public rites, respectively. In fact, the familiar conventions of stage plays and oral poetry are what make their popular forms widely accessible.[141] The repetitious quality of those conventions is counterbalanced by the ephemerality of performance. New interpretations vary the theme according to the rhythms of social life.[142] Genres, sequels, and series have something in common with the repeated but variable performance of plays and oral poems.[143]

Although most twentieth-century film theorists attended to the literary qualities of the record and the material apparatus, a civic humanist approach redirects inquiry to cinema's public aspect as drama. This approach follows Jacques Rancière's pivot from apparatus to dramaturgy. The French philosopher praises popular Hollywood movies such as Anthony Mann's westerns. By uncovering the complexity of character, situation, and themes of the genre, he draws attention back to the political importance of story.[144]

As a recorded dramatic performance, cinema has one democratic quality that many film theorists have overlooked. The civic screen involves an egalitarian space of performance: whether at the multiplex, drive-in, or home theater. Recall apparatus theory, which extended the culture industry argument by claiming that the technology of cinema itself constituted a mechanism of social control.[145] Because the recording and screen separated spectator from performer more than any previous dramatic art, it was presumed that the apparatus had more powerful means of manipulation and therefore more antidemocratic effects. However, the recorded performance can be seen in another light. By removing the performer from the scene of performance and leaving only their image, spectators regain their own potential to dominate the scene—a capacity highlighted by Stuart Hall.[146] My point is that spectators regain authority within the movie theater because there are no star actors in the building and no nobility in box seats. With the actors reduced to pictures, the projector now mostly automated in a booth, or the screen under your remote control, the apparatus restores a certain kind of civic freedom. Spectators may not interact with the performers, but everyone at the screening now has the same social status.

Home radio and television sets illustrate this strange dynamic. Recall President Franklin Roosevelt's fireside chats that were broadcast weekly on national networks. On the one hand, the voice of the head of state in your parlor has an unprecedented propaganda power. On the other hand, anyone might shout down the device in disgust, ridicule him with laughter, or not pay attention to the background noise of the broadcast as they change baby diapers or play spades. The greater freedom to behave in the performance space is a form of civic freedom. Also consider the ease in entering a cinema or streaming a movie compared to the rigid codes of the legitimate theater and symphony concert, with ushers and assigned seating. Cinema's freedom extends to the interpretive dimension of "reading" the film as well. Cinema veers closer to literature than oral performance in this regard. The social equality of the device allows the spectator to treat the meaning in their own grip. In other words, mass-produced automated recordings have less aura than live performance. Seen from this angle, cinema and television restore a democratic quality to the public ritual of drama.

Now I want to discuss cases where the civic screen does convey sacred meaning. Hollywood movies that express the American dream have special importance in the United States. In illustrating the national ideal, movies exemplify Aristotle's view that fiction represents universal truths, not the actual world. The happy ending, its defining feature, is simply a synecdoche for the dramatic form of comedy. Joseph Campbell advises that "the happy ending of the fairy tale ... is to be read, not as a contradiction, but as a transcendence of the universal tragedy of man."[147] Hollywood's sentimental form of comedy represents collective ideals that transcend the material necessities of labor and death. Northrop Frye adds, with a more practical focus than Campbell, that "the theme of the comic is the integration of society."[148] Hence, popular comedies cultivate solidarity through ideals that transcend and gather the audience.

Hollywood's ideal happy ending represents public happiness and recognition, not necessarily private gain and social power.[149] Among the sports movies under study it is noteworthy how many happy endings eschew victory. *Rocky* and *A League of Their Own*, in particular, evoke a grand sentiment that centers on recognition and egalitarian respect that can be described as public happiness. Horkheimer and Adorno are right to criticize the ideal of individual riches, but they wrongly assume that any commercial product affirms that ideal. From a civic humanist point of view, Hollywood fictions that embody ideals of equality and inclusion contribute to a democratic civil sphere in spite of their ticket price. Sports movies, as we will see, develop themes of equality and inclusion via off-field plots. Many of their heroes are not successful in their on-field competition but enjoy happy endings nevertheless.

As a ritual, comedy gathers everyone in celebration of given ideals. A successful celebration builds momentum for the next event, as any good party host knows. To the extent that Hollywood's popular comedies build a wider and wider circle of solidarity, they support the democratic republic. We must next address what the civic freedom of popular movies means for the hero, and the control the hero has over the audience.

The Hero

Drama's vehicle for solidarity is the hero. But the spectator's relationship to the hero raises a concern with control. Horkheimer and Adorno criticize the Hollywood star for presenting a model image to which viewers are persuaded to conform. The arbitrariness of the everyman hero, they argue, reflects capitalism's deceiving promise that anyone can succeed.[150] An affirmative hero thus becomes a tool for social control. Hollywood's sentimental and epic comedies exemplify such conformity whereas satire, tragedy, or avant-garde forms of anti-drama negate that subordination. This critical judgment again stems from an emphasis on the viewer's autonomy. Identification with a hero threatens the spectator's self-mastery. Forced to conform, the viewer can no longer appreciate the difference and autonomy of others, either.[151]

However, Horkheimer and Adorno oversimplify the relationship of spectator to hero. Northrup Frye's theory of dramatic modes offers a means to gauge the hero's power of action relative to the spectator.[152] And these different modes then correspond to forms of government, in my view.[153] Myth and romance have heroes with divine and magical powers who correspond to despotic and monarchical regimes.[154] Heroes in the high or low mimetic modes are leaders or simply one of us, respectively; they correspond to the republic's representative in more aristocratic or egalitarian ways. The hero in the ironic mode, who has less power than us, performs other political functions such as social exclusion, critical distance, or the anarchist rejection of government. Clearly, not all heroes are common types that invite identification. Hollywood sports movies nonetheless tend to the low mimetic mode, as we will see.

Reconsidering the hero on the basis of *la vita activa* discovers how the spectator may admire the hero without subordination. Drama ideally represents an autonomous action, not an autonomous character. Three democratic relationships can thus form between spectator and hero: general virtue, recognition, and cooperation.

First, the abstractness of the hero corresponds to an abstraction of the virtue that the dramatic action represents. For instance, a person that helps a stranger in need commits a benevolent act that merits admiration. The spectator can relate to that humane act without identifying with any other characteristic of the hero. In fact, the hazy biographies of Hollywood's fictional protagonists contribute to a focus on the action. While it is true that the star's ideal physical features induce conformity, those generic features also strip away identifying characteristics. In the same way that the fashion model serves as a mannequin for the clothes more than an actual person, the movie star is a vehicle for certain virtues.

Second, elevating one person can recognize individual difference in the hero's particular body, situation, and initiative. The word *identification* considers only sameness in the relationship of spectator to actor and thus overlooks the possibility of relating through difference. One may identify with the humanity of the other who has the same presence and potential to act in a democratic sphere, but the relationship to the other's particularity has a different character that might be called simply solidarity or admiration. Recognition is key to multiculturalism because it relates people, paradoxically, through difference.

Third, spectator and hero can relate as participants who cooperate in the same endeavor. Arendt notes that heroes do not author the total action. They are simply an agent who sets change in motion.[155] Therefore, the recognition afforded a hero does not necessarily upset the equality of a community. She notes that the word *hero* originally referred to all participants in the Trojan War, not to leaders or pivotal figures solely. A hero's initiative may prove crucial, like one inspiring charge in a pitched battle, but responsibility for the victory is shared by all participants. The celebration of public happiness can likewise be shared by everyone involved. A *hero* is simply "any person about whom a story can be told."[156] The enacted story recognizes the unique hero's initiative. Championing one person is not necessarily despotic or conformist, especially if that celebration comprehends the equal potential of any person to have acted or to act in the future.

In surveying these three possibilities we can see that the dramatic hero is an ambiguous social object. Admiration of abstract virtues, recognition of an admirable individual, and mutual participation in an endeavor all cultivate democratic alternatives to identification. While it is true that elevating any one person can imply a social mold, identification is not necessarily total or controlling. Furthermore, the civil sphere always involves identification and exclusion, as I mentioned earlier. Its democratic quality depends upon codes of conduct that vary with different texts and contexts. Stepping back from the deterministic view of the culture industry invites a fresh look at popular drama in American movies.

One general comment on race must be said before proceeding. I contend that Hollywood's ideal dramas exemplify democratic action. A hero who appeals to all spectators can maintain difference if universality is based in virtuous action and recognition, not in identity. On these bases the dramatic form of popular comedy favored by Hollywood can accommodate pluralism and minority heroes. And for this reason a diversity of personalities is important to the universality of Hollywood heroes. Without diversity, exclusive identity can take hold despite a focus on action. Diversity is necessary to hold viewer and character together through a common context and shared ideals.

The historical dominance of the Anglo male protagonist in Hollywood movies reflects the gender and racial discrimination that has dominated American culture. That statement contradicts the claim that racial disparity is a consequence of dramatic form. From that point of view, all diversity on screen is superficial because the deeper control of narrative form always fosters racial hierarchy. Horkheimer and Adorno's rejection of all forms as oppressive invites such a claim.[157] They see social form align with discursive form according to an economic impetus to conformity. However, I distinguish the social problem from the dramatic form. (The success of Hollywood films with non-white casts, notably *Black Panther* [2018], has also supported the economic counterargument that white dominance limits Hollywood's commercial potential.) Although Hollywood firms have had less conscience and courage to take the leadership that partisans of democracy demand, the culture industry stigma has led academic critics to underestimate positive qualities in popular movies since the 1970s.

In sum, Arendt's emphasis on public freedom and action has invited a reconsideration of popular art's public and political importance. Horkheimer and Adorno regard art exclusively as a formation for the autonomous individual; for them, mass culture products detract from their aim of contemplation. Yet art's role in civic life is of a different order that exceeds its economic and contemplative aspects. In the civil sphere, art recognizes difference, remembers action, imagines ideals, and builds solidarity vital to civic freedom. The heroes of popular drama are thus pivotal to the life of the democratic republic.

Civic Humanist Criticism

This introductory chapter has moved gradually from political philosophy toward drama to prepare subsequent analysis of particular sports movies. A word must be said about how academic criticism participates in the circuit of civic life through which popular culture legitimizes the nation-state and civic institutions (including academia). Affirmation, despite potentially serving economic hegemony, is necessary to the democratic agency of civil society. Critical work is done in judging the ideals of conduct expressed by a work, especially because one of art's special roles is to discover the good anew.[158] This vision of democracy places greater concern on solidarity and values than on self-consciousness or economic consequence.[159] Writing civic humanist criticism is itself a kind of action—speech—whose public engagement takes priority over judgments of esthetic pleasure or theoretical contemplation. Moreover, popular drama positions the critic at the same level as the spectators, not perched on a distant ledge. Only a difference in degree of analysis and supporting knowledge might separate the academic expert from the popular critic.

Horkheimer and Adorno are right to sound the alarm over an ideology of greed and vanity often propagated by mass culture.[160] Their school of criticism has drawn unprecedented attention to the economic conditions of the culture industry and its attendant political consequences. However, they go too far in claiming that the capitalist system determines the political quality of the works. I have also shown how their emphasis on autonomy and skepticism pose a danger to the civil sphere.

Of course it is not as simple as replacing an ethic of negation with one of affirmation. If one extreme succumbs to anarchy and nihilism, at the other extreme is a dutiful parroting of sober authority supported by blind faith. The alternative approach that this chapter has outlined aims to complement critical theory by reconsidering the democratic importance of Hollywood movies generally.

Overview of the Book

To some, it may seem absurd to have wandered so far intellectually in this introduction. But serious thought about society, political freedom, and the nature of reality has always been a part of film criticism. The stories told by the movies have a profound connection to the collective life of a people. Now that I have outlined alternative approaches to interpreting their political significance, we can turn to a given set of films with fresh eyes.

The following two chapters reconsider *Rocky* and *Slap Shot*, respectively. Their working-class white heroes have been read as metonyms of a conservative turn in American culture; however, the contemporary men's liberation movement frames the action in a new light. In fact, the protagonists develop from a mindset of conservative individualism to a more community-oriented, expressive camaraderie. Sylvester Stallone's Rocky Balboa grows into a representative for Philadelphia's working-class community similar to Jimmy Carter, although an ambivalent relationship to Black champion Apollo Creed complicates that leftist character. Meanwhile Paul Newman's Reg Dunlop develops a minor league hockey team from complacent employees into goons whose queerly performative brand of masculinity galvanizes the town. Shot on location in what has become America's rust belt, the realist satire reflects upon the effect that post-industrialism will have for masculinity and the social order. *Slap Shot* imagines a pathway for democratic reform that differs from both conservative toughness and the liberal new age.

A chapter on *The Natural* situates its legendary tale in the context of the 1980s farm crisis. Set in 1939, others have read its nostalgia as a pure expression of Reagan's conservative turn and endorsement of his neoliberal policy; however, they overlook details that point instead to Roosevelt's New Deal. And while the movie's happy ending is infamously unfaithful to the tragic realism of Malamud's novel, the more interesting difference from that midcentury source is the film's edification of small farm life as a minority culture. This angle on the rural subject integrates the logic of multiculturalism into the mainstream. The democratic politics of the small farmer offer a different perspective on American sports history films and on the complexity of minority politics.

White Men Can't Jump (1992) makes the discourse of multiculturalism more explicit than ever. In this chapter I introduce Jeffrey Alexander's theory of social incorporation via three modes—assimilation, hyphenation, and multiculturalism. I argue that director Ron Shelton's film follows the middle path of hyphenation, which has not received enough attention. The representation of a White outsider in a fantastically Black Los Angeles, subtle criticism of the liberalist political economy through street basketball, and a challenge to traditional masculinity voiced by Rosie Perez's character all contribute to a progressive vision of America. Yet the absence of good institutions represented in the story indicates a libertarian side of 1990s liberal Hollywood.

Released later the same year, *A League of Their Own* is a landmark sports movie about the women athletes in a 1940s baseball league that centers on one team and two sisters. Many have lamented the conservatism of the protagonist Dottie, played by Geena Davis. Initially reluctant to join, she retires after her husband returns from the war. In this chapter I step back to read her character within a deeper dramatic conflict established by the framing story. Director Penny Marshall concludes the film at the hall of fame decades later to emphasize collective effort and diversity over the individual and the drive to win. To interpret the political valence of this conflict I introduce Montesquieu, whose distinction between democracy and monarchy clarifies the aristocratic character of athletic competition. Marshall's film contrasts a traditionally masculine and aristocratic ethic of winning above all to a democratic alternative aligned with both wartime patriotism and 1990s feminism. The development of Tom Hanks's coach character into a "sideline man" also models how progressive men can support women as peripheral parts of a collective effort.

The subject of *Ali* (2001) has obvious democratic and multicultural qualities that self-consciously memorialize the 1960s. Michael Mann's film has been praised for representing the complexity of Muhammad Ali where lesser biopics present a conformist model. Yet how can a uniquely different and complex hero represent the people generally? I argue that the film represents Ali's 1964 and 1974 title fights as actions in Arendt's special sense of the word. This chapter details how key montage sequences connect Ali the unique individual to Black Americans, Black Africans, and to oppressed people globally. I also underline how Mann and screenwriter Eric Roth depict all institutions, both White and Black, with a skepticism whose extremeness has not been reflected upon sufficiently by previous critics.

A final chapter compares Ali's triumphal 1974 reception to the controversy surrounding Colin Kaepernick's national anthem demonstrations begun in 2016. Five issues concerning the political character of the United States since the 1970s emerge: multiculturalism, community, imperial legacy, liberalism, and civil religion. These key axes inform and complicate the partisan picture of two Americas.

Returning to the familiar subject of Hollywood cinema revises our general understanding and opens new avenues for critical debate. Even readers who disagree with certain interpretations should find an alternative perspective that enriches discussion of popular culture, critical method, and democratic politics.

2

Rocky (1976)

Tenderhearted Community and Racial Moderation in Bicentennial America

On the eve of *Rocky*'s release in November 1976, Sylvester Stallone opined: "He's understated, a common man, and that's why he won."[1] He was not speaking of his movie's underdog hero (who loses the climactic title bout, in fact), but of President-elect Jimmy Carter. "What about a guy like Carter? Who had heard of him eighteen months ago? That's part of the reason *Rocky* is going to go with audiences: the country has been through this terrible downer, and people are ready for a change."[2] Stallone's seemingly glib comparison of a movie hero to the nation's new leader foregrounds the political importance of popular drama. More surprisingly, the connection photographed in Figure 2.1 runs counter to Stallone's subsequent association with Reagan and America's Right that took hold in the 1980s. This chapter makes evident a political side of *Rocky* that has been long overlooked.

Carter, Stallone, and the Revival of the American Dream

Providence, in both senses of the word, characterized Jimmy Carter's project as president. In the years after Vietnam and Watergate, when many saw the federal government as a corrupt and wasteful military machine, the appearance of a "fresh-faced" outsider as the Democratic candidate did indeed seem providential.[3] As governor, the earnest and folksy Georgia peanut farmer had formed a broad coalition that represented a New South. "I say to you quite frankly, the time for racial discrimination is over," Carter once declared. "No poor, rural, weak or black person should ever have to bear the burden of being deprived of the opportunity of an education, a job or simple justice."[4] Like Stallone's film, Carter spoke to the disadvantaged with hopefulness as well as pragmatism. Trained as an engineer, Carter believed that providence and thrift would restore the federal state to economic health without sacrificing its means of providing for all citizens equally.[5]

Meanwhile, Carter invoked divine providence when he called upon faith itself as a key ingredient in national recovery. "The American dream endures," he proclaimed in his inaugural address: "We must once again have full faith in our country—and in one another. I believe America can be better."[6] And when

Hollywood Sports Movies and the American Dream. Grant Wiedenfeld, Oxford University Press. © Oxford University Press 2022. DOI: 10.1093/oso/9780197624920.003.0002

Figure 2.1 Stallone visits President Carter in the Oval Office on September 7, 1977. Courtesy Jimmy Carter Library and National Archives.

recession deepened in 1979, he reiterated this theme: "Restoring that faith and that confidence to America is now the most important task we face."[7] If Watergate and Vietnam had profaned the idea of America for many, Jimmy Carter combined the revival spirit of a minister with the modesty of a farmer to lead a successful presidential campaign in 1976.

At this providential moment Sylvester Stallone consciously represented himself and *Rocky* as exemplars of the American dream. As a struggling actor he had penned the film's original screenplay and insisted on playing the lead role. "I want to be remembered as a man of raging optimism, who believes in the American dream," he declared.[8] His scenario indeed gives an everyman from Philadelphia a shot at the heavyweight title and a girl-next-door love interest. To make the movie itself part of the dream narrative, Irwin Winkler and Robert Chartoff opted for a small production, shot on location in the hometown of the little-known lead actor.[9] The city known as the nation's birthplace is the cradle for his dream. In pre-release interviews Stallone would describe *Rocky* as a kind of Great American Movie: "If nothing comes out of it in the way of awards and accolades, it will still show that an unknown quantity, a totally unmarketable person, can produce a diamond in the rough, a gem. And there are a lot more people like me out there, too, people whose chosen profession denies them opportunity."[10] Despite only mild approval among critics, *Rocky* quickly became a runaway hit with audiences.[11] Still, many were surprised when it won the Academy Award for Best Picture of 1976 over more seemingly serious contenders.[12]

In the same 1976 interview Stallone extended the comparisons of the movie's hero to Carter. He described Rocky Balboa as "a simple man, a man [anyone] can identify with, a man who doesn't curse and who likes America, a man who's a real man. That's what people want to see these days." Reflecting on the drama's soaring optimism, Stallone said, "People require symbols of humanity and heroism."[13] When warned that such happy endings might give false hopes, Stallone replied, "A peanut farmer has just become President of the United States. That's the greatest inspiration story of all time."[14] It is therefore little wonder that Carter reacted very positively to the film. He sent Stallone a note (Figure 2.2) that read, "It is one of the best movies we've ever seen" and subsequently invited the star to the White House.[15] In 1976 and 1977,

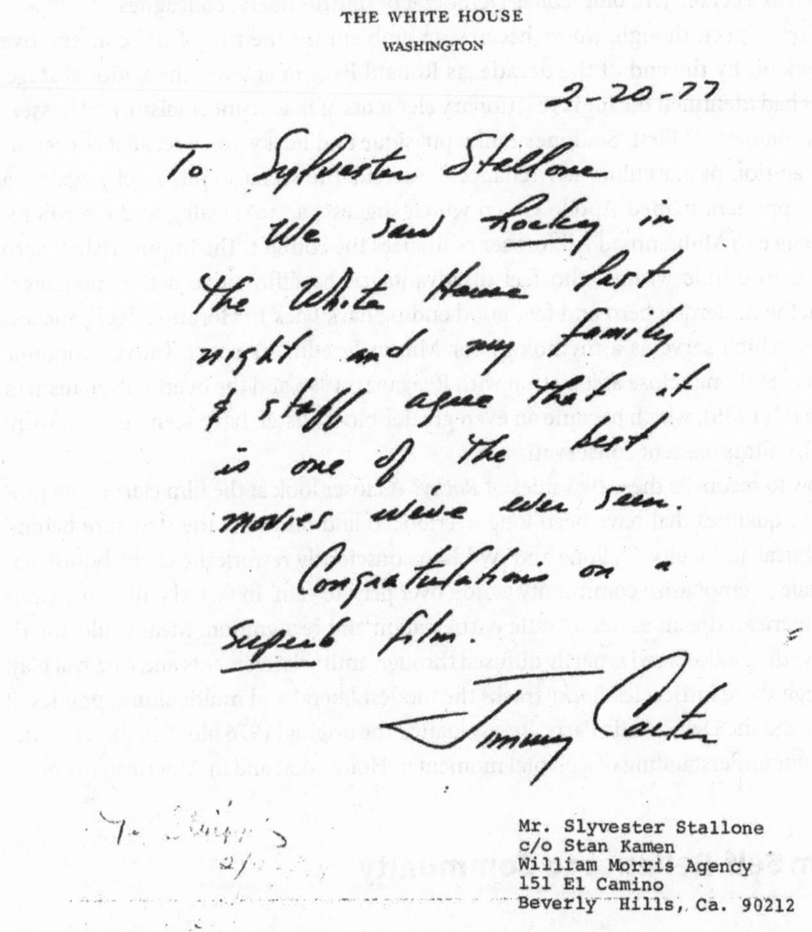

THE WHITE HOUSE

WASHINGTON

2-20-77

To Sylvester Stallone

We saw Rocky in the White House last night and my family & staff agree that it is one of the best movies we've ever seen.

Congratulations on a Superb film.

Jimmy Carter

Mr. Slyvester Stallone
c/o Stan Kamen
William Morris Agency
151 El Camino
Beverly Hills, Ca. 90212

Figure 2.2 President Carter wrote Stallone this note after watching *Rocky* in a private screening at the White House. Courtesy Jimmy Carter Library.

Jimmy Carter, Sylvester Stallone, and Stallone's onscreen character all embodied the American dream of a better future for the common man.

The filmmakers involved in *Rocky* all appeared to match this Democratic Party brand in 1976. Producers Irwin Winkler and Robert Chartoff, both Jewish New Yorkers, had established their reputation with *They Shoot Horses, Don't They?* (1969)—the story of a dance marathon in the Great Depression, directed by Sydney Pollack and starring Jane Fonda at the very moment she began to speak actively on the political left.[16] Winkler and Chartoff then hired "avowed liberal" director John G. Avildsen to direct *Rocky*.[17] Although Stallone defends the status quo when he says, "I've had it with anti-this and anti-that," in the same 1976 interview he praises Carter and also mentions his screenplay *Sinsilver*, "about a Hasidic Jew in the Old West, and based on a reinterpretation of the *Communist Manifesto*."[18] Thus Stallone positions himself as a center-left, blue-collar Democrat beside his liberal colleagues.

In retrospect, though, *Rocky* became an emblem for the rise of the conservative movement. By the end of the decade, as Ronald Reagan entered the national stage, critics had identified the film's reactionary elements of machismo, racism, and laissez-faire capitalism.[19] First, Stallone's bulky physique and husky voice recall a conservative tradition of masculine self-reliance.[20] Second, the scenario pits Rocky against a black opponent named Apollo Creed which suggests a race rivalry, and Creed's resemblance to Muhammad Ali further politicizes the conflict. The impoverished hero appeals to ethnic whites who feel disadvantaged by affirmative action policies.[21] Third, the underdog hero and feel-good ending hark back to Horatio Alger's success stories, which serve as a mythology for Milton Friedman's conservative economic policy.[22] Stallone's close association with Reagan in 1985 and the overt nationalism of *Rocky IV* (1985), which became an even greater blockbuster, have seemed to confirm the 1976 film's nascent conservatism.[23]

How to reconcile these two sides of *Rocky*? A closer look at the film clarifies its progressive qualities that have been long overlooked and discovers the structure behind its political ambiguity. Stallone and Avildsen consciously rework the cliché bootstrapping tale to emphasize community action over private gain. In fact, the film interprets the American dream as democratic participation and recognition. Meanwhile, the rivalry with Apollo Creed is partly diffused through antiracist elements and carnival play. Through these intricacies *Rocky* tracks the modest liberal and multicultural politics of Carter and the Democratic Party. Re-evaluating the original 1976 film will therefore develop our understanding of a pivotal moment in Hollywood and in American history.

From Self-Reliance to Community

Rocky inverts key components of the rags-to-riches legend to highlight the importance of community. Like its peers in the Hollywood Renaissance, this film deconstructs classical conventions; however, in eventually recuperating the comedic happy ending, it forms an adroit hybrid of mainstream and counterculture.

In the 1970s Hollywood cinema turned away from its tradition of lighthearted optimism. Thomas Elsaesser detected the emergence of two forms of negativity in its heroes: an "unmotivated hero" exemplified by Jack Nicholson's oil worker protagonist in *Five Easy Pieces* (Bob Rafelson, 1970), and a vigilante type exemplified by Clint Eastwood's *Dirty Harry* (Don Siegel, 1971).[24] Each breaks with the affirmative moral vision of the traditional American hero. The violent vigilante expresses a conservative political reaction to restore order, while the unmotivated hero expresses the liberal politics of the counterculture. The "non-committed hero" stands apart from the present state of crisis with a cool, almost analytical distance.[25]

In particular, an "offhanded" beginning structures the unmotivated hero movie. Entering upon a nonchalant situation invites skepticism about the consequences of the hero's actions and a more general skepticism about the established order. By contrast, the classical Hollywood intrigue opens with an incident that sets the hero forth on a meaningful journey. The Horatio Alger–type tale typically begins with a child or young man in low circumstances; then, a chance opportunity sets forth a rise to success that involves overcoming obstacles through self-discipline, moral conduct, and individual talent. Midcentury sports biopics, such as *Knute Rockne, All-American* (Lloyd Bacon, 1940), adhere to this pattern by starting from a boy playing on a sandlot and building to the hero's eventual championship. In drifting away from that classical structure, seventies Hollywood developed a "pathos of failure" that reflected broader "malaise" and uncertainty around the Enlightenment ideology of progress.[26]

Rocky initiates a liberal retelling of the American dream tale with realist pathos. The protagonist is introduced as an aging club boxer of limited talent, rather than a promising youth. This unmotivated hero inhabits a working-class world of exploitation where self-reliance yields only loneliness. He is no pioneer, no entrepreneurial climber. Opportunity will come offhandedly and will not be sufficient to inspire Balboa. Only through a slow process of bonding with others in his neighborhood will the narrative pivot toward a positive outcome. Stallone and Avildsen's opening act belongs to the new wave of urban realism in 1970s American cinema.[27]

The film opens on a grimy club fight that illustrates the inadequacy of self-reliance. Crass patrons call for blood as Rocky Balboa and Spider Rico clobber one another. Cinematographer James Crabe uses a single overhead light to mimic George Bellows' Ashcan School painting, *Stag at Sharkey's* (1909), illustrated by Figures 2.3 and 2.4.[28] Yet, unlike the heraldic brightness of the painting, Crabe's dimmer lighting conveys degradation. The camera watches Rocky's hulking body absorb punches. Between rounds his corner man offers advice but the self-reliant Rocky ignores him. Only when Rico cuts his face does Balboa respond with violent blows, until he fells the enemy and is declared the victor. Yet instead of a grand musical accompaniment we hear a woman in the crowd congratulate Balboa by yelling, "You're a bum!"[29] Indeed, she is right to see him as a bloody brawler and no master of the sweet science.[30] He mopes and wails boyishly but, at his advanced age, victory will bring neither joy nor opportunity.

Figures 2.3–2.4 *Rocky* cinematographer James Crabe evidently draws from George Bellows's 1909 painting *Stag at Sharkey's*, but the dim film image displays less enthusiasm.

The locker room scene that follows makes evident the exploitation both fighters endure. A medium-long shot shows the rivals resting placidly in the locker room, depicted in Figure 2.5. Their animosity evidently ended at the ring's edge. Neither reacts violently to the crowd or to the situation as a vigilante-type would. Rocky

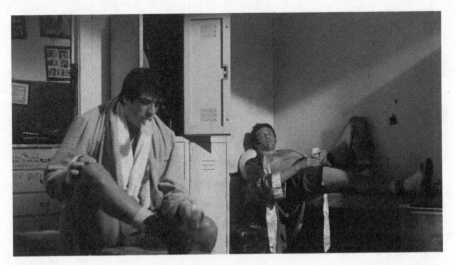

Figure 2.5 In the shared locker room after the fight, Rocky smokes a cigarette beside his opponent Spider Rico, who nurses a can of beer.

simply smokes a cigarette in silence. A weasely old man then pays each fighter a pittance, with fees deducted for the locker, cornerman, shower, towel, and tax. Whatever hope the boxers might have had of renown, in actuality they are just meat paid to entertain a bloodthirsty crowd. Rocky then trudges through the dark streets alone, accompanied by a somber piano solo, to a low-rent studio apartment where only his pet turtles await. This sequence reveals the dark, lonely, and oppressive existence of the common man.

Even fantastic opportunity brings no joy to Rocky, who perceives only further exploitation and shame. A slick promoter calls and Rocky trudges into his office, assuming that he is hiring sparring partners. When the promoter offers a title fight against heavyweight champion Apollo Creed, Rocky remains impassive, displaying neither surprise nor any desire for revenge. The poor boxer initially refuses the opportunity, acknowledging that he is outmatched. But the promoter is keen to exploit the mismatch, so he woos the desperate man: "Rocky, it's the chance of a lifetime. You can't pass it by. What do you say?" Unenthusiastically, Rocky assents by looking toward the camera, momentarily breaking the fourth wall, as shown in Figure 2.6. No inspiring music plays. His attitude is contrary to the self-confident hero just waiting for a break to prove himself. His glance toward the camera instead marks a nadir of self-reflection. Introspectively played by Stallone, Rocky looks as if he is a lamb for slaughter, destined to be a loser for life, so he grimly accepts the fight. Subsequent scenes depict his stubborn isolation and despondency. In this dog-eat-dog world, Rocky has no illusion of making it, so his purported self-reliance leaves him in a lonely state of depression. This narrative arc undoes the classic pattern of a talented young hero who only needs an opportunity to spark his rise to success. The over-the-hill

Figure 2.6 At the moment he agrees to fight the champion, Rocky looks almost directly at the camera with an expression of dismay.

fighter understands that the American dream is little more than a marketing tease, but the stoic rational man has no choice but to take what comes. Here Rocky exemplifies Elsaesser's "unmotivated hero" in his cool mistrust and uncertainty about the consequences of his actions.[31]

Rocky's lack of motivation demonstrates a fundamental opposition to conservative economic theory. It is well known that American conservatives abide by a laissez-faire school of thought. Their free-market theory holds that hard work will receive a just reward and that state interventions such as welfare only impair everyone's motivation to work. But *Rocky*'s sober opening scenes expose an unjust world that leaves a common individual alone and despondent. Stallone introduces an everyman in a system so rigged against him that he loses all ambition to better himself, even when granted a special chance. As a middling and fading fighter, Rocky lacks normal opportunity for advancement and his consciousness of being exploited further depletes his motivation. He resigns himself to suffer, lose, and collect his paycheck, and makes no effort to improve himself. The story does not offer any specific cause for his low state, such as a broken childhood or a previous transgression; instead, from a sociological perspective we observe the general state of the world through this typical figure. Rocky's despondency suggests that laissez-faire policy installs a state of inequality that requires stronger intervention to correct. The subsequent dramatic change will symbolize the kinds of politics and programs promoted by the Democratic Party throughout the twentieth century.

Rocky will discover a new motivation for its hero in an original way. In a supportive circle he will soften his classical masculine shell and find his spirit revived. While the film begins like a failure narrative of an unmotivated hero, it progressively develops a positive thrust. This hybrid composition ultimately reconfigures the form of the American dream. Rather than a hardened pioneer, tenderhearted Rocky learns to bond with others to become a civic leader.

The Tenderhearted Tough

Rocky's redemption takes root in a tender heart, not his tough hide, which has deep political significance. In the early twentieth century, stoic self-discipline defined traditional American masculinity and was incarnated by Hollywood's cowboys, especially John Wayne. In his portrayal of Rocky Balboa, Stallone combines that conservatism of yesteryear with a more forward-looking, liberal side.

Interestingly, the men's liberation movement that peaked in the mid-1970s informs the film. To extend the gender reform begun by women's liberation and feminism, liberal men led a complementary movement that advocated for male emotional expression, playfulness, and bonding as an antidote to toxic masculinity. Michael Kimmell has defined the movement as "a coherent critique of the self-made man."[32] The parallel names of the two movements underscore that women's liberation cannot be complete without men's liberation from an antiquated set of sex roles (what we might call gender norms today). Patriarchy thus affected not only women; its pitiless hierarchy also forced men into inhumane roles full of dreariness. For instance, Marc Fasteau diagnosed the problem of *The Male Machine*, a model of self-reliant toughness born in the industrial age. "Men's libbers" promoted cooperation, playfulness, and androgyny as alternatives to stoic self-discipline. "Becoming a liberated man," declared Warren Farrell in 1974, "is getting in touch with childlike and feminine parts of the self.... It is always working on the process of liberation rather than thinking one has reached it."[33] Reformers gathered male support groups and promoted community bonding to overcome the isolation, repression, and loneliness men experienced.[34]

The development of Rocky's character follows the arc of men's liberation. Introduced as a male machine in despair, his drive toward happiness will involve revealing his emotions to others, forming a supportive circle, and finding joy in play. He does not abandon his bulk or his toughness, but it is not those qualities that spark his growth. Instead, gentler elements provide the source of his motivation and self-worth.

Scenes of a dour day job show Balboa donning a mask of toughness then peeling it back to expose his tenderness. That same pattern was introduced in the opening club fight and locker room scenes. Pauline Kael succinctly describes his character and his job: "Stallone plays a waif, a strong-arm man who doesn't want to hurt anybody, a loner with only his pet turtles to talk to."[35] The job scenes begin when Rocky walks onto the dockyards to grab a feeble forklift driver who owes money on a loan. The heavy boxer raises his strong arm, but then lays it down when the skittish man begs for mercy. Rocky tries to convince him, "I ain't emotionally involved," but the heavy is evidently too sympathetic to break any bones. "Stallone is aware that we see him as a hulk, and he plays against this comically and tenderly," Pauline Kael observes. "He's

Figure 2.7 Rocky explains to his boss, a loan-shark, why he could not bring himself to break a debtor's thumbs.

at his funniest trying to explain to his boss why he didn't break somebody's thumbs, as he'd been told to."[36] Figure 2.7 shows this funny moment. Where one expects authentic toughness and phony sentiment, Rocky presents the opposite. A lead actor with a lithesome body would come across as maudlin, but Stallone's hefty physique creates a peculiar complement to his softness. "His unworldliness makes him seem dumb, but we know better; we understand what he feels at every moment," Kael continues. "Rocky is the embodiment of the out-of-fashion pure-at-heart." Stallone's performance enchants because his tenderness does not fit his tough character or hard body. His humanity stands out against the geometric industrial environment of metal fences, railcars, and girders, like graffiti without anger. As a hero Rocky therefore appeals to us through human sentiment, rather than through admiration for his mind or body.

Avildsen's depiction of Rocky's day job suggests a critique of "hard" masculinity. Immense steel hulls, rusting towers, and a gaudy Cadillac hint at big business and global capitalism that hang over the miserably poor workers. The Philadelphia location and Crabe's still compositions in Figures 2.8 and 2.9 recall the modernist smokestacks of Charles Demuth and Charles Sheeler, whose paintings were imbued with the optimism of Horatio Alger and Henry Ford. Avildsen's urban realism reduces those magnificent machines from crisp eidolons to banal apparatuses and crumbling ruins. Meanwhile, the men in this world face these big structures in hard shells of leather jackets and Cadillacs that publicize their machismo. When the debtor offers the jacket in lieu of cash payment Rocky refuses to accept it, underlining the symbolic importance of this modern suit of armor. The men's outer shells recall Jack Nichols' reflection, "In future decades today's male role will be remembered as a straight-jacket."[37] His study *Men's Liberation* criticized patriarchy for isolating men behind

Figures 2.8–2.9 Philadelphia's industrial backdrop recalls the Precisionist paintings of Demuth and Sheeler, but their optimism has been replaced by inhuman mass.

tough exteriors that causes them to eventually crumble on the inside. Presented with sparse musical accompaniment, the scenes of Balboa's day job suggest the weight that established industry and its adjacent tradition of masculinity bear upon every worker in the hierarchy.

In contrast to this unforgiving and hard world, Rocky shows a glimmer of a soft and playful humanity. He walks through the docks bouncing a rubber ball that indicates a boyish and fun-loving man. One can detect an allusion to Steve McQueen's gregarious hero in *The Great Escape* (1963), who bounces a baseball around his isolation cell to stay sane and inspire others. Kael remarks that Balboa has "a street-wise, flower-blooming-in-the-garbage innocence."[38] Nice guys should not walk these streets or box in these gyms, but here we find Rocky the tenderhearted tough. His surname Balboa, which derives from the Latin *vallis bona*, "pleasant valley," agrees with his kind nature. After his boss chastises him for not breaking the dockworker's thumbs, Rocky walks down the brick road alone, too dejected to continue bouncing his ball. Bill Conti's somber piano theme communicates this despair to the audience, who must wait uncomfortably for a solution. This character lacks the stoicism and relentless optimism of McQueen's midcentury hero. Hard masculinity has become part of an entrenched inequality and unhappiness where we meet Rocky at the beginning of the film.

Adrian

During the movie's middle acts, Rocky emerges from his forlorn state by forming relationships in his local community. He first reveals his insecurities to a young woman, Adrian, who accepts him and begins to restore his self-worth. Avildsen intersperses a series of encounter scenes throughout the first act. The narrative point of view shifts from Rocky to Adrian to underscore their delicate bonding as his hard shell beings to soften. This more progressive hero and narrative arc erodes the "masculine mystique" that men's liberation saw in old Hollywood.[39] In telling a love story about common people, the film recasts the American dream as an ideal of togetherness and humanity rather than social ambition or material gain.

Their courtship exemplifies Elsaesser's unmotivated hero and "pathos of failure." Their relationship is notably disinterested from classical narrative's external objective. Because the characters share the same low social status, their courtship has no direct consequences for the hero's actions. Instead, the characters develop interactively as perspective relays from one to the other. Rocky first meets Adrianna (Talia Shire) at a nondescript pet shop where she works. Avildsen first shows him preparing to address his crush, then we see the tough guy awkwardly flirt by telling bad jokes as she twitches nervously behind the counter. Next, her brother, Paulie, brings the two together at his house on Thanksgiving, but the crass older sibling embarrasses her. Avildsen and Crabe now frame Adrian at the center of the action and relegate Rocky to cutaways where he sympathetically witnesses her home life. The masculine spelling of her nickname, Adrian, does not seem to fit her mousy character at first, but she grows more resilient as their relationship develops, just as Rocky in turn becomes more pliant.

Their love (to say it plainly) becomes an independent source of motivation for the hero. Avildsen expands his play with point of view during a comically bad yet pivotal date. Rocky takes her to an empty ice rink, closed early for the holiday, but persuades the lingering employee to let them skate for ten minutes. The bystander then chaperones their date from a Zamboni. That neutral point of view and the cold setting accentuate the couple's budding warmth. A mural above the rink depicts a blissful winter park scene that hints at the pair's romantic dreams as it contrasts with the bleak reality these poor Philadelphians share. By highlighting this tension, Avildsen and Stallone suggest that the couple bonds over a shared feeling of individual shame that each other's company dispels.

Adrian's point of view predominates in the middle of the date to signal her lead in the relationship. The camera trains on her skating around the white expanse somewhat apprehensively while Rocky shuffles beside her in his street shoes and rambles on with dumb jokes. Afterward they walk to his apartment where Avildsen shows Adrian hesitate outside on the stoop. Rocky holds open the door, invites her up, and awaits her decision. Talia Shire performs her quiet trepidation brilliantly—the opposite of the raving daughter she played in *The Godfather*.[40] When they move inside, the point of view remains with Adrian, who watches Rocky try to conceal his embarrassingly shoddy bachelor pad. She moves to leave saying, "I don't feel comfortable." He replies, "I don't feel so comfortable neither." Rocky then removes his jacket and sweater to reveal a muscular chest to her, and slides off her glasses with a light touch. Nervousness suddenly overcomes her and she moves to leave but Rocky corrals her as if he were taming a filly. A close-up follows his face as he moves near hers and pauses; then she kisses him, music plays, and the scene ends suggestively. In narrating the scene primarily from her point of view, Avildsen demonstrates Rocky's frankness and caring, layering their perspectives. No longer is our point of view restricted to Rocky's, and no longer is he walled off within a hard masculine shell. The couple's awkward exchanges show how they bond through expressing their anxieties and uncovering their inner worth.

Rocky's dominant "taming" has been rightly criticized. It is precisely the male-centric presumption that a woman needs to be persuaded, even by strength, to lay down her guard and express her desire, that fosters toxic masculinity's rape culture. His blocking her nervous exit seems to jeopardize her free will. Without her consent, his muscular physique changes from object of desire to instrument of dominance. This moment clearly goes against the pattern of emo, liberal masculinity that has developed throughout their courtship. A more progressive type of 1970s man would let Adrian lead the way to physical intimacy.

Nevertheless, Rocky actually takes a small step forward from classical misogyny. Even as the dominant hunk leans over her, he pauses and she kisses him. Her perspective throughout the scene also suggests that he is acting out her fear and desire. An older type of Hollywood man has no need to pause, but simply imposes his will physically until the woman relents. Compared to the fraternity pranksters of *M*A*S*H* (Robert Altman, 1970), the false rape accusation in *The Graduate* (Mike Nichols, 1967), and the prudishness of Hollywood during the production code, *Rocky* is sensitive and refreshingly honest about sex. Neither Rocky nor Adrian suffers any feeling of social shame for engaging in an unmarried sexual relationship. The only prudish character is her brother, Paulie, an unhappy alcoholic whose older repressive mores contrast with the liberated, younger couple.[41] Although the taming moment reverts to a more conservative trope, Balboa's acknowledgment of discomfort around sex certainly opposes classical trends.

In Rocky's conflicting qualities one can recognize Stallone's attempt to develop an alternative masculinity that emphasizes emotional expression and sympathy without forfeiting strength. "Rocky represents the redemption of an earlier ideal—the man as rock for woman to cleave to," Kael observed.[42] Stallone attempts to fashion a hybrid between the emotional new age man and the old-fashioned hunk. For comparison, the Canadian hockey film *Goon* (2011) promotes the same type of strong protector in a more comedic context. Rather than a mid-century masculinity that employed stoic repression to maintain a public face of can-do optimism, Stallone's amalgam balances strength with emotiveness. Where older solidarity formed through rational notions of duty, purpose, and decorum, the liberated man must form communal bonds through emotional intimacy. This pattern of building self-worth through self-knowledge, emotional expression, and bonding is typical of liberal masculinity in the seventies. Consider Stallone's Rambo character in *First Blood* (1982) who has long, curly hair and cries in the arms of his mentor at the drama's climax. In intimate scenes Rocky will reveal to Adrian his public discomfort at the press conference and, on the eve of the fight, he confesses that he's nobody special next to the champion and expects to lose. That moment of clarity allows the hero to adopt a more modest goal of avoiding a knockout. In *The Liberated Man*, Warren Farrell contends that "Becoming a liberated man is never underestimating the complexity, the joy or the pain of getting in touch with one's humanity."[43] Though not the liberal ideal, at this point in his career Stallone portrays a hybrid, reformed masculinity.

Pets highlight emotional expression and bonding that extends from the couple to the city at large. Rocky's compassionate side is first revealed when he speaks to his turtles, Cuff and Link, at the outset. Adrian works in a pet shop, where as an excuse to flirt Rocky buys package after package of turtle food. The setting characterizes the two as slightly odd in that they bond more with pets than people. After their big date, Adrian buys Rocky a dog from the shop as a gift to accompany him on his runs, a moment shown in Figure 2.10. Rocky is never seen disciplining these pets, which might evoke a harder masculinity. The warmth he shares with these domestic companions expands the circle of emotional bonding and points to the hero's natural fellowship with the city at large. In fact, the dog creates a kind of public legitimacy and spectacle for Rocky's training, appearing in the ebullient montage. Significantly, when Adrian presents this barking gift she appears in a new outfit, and without glasses, that Rocky warmly compliments. The flourishing couple and pets imply that civic life takes root in everyday, personal bonds rather than family loyalty or institutional obligation. Their relationship with pets recalls the illicit affair between Petra Cotes and Aureliano Segundo in *100 Years of Solitude*, whose lovemaking magically proliferates their livestock and revives the agricultural town.

Adrian and Rocky's love represents, politically, a republican revival of liberal democracy. Theirs is not a glamorous romance.[44] Adrian is not a prize to attain, an obstacle to conquer, or a sweetheart taken for granted. Rocky and Adrian develop a relationship as equals in the neighborhood. In accepting each other just as they are, they each recover a basic sense of self-worth. Rocky's public acknowledgment of

Figure 2.10 Adrian gets a makeover and gives Rocky a dog, together symbolizing how the couple's love spreads outward to the city at large.

Adrian therefore has an egalitarian character. In the middle of his first televised press conference, he blurts out "Yo Adrian," and after the final fight concludes, he foregoes the attention of the press to seek her out. Their kiss is caught in a freeze-frame as the film's final image. Bill Conti's sentimental piano music further accentuates all these moments. The film's original posters also feature the couple holding hands in silhouette, not the rival boxers.[45] Their love promises a certain solution to the unmotivated hero that, unlike the pessimistic ending of *Bonnie and Clyde* (Arthur Penn, 1967), is realized in a happy ending. By focusing on the couple's authentically shared sentiment rather than external goals of social status or material gain, Avildsen and Stallone establish a democratic basis for their melodramatic American dream tale.

Mickey

Rocky's relationship with his trainer, Mickey, repeats the development from a hard to a softer masculinity and represents the authentic bond of local institutions. Their initial interactions demonstrate the pitfalls of hard masculinity. The brutally honest Irish gym owner (Burgess Meredith) berates Rocky the day after he wins the club fight. "You got heart but you fight like a goddamn ape. Nothing special about you," Mickey tells him bluntly. He gives Rocky's locker away to a younger fighter with more potential. "You had the talent to become a good fighter," Mickey scolds him, "and instead of that you became a leg-breaker to some cheap, second-rate loan shark." The trainer delivers hard truths without encouragement.

Rocky will attempt to respond in an equally hard way by deciding to train himself, but he cannot muster the requisite discipline. When Adrian's brother, Paulie (Burt

Young), hears about the title bout and asks if he wants people in his corner, Balboa shrugs, "Who cared about me yesterday? Nobody. I think I'm gonna train myself." In a Horatio Alger–type story the American hero would pull himself up by his bootstraps here. Yet our apathetic hero makes this declaration without any conviction. In an adjacent scene we see Rocky out socializing, smoking a cigarette, and pocketing training money from his slimy boss. If Rocky displays the harsh negative edge of old-school masculinity, he nevertheless lacks positive belief in himself. This leaves him indifferent and acrimonious.

When Mickey hears about the title shot, he attempts to repair his relationship with Rocky, but the old man's sternness backfires. First, he insults Rocky by calling his title shot "freak luck." However accurate, the Irishman denies the Italian any credit. In Rocky's apartment, the hero sweetly introduces his pet turtles and Mickey replies offhandedly, "They make good soup." Meredith then delivers an exemplary line: "Like the Bible says, you ain't gonna get a second chance." Of course, the Christian doctrines of afterlife and forgiveness are precisely second chances. This line reveals Mickey's unforgiving worldview. He refuses to apologize to Rocky for taking away his locker or for anything else. The trainer's verbal attacks aim to subordinate his charge and to motivate him through fear and anger, not through encouragement.

Rocky responds in kind by candidly and angrily rejecting Mickey. "I needed your help about ten years ago," he snaps. "You never helped me none." With the fight already set, Rocky suspects that Mickey seeks a cut of the payout and publicity for his gym. As Mickey departs, Rocky howls angrily through the thin walls, "I ain't had no prime! I ain't had nothing! Legs are going, everything's going!" He repeats that he is "going to get my face kicked in" by the champion. This moment epitomizes the isolated male machine—deliberately walled off from everyone, whose only coping mechanism is to inflict more pain on himself.

Yet a dramatic change occurs immediately after Rocky has expressed his rage and frustration. His anger spent, Rocky runs out of the apartment to find the older man. In a long shot accompanied by sentimental piano music we see the men shake hands and agree, signaling the hero's momentous decision to commit to training with Mickey. In this epiphanic moment Balboa drops his mask of toughness, his grudge, and his self-reliance.[46] No sooner has the scene ended than Avildsen immediately cuts to Balboa beginning training the next day. This sequence effectively communicates that tenderheartedness and intimate bonding motivate Rocky more than tough discipline. Henceforth Mickey will train and support his protégé with encouragement rather than rejection. Rocky's training therefore represents an emotional liberation and collective effort of the local community. In this way the film reverses the bootstrapping cliché and points toward a new masculinity.

Paulie

Adrian's brother, Paulie, represents the decline of traditional masculinity, and his relationship with Rocky demonstrates reform led by a new generation. Burt Young plays the Korean War veteran, whom we first encounter as a drunk at the local pub. Single, he works at the Shamrock Meats company and shares a duplex with his sister. When Rocky visits on Thanksgiving, Paulie humiliates Adrian as a perverse means to persuade her to go out on a date with the fighter. "I'm tired of you being a loser," Paulie tells her in front of Rocky. When she cries, Paulie screams at her so aggressively that she retreats, cowering, into the back room. Rocky coaxes her out with sympathy, and thus offers a contrast of a kind masculinity to Paulie's hardheartedness.

Another violent scene at Paulie's duplex showcases the toxicity of his traditional masculinity. The three are watching Rocky's press conference on television when Paulie turns caustic. He criticizes the naive contender's media performance and offers to help, but Rocky criticizes Paulie in turn and the conflict escalates to the moment shown in Figure 2.11. The drunkard suddenly grabs a baseball bat and bashes apart the decor of his house. Desperate and full of self-pity, he even cries that his sister is "busted" for losing her virginity. She will respond by moving in with Rocky. In these outbursts, Paulie epitomizes the insensitive patriarch who walls off his own emotions only to lash out tyrannically. Prudishness about his sister and concern for his social rank also reflect traditional patriarchy. He suffers from public shame for his unglamorous job at the meatpacking plant and lack of standing in civil society, then channels his despair into drink, verbal abuse, and violence in his domicile. In depicting Paulie's downward spiral, Stallone's drama clearly portrays traditional American masculinity as needing reform.

Paulie recovers somewhat after Rocky reaches out. The boxer offers him a job handling publicity for the fight and assisting Mickey as a cornerman. At the title bout Rocky enters the arena wearing a robe with his meat company logo, with Paulie strutting beside him smoking a cigar and boasting about the sponsorship deal. Here

Figure 2.11 Adrian's brother Paulie grabs a baseball bat in a drunken rage. Juxtaposed with a quaint "God Bless Our Home" picture, he represents the problem of traditional masculinity.

Avildsen satirizes Paulie lightly, who is living his own rags-to-riches dream narrative. Without buying into such glamor, Avildsen's cool perspective demonstrates how Paulie's inclusion in Rocky's circle has alleviated the man's despair and transferred leadership to the younger generation.

Philadelphia

Two montage sequences of Rocky training signify the hero's representation of the wider community of Philadelphia and the civic revival he initiates. Realist elements add to his symbolism. Beyond Adrian, Mickey, and Paulie, the appearance of minor local characters and extras—for instance, Mickey's assistant at the gym, workers at the docks, and teenagers Rocky encounters on the street—imparts a sense of a real community to the drama. Filming on location also authenticates Rocky as a part of the greater Philadelphian community. The twinned sequences therefore become a civic ritual like a parade through the city. Often misinterpreted as the accomplishment of a bootstrapping individual, a closer look at these montages shows how they signify communal uplift like a civic monument.

The first sequence characterizes Rocky as a collective hero. Following his reconciliation with Mickey the night before, a four o'clock alarm wakes Rocky, who turns on the radio and shivers. "Twenty-eight degrees, it's cold out there! Well, we deserve it," announces actual WIBG morning radio host Don Cannon.[47] By speaking in the first-person plural, his narration identifies Rocky as a representative of "us." As the radio speaks Rocky walks to the fridge, cracks open five eggs into a glass, and drinks them raw, all filmed in one long take. Here Stallone cites Paul Newman's hero from *Cool Hand Luke*, a victimized common man who eats fifty eggs to raise the spirit of fellow inmates.[48] Then we see Rocky begin a slow jog down his block and through City Hall, alone on the dark streets except for a newspaper truck dropping a bundle on a curb. Avildsen again hints at the hero's civic representation when he points the camera at the red letters on the side of the truck that read, "Philadelphia Daily News: The People Paper." On the soundtrack, a hopeful horn gives way to strings and a somber piano melody that express his acceptance of shame and of training's difficulty. Next, long shots show the boxer struggle up the steps of the Philadelphia Museum of Art before a gray dawn, exposing his weakness to the entire city. But in that *unconcealment*, as Heidegger might call it, the hero furthers his liberation from a masculinity that fronts toughness at all times. He leaves the privacy of his apartment, symbolically adopts the collective voice of radio and newspaper, and parades through the city center to its monumental art museum. All these elements in the first montage paint Rocky as a hero who represents Philadelphia's collective struggle.

When the second montage sequence repeats the pattern, sunnier scenes and Conti's upbeat score indicate that positive development has occurred. Rocky begins jogging through the rubble beside a factory with bricks in his hands, as if rebuilding the city. The Steadicam panning shot reinforces the symbiosis between Rocky and

Philadelphia, leading the eye from the warm-hearted hero to vapor pumping from distant chimney stacks; in the middle of the shot he veers to the right as an elevated train serendipitously propels through the background. Then Balboa jogs through a street market where one kindly bystander spontaneously tosses him a tangerine. Next, we see him jog through Fairmount Park, where Avildsen frames a stone arch viaduct behind the hero to signify collective strength.[49] A few shots in the gym show him sweat and do one-armed pushups under Mickey's watchful eye and the appreciative smile of a young assistant, indicating their team effort. Conti adds the buzz of an electronic synthesizer and a virtuoso electric guitar to give the orchestral score a modern, almost futuristic sound. Finally the hero sprints along the wharf and once again up the stairs of the art museum. The montage climaxes with Balboa overlooking the city at sunrise as a choir sings "Gonna Fly Now," figuratively giving him wings. This time the camera floats up the steps to the top level and spins around; its panoramic view is synthesized into a moving cityscape by the music. Rocky's gaze upon this skyline radiates his new confidence to all of Philadelphia. He prances with raised arms and then releases his fists at the instant captured in Plate 1; Avildsen then cuts to a reverse angle to suggest that all the city watches Rocky dance, as though he embodies its collective hope and joy.[50]

Since losing its position as the nation's leading city, Philadelphia has harbored a certain inferiority complex.[51] Its sporting heroes promise redemption for this lost honor but suffer defeat more often than not.[52] Balboa may be fictional, but the movie and this sequence in particular create a special point of civic pride.

The final fight confirms Rocky's importance as Philadelphia's native son. Apollo Creed chose a local underdog to give rise to an American dream scenario (I discuss that Apollo scene later in this chapter). When Rocky enters the ring wearing an "Italian Stallion" robe with a "Shamrock Meats" company logo, he certainly appears like a local—the national announcers try not to laugh at this unsophisticated urbanite. Knowing the backstory between Paulie and Rocky situates us as locals, too, so that we feel their slight embarrassment before the wider audience. During the big fight Avildsen highlights the connection of Rocky to the neighborhood by cutting away to the local pub where all the locals watch their hero on television, as depicted in Figure 2.12. The camera films them, cheering, from the elevated position of the barroom television mounted on the wall. Earlier, we saw Rocky encounter Paulie at this pub and watch an interview with Apollo on that TV; now the locals appear on sports media's elevated stage.

Rocky's goal of avoiding a knockout and earning respect as a fighter also signifies respect for Philadelphia's working classes. He does "go the distance" of fifteen rounds but ultimately loses the fight. The ring announcer implicitly recognizes this community when he declares, "Tonight we have had the privilege of witnessing the greatest exhibition of guts and stamina in the history of the ring!" Guts and stamina are, of course, fundamental qualities of the physical laborer. That comment and the fight's result also recall the performance of Philadelphia boxer Joe Frazier, whose 1975 "Thrilla in Manilla" bout against Muhammad Ali is widely admired as one of

Figure 2.12 Patrons at Rocky and Paulie's local pub are shown rejoicing as they watch their hometown hero perform well in the televised fight.

the best and most grueling boxing matches of the modern era.[53] Frazier appears in the film as a ceremonial guest in the ring, inviting comparison to Rocky. Finally, Avildsen closes the film upon a freeze-frame of the battered fighter shrugging off the press to embrace his working-class lover, shown in Plate 2. Rocky's achievement does not elevate him to a higher social rank or transport him to another place; instead, the final shot affirms the worth of his own community. These elements of the final fight reinforce the idea that Rocky is Philadelphia's hero. His moral victory—and Stallone's movie—merit national recognition as authentic, vernacular culture.

The training montages approximate the civic ritual of the procession. The hero parades through key civic sites, all filmed on location: residential streets, industrial zone, city hall, parks, docks, and the museum. The montage sequence performs a virtual parade by stationing the public in all these places as observers; and the everyman hero invites us to imagine ourselves as Rocky. Repetition is a fundamental feature of ritual, so the twinned training montages take on added significance. Similar training montages in the sequels have cemented the ritual to the point that tourists now perform it themselves by running up the "Rocky Steps" (as they are now called), raising their arms in triumph and snapping photos.[54] In representing an American everyman, *Rocky* shares the ethos of the civic festival that involves all citizens as participants. For Rousseau, such civic rituals were crucial to the health of an egalitarian republic.[55] In elevating Rocky's training to a formal procession, the hero takes on a civic significance beyond his particular, private story. Indeed, any tourist can perform the role of this egalitarian hero by climbing the steps. The festival atmosphere that concludes the final fight also expresses this democratic spirit, which extends to the movie itself as popular culture.

Bill Conti's theme song, "Gonna Fly Now," epitomizes the drama's sense of civic reformation. All conventional scores fulfill the public role of a chorus that interprets the action for the audience, but Conti's score cultivates a particular civic sentiment through its heraldic brass, choral voices, pop funk sounds, and its direct channel to the heart of an everyman hero.[56] *Melodrama* literally means musical drama, and Conti's score makes its presence known at the opening title sequence when the "Gonna Fly Now" fanfare plays, teasing the song's full performance during the training montage. The synthesizer that grows prominent during the training montage imitates the Kool & the Gang song "Summer Madness" (1974), which plays in the background earlier in the film. Conti's blend of Black funk and choir with traditional brass recalls Romanticism's combination of medieval folk culture with classical grandeur. The hybridity of the song reflects the hero's masculinity, urban setting, and the new version of the American dream for which it serves as an anthem.

Philadelphia's civic sites and the upbeat training montage call to mind American Progressivism. Fairmount Park was the site of Philadelphia's 1876 Centennial Exposition, whose promotion of technological "progress" would expand into a political theme for populists and progressives alike.[57] The city's art museum was established at that event. Progressives involved in the City Beautiful movement later commissioned a plan for the museum building and a new parkway connecting Fairmount and Center City, now known as Benjamin Franklin Boulevard. Both pragmatic and monumental, their plan illustrates the sacred importance of the republic as a collective entity during the Progressive Era.[58] Sporting culture also grew widespread in American life during the Progressive Era as a part of education reform and social outreach. The explosion of exercise culture in the 1970s revived that spirit, especially evident in the new civic rituals of the charity run/walk.[59] Beyond the film's particular importance for the city of Philadelphia, on a national level its civic revivalism resonates with the new, progressive spirit of Jimmy Carter and with the 1976 Bicentennial celebration.

Surprisingly, a temptation to fix the fight never enters into the drama. The mafioso fight fixer played a dominant role in the midcentury boxing genre, whose hero faced a dilemma between easy money or dutiful integrity.[60] With an Italian-American protagonist who works for a loan shark one might have expected dishonest gambling to play into *Rocky*'s plot. Its absence marks a new turn for the boxing genre. Moreover, the faith *Rocky* holds in the integrity of sport translates to a faith in the civic institutions of business and government. In contrast to midcentury Hollywood that found in boxing a setting for economic tragedy, the bicentennial movie recovers in sport a locus for civic comedy.

Overall, what distinguishes Rocky Balboa from the traditional American hero, and the typical quest centered on accomplishment, is his liberal masculinity and playfulness. In particular, the training montages effectively shift the emphasis from outcome to process. The classical discipline of athletics subjugates the body to the individual will, in order to accomplish a clear objective. Philosopher Wolfgang Welsch has

identified a historical shift away from sport's classical discipline with the rise of exercise culture in the early 1970s.[61] The second training montage exemplifies that culture's new celebration of the body's emancipation. For example, Rocky sprints down
the wharf without any finish line—he sprints simply to sprint, as if Stallone were
racing the vehicle holding the camera. The pleasure of this moment reflects the sheer
joy of his athletic capacity to perform, rather than attaining a concrete objective.[62]
Furthermore, Balboa's modest goal for the title fight, to go the distance without regard
to winning or losing, echoes the new emphasis on process. The wounds he suffers do
not show a disciplined hardness as much as they display his emotional wounds and
a doggedness that represents the city in all its humanity. What Rocky Balboa accom-
plishes is not victory but emancipation from an old system that devalued "losers."
Despite the hero's defeat, the film closes by celebrating the inherent worth of Balboa,
his city, and all his people.

Rocky revives the affirmative hero type by blending old and new characteristics. Previous critics are right to notice a change from the 1970s unmotivated hero;
however, Rocky does not simply revert to an older type. He retains the strength
and honesty of the old Hollywood hero but replaces a stoic demeanor, clear objective, and cool-minded expertise with a liberated masculinity that emphasizes process over goal, emotional bonding over discipline, and the everyman over expertise.
Considering the progressive side to this pivotal character in American popular culture points toward a more complex understanding of the nation's development from
the 1970s to today.

Race Rivalry and Antiracism

One crucial dimension of *Rocky* remains to be analyzed—"race."[63] I have chosen to
treat it separately, in the second half of this chapter, for two reasons: the movie itself
treats race separately from Rocky's masculinity and community; and its combination
of implied racism and explicit antiracism complicates judgment in a curious way.

Rocky implicitly appeals to White racists through its light-skinned hero and darker
opponent. In boxing, race rivalry reared its ugly head when the first modern heavyweight champion, John L. Sullivan (1882–1892), refused to face nonwhite challeng-
ers. Tensions peaked with the rise of Jack Johnson (1908–1915) and would persist
through a series of African-American champions that includes Muhammad Ali
(1964–1967, 1974–1978, 1978–1979).[64] Against these Black champions, White racists
would promote a fair-skinned challenger as a "great White hope."[65] Stallone structures the drama around a race rivalry by pitting his Italian-American hero against
an African-American opponent, Apollo Creed (Carl Weathers). Creed's obvious
resemblance to Muhammad Ali, an outspoken critic of the White establishment in
the 1960s through his prominent position in the Nation of Islam (staunchly Black
nationalist at that time), increases the racial tension. Numerous critics have noted
how *Rocky's* race rivalry scenario speaks to white working-class resentment over

affirmative action, welfare programs, and other state benefits that they perceive as helping minorities at their expense.[66]

Yet *Rocky* takes pains to diffuse the race rivalry in ways that have received less attention.[67] A reactionary version of *Rocky* would have stressed Creed's villainy and rooted the hero's motivation in White rage.[68] Instead, the principal drama concerns masculinity and relationships internal to the hero's Philadelphia community. Moreover, racial tension is neither heightened nor resolved by the three scenes in which Rocky and Apollo do interact: first, when Apollo appears on television in the local pub; later, in the promoter's office, when Apollo selects Balboa as his opponent; and finally, when Apollo enters the title bout in patriotic costumes. Neither character ever expresses racial hostility. Their actions in each scene invoke both color-blind merit and a multicultural recognition of difference. But these parallel strategies of antiracism are not coordinated and do not fully diffuse the race rivalry. Analysis will show how racial tension is partly diffused yet floats adjacent to the central drama.

Cassius Clay, Apollo Creed, Muhammad Ali

One ambiguity springs from the fictional character Apollo Creed. Creed's resemblance to Muhammad Ali, the reigning heavyweight champion in 1976, was obvious to all. From the outset Stallone acknowledged that Ali's 1975 bout against journeyman Chuck Wepner had inspired his script.[69] However, Ali's complex persona and evolving political positions complicate interpretation of *Rocky*'s politics, especially with regard to race. Creed resembles a moving target.

By 1976 Ali's politics had developed through three stages. Early in his career he had aligned with liberal establishment politics. Upon winning an Olympic gold medal in 1960, Cassius Clay (as he was then known) had famously delivered a patriotic poem. His sponsors at the time also had ensured that his public persona was a clean all-American one.

The day after winning the heavyweight championship in 1964, Ali publicly announced his conversion to Islam and the mentorship of Nation of Islam minister Malcolm X. A name change would soon follow. Muhammad Ali became an outspoken anti-establishment critic. His objection to being drafted during the Vietnam War made him public enemy number 1 for mainstream America but a hero for opposition movements.

In the 1970s Ali returned closer to the nation's political center without abandoning oppositional politics. In 1971 the U.S. Supreme Court overturned his conviction for draft evasion and affirmed his conscientious objection as a Muslim pacifist. Meanwhile, the United States was pulling out of Vietnam and public opinion turned against the war, exemplified by the amnesty program for draft dodgers passed by President Gerald Ford in 1974. That same year Ford also invited Ali to the White House when the boxer unexpectedly regained the heavyweight title. As the political center shifted, Ali emerged as a political leader for the entire nation. He had built relationships with African and Islamic heads of state and now aspired to become a "Black Kissinger."[70] Jimmy Carter would send Ali to Moscow in 1978 as an "unofficial ambassador" and then to Africa as a diplomatic envoy in 1980.[71] Stateside, Ali led protests such as the call for boxer Ruben "Hurricane" Carter's release from prison because of a racist justice system.[72] It became clear that Ali's political position was no longer a simple matter for the mainstream public. Ali had evolved into a political leader who walked a delicate line.

Ali's complexity and Creed's fictional difference add ambiguity to *Rocky*. Which Ali does Apollo Creed represent? The name *Apollo Creed* certainly captures the classical ring of *Cassius Clay*, and thus invites one to see Creed as the counterfactual version of Clay who embraced mainstream cultural values as a model minority but never joined the Nation of Islam. However, Creed's dramatic role as antagonist aligns better with the oppositional Ali of 1964–1971. Having such a close resemblance to Ali while changing the name opens a gap that is not resolved. His half-resemblance to Ali complicates the racial implications of the film. A closer look at Creed's three principal scenes demonstrates this equivocation at play and illustrates competing antiracist strategies.

Class Distinction and Color-Blind Individualism

Apollo's first appearance immediately establishes class and race distinctions between himself and Rocky. During the opening act's realist portrait the protagonist saunters into a neighborhood pub where he sits at the bar and orders a beer. On the barroom television shown in Figure 2.13, the local news interviews Apollo for a spot about the upcoming title fight. Dressed in a business suit, the champion looks directly at the camera with advice for young people:

APOLLO. Stay in school and use your brain. Be a doctor, be a lawyer, carry a leather briefcase. Forget about sports as a profession. Sports make you grunt and smell. Be a thinker, not a stinker.

Like a model minority, Apollo promotes conventional education and professions over sports. No cleaner expression of professional-managerial class values could be made. There is no trace of Ali's anti-establishment rancor or lack of education.[73] Although they share poetic speech, captured in a catchphrase, Creed presents a more mainstream black figure than Ali. Stallone's scenario touches another nerve of white racism by making Apollo into a respectable middle-class character. The 1970s economic downturn exacerbated the resentment many poor whites felt over civil rights legislation and welfare-state programs that they perceived as unfair advantages to upwardly mobile blacks.

Figure 2.13 Rocky first encounters Apollo on the barroom television. The champion advises kids in the audience to use their brains rather than their fists.

Indeed, Rocky appears to represent precisely the kind of "stinker" Creed describes. The bulky Italian has been seen sweating and bleeding in a gritty ring, then dragging his knuckles around the dockyards. In a previous scene he struggled to spell "Del Rio." People call him a "creep" and a "meatbag." Balboa epitomizes a poorly educated, lower class grunt with no professional prospects. In this way Stallone's scenario inverts the common social structure of a white professional class and a black underclass. That reversal of stereotypes sets up both racist and antiracist interpretations.

The white bartender raises the issue of race obliquely. Figure 2.14 depicts a moment when he shakes his head at Apollo on the television and says, "All we got today are jig clowns." The epithet *clown* can be read in two ways. It may criticize Creed as an insincere politician, reflecting Ali's new presence in the mainstream; in fact, Ali was the first to admit that he would "clown" around.[74] However, *clown* can also insinuate that Creed is not a legitimate fighter but merely a poseur. The bartender thereby hints at a criticism of affirmative action policy for granting positions to unqualified minorities. Furthermore, reading *jig* in reference to dancing alludes to black minstrelsy; taken on its own, *jig* is a shortened form of the offensive label "jiggabo" and also rhymes with a more severe slur.[75]

However, Rocky snaps back at the bartender to defend Apollo: "Are you crazy? He's champion of the world. He took his best shot at becoming champ. What shot did you ever take?" Rocky affirms his respect for the black man and implies the color-blind merit of sport. This racially charged scene thus establishes Rocky as an antiracist hero.

Color-blindness and merit belong to an individualist strategy of antiracism. By suppressing group categories that form the basis of racism, this strategy promotes the treatment of each person as a unique individual. Leah Gordon explains that the

Figure 2.14 The white bartender looks at the television and dismisses Apollo Creed with an insult, prompting Rocky to come to the champion's defense.

liberal consensus implemented the strategy of "racial individualism" after 1945 and that it shaped civil rights legal reforms through the 1960s.[76] The idea behind this strategy is that blindness to "color" will slowly erode prejudice from everyone's mind. Where prejudice constituted an error in judgment, color-blindness aims to restore neutrality so that individuals can be judged purely on merit. Since the 1970s, individualism has been the preferred antiracist strategy of mainstream conservatives, while the left began to prioritize multicultural and economic strategies.

Disregarding race risks turning a blind eye to all social phenomena. Individualism has been criticized for oversimplifying racism and ignoring minority culture. For the multiculturalist, color-blindness denies public recognition to minority cultures, denies the importance of culture to individual identity, and cuts off deliberation over national identity. Moreover, conceiving of racism solely as a matter of individual morality overlooks systemic aspects of the social problem. Kelly Madison criticizes antiracist Hollywood movies in the 1980s and 1990s on these grounds. For instance, *Mississippi Burning* (1988) and *A Time to Kill* (1996) feature blatantly White supremacist villains and heroic white saviors while relegating black characters and African American culture to the background.[77] The dramatic structure of these films reduces racism to a personal demon, and casting a white protagonist disempowers African-Americans in another way. The pub scene in *Rocky* echoes that pattern by having Apollo appear only on television, while the conflict plays out between the white bartender and white hero.

If we were to evaluate the film's racial politics from this scene alone, its individualism would qualify as center-right. Apollo's next appearance complicates things by addressing race and ethnicity explicitly.

Affirmative Action and Pluralism

The drama breaks with an individualist ethic when Apollo intentionally selects Balboa to be his opponent because he is a local white fighter. This action instead resembles affirmative action, but inverts the usual stereotypes.

This moment is worth examining in detail. The scene begins as the fight's promoter informs Apollo and his entourage that the original opponent, another black boxer, was injured and can no longer fight. (This narrative device is a patent *deus ex machina*.) No other contenders are available on such short notice, so they mill about the office, hankering for a solution. Figure 2.15 captures the moment when everyone looks to ruminating Apollo, who responds:

APOLLO. Without a ranked contender what this fight is gonna need is a novelty. This is the land of opportunity, right? So, Apollo Creed on January 1st gives a local underdog fighter an opportunity. A snow white underdog, and I'm gonna put his face on this poster with me. And I'll tell you why: because I'm sentimental. And a lot of other people in this country are sentimental, and there's nothing they'd like better than to see Apollo Creed give a local Philadelphia boy a shot at the biggest title in the world on this country's biggest birthday.

Creed selects a "snow white underdog" with full understanding of the race rivalry the matchup implies. He evidently wants to exploit the race rivalry, the fantastical underdog scenario, and the national political implications of both elements.

Figure 2.15 When his original opponent is injured, Apollo Creed hatches the idea of recruiting a "snow white underdog" during a meeting at the promoter's office.

Creed performs another twist on Muhammad Ali here. Ali was well known for his promotional bombast that played upon racial tensions with white as well as black opponents. For instance, Ali would bait fight audiences by casting his darker-skinned black opponents as Uncle Toms or brutes, and himself as the hero.[78] Yet Ali would never deliberately cast himself as the black villain against an underdog American hero, as Apollo does. Nor did Ali treat racial difference so flippantly. Carl Weathers performs a cerebral Apollo character in a way that tosses off the race rivalry scenario as a mere ruse, at least within the private office. These twists complicate the character of Apollo, who is no simple race villain.

Apollo's selection of Rocky mimics affirmative action in reverse. A shorthand term for federal civil rights policies adopted in the 1960s to increase employment of minorities, *affirmative action* refers to what might be more accurately described as positive discrimination or preferential selection that corrects for negative discrimination and unjust preference. The Civil Rights Act of 1964 prohibited discrimination on the basis of race, color, religion, sex, or national origin. To complement the law's negative prohibition, executive policies affirmed compliance by setting out positive measures for representation that courts could enforce. Since the 1972 expansion of federal policy, affirmative action has generated intense controversy because it can conflict with judgment based purely on individual merit and because white Europeans were not a protected class of minority under federal policy.[79] Apollo's selection of Balboa as challenger clearly breaks with a merit-based system that would only allow a ranked contender. The champion and the promoter grant Balboa a special opportunity because of his race, local origin, and underdog status. Furthermore, invoking patriotism around Apollo's decision highlights the resemblance to affirmative action.

High-level American sports have most often symbolized merit-based evaluation, so *Rocky*'s positive invocation of affirmative action is especially meaningful. Conservative beliefs in individualism, the free market economy, and aristocracy cohere in the ritual of competitive sports. (Recall that *meritocracy* is a euphemism for *aristocracy*, a Greek word that literally means rule by the "best" [*aristos*].[80]) Men's professional sports became a rare and visible example of rapid minority advancement after racial integration as African-Americans dominated the ranks of boxing, football, basketball, and baseball by the 1970s. For its conservative opponents, that rapid change seemed to prove affirmative action unnecessary. Against the call for pure merit, Apollo's artificial selection of an unranked contender endorses affirmative action. His patriotic motivations blend his individual interest with the egalitarian interest of the everyman. Although the racial structure is reversed in this exceptional sports situation, sowing more ambiguity, Apollo implies that affirmative action truly adheres to the egalitarian ethos of the American dream.[81]

Rocky's obvious ethnicity highlights multiculturalism in this scene. Apollo not only selects a local white adversary, he specifically chooses an Italian-American. The big fight has been billed as the "Bicentennial Super Battle" shown in Plate 3. Set for New Year's Day 1976, the event will inaugurate bicentennial commemorations for the 1776 signing of the Declaration of Independence in Philadelphia. Apollo devises a way to add to the heritage novelty.[82] "Now who discovered America?" he asks rhetorically. "An Italian, right? What would be better than to get it on with a descendant?" Jergens and the others agree that Apollo's casting adds another layer of significance to the fight. This clever, meta-cinematic moment reflects on the ethnic and local authenticity Stallone brings to the film as an actor.[83] In addition, Italian-Americans Talia Shire and Burt Young play Adrian and Paulie.[84] Mickey's Irishness could not be more overt. *Rocky*'s emphasis on different ethnicities and races exemplifies the recognition of plural cultures in America. The film does not ignore the social tension created by pluralism, as an ideally color-blind drama would do.[85]

The visibility of race and ethnicity in *Rocky* reflects the mainstream acceptance of multiculturalism in the 1970s and the ongoing controversy over national identity. The 1976 Bicentennial celebration embodied the celebration of a panoply of ethnic cultures. Rather than organize a central event like Philadelphia's 1876 Centennial Exposition, the federal government created an agency, the American Revolution Bicentennial Administration (ARBA), that catalogued and distributed financial support to local community celebrations that emphasized tradition and heritage.[86] ARBA's catalog listed over 55,000 events, such as a Norwegian-American Lecture Series in Decorah, Iowa, and a Mexican Heritage Day in Oelwein, Iowa.[87] This grassroots approach to the Bicentennial typified both the liberal ideal of a neutral state and a multicultural, communitarian ideal of festive tradition. Another contemporary trend that illustrates the acceptance of multiculturalism is that of immigrant narratives, such as Alex Haley's *Roots* (1976) and Maxine Hong Kingston's *Woman Warrior* (1976). Haley's book was adapted into a wildly successful television mini-series in 1977. The mainstream white public, who had had its own immigrant narratives since Horatio Alger at the end of the nineteenth century, could perceive something similar in these nonwhite immigrant stories, which effectively integrated African-Americans and Asian-Americans in the mainstream imagination. Yet these new works differed from earlier immigrant narratives in their ostensible pride in minority, ethnic cultures.[88] Minority cultural memories of racial oppression nevertheless conflicted with the celebration of European heritage in America. Sociologist James Davidson Hunter etched a name for this conflict in the title of his 1991 study *Culture Wars: The Struggle to Define America*. Stallone's setting the story around the Bicentennial probes the deep tensions of multiculturalism felt by mainstream white America.

Apollo's selection of a local Italian opponent invokes the antiracist strategy of multiculturalism in an unusual way. Multiculturalism refers to the principles of recognizing and protecting minority cultures from the tyranny of the majority.[89] It aims to create peace between plural social groups through a mutual recognition of cultural difference. Such pluralism contrasts with the borderless ideal of individualism, and resists assimilating minorities into a majority monoculture.[90] While one might criticize pluralism for impeding the coherence necessary for a good state, advocates maintain that multiculturalism acts to incorporate diverse social groups in a nuanced, authentic way. Whereas assimilation conforms all people to the same values and characteristics, multiculturalism finds agreement, paradoxically, in the mutual recognition of difference. Using a concept from Gadamer, Charles Taylor explains this nuanced agreement as a "fusion of horizons."[91] Multiculturalism aims to create a form of solidarity that tolerates difference rather than stamping it out. The salad bowl whose various ingredients remain intact while blending their flavors has been one metaphor for multiculturalism in contrast to assimilation's melting pot. (Subsequent chapters on *The Natural* and *White Men Can't Jump* will expand discussion of multiculturalism.) If the white majority set European-American culture as a standard for assimilation that implied its superiority, multiculturalism combats racism by accepting cultural difference, recognizing minority cultures publicly, and prompting critical reflection about common culture.

The different narrative perspective in Apollo's first full scene both supports and diffuses the race rivalry. At this juncture Avildsen shifts the focus away from Rocky for the first time. Leaving the hero unaware for the moment, Avildsen transitions to the office of the fight promoter to open a new line of action. The musical score that had located our point of view and sympathy with Rocky likewise disappears in this new locale. The narration's cool detachment thus mirrors Apollo's cerebral mindset and posits a difference from the warmer hero. In line with multiculturalism, this critical perspective fuses with the patriotic theme to suggest solidarity through difference. Invocation of the American dream suggests to the audience that Apollo is also one of us, not some foreigner to be hated for his difference. In a self-referential way, the scene even aligns Stallone the screenwriter with Apollo who authors the fight scenario. Nonetheless, the cool indifference of the narration can also allow for negative attitudes toward Apollo. From this distance, he can be recognized as a fellow American or suspected as a devious villain.

Throughout this scene *Rocky* openly reflects on its own suggestive design. With Apollo Creed as their proxy, Stallone and Avildsen wink at their own conscious exploitation of race rivalry, underdog fantasy, and nationalism. Stallone must have had this scene in mind when he reflected on his screenplay in an interview, "I pitched it straight at the sentiments of a mass audience."[92] Stallone and Apollo employ the same key word, *sentiment*, and the same rationale. And yet this scene dispels any sense of mysticism about the opportunity granted Balboa. Apollo the showman, and behind him Avildsen and Stallone, give the audience what it desires. One desire is the taboo of racial conflict. A second desire, more democratic, is the dream of opportunity. The film's reflexive wink suggests that the nation, or at least its leaders, have the power to create opportunity for everyone. They only require the proper sentiment to bring that dream to life.

In sum, the office scene further complicates the film's racial politics. With a playful touch it brings affirmative action and multiculturalism into the center of the film through Apollo's character. His speech and action, couched in a patriotic sentiment, represent mainstream acceptance of minority heritage and the special minority policy of affirmative action. If *Rocky* plays a dangerous game in evoking racial sentiment, it is now a game situated within the playing field of multiculturalism. The grand finale scene will not resolve the tension between individualism and multiculturalism in the film; irony confuses the picture in yet another way.

Bicentennial Satire

Apollo's spectacular entrance to the fight satirizes national identity with an intent impossible to pin down. It repeats the pattern of introducing controversy but diffusing it through the characters' playful and non-hostile temperaments. The champion parades into the ring garbed in patriotic costumes that raise the issue of race and national identity. Playing on the well-publicized backdrop of Ali's politics and his wittiness, Creed's lightheartedness creates a confusion that is best described as carnivalesque, in a very specific sense of the word.

For Russian literary critic and philosopher Mikhail Bakhtin, carnival operates as a radical complement and antidote to formal speech and ceremony. In medieval Europe the ruling establishment generally suppressed folk culture, but held carnivals on special occasions to provide a release that revitalized the community. The nature of the festival is to mock seriousness and to dissolve social hierarchies. A logic of inversion and reversal drives this liberation and renders a "world inside out."[93]

Rocky employs the logic of inversion in several ways. We have seen how it reverses stereotypical race and class roles by situating the black champion as a benevolent middle-class liberal who grants an opportunity to an underprivileged white underdog. Here in the festive pre-fight scene Apollo dons costumes that recall a white national heritage and thus multiply the inversions.

The carnivalesque atmosphere of the scene develops from the contrast between Apollo's provocative costumes and the ringside announcers' innocently merry tone. Their television broadcast intervenes within the drama as a neutral narrative point of view coded in the conventional voices of white sports reporters. They receive Apollo's stunning entrance with good humor. "He's doing an imitation of George Washington," the announcers explain, chuckling. Figure 2.16 shows the parade float disguised as a boat that carries the black champion poised atop the prow and dressed in a white wig. Evidently part of the event's Bicentennial theme, this elaborate getup echoes Emanuel Leutze's hallowed 1851 painting Washington Crossing the Delaware that memorializes a surprise victory launched against the British from Pennsylvania during the Revolutionary War. To play off another Washington myth, of the young leader throwing a silver dollar across a river, Creed tosses coins into the crowd. "A dollar in those days went a lot further," the reporters quip, joking about the 1970s inflation crisis. Avildsen fills out the soundtrack with ambient laughter and commotion that envelop the whole scene. Carl Weathers performs everything with a charming smile and camp jocularity that draw attention to the spectacle. The lighthearted atmosphere contrasts with the potent racial significance of an Ali-like boxer in the costume of a founding father widely known as a slave owner, symbolically flaunting his wealth during a recession.

Stirring the pot further, Apollo dons an Uncle Sam costume once he enters the ring. "During World War I there was a picture of Uncle Sam," the announcers explain, ". . . a recruiting poster for our fellows in the army and the navy. 'I want you!' That's what he's doing a take on." Plate 4 captures a medium shot of Apollo's top hat, coattails, and

Figure 2.16 Perplexingly, Creed enters the ring dressed as George Washington on a float representing the crossing of the Delaware River—the start of a surprise victory in the Revolutionary War.

glittery lapels as we hear him shout the slogan "I want you" at his opponent and then "I want all of you" to the crowd. The point of view then shifts to Rocky, who whispers to Mick in a medium close-up, "He looks like a big flag." Rocky appears amused, and even plays along with his opponent's theatrics by questioning, "Is he talking to me?" The act and response are nonsensical because the publicity character recruited allies, not opponents. The ring announcer then sobers the scene by starting the formalities of the fight. The shadow of Muhammad Ali makes the Uncle Sam costume particularly controversial; he was convicted for resisting the draft in 1967, and although the Supreme Court exonerated him in 1971, his anti-war reputation persisted. Yet here again the main characters show no personal animus. Their theatrics simultaneously inflame and extinguish the race rivalry, moderating their relationship.

Apollo's spectacle also satirizes Bicentennial festivities that had saturated the country prior to *Rocky*'s release. The year 1976 witnessed a surfeit of events owing to the decentralized approach of the American Revolutionary Bicentennial Administration. ARBA also licensed official Bicentennial imagery and designations, encouraging commercial exploitation of the occasion through commemorative products and corporate-sponsored events. For instance, one particularly chintzy commemorative product was an eagle-themed ice gusher.[94] Rabid commercialization already during the years preceding 1976 led critics to rail against the "Buycentennial." Activist Jeremy Rifkin even formed a commission to highlight corruption by official planners, which led to congressional hearings.[95] By the time *Rocky* was released in late November 1976, audiences would have understood the mockery of this commercial spectacle, especially when the ringleader throws money at the crowd. Yet it is not clear if Apollo is meant to represent a corporate elite and corrupt establishment that was exploiting the occasion, or to mock them.

Moreover, some commercial Bicentennial events had undeniable civic importance. For instance, Pepsi, GM, Kraft, and other companies launched a cross-country "Freedom Train" whose exhibits included film screenings of Dr. King's nonviolent protests and DeMille's personal script of the 1956 Hollywood blockbuster *The Ten Commandments* to memorialize the civil rights movement.[96] Apollo's "Bicentennial Super Battle" likewise mixes commercial novelty with serious symbols and social questions, but in a beguiling, carnivalesque atmosphere.

On the one hand, Apollo's costumes can signal his villainy. Interpreted from a reactionary perspective, Apollo masquerades as Ali the Black nationalist and draft dodger in costumes that sardonically mock White America and its sacred traditions; he also represents the new establishment Ali who hypocritically ignores his past treason and a cynical liberal elite that has corrupted the country with lucre and multiculturalism. Against such villainy the hero represents a great white hope to restore the nation's sacred White tradition. The scene's ambiguity admits such an extreme view.

On the other hand, the cerebral Apollo character makes a clever leftist critique of American tradition. His black George Washington demystifies the founding fathers who did not treat nonwhites as equal men. (In his 2015 play *Hamilton*, Lin-Manuel Miranda provoked a similar critique by casting nonwhites as founding fathers.) Apollo's black Uncle Sam also jabs at the imperialist and racist history of American military force; historically aware viewers might know that the culturally conservative Army was segregated during World War I and had race-related controversies such as the Camp Logan mutiny. Furthermore, Creed's spectacle derides the commercialism of the Bicentennial and the patriotism around sports. Through his association with Stallone as the author of the event, Creed also reflexively mocks the movie itself, which was widely criticized for being "oversold" owing to a marketing blitz upon its release.[97] Weathers' cool performance of the ringmaster character in these ludicrous but deadly serious situations sublimates into the same cynicism that Elsaesser located in Hollywood's liberal antiheroes.

Yet the mild attitudes of Apollo and Rocky reign in these extreme interpretations. Reading Apollo's good humor at face value, he makes an earnest demonstration of patriotism by embracing the superficial role of founding father and recruiter. This earnestness certainly fits with his characterization as a version of Cassius Clay. Rocky's mild amusement testifies to his respect for Apollo from a cool distance. Their lightheartedness relays an acceptance of establishment policy of liberal multiculturalism, without resolving its internal conflicts. Such nonchalance also downplays the importance of national culture, as if laughing away all the controversy the scenario has stirred up. In this milder reading, there is no deeper sense to Washington's conflict with a local Italian-American, nor to Uncle Sam recruiting Balboa who will fight against him, not beside him—the whole charade is absurd. Avildsen and Stallone are aiming for this moderate interpretation, in my view; such moderation complements the main arc of the film by floating in the background. The controversial spectacle abruptly ends and the action re-centers on Rocky's melodrama. In this way the pre-fight festivities epitomize the carnivalesque. Apollo turns national identity inside out and generates a confusion that has no real consequence beyond revitalizing the principal civic drama of the hero.

Apollo Creed could have made the perfect race villain, and the film could have been an incendiary political anthem. Instead, *Rocky* sets up a controversial situation and then plays out the drama in a way that dissolves race rivalry in uncertainty, effectively diverting attention toward the masculine liberation plot. Stallone and Avildsen simply leave the question of national identity unresolved. Rocky is clearly a collective hero, as an everyman who has been integrated in the community and uplifted it, heralded by Conti's brass fanfare, synth, and choir. However, in 1976 Rocky is not yet a full-fledged patriot. Such skepticism around national issues reflects popular mistrust of government and elites generally in the 1970s. *Rocky IV* (1985) will adopt a frank nationalism and repackage that skepticism in another way.[98] The first film offers a fascinating exercise in moderation by inciting controversy but then allaying it.

Evaluating the film's racial politics overall, *Rocky* and its characters are evidently hyperconscious of the social division between blacks and whites in America. However, the drama does not center around a conflict and resolution of racial tension. It therefore marks a step beyond Hollywood's traditional idealism and color-blindness, but a long way from the casual multiculturalism that emerged at the end of the century. Ultimately, its race rivalry scenario and conventional white male hero strike a distinctly regressive chord. Nevertheless, Balboa's attitude toward Apollo is neither hostile nor amiable; Stallone performs something akin to the "grudging respect" that earned Democratic politicians like Joe Biden the support of African-Americans in this era.[99] The hero does not expel his Black foe from America, nor does Rocky's achievement lead to a White suburb. The moderate conclusion simply leaves racial tension latent and lingering. In this respect, *Rocky*'s ambiguity and incoherence around race reveals limitations and problems within the ideology of multicultural liberalism that has defined centrist American politics since the 1970s.

Conclusion

Comedy, in the formal sense of the word, sews together the two halves of *Rocky*. Following Aristotle, literary scholar Northrop Frye defines comedy as a kind of social ritual. "The theme of the comic," he explains, "is the integration of society, which usually takes the form of incorporating a central character into it." Frye classifies the everyman hero who inhabits the same strata as the audience as the "low mimetic" mode of comedy, which typically involves "the incorporation of an individual very like the reader into the society aspired to by both, a society ushered in with a happy rustle of bridal gowns and banknotes."[100] Frye's definition makes clear that the happy ending is not an American or Hollywood invention but a common mode of popular comedy.[101]

As a ritual, low mimetic comedy serves to affirm the goodness of a given society—its ethos, identity, and values.

In this light *Rocky*'s central drama interprets the American dream as democratic participation. It therefore revises the Horatio Alger version that emphasizes the self-reliant individual and material success, as this chapter's detailed analysis has demonstrated. Initially isolated by circumstance and by a hard masculinity highlighted by the name Rocky (which also recalls 1950s heavyweight champion Rocky Marciano), Balboa opens up emotionally and forms bonds with Adrian, Mickey, Paulie, and the city at large. The hero and the working-class community he represents are symbolically integrated into the nation. Rocky loses the fight, but the optimism of Bill Conti's score remains, surprisingly, undiminished. Bridal gowns and banknotes are eschewed in favor of a romantic embrace between Adrian and Rocky. Stallone's drama begins with realism but follows the archetypical form of comedy to a happy ending. This democratic interpretation of the American dream idealizes egalitarian civil society—the everyman worker ascends and the elite descend to meet in a middle ground.

It is significant that a local, ethnic, working-class type like Rocky appealed to the American public. As an Italian-American, he falls among the contemporary film characters of Francis Ford Coppola and Martin Scorsese. In his history of race and Hollywood, Greg Garrett identifies *The Godfather* (1972) as a turning point for the self-representation of minorities. A bigger step forward from ethnic Italians to African-Americans took place in the 1990s, although European ethnicities still remain dominant in Hollywood today.[102] Moreover, Biskind and Ehrenreich see the 1970s laborer-hero as a replacement for the cowboy, and they observe that a large portion of the audience for boxing and for *Rocky* were middle-class patrons.[103] Here again Rocky compares to Jimmy Carter, an outsider characterized as a peanut farmer during his 1976 campaign. Populist energy at this moment gravitated to the Democratic party, where the romantic image of the laborer-hero represented progressive politics.

But the film's representation of Blackness does not fully cohere with this ideal. The hero and his community have exclusively European ethnicities, which can suggest the exclusion of others. The main Black character does not resolve this ambiguity. Avildsen depicts Apollo Creed according to a different form of comedy—satire. In its formal sense, satire is an ironic mode of comedy whose meaning can vary from savage mockery to light humor. The realism of the opening act also constitutes an observational form of satire that shares something with the cool representation of Apollo in the office scene. But the move to the carnivalesque diverges from the central drama's affirmative mode of comedy. Avildsen and Stallone attempt to create a moderate pluralism by balancing the provocative race rivalry with good humor and tempered attitudes, leaving the ambiguity unresolved. Creed's pivotal selection of Balboa, motivated by patriotic sentiment, indicates that Creed is not symbolically excluded from the nation; however, as an opponent he does not integrate into the hero's circle. The end result of the drama is confusing because it neither addresses the sins of racism in the national tradition nor demonstrates racial reconciliation in its idealized conclusion. The franchise will eventually correct this deficiency by having Rocky and Apollo develop a friendship in *Rocky III* (1982), then go a step further by promoting Apollo's son Adonis as the primary hero in *Creed* (2015), a film written and directed by Ryan Coogler, a Black American filmmaker. The original *Rocky*'s racial politics have progressive and regressive elements, and they appear simply incomplete in hindsight.

At the moment of the Bicentennial, *Rocky* wanted to imagine an America that has matured from the crises of the 1960s. Its aging hero, urban realism, and community development reflect the nation's inward turn after Vietnam; it avoids the imperialistic adventures of a young hero in a coming-of-age tale. Traces of men's liberation and multiculturalism indicate reform from the hard heroes and racial villains of the past, although these incremental steps do not appear so significant in retrospect, nor were leftist critics at the time convinced.[104] The film's guiding theme of moderation amid controversy might perfectly summarize the decade. For the radical, such moderation is conservative; yet for the progressive it constitutes an early phase of integrating radical changes into the main stream of the nation. Furthermore, the film's hybrid ideology testifies to the era's unstable political state. *Rocky*'s unbounded optimism does not cohere with the serious social issues it raises, which compares readily with Jimmy Carter's promise of renewal that would struggle for fulfillment.

Historically, *Rocky* represents a breakthrough success for the sports genre that would inherit the mantle of the Hollywood western. Having clarified the progressive elements of the film invites further reconsideration of Stallone's work overall. A tender heart remains a fundamental part of Rocky throughout the franchise[105]; carnivalesque inversion also operates in his 1985 blockbusters *Rocky IV* and *Rambo* to complicate their political significance[106]; and Ryan Coogler's reboot of the franchise around Apollo's son Adonis with *Creed* (2015), in perfect continuity with the 1976 film, suggests that a seed of multiculturalism was present from the start. One way to move forward would be examine the politics of the *Rocky* franchise as it evolved across four decades, but its particular history would distort our view of Hollywood and the nation in general.

This chapter has served to introduce the main concerns of this study: masculinity, race, class, and civic community (especially the nation). It therefore provides a vantage upon further development in other works we will now consider. First, its near contemporary *Slap Shot* migrates urban realism to a Pennsylvania steel town; rather than focus on a tender heart, it aims to liberate masculinity through a playful approach to toughness.

3

Slap Shot (1977)

Deindustrialization, Goon Masculinity, and Yankee-Doodle-Disco Patriotism

A steam whistle signals a shift change at the steel mill, as the town's star hockey players idle past. "What are these poor fuckers gonna do when they close the mill?" wonders one teammate to another.[1] The athletes appear oblivious to their own dependence on the local steel industry for the team's sustenance.

But the hockey players do understand the plight of the workers. Male icon Paul Newman stars as aging player-coach Reggie "Reg" Dunlop, flanked by phenom and Princeton graduate Ned Braden (Michael Ontkean):

REG. They ain't closing [the mill], just jacking the guys around so they'll feel happy they got jobs. It's the old tactic, the mind fuck.
BRADEN. Announced it today. April 1, they shut it tight. Ten thousand mill workers placed on waivers.
REG. That's a big surprise. What the hell are they gonna do with them?
BRADEN. I don't know. Every sucker for himself, I guess.

Newman's stunned look and rapid shift in tone make evident that the mill closure is no bluff. Figure 3.1 captures his change in attitude. Notice how screenwriter Nancy Dowd's line "every sucker for himself" cleverly twists the maxim "every man for himself" to suggest a crisis of masculinity. The disappearance of steady union jobs with deindustrialization will reduce the workers from men to dependent and gullible "suckers." These blue-collar types do not share the optimism expressed in Daniel Bell's *Post-Industrial Society* or Richard Florida's *Creative Class*.[2] In losing their livelihood, these workers will lose the very basis of their manhood.

Cinematographer Vic Kemper tracks the two men in a long take that visualizes the correlation between the hockey team and the rusting mill town. Men in hard hats glide past them in the foreground of Figures 3.1 and 3.2—likely actual mill workers hired as extras on location in Johnstown, Pennsylvania. The red paint coating the ducts, Braden's maroon vest, and the drab background seen in Plate 5 together evoke iron oxide rust. These images announce deindustrialization in parallel with the dialogue.

The steam whistle in this scene recalls an important symbol in literature and cinema. That icon of modernity has typically represented the dawn of industrialization in a given place or epoch. In Flaubert's realist novel *A Sentimental Education*, a

Hollywood Sports Movies and the American Dream. Grant Wiedenfeld, Oxford University Press. © Oxford University Press 2022.
DOI: 10.1093/oso/9780197624920.003.0003

Figure 3.1 A walking conversation between hockey players is staged outside the steel mill whose imminent closure will incite the dramatic action.

Figure 3.2 Steel workers, probably local extras, interrupt the foreground to create a realist presence.

steamboat inaugurates the coming-of-age tale; the steam engine of a train likewise breaks into the countryside in Satyajit Ray's film *Pather Panchali*. This key scene from George Roy Hill's film sets in motion a plot to save the season and the team. The steam whistle pierces the sequestered world of sports to signal the historical change of deindustrialization.

The players respond to the crisis in a radical way. Paul Newman's character Reg will lead them to become goons who perform male violence and sexuality to the desperate mill town's delight, and they win the championship in ridiculous fashion. Already in its opening title sequence, Hill's sports movie announces a political statement with the national anthem and the flag, depicted in Figure 3.3. But the nature of that statement has not been well understood.[3]

At first glance, male hockey violence recalls the conservative masculinity of Teddy Roosevelt who championed a "strenuous life" of hard work and physical striving. Academic critics initially associated the rage for white working-class subjects in 1970s Hollywood with the rise of Reagan and the New Right, who wed conservative social views to neoliberal economic policy and nationalism. For example, Peter Biskind and Barbara Ehrenreich read macho men like Rocky Balboa as fantasy avatars for an anxious middle class, akin to the self-made western hero who became legend at the moment the frontier closed.[4]

However, more recent studies have underlined the expressive range of 1970s cinema, especially its working-class subjects. Derek Nystrom highlights queer, female, and nonwhite characters that present strong counter-examples to Biskind and Ehrenreich's argument. John Bodnar surveys working-class representations across five decades to demonstrate how movies resist simple reflection of partisan ideology and narratives.[5] Following in this vein, a closer look at Hill's film will reveal an unusual political vision.

This chapter argues that *Slap Shot*'s goon masculinity satirizes conservative American sports culture from a populist left angle. Moreover, a progressive patriotism emerges from its zany comedy.

Figure 3.3 A downbeat title sequence announces the film's serious meaning by placing the title upon the flag.

Rust Belt Realism

Sports comedy was a novel subject for realist cinema in the 1970s. *Slap Shot* appeared in the wake of *The Bad News Bears* (1976) and *The Longest Yard* (1974), cementing a team comedy formula that combined burlesque secondary characters with satirical situations. Rather than centering the stories on workers or on mythic high-profile teams, sports such as little league baseball and minor league hockey create an occasion for comedy and performance. Cervantes's Quixote or Chaplin's idiosyncratic tramp character initiate a similar kind of play. The comedic strand of realism runs from Rabelais through Flaubert in French literature, with satire that punctures lofty dreams to reveal the brute everyday.[6] Literary scholar Northrop Frye would add that their irony turns on a hero who is inferior to the reader, like all comedy.[7] From this angle, it will be clear that *Slap Shot*'s goons mock the ideals of sportsmanship and fair competition to reveal the absurdist suffering of workers.

Director George Roy Hill and star Paul Newman followed up their successful collaborations *Butch Cassidy and the Sundance Kid* (1969) and *The Sting* (1973) with this contemporary hockey picture. Screenwriter Nancy Dowd spent a month with the Johnstown Jets minor league hockey team; her brother Ned played a few seasons there and served as the basis for the Ned Braden character.[8] They each contribute progressive elements to this Hollywood romp.

Johnstown, Pennsylvania, is one of many cities in the region that would be drastically affected by deindustrialization. A "Steel Belt" of heavy manufacturing once stretched across the Great Lakes region to the urban northeast, until a wave of older factories and mills closed in the late 1970s and 1980s. Subsequently, the region became known as the "Rust Belt" for its hulking ruins and corroding social environment.[9] For instance, Bethlehem Steel Corporation operated large mills across the country, including one in Lackawanna, New York, and several in Pennsylvania. In 1977, a year after filming, Bethlehem scaled back mill operations in Johnstown, and the Jets hockey team also folded. In retrospect *Slap Shot* is realistic to the point of being predictive.[10]

Extensive location shooting sets Hill's film apart from old Hollywood studio dramas, following the post-1945 trend sparked by Italian neorealism. More specifically, Hill's ironical and ambivalent depiction of middle America takes cues from postwar documentary photographers Robert Frank and the New Documents trio. The film merely changes the name of town to "Charlestown," locating its fictional world in close proximity to actual Johnstown.[11] *Slap Shot* memorably offers one of the first depictions of the Rust Belt in mainstream culture.

Realism, as I am using the term, describes an artistic representation that uncovers the lives and environments of common people. The naturalist movement in literature, led by Zola in France and by Dreiser and Norris in North America, even aspired to perform sociological study through fictional novels.[12] More than simply displaying authentic details or communicating information about social issues, artistic representation presents a holistic microcosm where class and group dynamics can be observed by a general public. And, of course, naturalism in Zola's hands was also seen to be predictive, guiding action and policy reforms. Realism often carries a shock in revealing common lives not represented previously in public and in art (that traditionally represents divine ideals or glorious historical leaders). Midcentury Hollywood boxing melodramas such as *Champion* (1949) or *On the Waterfront* (1954) established a realist tradition in sports cinema that Scorsese revived with *Raging Bull* (1980); however, that particular strain is serious tragedy. *Slap Shot* belongs to the Chaplin tradition of realist comedy.

Beyond the steel plant's gigantic pipes and geometric blocks, the film depicts everyday life in the town square and its small shops. Hill and Dowd present players hanging out at the local drug store, drinking sodas and watching soap operas. For instance, Reg visits his ex-wife Francine (Jennifer Warren) at the hair salon on the square where she works. Francine's coolness conceals a bitterness about both the town's prospects and the hero Reg. In another sequence, depicted in Plate 6, Ned Braden's wife Lily (Lindsay Crouse) saunters from the state-regulated liquor store to a bench on the town square. Educated and liberal, she complains cynically about her rotten destiny in Charlestown as a mere wife. The austere sign "State Store" and the medical green lights ironically suggest that the state aims to anesthetize its provincial citizen consumers.[13] Hill does not romanticize Main Street America, and he employs a neutral soundtrack in these scenes to present quotidian, provincial life as it is.

Nancy Dowd's screenplay also conforms to literary traditions of realism in its vernacular language and contemporary setting. First, the vulgar dialogue mimics the speech of ordinary people. Historically, literature privileged formal speech for serious subjects and relegated low speech and everyday subjects to frivolous or grotesque comedy.[14] No respectable text would have showcased dialogue like this exchange between hockey players:

OPPOSING PLAYER, *angrily*. Dunlop, you suck cock.
REG DUNLOP. All I can get!

Reg's sly comeback reclaims queerness as a strength and taunts homophobes—a subversive attitude I discuss in the next section of this chapter. Profanity had been censored in Hollywood until the late 1960s, so the vulgar dialogue prompted angry letters from some older Paul Newman fans. In interviews, Dowd authenticated this sort of coarse exchange by mentioning the fact that she had given her brother a tape recorder to capture actual talk in locker rooms.[15] Against the classical doctrine of levels of style, Dowd's realism mixes low culture with the most serious of subjects, the steel mill closure.

Dowd's Rust Belt plot has a realist relation to history. Bakhtin observed how coming-of-age novels usually set the hero's lifetime in parallel to a general epochal shift.[16] Unlike adventure stories that unfold in an infinite time, with endless episodes, realism's dynamic world situates the characters in an evolving historical context. In this way *Slap Shot* aligns its dramas of mill closure and team crisis with the historical shifts of deindustrialization and neoliberalism.

For his part, Paul Newman breathes dynamic life into the vernacular speech, historical dynamism, and satire of literary realism. His star persona included a small dose of counterculture without radically rejecting common values, making him perfectly suited to express the resentment and stubborn hope of middle America. *Hud* (1963), *Cool Hand Luke* (1969), and *Butch Cassidy* each cast Newman as an endearing petty crook who suffers at the hands of a belligerent establishment. These antihero roles blended outsider rebellion with the universal looks, charm, and social acceptance of the Hollywood golden boy. He "embodied a mainstream version of non-conformity," as Christine Becker describes it.[17] To perform that balance he had developed an underplayed comic style that exuded charm while avoiding inner turmoil and severity. Compared to the aloofness of Clint Eastwood or Steve McQueen, stars such as Newman and Warren Beatty offered more humane antiheroes. In this way Newman's star persona translated well to a Rust Belt hero for marginalized labor.

In his (publicized) personal life Newman simultaneously represented a rebel outsider and the marrow of middle America. Newman and his wife, the actress Joanne Woodward, resided with their children in pastoral Connecticut, far from Southern California and its glamorous celebrity scene. Newman nonetheless became actively involved in public life by protesting the Vietnam War and advancing progressive causes at the United Nations—endeavors that must have given his agent a heart attack, but proved well timed to the general public's turn against the war. Like other rat pack stars, he took up car racing, a sport simultaneously blue collar and aristocratic, when he starred in *Winning* (1969). By 1977 he retained the image of a progressive new man, but, now past fifty, also spoke to older audiences and to tradition. Though much less cartoonish than Chaplin, Newman plays the lovable loser with just as much charm.

Nowhere are Newman's ambivalent qualities more evident than in his costumes for *Slap Shot*. Off the ice, costume designer Tom Bronson dressed him in flamboyant materials with patterned fabrics and wide collars. For instance, his full leather outfit chafes against a bourgeois dining room, shown in Figure 3.4. Outside the mill he wears a coat whose fur collar recalls "Broadway Joe" Namath, the New York Jets' dandy quarterback who famously wore fur on the sidelines; compare Figure 3.5 to Plate 5.[18] These styles speak to a masculine tradition of wild and tough men, whether on Teddy Roosevelt's western frontier or in the urban subculture of the gangster film.

Yet Newman's character also dons pendants that resemble hippie beads via Madison Avenue, as Figure 3.6 displays. Both fur and pendants would normally be considered feminine, but male iconoclasts like Namath and Newman reverse that coding. Never the prim organization man off the ice, Dunlop's sartorial choices combine small-town swagger with distinct, cosmopolitan chic. On the ice, a hockey uniform tamps down individual style to portray him as one of the guys. The combination of uniform and crossover styles dress Dunlop as both swanky working man and collective hero.

Figures 3.4–3.5 Newman's swashbuckling costumes recall the wild masculinity represented by Joe Namath. Photograph credit: Associated Press.

Figure 3.6 Fur and pendants give Newman's manly swagger an almost queer edge.

All this is to say that *Slap Shot* has a serious intent beneath its comic hijinks. For a Hollywood comedy, it trades a glamorous locale for the crumbling reality of the common man. The cinematography, screenplay, and star situate the drama deep inside the late 1970s Steel Belt. Hill and Dowd aim to paint a realist portrait of an age we now call deindustrialization or neoliberalism. Their fictional work also points toward a possible future whose realization has been less evident. Key to their imagined new America is gender. What seems comically out of place in this "flyover" state and hockey movie are unmistakable feminist and queer themes.

Queerness, Feminism, and Goon Masculinity

SUZANNE. You're the first man I've slept with since I left Hanrahan.
REG. A beautiful woman like you?
SUZANNE. I've mostly been sleeping with women. [...] Are you shocked?

After a road game, Reg receives a phone call, out of the blue, from a rival player's ex-wife, Suzanne (Melinda Dillon). Hill cuts immediately from the hotel to Suzanne lying in her bed as Reg crawls up from beneath the sheets. Here she reveals that she is bisexual and recounts her story: miserable with their husbands on the road, Suzanne and another player's wife would get drunk, until one day they began playing with each other "like kids." Repeated sober, they discover a "terrific" lesbian relationship that liberates them psychologically. But her husband Hanrahan goes berserk: "He said if I was a dyke, that made him a queer! He started slapping me around, and I ended up in the hospital." Reg listens with tender sympathy beside her in bed.

Their pillow talk softens Reg's view of homosexuality. Suzanne initially asks if he is attracted to men, and Reg says no. After she recounts her story, she concludes by asking if he would ever sleep with a man. Reg then concedes openly, "Maybe it will change, and I'll wind up sleeping with old goalies. Things being what they are, who knows?" By the end of the film, although he doesn't kiss any men, Reg will pretend to be proudly gay to goad homophobic opponents who insult him. At one point he declares, "Now that I'm sexually liberated I don't care who's a fag no more. I mean, who cares? It's natural; it's all around us."

Suzanne's coming-out story and Reg's reaction express the flourishing of radical feminism in 1970s America. A new generation of activists saw the family and its traditional roles as a fortress for patriarchy while queerness offered a means of sexual and political liberation. Hill and Dowd might have read Shulamith Firestone, Kate Millett, or Julia Kristeva, who advocated class solidarity among women, queer transgression of social convention, and embodiment through play.[19] They challenged the moderate feminism of Betty Friedan, author of *The Feminine Mystique* (1963) and the first president of the National Organization for Women (N.O.W.), who regarded lesbianism as a threat to the family. The radical leftists pushed N.O.W. to officially accept lesbianism in 1971, and to focus on poverty and racism.[20]

Suzanne's tale exemplifies the radical break with family values: two oppressed hockey wives liberate themselves from a subordinate family role and abusive husbands, then soberly take control of their lives and pursue sexual partners freely. Nancy Dowd does not reveal any source for this character, but it clearly follows the lead of radical feminism. Hill's choice to withhold the sex scene (from a movie whose language was so vulgar it risked an X rating!) could also be read as a corrective to the typical objectification of women.[21] The movie only gives the audience nudity during a pillow talk scene, upsetting the classical coding of nudity equating to sexual desire. Cinematographer Vic Kemper throws shade over Suzanne's body to instead code their nakedness as intimacy and unguardedness. By setting the scene this way, Hill suggests that Reg's feelings about homosexuality are a matter of discourse, rather than brute instinct—a guiding principle for Kristeva. Suzanne's persuasion to accept her queerness (and potentially his own) happens in the intimate space of emotional closeness and in dialogue. Reg's playful bickering with opponents likewise makes public queerness an asset for the hero and casts the villains as bigots.[22] In all these ways, Suzanne's encounter with the hero points to radical feminist and queer themes at the heart of the film.

This queer character imparts the value of *play* to the hero, which is crucial to understanding the drama. Suzanne meets Reg at a crucial point in the story. He has just discovered that his hockey team will cease operation along with the steel mill. In his anxious and desperate state, Suzanne appears unexpectedly. Like a *deus ex machina*, she offers Reg advice based on her coming-out story: "Use your imagination! That's what I've been doing." Her counsel pivots from sexuality to labor and economics—an important relationship in feminism's socialist tradition and in queer theory. Queer, in this sense, is to resist the normative.[23] Suzanne leads Reg to transgress conventional morality in a sphere different from the bedroom—sport.

Reg uses his imagination with two ruses that alter the fate of the team. First, he fools the town sportswriter Dicky Dunn into believing that a Florida retirement community may buy the hockey team. After convincing Dunn, the team, and the town of the potential sale, Reg almost expects the rumor to take hold and become a reality, like the mythical town in Jules Romains' *Donogoo Tonka* or the *Field of Dreams* ("If you build it, he will come"). The ruse suggests James Carey's theory of media as a ritual that has the power to create reality.[24] In the meantime, before the rumor is discovered, the Florida prospect lifts the cloud of the mill closure and lifts the spirits of the team. Imagination has a real effect.

Second, Reg encourages his teammates to become goons who provoke their opponents to brawl. Imagination comes into play here, too: Reg merely performs anger and violence, with no real animosity. It begins when he taunts the opposing goaltender, Suzanne's abusive ex-husband Hanrahan. In the midst of the hockey game, a moment shown in Figure 3.7, Reg yells at him, "Hanrahan! Suzanne sucks pussy!" Hanrahan scowls, so Reg continues shouting across the ice, "She's a lesbian! A lesbian!," until the bigoted ex-husband reacts furiously. Hanrahan gives up a goal and instigates a fight, losing the game. Through cuts and bruises and cutaways to the onlookers, Reg recognizes how the fight catalyzes the fans and his team. Whereas fear motivates their opponents to fight, a playful aggression motivates the goons. So he goads them along in subsequent games, changing the course of the season.

By ridiculing Hanrahan, the film aims to teach viewers a lesson. The locker room scene after the game reinforces the notion that bigotry is childish and weak. Teammates ask, "What did you say to him?," and Reg explains Hanrahan's homophobia. Everyone laughs. To repeat the punch line, one sincere older teammate asks

Figure 3.7 Reg (Paul Newman) provokes Hanrahan by saying behind his back (literally) that his wife is a lesbian. The goalie mask emblematizes Hanrahan's insecurity.

if the woman's lesbianism really does make Hanrahan gay. With a deadpan beat, editor Dede Allen lets the viewer laugh at this simpleton. Neither man is mocked for being gay; Reg teases them for their prejudiced fear of homosexuality. Dowd's satire reverses the typical homophobic locker room where alpha men mock weak "fags"—a slur still tolerated at the time; those bigoted men are now the butt of the joke.

Goon masculinity expresses the 1970s men's liberation focus on noncompetitive play. Marc Feigen Fasteau led an important wave of scholars and activists who criticized "the male machine" as a role that patriarchy thrust on men. Their advocacy focused on liberation through communal bonding and emotional expression, which were highlighted in the previous chapter's analysis of *Rocky*'s principal melodrama. The clownish violence in *Slap Shot* instead emphasizes spontaneous play and physicality. For instance, gay rights activist Jack Nichols highlighted play as a "missing ingredient" in masculinity, and called for activities that cultivate flow and spontaneity rather than a single-minded focus on winning. Nichols explains that rational structures inhibit leisure and reduce men to "dull boys" who become neurotic in unstructured environments—a nightmare epitomized by Jack Nicholson's character in *The Shining*. By contrast, the liberated hockey goons in *Slap Shot* fight spontaneously, for no reason. Their physicality and aggression represent an answer to Nichols' call for free play.[25]

Goon masculinity fits within the countercultural movement for "noncompetitive" play. San Francisco radical Stewart Brand led one current of this movement, beginning with a 1966 anti-war event ironically titled World War IV. Concerned with " 'peaceniks' who seemed out of touch with their bodies in an unhealthy way," Brand created an antiwar parody game that offered "intense physical interactions" and the "opportunity to express aggression."[26] He called the game *Slaughter*, with forty barefoot players on their knees on a wrestling mat, four balls, two moving baskets, and the only rule that pushing another player over the edge "kills" them. From this event was spawned a New Games Tournament and foundation that flourished in the mid-1970s. To Brand's belief in physicality, George Leonard added a belief in creative play and Pat Farrington a focus on trust and cooperation. Similar movements and publications also appeared through the mid-1980s, such as Terry Orlick's *Cooperative Sports and Games*, Bernie DeKoven's "Games Preserve" in eastern Pennsylvania, the Friends Peace Committee Collective, and the Sagamore Institute's book *Playfair*. The latter's critique of mainstream sports culture is summed up in the phrase, "victory ... has spoiled play altogether."[27] These movements shared a commitment to developing inclusive communities through activities that avoided the "survival-of-the-fittest" paradigm so central to strenuous masculinity. Advocates saw physical and psychological health benefits in getting people off the couch and in removing the fear of failure. They also saw political effects in the practice of democratic participation and in the antiwar ethos.

Crucial to these noncompetitive forms of physical play were the promotion of awareness and consciousness over rational objectives. Such mindfulness aims to distinguish spontaneity from impulsiveness, and physicality from violence.[28] Advocates differentiated "releasing" physical aggression in noncompetitive play to "teaching aggression" in conventional sports.[29] The playful goons in *Slap Shot* yoke the game in this new direction by abandoning the basic objective of putting the puck in the net to brawling with abandon. In so doing, they discover one alternative to the traditional male machine. Hill focuses on the brawling and resists showing goals or the scoreboard. Although the goon attitude sparks a winning streak, by deemphasizing the score Hill promotes physical play for its own sake. While some critics on the left (whom Brand might describe as "peaceniks") associate any male aggression with patriarchy, the parody and irrationality of the goons seeks to align with countercultural masculinity.

Significantly, it is younger players Mike "Killer" Carlson and the Hanson brothers who respond to Reg's call to brawl. The Hanson brothers are the most cartoonish models of playful violence. Hill first presents them playing with their toy cars in the hotel room, to imply that their violence on the ice is equally a form of childish play. Plate 7 depicts this three-headed monster sitting rinkside. Like a comic strip, a montage highlights their egregious body checks, high sticks, and outright fouls that lead the referees to eject them from their first game. The Charlestown fans had begun the movie heckling their own losing team, but they now embrace the goons whole-heartedly. Women admire the players' cuts and bruises. The hockey players confront the economic crisis by becoming *goons*: they play dirty, start fights, and entertain the bloodthirsty crowd. Figures 3.8–3.10 illustrate these cartoonish moments.

The team's goon agitation represents a surge of populism. The film's middle act climaxes in a game against the Hyannisport Presidents, a direct reference to the Kennedy family. The New England locals protest the Charlestown team and their supporters, but the goons playfully moon them through their bus windows, as depicted in Figure 3.12. Outside the arena before the game, fistfights, sirens, and police with German shepherds (shown in Figures 3.13 and 3.14) suggest that goon masculinity foments general unrest. Then, once the game has begun, one Hyannisport fan incites a massive brawl inside the arena, egged on by the animated local radio announcer. The wild goon performers seem to channel public anger against an oppressive state of affairs.

If this film had been about Black football players instead of white hockey players, its radical politics would be recognized immediately. It is not a Democrat/Republican issue so much as an agitated working class that is rejecting an elite liberal establishment represented by the Hyannisport Presidents. Such anarchistic popular enthusiasm recalls the news anchor hero in *Network* who rants, "I'm mad as hell, and I'm not going to take this anymore!"[30] The milieu of minor league hockey situates local resistance to a plutocratic moral and economic order.

One player's resistance to goon play reveals the class conflict at stake. Star player and Ivy League graduate Ned Braden refuses outright at one point, telling Reg, "I won't goon it up for you." From a wealthy family, Ned scoffs at the unethical tactic of deliberately playing dirty and transgressing the rules of fair play. It's not the clean and technical "old time hockey" of Eddie Shore but a disgrace that Braden derides as "wrestling shit." His comparison to professional wrestling underlines the theatrical

Figures 3.8–3.10 The Hanson brothers are shown behaving like comic children who land heavy blows for fun and for cheers.

Figure 3.11 Charlestown fans embrace the capricous goons.

Figure 3.12 Charlestown players and supporters turn their backs on the respectable people of Hyannisport, amusingly.

performance of male violence and suggests a lower class audience. Moreover, Ned refuses to "goon" because the tactic draws attention away from his refined skills. "We win because I score goals," he complains to Reg. The player-coach holds his ground and replies, "We win because I make them crazy." It takes no special talent to be a goon, so Reg's tactic undermines Ned's special skillset and threatens his social status as a professional.

Figures 3.13–3.14 The hockey goons create a riot-like atmosphere before the games, indicating the political dimension of their sporting transgression.

Ned represents the conservative, American tradition exemplified by Teddy Roosevelt's speech "The Strenuous Life." Roosevelt encouraged aggression and physicality as a vital male force that urban life threatened to extinguish; the higher mind of logic and reason disciplines this brute force. The "clean, vigorous, healthy lives" that Teddy Roosevelt admired do not square with the dirty play of goons. His regime also conveys a strong paternalistic quality that is reflected in the central control of large organizations. In government, Roosevelt greatly expanded the executive branch of government. Large, technocratic agencies such as the military epitomized this chauvinism. The old colonel also linked the individual strenuous life to national greatness amid the global "struggle for naval and commercial supremacy." In the same vein, Lyndon Johnson and Richard Nixon defended their dogged persistence in Vietnam as manly, and labeled antiwar critics as sissies.[31] Ned reflects this attitude in his marriage. When his wife Lily complains at being stuck in a provincial town, with no occupation of her own, he stubbornly refuses to accommodate her. "You're drunk," he says to end one argument with her.[32]

Roosevelt's brand of masculinity aligns with large corporations, exemplified in his era by the Ford Motor Company. Fordism even became a name for a paradigm that subordinated woman to man, and that subordinated the individual to central control. In concert with labor unions, Ford privileged male workers with head-of-household status over women, whose labor was restricted to the domestic realm (except during World War II). Hence the old morality around male toughness meant a power over women, yet a subordination to higher male authority. Male sports culture reflected that paradigm in the ethic of "sportsmanship" and in the military authority of coaches and commissioners.

From this angle, Dowd and Hill's film criticizes the Roosevelt tradition of masculinity by pointing to its self-destruction. The mill closure disrupts the old work ethic and hierarchy of Fordism. Toughness consequently runs amok with the goons. Their antics unleash a populist rage that lampoons sportsmanship and respectability. In the story this rage is directed at the neoliberal executives who close the mill and fold the team. And within the context of the Watergate scandal and defeat in Vietnam, the goon characters mock the chauvinist tradition of national righteousness. Although goon masculinity shares physicality and aggression with the classical American tradition, it operates through mindful and embodied play, rather than the dialectic of violence and discipline.

As a band of buddies, the hockey goons compare to the democratic character system of old-time Hollywood director Howard Hawks. Peter Wollen distinguishes Hawks's collaborative male team from both Bud Boetticher's radical individualism and John Ford's imperialism.[33] "For Hawks," Wollen writes, "the highest human emotion is the camaraderie of the exclusive, self-sufficient, all-male group."[34] The group is united by pride in their professional skill, by folksy rituals such as communal songs, and by a nihilistic love of danger and fun. Hawks's model for masculinity suits the team sports movie with its variety of subplots for minor characters. For instance, *Slap Shot* centers on a heroic group of outsiders who play the adventurous game of hockey. They wear the same uniform, drink beer in the same bar, play cards together on the bus, and talk over the television at the hotel—all little rituals that bind them together.

The goons' solidarity translates to civic republican politics, best expressed by their patriotism. A fight breaks out during the warmups before one game, hilariously offending everyone. But Hill then cuts to the pregame national anthem ceremony where the Hanson brothers insist on standing reverently. A referee interrupts the anthem to scold the goons, but one brother hisses defiantly, "I'm listening to the fucking song!" One might not expect goons to respect any rules or formalities, but these teammates are not anarchists or outsiders. Their goon behavior is grounded in spontaneity and solidarity, with some sentimental attachment and respect for collective symbols, though tempered by their discontent. Like the revolutionary French republicans who attacked aristocrats, the people's team sticks it to the Hyannisport Presidents, in the name of the republic.

However, our heroes do not possess the superior skills of Hawks's heroes. They lose terribly in the first game we see and do not expect to do better. They are just goons, bound together not by professionalism but by ludic enthusiasm and shared suffering. Their bad performance, that nevertheless results in success, satirizes the meritocratic myth of sports. These hockey players are not pitted against female antagonists, as Hawks's men so often are. In fact, the goons build positive relationships (if superficial) with women such as Suzanne and with a group of fans who share in the adventure. Such relationships soften the sexism of Hawks's world, underlining the arbitrariness of the team's maleness. In fact, other team sports movies introduce female players onto male teams, such as *The Bad News Bears* and *The Mighty Ducks*. Despite not taking that step, Dowd and Hill's character system develops Hawks's male team into a more gender inclusive and proletarian bunch.

The championship scene ridicules the lore of victory so central to American sports. Before the game, Reg reveals that the owner will fold the team and that he invented the Florida rumor. Then he convinces them to play clean "old time hockey" for his swan song game. But their attempt to revert to clean tactics backfires when the opponents field a squad of ultra-goons. A glimmer of hope comes when the team learns that NHL scouts have come to recruit toughs. Immediately the game degenerates into a brawl, and the crowd relishes in the violence. The environment has evolved such that technical, clean hockey is no longer possible. Victory has consequently lost its moral significance. This ending suggests that deindustrialization and its crisis for middle America have made ironic performance the only reasonable conduct in an upside-down world.

Braden's spontaneous striptease creates a climax that takes the farce of sport beyond fighting. He sits on the bench, still refusing to play dirty, when he sees his estranged wife enjoying the spectacle of the brawl. The sight of her inspires him to jump on the ice and slowly remove his clothes as he skates around the rink, past the clashing goons. The band even strikes up a seductive soundtrack to accompany him. All the players stop fighting, agape at Braden stripping down to his jockstrap. Radio announcer Jim Carr (Andrew Duncan) chastises him: "I'm glad Mrs. Carr isn't here tonight, because this is a lascivious display!" The striptease brings the house down, indicated by a montage of excited faces among the buzzing crowd.

An absurd turn of events brings victory to Charlestown. Braden's lasciviousness enrages one enemy goon who punches a referee. The official promptly disqualifies the opposing team and awards the championship to the Charlestown heroes. Figure 3.15 depicts a nude Braden proudly hoisting the trophy and basking in the roar of overjoyed fans. The foolish announcer flips from condemning to praising Braden now that they have the championship in hand.

Ending so absurdly, *Slap Shot* clearly does not take winning seriously. Dowd and Hill present the game as a comic performance. They parody a conservative masculinity and a work ethic that neoliberalism has stripped bare. Before the game, Reg

Figure 3.15 Braden (Michael Ontkean) performs a striptease amid a mass brawl that ironically wins the championship by forfeit—an apogee of men's liberation. Ontkean later starred in *Making Love* (1982), one of Hollywood's first gay dramas, in a coming-out story.

even admits to the team, "We've been clowns ... we've been goons ... we're the freaks in a fucking sideshow." Like professional wrestlers, they ultimately win for giving the most uproarious performance, not for their hockey skills. In this way the film subverts the ideal of athletic competition, laser-focused on winning, and its masculine codes of honor.

Judith Butler concludes *Gender Trouble* with a section entitled "From Parody to Politics." She explains the subversive potential of laughter: "Just as bodily surfaces are enacted as the natural, so these surfaces can become the site of a dissonant and denaturalized performance that reveals the performative status of the natural itself."[35] In other words, performance reveals the contingency of what seems normal and natural, thereby opening the door to change. Of course, Butler's text is from 1990; perhaps Dowd had read Butler's influences Kristeva, Foucault, or Bakhtin as a Smith College student. More likely, the carnivalesque spirit of the film came through popular culture itself. The subversive tradition of the festival turns everyday morality on its head with a playful spirit that can spur radical politics.[36]

Slap Shot laughs at traditional masculinity from start to finish. Aided by the critical eye of female characters, the film denaturalizes the conservative masculinity that reigned in North America from Teddy Roosevelt to Nixon. Although the spousal relationships of Reg and Ned are not explored in depth, the goon drama unmasks the arbitrariness of old masculine codes by celebrating liberation. The hockey players triumph without conventional skill, without respectable conduct, and without achieving the rational objective of preserving the team. What they have is their humanity and solidarity, achieved through play rather than through classical discipline.

"My Accountant Is Certainly Pleased"

A verbal showdown between Reg and the team's owner crystallizes *Slap Shot*'s leftist critique of the new finance capitalism. To spin his rumor of a Florida sale, Reg has pretended that he had befriended the owner. "He's neat, and looking to get us bonuses," Reg lies. But when it is revealed that an anonymous corporation owns the team, just before the championship game, Reg ascertains the true owner's home address. He drives out to a site that could figure in *Better Homes and Gardens* magazine and is surprised to discover that the owner is a woman.

The only female antagonist in the film, the shrewd Anita McCambridge (Kathryn Walker) represents an interesting double for Reg. With her closely cropped hair, Anita appears confident in a chic pantsuit depicted in Plate 8, the very image of Betty Friedan's smart businesswoman. The wide collar on her blouse rivals Reg's panache but is coolly tucked behind a mauve suit jacket. Her attire highlights the classical discipline of a professional vanguard, in contrast to Reg's proletarian flamboyance and impetuousness.

But the new owner lacks the old aristocracy's paternal responsibility to its workers. Anita shares Reg's cynicism without any solidarity. He is unsure of how to confront her and express the interest of his comrades. First he curries favor by carrying her groceries and showcasing the tickets sold through the team's turnaround. But Anita proves to have been fully aware of his Florida sale bluff as well as his goon shenanigans. She only offers mild kudos for the increased revenue, telling Reg, "My accountant is certainly pleased." This line belittles their accomplishment and illustrates her amorality. The owner evidently does not take pleasure herself in the revenue. Rather than being driven by the vice of greed, the owner follows a coldly instrumental logic—pure nihilism.

As they turn from pleasantries to economics the conversation highlights the underlying cause of the Rust Belt. Reg inquires if Anita will sell the team, and she replies that her accountant advises her to write it off as a loss instead. Dumbfounded that anyone would dispatch a profitable business, Reg protests, "We're human beings, you know." When he insists that she could sell the team, Anita replies coolly, "I don't think you understand finance." Paradoxically, she makes more money by folding the team than by retaining it—purely a question of profit margin. "My accountant tells me I'm better off folding the team and taking a tax loss," she explains matter-of-factly. The goon intervention has made the team profitable but not as profitable as other investments. The closure of older, less profitable steel mills in the Great Lakes and Northeast regions followed the same logic. Sun belt cities and locales further south enticed companies to build new facilities with more efficient technology on top of cheaper land, with cheaper labor.[37] In this dialogue Nancy Dowd not only stages the conflict of people versus profits, but she also upends traditional gender stereotypes of stoic masculine pragmatism and feminine sympathy. Moreover, having the owner's decision hinge on a "tax loss" attacks government corruption and the unjust manipulation of finance capitalists.

The argument then escalates beyond finance to social politics. With even more condescension, Anita declares that she does not allow her children to watch hockey on television because she considers it a bad influence. "I have a theory that children imitate what they see on a TV screen," she explains. "They see violence, they'll become violent." In response Reg stands up and insults her by saying, "Your son looks like a fag to me ... he'll have somebody's cock in his mouth before you know it." She exclaims, "How dare you!" as he storms out.

Let us unpack these piercing insults. Anita's moralism evidently matches her disdain for proletarian culture. At first glance, Reg's reply seems purely bigoted and could be read as a conservative swipe at the liberal elite. But given his goading of the homophobic Hanrahan and Anita's sore reaction, I see him performing the same provocation here. The liberated Reg attacks the repressiveness of the conservative plutocrat by suggesting a nightmare scenario in the 1970s, when polite society remained closeted. Newman hits a countercultural note by ruffling the feathers of the old establishment.

Anita prefigures Gordon Gecko as a character who represents late capitalism. She can make *more* money with a tax write-off than keeping the profitable team. Her accountant would probably say that folding the team reduces fixed, overhead costs and makes her assets more flexible. If the old, capitalist owner resembled a feudal lord, this new incarnation has become an itinerant prince who no longer possesses an estate or subjects, only abstract assets. Kathryn Walker performs terrific aplomb that compares to Michael Douglas' Gordon Gecko character in *Wall Street*, known for his sardonic mantra, "Greed is good."[38] Gecko and Anita relinquish Fordism's pact between big business and big government—indeed, the state's only presence in *Slap Shot* is the state liquor store, some police, and a few military men at a parade. There is no visible welfare state, only the neoliberal prospect of "every sucker for himself" as Ned Braden predicted.[39] What distinguishes Anita from Gecko is her apparent lack of acquisitiveness. Gecko represents the patriarchal center of the whole capitalist system, operating on a nihilistic craving for power.[40] In contrast, Anita presents as a modest functionary who simply does her job as owner, in perfect ethical standing. She represents a genteel class blind to its own moral corruption. For this reason she epitomizes the Frankfurt School's criticism of reason's corruption through the mechanical logic of modernity; appearance triumphs while her humanity has been calculated out of existence.[41]

Some have criticized Nancy Dowd's decision to cast the owner as a woman. Viridiana Lieberman, for instance, observes that female team owners like Anita "continue the tradition of separating women from sports." Furthermore, their shrewdness is set in opposition to the team itself, which creates a gender rivalry.[42] The screenwriter anticipated criticism that the film was sexist, and affirmed her own feminism in interviews. "The only scene I thought twice about writing was making the team's rich, uncaring owner a woman," Dowd said. "... But I've seen that woman's attitude so many times: 'I never let *my* children see a hockey game.'"[43] Dowd criticizes moderate and conservative women types of the era: the women's liberation of Betty Friedan that once saw lesbianism as a threat to the family; the modest "peacenik" who sees all physicality as inherently violent; and the new conservative Phyllis Schlafly, whose campaign sunk the Equal Rights Amendment.[44] Anita thus represents the liberated woman plutocrat against which leftist feminists struggled in the 1970s. Moreover, casting the owner as a woman indicates a new era after the 1960s and calls for new political action.

Anita symbolizes the conservative individualism of late capitalism. Dowd's scenario avoids a brawny showdown between Reg and an older man, while accentuating the moral aspect of the conflict. If Fordism had a father-son relationship of owner to worker, the female owner represents the pure individualism of late capitalism. She has no relationship at all to the workers, who are mere numbers on a page. Anita does not represent all women, but rather an owner class whose business savvy comes at the workers' expense.[45] Dowd's Anita character underlines a Marxist critique of late capitalism, more than a conservative satire of women in a traditionally male public world.

The owner effectively spoils the American dream for the hero. The victory plot is a seminal aspect of the sports movie genre, but *Slap Shot* is fundamentally anti-climactic. The owner's steadfast decision to fold the team drains all drama from the upcoming championship game. The players cannot overcome her power, no matter their tactic. This season will be the team's last one even if they win. Most critics compare the victory plot to Horatio Alger's rags-to-riches formula and read in that myth the liberalist belief in free markets and meritocracy. Dowd's scenario instead locates those conservative beliefs with the aloof owner who actually destroys the common hero's hope for advancement. The Anita character therefore suggests that a neoliberal class of oligarchs are the only ones with access to the dream of a better life. Read in the historical context of political economics, the nontraditional owner accentuates a new threat to the treatment of workers as human beings. According to the codes of the genre, Dowd's story design is boldly critical of neoliberalism.

The film's leftist critique remains, however, muted. Appearing in only one scene, Dowd's Anita character is not as developed as Gordon Gecko and resembles too closely the "society women" antagonists of old Hollywood (such as the respectable ladies in John Ford's *Stagecoach* [1939]). The other female characters (Suzanne, Lily, and Francine) do not counter the dramatic weight of Anita. The film therefore risks confusing its radical left picture of a liberalist elite with a reactionary image of a femme fatale. Meanwhile, Reg is clearly a populist but no model socialist. Despite its leftist elements the film evinces a certain ambivalence; that ambivalence may have been a calculated effort, as with *Rocky*, to appeal to a broad audience.

Yankee-Doodle-Disco Patriotism

Slap Shot concludes with a town parade that expresses a popular democratic spirit, despite the closure of the mill and disbandment of the team. Maintaining the satirical tone from Braden's striptease, the parade showcases the lingering tensions of Rust Belt America. Figures 3.16–3.19 illustrate the zany event. School bands march down a sunny thoroughfare playing "Yankee Doodle," the merriest of patriotic anthems.

Figures 3.16–3.19 The Charlestown parade's conventional marching band and military men are set against the champion goons and marquees advertising pornographic movies.

Figures 3.16–3.19 Continued.

A cutaway shot subtly mocks some old Army officers who stand in front of a movie theater showing a pornographic film whose title, *Deep Throat*, parodies Watergate. The old guard observes a new set of heroes, the Hanson brothers, floating atop a gigantic nose and spectacles that recall Groucho Marx. Heroes Reg, Ned, and Lily appear reveling in the festivities as they ride in a large convertible with beers in hand. By sidelining the military men the parade suggests that the goon hockey players have become the new community leaders. The porn movie marquee can either be associated with the degenerate military men or with the liberated heroes. In his mise en scène George Roy Hill cultivates this carnivalesque ambivalence.

Reg's ambivalent fate tempers the happy ending and incites critical reflection. At the parade he happily announces that he has accepted an offer to coach a team in Minnesota, where he plans to hire his old teammates. His hopefulness might suggest that an attitude of carefree levity will solve all problems. However, Reg's ex-wife interrupts the parade with a dose of uncertainty. Her car pulls onto the route, packed with belongings as she leaves for a better life in Long Island. Reg bounds over to her window and insists that she call him after they settle in their new cities, but Francine only smirks at his naïve optimism. Her frank look hints at unexpressed, deeper problems. Dowd and Hill deny us the old Hollywood remarriage plot (though Lily and Ned Braden do reconcile) and thereby dampen the victory parade.[46] Figure 3.20 depicts a long shot that places Francine's departing vehicle against the backdrop of the closing steel mill to suggest the town's demise.

A closing credits montage restores the horizon of patriotic faith. Editor Dede Allen pairs close-ups of children at a Bicentennial parade with upbeat "Yankee Doodle," as shown in Plates 9 and 10. The soundtrack then transitions to Maxine Nightingale's gay disco tune, "Right Back Where We Started From." Her song also features prominently in several earlier montages of the team traveling by bus, in addition to the closing credits. A female vocalist and the liberal connotations of disco music are not

Figure 3.20 The final shot of Reg's ex-wife Francine departing for New York City, passing by the steel mill in the background, is an omen for the declining rust belt.

what traditionalists would associate with men's ice hockey. Barbara Ehrenreich has shown how the sports world adopted counterculture in the 1970s, especially music, to diffuse its Cold War conservatism.[47] The collage of Yankee Doodle, disco, and youth forges a new patriotism. It does not express a clear policy, but the solidarity of carefree people makes its own political force.

The Yankee Doodle Disco parade points to popular culture as a fundamental civic institution, revising the old Hollywood tradition of John Ford. Peter Wollen observes that Ford's heroes locate transcendent values in ritual U.S. institutions such as "the wedding, the dance, the parade."[48] Hill and Dowd's heroes would not be welcome in Ford's respectable churches. The goons grasp performance and festival as means of liberation, both collectively and individually. They would fit in better at gay pride parades, which began to develop in the 1970s and which share the same political force of festive gathering.

From this angle, cinema itself can be seen as a civic institution. Sociologist Jeffrey C. Alexander agrees that popular culture binds society through a feeling of solidarity. Prior to the formal dogmas of legal, partisan, and religious institutions there exists what he calls "a cultural structure at the heart of democratic life."[49] If *Rocky* represents that heart's sentimental aspect, *Slap Shot* represents its ludic quality. Hill's decision to close with a parade underlines the idea of cinema as a civic celebration.

Conclusion

With a realist eye on the U.S. Rust Belt, *Slap Shot* integrates themes of rebellious populism and liberated gender norms into a mainstream genre comedy. Though not an avant-garde documentary or radical manifesto, it tweaks the male sports world with some feminist and Marxist ideas. It is significant that Suzanne's character instigates change within the dramatic arc. Of course, no amount of secondary women characters add up to a woman protagonist; nevertheless, it is remarkable that Dowd and Hill imagined a Hollywood sports movie as a vehicle for some queer themes of performance, play, and parody.

The film's populist Rust Belt goon ethos of progressive politics raises the issue of populist politics in the United States. One relevant figure here is Jesse Ventura, former professional wrestler and Reform Party governor of Minnesota from 1999 to 2003. Since 2016 populism has become the dominant theme of several presidential campaigns, most notably those of Donald Trump and Bernie Sanders. But *Slap Shot* resorts to comedy in a way that presidential candidates cannot. The film does not stake out any policy positions but simply underlines the humanity of its characters, the absurdity of modern life, and the sheer joy of comedy—a tradition in American cinema most closely associated with Chaplin and on television with NBC's *Saturday Night Live*. In his own way, Paul Newman's charming character meets systemic crisis with a boyish exuberance that is undiminished by his certain failure. Laughter in the face of misery is a traditional spirit of the popular classes that this film tries to harness.

Slap Shot stands among a string of burlesque sports comedies: *The Longest Yard* (1974), *The Bad News Bears* (1976), *Semi-Tough* (1977), and *Caddyshack* (1980). All critical of an old establishment, they integrate characters with marginal identities and manage to celebrate silver linings in a decade of expectations diminished by recession. *Major League* (1989) and several kids' comedies in the 1990s revived the formula, whose optimism seemed to grow with the sub-genre's success. With a more direct inheritance, *Goon* (2011) and its 2017 sequel develop a tough yet progressive masculinity based on protectiveness. Cultural Studies critics such as Robin Wood have been quick to interpret these happy endings and aggressive male heroes as part of the conservative backlash to the civil rights and women's movements. However, this chapter has shown how *Slap Shot* complicates their reading and even undermines it. The Hanson brothers eloquently express this leftist impulse when they congratulate Reg for enraging Suzanne's homophobic husband: "You nailed him, Coach, in the fucking head! Right in his mind! ... He deserved it!"

4

The Natural (1984)

Farm Crisis and Minority Culture in a New Deal Legend

ROY. Did you sell the farm?

IRIS. No, I'll always have that. It's home. It's my son's. He means the world to me.[1]

This exchange between the hero and his childhood sweetheart does not appear in Bernard Malamud's 1952 novel, *The Natural*. In their movie adaptation director Barry Levinson and screenwriters Roger Towne and Phil Dusenberry make three major changes: they invent a flashback to a rural childhood that opens the film (depicted in Plate 11); they shift the main setting back to 1939; and they infamously reverse the ending. Whereas Malamud's protagonist ends up a penniless failure, his Hollywood counterpart triumphs and then returns to the heartland. The movie scenario therefore arcs from a family farm back to the Arcadian prairie, turning on the foregoing conversation. How do we understand the political significance of these alterations from the novel?

At first glance, *The Natural* makes another emblem for the conservative movement that swelled during Reagan's presidency. Rural whites became the cornerstone of the Republican Party, which represented resistance to urban, liberal social movements.[2] From this angle, *The Natural*'s blond heroes, played by Robert Redford and Glenn Close, paint an idyllic picture of a White American past, which appealed to conservatives nostalgic for an era before racial integration and immigrants of color. (No such White utopia ever existed, of course, so this nostalgia itself represents a White supremacist fantasy.) For many, the movie adaptation's happy ending epitomizes the vulgar commercial motive of the culture industry, as well as reflecting Reagan's callow optimism.

While it is true that its halcyon images have a simple appeal to country folk, when read through the context of the 1980s farm crisis *The Natural* tells a surprisingly progressive and multicultural legend. Rural Americans turned against Reagan's free market policy and "yuppie glitz" with nostalgia for Roosevelt's New Deal.[3] The film portrays the small family farm as a minority culture—a curious and controversial multiculturalism.

Moreover, the concept of civil religion shines a new light on Hollywood's important promotion of higher, democratic ideals. Against the presumption that leftist politics on screen are confined to realism or satire, this chapter demonstrates how the

Hollywood Sports Movies and the American Dream. Grant Wiedenfeld, Oxford University Press. © Oxford University Press 2022.
DOI: 10.1093/oso/9780197624920.003.0004

romantic elements of Levinson's adaptation add to its progressive allegory. Beneath its boyish fantasy, the heartland legend develops a faith in collective action that symbolizes the righteous republic.

An Allegory for Foreclosure on the Family Farm

In the 1980s, agriculture in the United States experienced an economic crisis that hit small family farmers especially hard. During the previous decade agriculture had dodged the recession; when the USSR began importing grain in 1972, commodity and land prices soared, which afforded American small farmers credit to upgrade machinery and expand operations. Their fortunes reversed, however, by the end of the decade as prices plummeted. While the rest of the nation's economy boomed, Reagan's administration refused to budge from its laissez-faire policy. Now the family farmer faced escalating debt and foreclosure by banks who vacuumed up small holdings, then consolidated and sold to larger agribusiness operators.[4] Large operators could survive owing to their scale, better credit, and cheaper land acquisition. Their ascendance only deepened the crisis for small operators.

Grassroots advocacy groups such as the American Agricultural Movement, Iowa Farm Unity Coalition, and Rural America pushed for federal intervention. In March 1985, for instance, two thousand farmers marched through Washington, D.C., with white crosses, each of which represented a colleague whose family farm had been foreclosed on. Reagan used his veto power to resist congressional aid packages because his administration favored a free market.[5] It marked a change of course from Carter, whose Democratic administration had increased subsidies for farmers.[6] In September 1985 the campaign spilled over into popular culture with the first Farm Aid benefit concerts. That year Neil Young published an open letter to Reagan: "Mr. President, you have a decision to make. Will the farmer be replaced by the farm operator? Will the family farm in America die as a result of your administration?"[7] Advocates sought legislation that would extend credit to farmers, subsidize price increases, conserve land, and provide assistance such as the school lunch program.[8] Congress would pass a bipartisan farm bill in late 1985, followed by similar measures annually as the crisis endured.

From this perspective, Levinson's movie adaptation of *The Natural* campaigns strongly for farm legislation. Its central conflict even parallels that of the small farmer versus the big banks. The New York Knights' longtime manager, Pop Fisher (Wilford Brimley), has been perennially unlucky. He had to sell the majority of team ownership to "The Judge" to stay afloat; however, a special clause in their contract will restore Pop's ownership if the Knights win the pennant this season. Like a Frank Norris novel, this peculiar scenario pits a heartland hero and a mom-and-pop entrepreneur against an archetypal villain financier.

A love for small farm life characterizes the heroes. New York Knights manager Pop Fischer repeats the line "I should've been a farmer" so often that it becomes his mantra. Wilford Brimley performs the part by shaking his head and heaving his shoulders in front of his players on the bench, who chuckle at his exasperation. As his team struggles initially, the manager eulogizes the pastoral life cultivating plants and animals. "Nothing like a farm," Pop says wistfully. Figure 4.1 illustrates the supporting character's folksy cheer. Similarly, Roy's rural character is immediately highlighted by the opening flashback to his bucolic childhood and ultimately by his return to the countryside in the epilogue. That setting evokes the myth of baseball's rural American origin in a field near Cooperstown, New York, in 1839.[9] Pop initially receives Roy with hostility because he mistakes the middle-aged nobody as a ploy by The Judge to drag the team down further. Nonetheless a dramatic irony develops against that initial hostility because the audience has seen Roy's rural origin and therefore knows the common dream that Pop and Roy both share: to win honorably, retire from baseball, and live on a farm. Indeed, their love of small farm life and values will unite them, and their triumph over the urban financier will signify their heartland sentiment.

By contrast, The Judge (Robert Prosky) is a squat capitalist with a serpent's tongue. Figure 4.2 depicts a noir office that recalls *The Godfather*, composed by cinematographer Caleb Deschanel. The Judge's evil associates are a wealthy one-eyed gambler, Gus, and a blonde vixen, Memo Paris. These characters might have been lifted directly from a children's comic book or *A Corner in Wheat* (1909).[10] The dramatic conflict has no moral ambiguity. Levinson's film self-consciously adopts the clear villains and heroes of folklore.

The dramatic conflict combines themes of geography, class, and culture. America's urban/rural tension has been described by G. Edward White as the eastern establishment versus the western experience.[11] The contrast between greedy elites and wholesome commoners involves class and moral elements, as well as a more general mindset that becomes a cultural difference. Pop expresses these themes in a conversation with Roy: "You know, my mother told me I ought to be a farmer," Pop confesses. "My dad wanted me to be a baseball player." He correctly associates baseball with city life, from which he now desires escape. Spoken amid the team's struggle in the league and their internal struggle with The Judge, Pop disparages the sport as pure competition. He admires Roy as a truly natural talent whose source of goodness is Mother Nature, in opposition to the cold rationalism of the urban rat race. Hence the heroes represent a good tradition of farm life and pure play that could be called "conservative" in its focus on community but progressive in its elevation above political economics. In contrast, the villain financiers represent the ethos of Milton Friedman's free-market capitalism under Reagan.

The movie's plot allegorizes the disastrous foreclosures faced by small farmers. In Malamud's novel, the conflict between Pop and The Judge was simply a long-term war of wills that had no association with agricultural policy.[12] The screenwriters invent a contract clause whereby ownership reverts to Pop if the team wins in this 1939 season. This clause shifts the meaning of the conflict from general authority to ownership. Such a scenario puts special emphasis on *the season* as a decisive event—just as the outcome of the Knights season determines team ownership, the farmer's yield

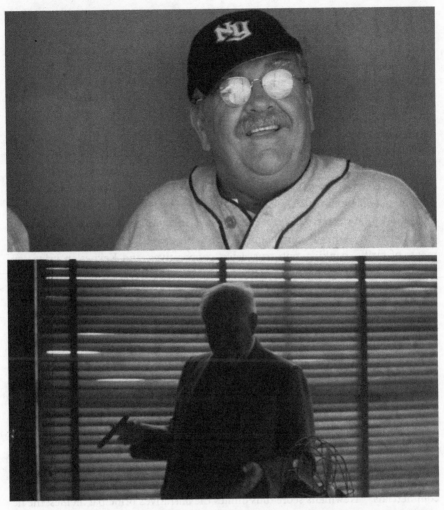

Figures 4.1–4.2 Secondary characters Pop (Wilford Brimley) and The Judge (Robert Prosky) contrast good country idealism with evil city ambition.

for the season could determine their land ownership. Such an improbable dramatic scenario would appear no more than a fantastic contrivance and a *deus ex machina*, if not for the real context of the farm crisis.

To the farmer facing foreclosure, a judge represents a justice system rigged to serve big-money interests. For example, a legendary incident occurred in Le Mars, Iowa, during the Great Depression. To resist banks foreclosing, a mob of farmers captured a county judge and almost lynched him. One local man described the "hard feelings" of people who were working fourteen-hour days to survive on acreages cleared by their pioneering grandparents; they saw little justice in the fine print of bank contracts.[13] *The Natural* stages this conflict in the New Deal era, linking the 1980s crisis to a progressive tradition of state intervention. The character name of "The Judge," whose full name, "Goodwill Banner," is dropped from the movie, suggests his impersonal, purely instrumental function like that of a foreclosure court. (Another rural baseball movie, *Field of Dreams* [1989], highlights the farm crisis in its contemporary Iowa setting; its plot revolves around the threat of foreclosure on the hero's land—the site of the mystical field.)

Historically, small farmers have been at the core of progressive political action in America. Elizabeth Sanders' *Roots of Reform* and Charles Postel's *The Populist Vision* trace these republican movements back to small farmers who banded together to advocate for political reform.[14] Looking back even further, economist John Galbraith says, "The effort of longest standing to develop countervailing power, not even excepting that of labor, has been made by the farmer."[15] Galbraith refers to policies and institutions that countervail the power of capital's dominant market forces, without turning to communism's command economy. He notes farmers' political achievements of tariffs, banking, anti-trust laws, cooperatives, and Keynesian price controls enacted during the 1930s. Although upper-class reformers eventually yoked the movement to their own interests, the zeitgeist for American Progressivism was agrarian populism in the mid-nineteenth century. Their greatest political accomplishment may be the New Deal policies of the 1930s and 1940s. In its golden age setting, *The Natural* nostalgically reminisces about the New Deal's preservation of small farmers, above all.

Randy Newman's accompanying score also recalls the New Deal era. He pastiches Aaron Copland so closely that certain passages feel lifted directly from *Fanfare for the Common Man* (1942). Strings sentimentalize every other scene, while the powerful brass theme is reserved to punctuate mystical moments. Latham Hunter notes that Newman's music in the Whammer scene riffs on Aaron Copland's "Hoedown" song from *Rodeo* (1942). Hunter also remarks that the 1985 farm bill created a federal "Beef Checkoff" marketing agency that would famously use Copland's tune in its television commercials.[16] Newman's score thus unifies the narrative's principal themes: the heroic common man, rural America, New Deal–era optimism, and a federal government response to the 1980s farm crisis. Within the history of film music, Newman builds upon John Williams's revival of keynote heraldic scores in New Hollywood cinema. His score represents an American vernacular, as does Bill Conti's *Rocky* theme, but Newman's retro flavor matches the historical setting. Etymologically, the word "melodrama" derives from music or song that accentuates emotion and sentiment in the drama; such moral clarity can feel oppressive to finer tastes but democratic and uplifting to popular audiences. Newman's prominent brass theme gilds all the action with a hopeful sentiment not yet boastful in its power but confident in its modesty, reviving Copland's democratic anthem for this sports melodrama.

Hero Roy Hobbs epitomizes the common man of the New Deal era. Everything about him is common, almost generic: his childhood, his laconic manner, and his names. Despite the regal connotation of his given name *Roy* (from the Anglo-Norman word for king—*roi*), being as crisp as a nickname identifies him as a prototypical

American boy. In the film's opening shot, cinematographer Caleb Deschanel depicts Hobbs in a railroad station that has the archetypical setting of a Norman Rockwell illustration, yet without his light optimism. Plate 12 shows the camera's frontal angle at the rail station wall, with the solitary hero leaning casually under his hat brim and an attendant off-center in the darkened station window.[17] With a color palette drained of bright tones and a soundtrack without music, the sparse scene also recalls the nameless and lonely urban figures in an Edward Hopper painting, as if shifted to the abandoned provinces. Redford's subtle movements and wrinkled face breathe authentic life into a mold that is decidedly common.

It must be said that the small farmer's politics involve a fundamental paradox. On the one hand, agrarians believe in an idealized liberal market whose invisible hand should reward individual success. In fact, Galbraith explains that the classical liberal economic theory, namely Say's law of supply and demand, was modeled on a market diffused across a panoply of small farmers; therefore, liberalism and the family farm go hand in glove. For this reason Marxists and small landowner farmers have traditionally had a deep antipathy. On the other hand, the dominance of the actual market by oligarchs in one form or another—railroad tycoons, commodity traders, or banks, along with the vicissitudes of weather, leave the small entrepreneur with an uncomfortable but necessary dependence on state regulation and subsidy to protect their livelihood. As mentioned previously, the American Agricultural Movement championed a patently Marxist concept of "parity" in their campaign for federal aid to redeem the surplus value exploited by merchants and landowners. American Progressivism is riven with such paradoxes; their most successful resolution would come through Keynesian economics and New Deal legislation, branded at the time as "controlled capitalism," that used state intervention to preserve autonomy. The 1985 farm bill simply updates that policy with a new intervention.

The drama of *The Natural* encapsulates the political paradox of Keynesian economics. The "love of the game" shared by Roy and Pop involves a moral code that compels them to play fair, without artificially fixing the outcome. This ethos reflects a liberal faith in merit and the justice borne of competition. Yet the hero prevails through a supernatural ability and the moral intervention of his sweetheart Iris.

Indeed, Iris symbolizes the virtue of state intervention through her dramatic actions. She brings Roy moral support in Chicago when he is being consumed by vanity. Depicted with the halo of a setting sun behind her white dress and hat in Figure 4.3, like an angel of virtue, she inspires him to hit a great home run that rights the team's season. Then, at the climax, she comes to tell him that they have a son, inspiring a greater home run that wins the pennant and resolves the overall conflict in favor of Pop and the players. Her virtue parallels the principled intervention of the state that restores justice and stability to the world. Remember that she reassures Roy when he anxiously asks if she had sold her family farm: "No, I'll always have that." The story ends with Roy's home run ball floating out to that halcyon field via a match cut styled after *2001: A Space Odyssey*. Figure 4.4 shows Roy playing catch with his son as Iris looks on, completing the generational circle begun

Figures 4.3–4.4 Iris (Glen Close) symbolizes state intervention as angelic. She restores Roy (Robert Redford) to their Edenic small farm.

in the opening flashback. Iris thus represents the virtue of both rural culture and the federal state that protects it.

Levinson's pastoral scenes suggest that the countryside, preserved in the baseball field, is a maternal source of goodness. Tellingly, these scenes are absent in the novel—Malamud characterizes Iris and Roy as naïve provincials destined for disillusion. Transforming the character for the movie, Glenn Close plays Iris with hardscrabble poise and folksy charm. Her common woman represents both Mother Nature and the virtuous welfare state—the opposite of the "nanny state" portrayed by Reagan's GOP. In sum, the movie elevates the image of the family farm to a poetic object of national tradition. The fantastical drama thereby implies the highest stakes for legislation to alleviate the farm crisis.

The Natural belongs to a 1980s cycle of historical sports dramas based on popular legends in the tradition of Hugh Hudson's enormously popular *Chariots of Fire* (1981). That film combined nostalgia for British greatness with Jewish and Scottish evangelical protagonists who simultaneously represented a break with imperial tradition. *The Natural* depicts a midcentury golden age as a way to revive the paradoxically modern tradition of progressivism in response to the 1980s farm crisis. More Hollywood history films followed in this vein: *Hoosiers* (1986) has as its hero a coach who represents the liberal faith in central authority; *Field of Dreams* (1989) presents baseball as a sacred ground for civic consensus; and *A League of Their Own* (1991) remembers the success and independence women achieved in 1940s America. Seen as an ensemble, these historical sports dramas use a rustic past and national pastimes to chart a heroic tradition from the Progressive Era to the present.

Yet the nation's history of racism tarnishes any romantic image of the past and complicates interpretation of the film's political values. Although *The Natural* clearly expresses democratic values with regard to class, at first glance its Anglo heroes could be read as an equally clear expression of racial pride. A closer look reveals an emphasis on culture that points toward a progressive understanding of race.

Liberal Multiculturalism and the New Minority

Farmers came to inhabit the political position of a minority group during the post-Vietnam era. However, for predominantly white farmers to cast themselves as minorities would certainly sound queer to Native Americans, Black Americans, Asian Americans, and others who had a long history of being marginalized by European men. Indeed, Jesse Jackson faced that specific problem in his effort to form a Rainbow Coalition that would support his 1984 presidential campaign. Although the historical film does not confront the historical reality of segregation, close examination demonstrates the film's sympathy for such a Rainbow Coalition.

Small farmers in this era adopted advocacy methods and rhetoric from other minority activists. For instance, in the late 1970s the American Agriculture Movement (AAM) organized "Tractorcade" marches on the mall in Washington, D.C., that echoed landmark civil rights and anti-war marches of the previous decade. The AAM demanded progressive farm policy to counter what they perceived as Eastern establishment indifference to the needs of middle America. Gilbert C. Fite even titled his 1981 study *American Farmers: The New Minority* for a Minorities in Modern America series at Indiana University Press. Mass migration to cities over the span of a century had made small farmers a numerical minority for the first time by the 1980s.

Moreover, the appeal to preserve a particular *culture*, the family farm, positions the rural minority under the umbrella of multiculturalism. Will Kymlicka theorizes multiculturalism through a picture of individual development within communities that differ from the dominant social group. Specific social practices can be legally protected.[18] Charles Taylor underlines the importance of public recognition for minority groups and their cultures, through the law or elsewhere in the hegemonic culture.[19] Recognition validates a person and group as equal members of the political community. In fact, civil rights legislation simultaneously protects an array of minorities and invites comparison between different groups.[20] On the one hand, then, the farmers' appeal for recognition and state intervention to preserve family farm culture is patently multicultural. Although some see nostalgia as an element of reactionary politics, cultural remembrance is in truth common to all minority groups. To the degree that small farmers saw their culture as one among a plurality (rather than restoring its dominance), they exemplify the progressive spirit expressed by the very name *multiculturalism*.

On the other hand, Native Americans, Blacks, Hispanics, women, gays, and the disabled were among the most visible minority groups of twentieth century America, and they all share a fundamental difference from small farmers. These groups' minority identity is rooted in the body, not in an occupation; moreover, a long history of marginalization attests to their minority status within the social structure. White European race/ethnicity was not an explicit aspect of the rural life that late-twentieth century small farmers cherished explicitly; and if whiteness had been important, it would negate claims to be a subaltern culture. Furthermore, rural American culture has a reputation (deserved or not) for being intolerant of racial and ethnic minorities, and for oppressing marginal identities generally.[21] From this point of view, farmers positioning themselves as a new minority appears absurd.

In comparing farmers to other minority groups, the general question becomes how to evaluate and position the farmers' claims for recognition and policy intervention. How do their claims converge, conflict, or move in parallel with other minorities? That question exceeds the scope of our study, but I have indicated some parallels and conflicts. We can nevertheless apply that question to our context by asking: How does the film perceive the relation of its small farm culture to other minority cultures?

Levinson's film makes subtle appeals to the minority causes of age, racial, and sex discrimination but avoids directly confronting the important issue of race. First, the hero encounters age discrimination in a scene that makes a subtle comparison to racism. Roy arrives at the Knights ballpark as a rookie in his thirties and Pop immediately rejects him because of his age, rural origin, and different path to the league. Pop suspects that the owner is planting Roy as a poison pill to drag down the team and questions the legality of his contract—precisely the kind of bad faith attitude that plagued racial integration and other progressive minority programs. Pop reluctantly accepts the contract but defiantly sits Roy on the bench, not even allowing him to participate in batting practice. Only the ulterior motive of another player's insubordination leads Pop to have Roy bat. The opposing players taunt him as "grandpa," but the aging hero stuns everyone with his performance. He hits the ball so hard that he literally "knocks the cover off" of the baseball—a marvelous feat captured in Figure 4.5. Made of white rawhide, the covering becomes a subtle symbol of racism. The opposing pitcher fondles the empty ball skin dumbstruck, confronting the emptiness of

Figure 4.5 The hero dispels prejudice against his old age by knocking the white leather cover off of the ball, hinting at white racial prejudice.

his own misconception. Through invocation of prejudice, legality, and opportunity, this baseball legend acts as a parable against racial discrimination.

Moreover, the fictional New York Knights team recalls the Brooklyn Dodgers, as Harley Henry has noted.[22] Dodgers manager and owner Branch Rickey hired Jackie Robinson despite resistance from teammates and other managers. Levinson uses Pop's age discrimination as a metonymic gesture to that pushback. That is not the situation in the novel, in which Pop keeps Roy from playing because of superstition surrounding his bat.[23] Homages to *The Natural* in the Jackie Robinson biopic *42* (2013) also support this interpretation of age discrimination as an allegory for racial discrimination and integration.[24]

Yet for all its subtle gestures to discrimination, *The Natural* sidesteps the historical reality of racial segregation. The centrality of white, blond characters makes no significant break against the privilege they have traditionally held in Hollywood. In fact, some scholars consider Redford's blondness and whiteness key to his star persona.[25] While Levinson's film does not appear to be intentionally White supremacist or masculinist, judging by the subtle references to other minorities, its lack of nonwhite characters is nonetheless complicit in a vicious national trend. The 1970s and 1980s had no major Hollywood sports movies centered on black or women characters, so every film that was produced contributes to that imbalance. *The Natural* could have at least acknowledged the exclusion of black players that was happening in 1939, as *A League of Their Own* (1992) does in one small scene that will be discussed in the chapter on that film.

Failure to directly confront historical discrimination can signal complicity. Everyone agrees that White racism was endemic in the United States historically, which required reforms from the constitutional amendments of 1865 to the civil rights legislation of the 1960s. Historical drama that depicts the eras of segregation or slavery as a golden age will automatically endorse that once-normative racism and will deny the existence of injustice if not corrected. *The Natural*'s subtle allegory for discrimination echoes the liberal coalition that formed in the 1940s and continued in Jackson's 1984 campaign; in retrospect, however, the film neglects its civic responsibility to acknowledge and condemn America's racist past.

Subtle Feminist Appeals

The film also invites feminists to sympathize with its characters, even its femme fatales. Consider the mysterious Harriet Bird, who targets top male athletes.[26] Her use of silver bullets, a folkloric weapon for slaying monsters, identifies her quest as a moral one. Both the Whammer's superficial flirtation with her and Roy's arrogant goal of besting all others exemplify masculinist culture. Her murders, shooting Roy, and jumping out a window to her death outline a feminist tragedy. And she is not simply a feminist villain, either. Her implied criticism of Roy's youthful arrogance will be confirmed by the drama, structured around his selfless sacrifice to the team.

Patriarchy appears more explicitly around the character of Memo Paris, who believes that her only path to success is through submission to powerful tycoons. She paints a picture of an unhappy childhood, fatherless and poor, before beauty contests and male admirers gave her nice things. "I'm not waiting for true love to come along, Roy," she tells him bluntly. "Anything wrong with that?" As the drama unfolds, Kim Basinger performs Memo's inner torment in a compelling way that makes her much more human than the male villains who exploit her. Memo and Harriet garner sympathy to the degree that they also navigate an unjust world ruled by patriarchs. Given that the femme fatale typically represents a threat to male hegemony, Levinson counterbalances these minor female villains with larger male villains.[27]

Another surprising moment breaks with the tradition of male hegemony in baseball. A newsreel segment during Roy's rise to fame includes a scene with youngsters that highlights one girl fan, as shown in Figure 4.6. One cannot imagine that the actual Fox Movietone or March of Time newsreels that Levinson imitates would have featured a token girl like her. Even though the film overall emphasizes Roy's influence on boys, the spotlight on a young woman during this hopeful sequence plants a seed of progressive change.

One can also detect a coded reference to the Equal Rights Amendment in the film. Passed on to the states in 1974, its deadline for ratification was 1984. It would have made maternity leave a right, among other provisions. When Roy is poisoned and falls ill just before the final game, he is taken to the nearest hospital, a maternity ward. A reporter's cartoon of his convalescence depicts him pregnant with a baseball, illustrated by Figure 4.7. Levinson thus draws an uncanny parallel from the hero to the unjust treatment of pregnant workers. These resonant meanings differ markedly from

Figure 4.6 Levinson features a girl fan in a newsreel segment, which appears to be a deliberate anachronism.

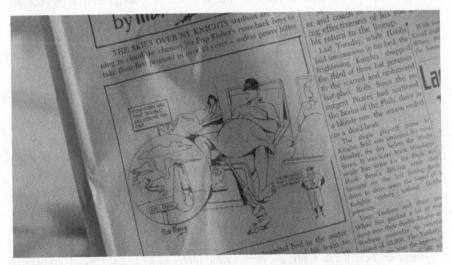

Figure 4.7 The convalescent hero is depicted as an incapable pregnant woman in a satirical cartoon, positioning the hero against patriarchal power.

the novel, in which the maternity ward is explained as a low-cost option for The Judge and symbolizes his feminization of the players.[28] Furthermore, the movie contrasts Roy's modesty to the machismo of Bud, a star hitter and a bad apple. The film thus portrays the hero as an almost maternal savior.

Lastly, Glenn Close's Iris character becomes much more admirable than her equivalent in Malamud's book where she is portrayed as a naïve country rube bumbling through city life. The novel's protagonist tolerates her having a daughter but recoils when he learns that she is a grandmother.[29] Her dour fate consists in being smacked in the face by Roy's foul ball, while her faith in him goes unrewarded. In contrast, Levinson's character is a respectable single mother who shows no regrets or weakness. She does not need Roy, but helps him magnanimously. Rather than provincial naïveté, she projects public strength and righteousness. It is *her* farm to which they return in the end, upending the patriarchal stereotype of male land ownership. In the historical setting she represents the feminist vanguard of the World War II years, and in the romantic legend she represents Mother Earth. Iris emerges as a civic and spiritual anchor in the film.

Viewed from a feminist perspective, the hero's drama arcs from patriarchal tradition toward an egalitarian or even matriarchal future. The villainy of femme fatales Harriet and Memo is traced beyond the characters to a hegemonic masculinist world. Even the antagonist women are more sympathetic than the villains Gus and The Judge, who appear motivated by pure greed and power. Roy's righteous quest to overcome the established powers is associated with Iris, and her virtue is associated with noble aspirations and with her farm. Of course, a movie centered on a male protagonist can hardly be praised as feminist. But Roy is clearly designed to represent the struggle of the marginalized in a hierarchical society. Levinson affiliates his underdog hero with women, racial minorities, and a higher purpose.

National Legend and Civil Religion

The previous sections have made evident *The Natural*'s appeal for progressive intervention in the 1980s farm crisis through a New Deal–era setting and through positioning its heroes as a cultural minority group. Yet many critics would consider such invocation of real social struggle at cross purposes with the film's fantastical elements—especially the improbable happy ending that reverses the outcome of Malamud's novel. Based on the view that realist tragedy is the best means to stimulate democratic political action, that school of criticism judges Hollywood fantasy and comedy equivalent to opiates that render the public impassive and inhibit sociopolitical reform.[30]

However, fiction can represent democratic ideals in its fantasy world, and those ideals have real importance to civil society. This section argues that *The Natural* spins a progressive American dream legend through Roy's mythical bat, Wonderboy, and the plot's marvelous ending. The film's fantasy elements therefore add hope and transcendent purpose to the allegorical call for state intervention in the farm crisis.

Fiction's relevance to political life is outlined by Montesquieu. In *The Spirit of Laws* he locates the ideal of justice in the realm of the possible above all:[31]

> Before laws were made, there were relations of possible justice. To say that there is nothing just or unjust but what is commanded or forbidden by positive laws, is the same as saying, that before the describing of a circle, all the radii were not equal.

He refutes the nihilist argument that justice is whatever is prescribed by legal codes and points to a higher ideal. Such an ideal may not be realized in experience, but its being can be known as a possibility. Extending Montesquieu's insight from law to knowledge generally, all moral ideals and truths have a possible being that precedes their existence.[32]

Fiction is a form of play with the possible through dramatic representation. Liberated from determined existence, a fictional world can more easily represent the moral and political ideal of democracy. As a form of collective imaginary, fictional worlds can articulate how things should or should not be, in the ideal. Aside from communicating ideals, dramatic fiction's positive form of comedy cultivates solidarity and faith that are necessary for civic institutions based on the rule of law. In contrast, realist drama tends to tragedy that represents actuality falling short of the ideal. The journalist's binary trope of fact versus fiction confuses understanding of these forms; dramatic fiction exists prior to truth and falseness in the realm of the possible. Drama comes closer to concrete existence than pure philosophy's abstract contemplation, but drama's possible world shares the freedom of play.

All this is to say that the political meaning of *The Natural* can be judged from the ideals it represents.[33] To exclude the affirmative forms of comedy and fantasy from democratic life is a mistake; the introduction argues this point in detail. Roy's underdog persona and improbable victory clearly belong to comedy. Recall that Northrup Frye says the comic genre is "usually based on the Cinderella archetype" that often culminates in the festive gathering of the wedding.[34] Roy's quest as an older player and the grand celebration of improbable victory fit the archetype perfectly (as do *Rocky* and *Slapshot*, as previous chapters have shown). Besides the comic structure, the legendary elements of Roy and his bat, Wonderboy, invite our judgment from a political perspective.

More than an all-American hero, Roy is almost a superhero. The opening scene at a train station uses a simple cut to transport Roy from quay to train, like an apparition. The ensuing flashback depicts his childhood in a series of tableaux, much like a tale. First we see the boy catch the ball in a wheat field, as shown in Figure 4.1. Then young Roy hurls a fastball hard enough to break the boards of the henhouse—a subtle foreshadowing of his weakness for women. Next, his father (Alan Fudge) sits him down like an elder mage delivering a serious message: "You've got a gift, Roy; but it's not enough. You've got to develop yourself." His statement can also be heard as "develop your *self*," implying moral development. Flashing forward, the old farmer suddenly keels over and clutches his heart; in a long shot we see Roy rush to his side as the music swells. Levinson directly lifts this scene from *Superman* (1978). The father's brief role in the childhood scenes structures the story like a fable. This flashback, absent in the novel, has the episodic structure, melodramatic range, and incredible action of myth-making folktale.

Wonderboy first appears as a magical talisman but evolves into a symbol of enlightened demystification. A prophetic storm follows the death of Roy's father. Lightning strikes a tree that we then see Roy carve into a bat. He christens his enchanted weapon

"Wonderboy" and carves into the pale wood its name and the figure of a lightning bolt—a symbol that would recall Thor or Harry Potter for children in the 2000s. In the context of the father's message about moral development, his death portends Roy's susceptibility to temptation. Both the selfish ambitions that Roy will announce to Harriet Bird and his seduction by bombshell Memo Paris block his natural path to success, suggesting that Roy's tragic flaw is vanity. Wonderboy appears to magically concentrate Roy's talent yet fails to perform when the hero indulges his vice, as if the object has a mind of its own.

In the specific terms of genre study, *The Natural* falls one level below "myths" proper, as legend. Northrup Frye explains that myths tell of divine beings—a category to which most superheroes belong. In his definition of the legend or romance, Frye inadvertently justifies the film's title:

> If superior in *degree* to other men and to his environment, the hero is the typical hero of *romance*, whose actions are marvelous but who is himself identified as a human being. The hero of romance moves in a world in which the ordinary laws of nature are slightly suspended: prodigies of courage and endurance, unnatural to us, are natural to him.[35]

Fittingly, Roy will play for the Knights, a fictional New York team. Levinson characterizes Roy as a good knight by showing his natural affinity with children in the Whammer scene and through his relationship with Bobby the batboy. Roy represents the American everyman who has an ideal degree of baseball talent that is tied to his moral being in a marvelous way.

In his commonness and sensitivity Roy's tale doubles as an allegory for the nation. The team will put lightning bolt patches on their jersey sleeves as a symbolic extension of Wonderboy. After Roy's initial burst of success with Wonderboy, his teammates perceive the icon as a source of good luck. One teammate says the bolt emblem reminds him of "squadron insignias," a reference to a similar practice in the military. In a montage sequence, the teammate breaks out of his slump with a hit, and another player remarks that "it must be the patch." In the next shot, the entire team has lightning bolt patches on their arms, as depicted in Figure 4.8. The camera tracks horizontally down the line of players with patches on their sleeves and their hands on their hearts as they sing the national anthem. (The day should be July 4, because the anthem was not played daily before World War II.)[36] A "win streak" montage follows, suggesting that the patches share Roy's magic with everyone. However, Roy soon falters when vanity consumes him, and the team falters in lockstep. This sequence plays with their superstition but ultimately dispels it. Newman's score adopts a playful tone to make light of their superstition. There was no real magic, but the noble lie acted indirectly to bring them together.

The patches add mystique to the basic civic ethos of the sportsman's uniform. Michael Mandelbaum explains the egalitarian quality of team costumes: "Like the citizens of Western countries in the modern era, the wearers of such uniforms are, in an

Figure 4.8 A pregame anthem singing moment reveals that Roy's entire team has adopted the lightning bolt emblem, a coincidence that reflects upon civil religion.

important way, equal."[37] The patches crystallize the same quality of solidarity. In their ultimate inertness, the patches recall Clifford Geertz's remark that national symbols like flags are empty vessels. What fills them is the collective being that all take part in—an experience Durkheim called "collective effervescence." The true mystery lies in the life of collective being that grows, shrinks, and transforms in dynamic relation to everyone's part in it. Singing in unison was a common ritual to cultivate solidarity, especially for the national anthem before modern loudspeakers shifted attention from the collective to an individual performer. Levinson unveils the team patches during the singing of the anthem to suggest that artificial icons and rituals create a unity that empowers the group.

Levinson designs other moments to suggest that spontaneous effervescence, rather than mere will, is the source of the hero's success. Roy's tremendous strike-out of the Whammer, his first major league hit, home runs in Chicago, and the climax all happen in slow motion. Levinson adds suspense to these moments with anticipatory silence, muffled environmental sounds, and uncanny decoupage; then Newman's brass themes herald each feat. In Chicago, for instance, Iris stands up in the bleachers as Roy comes up to bat. Levinson cuts to a shot of her glimmering figure, haloed by a setting sun and wide-brimmed white hat that was shown in Figure 4.3. He then cuts back to a medium shot of Roy to record the strange effect she enduces. Figure 4.9 illustrates Redford looking about as if a butterfly has floated past, before returning to his task with a different rhythm. Redford's laconic performance excels in these subtle moments—medium close-ups capture the ineffable in his face and posture. But Levinson counterbalances these sublime moments with Pop's light comic relief, an ironic homage to a dead teammate, and a midseason slump into indifference. What holds the film together stylistically are Newman's wide-ranging score

Figure 4.9 A moment of effervescence is depicted by an uncanny pause. Before stepping to the plate Roy looks around as if a ghost had swooped by.

and Redford's introverted performance; their exquisite contours elevate the work above blunt clichés.

The 1939 setting also adds to the romance of the aging hero. All the games were filmed at Buffalo's War Memorial Stadium, a place itself mythical in being unaltered since midcentury.[38] Levinson specifically sets the story in the centennial of baseball's mythical invention in Cooperstown, New York, 1839. That national heritage would seem to evoke nostalgia for Horatio Alger's American dream, except for the fact that the hero, Roy, begins the story as an old man. His second-chance narrative denotes a post-war period, rather than youthful innocence. When he first steps on the baseball field, he is framed walking down the stadium tunnel in wide angle, like a birth canal or a passageway to the afterlife, suggesting that the hero has been born again.[39] Moreover, the character name Pop Fischer alludes to the Fisher King myth of Arthurian legend, reinforcing the call to revive the bygone New Deal era. This romantic picture of 1939 would appeal not only to farmers in crisis but also to Rust Belt cities like Buffalo. Of course, Ronald Reagan embodied a legendary midcentury hero for many, but his small government conservatism stood in stark contrast to the progressive state that most associate with 1939.

Despite its extravagant romanticizing, *The Natural* demonstrates an enlightened self-consciousness through the fate of Roy's special bat, Wonderboy. Coming up to bat at the climax, Roy first hits a foul ball that splits Wonderboy in two. The point-of-view shot shown in Figure 4.10 emphasizes this dramatic moment. In the novel, that fracture reflects Roy's anger toward a heckler; he is handed a generic Louisville Slugger and promptly strikes out.[40] In the movie, however, Roy never lashes out; the fracture represents fate and the limits of his superstitious childhood faith. He turns to the chubby bat boy who has followed him all season and says, "Pick me out a winner,

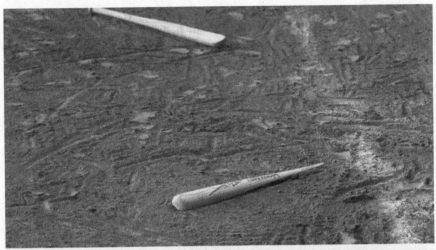

Figures 4.10–4.11 When Wonderboy breaks, Roy accepts a handmade replacement from the batboy to signal that the team's faith in each other, not a mystical bat, is the source of their success.

Bobby." Bobby Savoy pulls out his own handmade bat, created earlier under Roy's tutelage and engraved with his own surname, the "Savoy Special." Figure 4.11 shows the hero looking it over. Its mystical power is merely a boy's fancy, suggesting the same of Wonderboy. But this demystification does not lead to failure. With the boy's bat Roy strikes his legendary home run.

Bobby's Savoy Special symbolizes Levinson's liberal adaptation and his more modest hero. The Hollywood movie takes the broken faith of Malamud's novel and substitutes its own version, one generation later. The Savoy Special's mystique derives solely from the personal bond between the characters. Hence the film does not champion any other-worldly superstition, but sees itself as an optimism born from faith in fellow man. Rather than Zeus firing lightning bolts from the sky, Roy sets off a man-made equivalent when the ball crashes into the stadium arc lights. Levinson apparently agrees with Malamud that a hero who believes himself to be a prophet must be tragically arrogant. The filmmaker substitutes a more modest hero. Redford's Hobbs realizes his power as a leader for others and succeeds through their collective faith in him, not his own fantasy. The dimness and distance of the hero's figure at the moment of victory, as depicted in Figure 4.12, illustrates his modesty. His tragic fall as a young player at the hand of Harriet Bird symbolized the fantasy of arrogance, while his epic triumph as an aging hero represents his virtuous altruism. So while the bat is the most romantic symbol in the story, the climactic moment of the movie tempers the mystique by shifting attention to the human agents and their just cause.

Roy's modesty contrasts with *Slap Shot*'s wild goons, but their politics are not necessarily opposites. As a hero of a legendary tale, Roy comes closer to representing the ideal and the nation as a collective. Meanwhile the hockey satire represents real men as they are with an ironic laugh at the ideal. But both films target an elitist hierarchy on behalf of the common man. The villainous owners have identical motivations—greed and autonomous power. One film operates in a satirical mode of realism and the other in the legendary mode of romance; one focuses on gender norms and the other on higher purposes. Yet both dramas develop team solidarity through charismatic change and both endorse democratic political principles.

The political importance of legend can be understood through the concept of civil religion. In early modernity Machiavelli, Hobbs, and Rousseau articulated the concept of civil religion as a means to wield devout beliefs and practices to civic ends.[41] This relationship of religion to the state lies midway between liberalism's radically secular wall between church and state (exemplified by French *laïcité*) and

Figure 4.12 The hero's modest reaction to victory demystifies his personal action, shifting attention to the team and its virtuous aim.

the theocratic despot who claims supernatural authority. Sociologist Robert Bellah revived the concept of civil religion to understand American state ceremonies like the presidential inauguration and the religiosity of language in patriotic speech. While relatively little attention has been paid to popular culture, Jeffrey Alexander underlines its importance in cultivating the feelings of solidarity that undergird civil society.[42] The sentiments expressed by mainstream movies create public meaning that concerns the people's relationship to law and to political ideals in situations less abstract than the paradigmatic cases of statutes or philosophy.[43] At the center of the legendary mode of romance is the hero, whom Northrup Frye reminds us is admirable by definition. Criticism of popular movies in this vein compares to fables or folklore, comparable to biographies of saints, that nevertheless express meaning for a secular world.

The Natural constitutes a sacred and popular American legend. Roy's inspired home run encapsulates a faith in the common man's capacity to achieve the American dream of an egalitarian republic, overcoming the political obstacle of tycoons and the moral obstacle of vanity and greed. Though told through a romantic legend with outlines simple enough for children to understand, the implied narrator never takes too seriously the superstitions of the players wearing patches, Pop's sense of luck, or Roy's magic bat. Instead, the film's plot and symbolic subtleties present a mature understanding of effervescence that has its roots in civic solidarity.[44] Perhaps surprisingly, the film makes no mention of Christianity or any religious doctrine. Being thus neither atheistic nor overtly religious but grounded in a tradition of progressive politics, the popular legend of *The Natural* speaks to a belief in the American nation as an evolving project of democracy.

Conclusion

The Natural tells a multicultural legend that understands American family farmers as a new minority, and recalls the triumphant past of the New Deal to advocate for a policy solution at odds with Reagan's neoliberalism. Levinson alters the source material by adding a golden image of rural life as a pervasive background to the drama and by setting the action back in 1939. With the movie's release occurring within the context of the 1980s farm crisis, these elements reveal the plot as a poignant allegory for state intervention. Romantic invocation of America's progressive past couples with a multicultural view toward protecting minority ways of life.

However, the film's progressivism and its whiteness are at cross purposes in terms of democratic politics. With a cast dominated by European-Americans and with the reluctance of the historical drama to confront the era's racism, it cannot represent a multicultural American dream legend. Indeed the film appears antithetical to multiculturalism on those basic grounds. But a closer examination reveals its own multicultural logic in treating family farm culture as a minority cause and its subtle sympathies for other minority groups.

Judging these mixed messages within a broader arc of Hollywood in the late twentieth century, *The Natural* takes part in the slow acceptance of multiculturalism that would flourish in the 1990s. It should come as little surprise that Hollywood adopted white kinds of minority protagonists before women and people of color, moving from center to periphery.

The development of multiculturalism in mainstream American culture follows a logic of privilege rather than a logic of justice. During the 1960s and 1970s, Hollywood had engaged with minority characters and issues on various levels, in parallel to the civil rights movement and passage of major legislation. When the sports movie appears in the mid-1970s it begins with a liberal white male hero and moves slowly outward. In *The Longest Yard* (1974), Burt Reynolds allies his misfits with black players who turn the tide against their oppressive villains. With *Rocky* and *Slap Shot*, the hero moves outward to ethnic Roman Catholic Europeans and working-class men. In the 1980s, more white minorities appear with the bisexual hero of *Personal Best* (1982) and the rural Americans in *The Natural*, *Hoosiers* (1986), and *Field of Dreams* (1989). Not until the 1990s do women, the disabled, and people of color become protagonists in major genre films: *A League of Their Own* (1992), *Forrest Gump* (1994), *Space Jam* (1996), and *The Hurricane* (1999). The large productions of *Remember the Titans* (2000) and *Ali* (2001) mark an apogee for diversity on screen. Rather than a radical shift from white supremacy to antiracist pluralism, it appears that activists in film and culture drove incremental progress in the mainstream, which did not proceed automatically. Furthermore, the continued dominance of white men in the genre indicates the long distance from the realization of a democratic republic and from its representation on screen, even with the freedom of Hollywood fiction.

Our complex picture of 1980s cinema agrees with Stephen Prince's historical overviews. Prince complicates the old narrative of a Hollywood dominated by Reagan's Right; for instance, he points to director Tony Scott's queer gaze in *Top Gun* (1986), exemplified by a sand volleyball sequence that undercuts the conservatism associated with male battle.[45] This chapter has likewise demonstrated the myriad progressive aspects of *The Natural* without, however, denying its complicity in the general whiteness of Hollywood. The next step will come with films that directly address the question of social incorporation and cast minorities of color in major roles.

5

White Men Can't Jump (1992)

"Winning and Losing Is One Big Organic Globule"

"Why are you playing Jimi?" asks Sidney (Wesley Snipes) of his counterpart Billy (Woody Harrelson), who had popped a Jimi Hendrix Experience audiocassette into the car stereo and was jamming to the song "Purple Haze."[1] The white man replies matter-of-factly, "Because I like to listen to him." Sidney shakes his head and raises the issue of cultural difference:

SIDNEY. That's the problem. Y'all listen.
BILLY. What am I supposed to do, eat it?
SIDNEY. No, you're supposed to hear it.
BILLY. I said I like to listen to him.
SIDNEY. There's a difference between hearing and listening. White people can't hear
    Jimi. You listen.

The hearing-versus-listening motif evokes the challenge that a new Black film wave voiced to white America and old Hollywood tradition in the late 1980s and early 1990s. Led by Spike Lee's *She's Gotta Have It* (1986) and Julie Dash's *Daughters of the Dust* (1991), independent filmmakers reemerged at the vanguard of American cinema. Black filmmakers then entered the mainstream with realist youth and crime dramas that featured hip-hop artists. Snipes and Ice-T starred in *New Jack City* (Mario Van Peebles, 1991), Ice Cube and Cuba Gooding Jr. debuted in *Boyz n the Hood* (John Singleton, 1991), and Omar Epps and Tupac Shakur first appeared in *Juice* (Ernest Dickerson, 1992). If African-American cinema had receded after a boom of independent production and a blaxploitation cycle in the 1970s, this new wave atavistically reasserted the presence and autonomy of Black culture in the United States.[2] Sidney follows in this vein by asserting that white people don't appreciate the cultural difference of Jimi Hendrix.

But *White Men Can't Jump* is a more mixed work. Sidney and Billy's argument develops in a way that winks reflexively at the film's diverse cast. Billy's Latina girl-friend Gloria (Rosie Perez), also riding in the car, interjects that Jimi's drummer was white. She points to the U.S. album cover of *Are You Experienced*, shown in Figure 5.1, where a white British drummer and bassist flank Jimi, all in a psyche-delic style.[3] Comparison with their own trio—a white man, a black man, and a

Hollywood Sports Movies and the American Dream. Grant Wiedenfeld, Oxford University Press. © Oxford University Press 2022.
DOI: 10.1093/oso/9780197624920.003.0005

Figures 5.1–5.2 As Sidney and Billy argue over whether white people can truly *hear* Jimi Hendrix's music, the multiracial trio implies a comparison to Jimi's band.

Latina (illustrated by Figure 5.2)—is obvious. Sidney shrugs off her comment and the matter is left unresolved. What do this scene and the film overall say about race and popular culture?

On the one hand, writer-director Ron Shelton seems to temper Black resistance. Considered in a broader context, this scene illustrates Hollywood's move to tame and appropriate a Black film wave defined by its resistance to a White-dominated industry.[4] Here Sidney challenges the white protagonist to acknowledge the cultural difference in Jimi Hendrix's Blackness, but his words fall on deaf ears. Aaron Baker compares Shelton's film to the whitewashing of Black culture by the NBA and Nike. They incorporated Black style and stars in the 1980s and 1990s but the White owner-ship of the sports, apparel, and media industries was not altered.[5] Baker also recognizes a similar dynamic in the film's cast of non-white characters who surround an Anglo protagonist:

> Multiracial support groups would become a convention of the sports film, turning up in *Body and Soul* (1947) and *The Harder They Fall* (1956), as well as *Rocky III* (1982), *Field of Dreams* (1989), and *White Men Can't Jump* (1992); most of the time these groups allow female and black characters to contribute to the success of the white protagonist without challenging traditional gender roles or the racial status quo.[6]

To alleviate his anxiety of insufficiency the white hero is furnished with a black sidekick who helps him on his quest for self.[7] From this postmodern perspective, Shelton's film fits a common pattern of neutralizing resistance to a White-dominant cultural order.[8] Its token diversity does not represent any significant difference.

On the other hand, Sidney does appear to upset the racial status quo of colorblind universalism. Although he does not immediately convince Billy, the main narrative arc follows the protagonist's growing awareness of whiteness. The satire operates through dramatic irony as we witness Billy obsessively dig himself into a deeper hole financially while Gloria and Sidney come out ahead. The hero asks Sidney for a job in the end, effectively becoming the sidekick. Happiness appears as friendship rather than dollars or conquest. Although the mixed production is not as bold as new Black cinema, Shelton's film does differ from the classic patterns of assimilation in ways that have not been fully appreciated.

This chapter argues that *White Men Can't Jump* develops a new version of the American dream based on cultural diversity, community, and honesty. It subtly questions the older model of colorblind assimilation and individual self-interest to develop an alternative. To parse the film's complex play with race, culture, and economics I first introduce Jeffrey Alexander's triadic theory of social incorporation, followed by close examination of the ways that liberalism's competitive model and sham neutrality appear in the street basketball drama.

Three Modes of Social Incorporation

The American dream is positively associated with immigration, but the means of incorporating the foreigner into the nation are more obscure and contentious. Sociologist Jeffrey Alexander identifies three pathways of social incorporation: assimilation, hyphenation, and multiculturalism.[9] The rise of multiculturalism in the United States involved criticism of assimilation as a form of white supremacy. The subsequent backlash and culture war have provoked intense debate on national identity, race, and immigration. Alexander's triadic approach restores some nuance to what has often devolved into a binary standoff and will thus illuminate the alternative American dream worked out in *White Men Can't Jump*.

Assimilation

Strong and weak forms of assimilation predominated in the late nineteenth- and early twentieth-century United States. *Americanization* named a strong assimilation that shed away foreign characteristics; in his play *The Melting Pot* (1908), Israel Zangwill imagines the process of assimilation as a hard, heated molding that homogenizes whatever it contains.[10] Weaker modes of assimilation merely shield foreignness from public life without entirely erasing those characteristics. In sports, team uniforms exemplify the egalitarian and conformist qualities of weak assimilation. Refusing to wear the uniform offends the entire team; in stronger atmospheres, even individual hairstyles are taboo. The modern business suit fulfilled a similar function by replacing the ostentatious public dress of old Europe's nobility, and thereby creating a more egalitarian public sphere.[11] Assimilation undergirds the liberal political theory of a public sphere where individuals meet on neutral ground. However, assimilation also threatens individual freedom with the pressure to conform. This fundamental conflict in liberal theory existed long before debate arose over *multiculturalism*.

Hollywood movies before midcentury combined strong and weak modes of assimilation. For instance, the landmark sports biopic *Knute Rockne: All-American* (Lloyd Bacon, Warner Bros., 1940) takes as its subject a Norwegian immigrant who rose to prominence as a football player and coach at the University of Notre Dame. A family dinner scene illustrates assimilation and the cultural tensions it involves. After being scolded by his father for coming home late to dinner from a sandlot football game, the boy hero replies: "Papa don't talk Norwegian, talk American. I'm American now, I'm left end." Both adopting English as a national language and shaming his father for speaking a foreign tongue demonstrate strong assimilation. Young Knute also implies that a national sport, football, has assimilated him to American life by assigning him to "left end," a specific position on defense. Knute's young age in the scene makes light of the conflict and also weakens the stakes of assimilation that it represents. It is interesting that the youngster rebels against his father through an act of conforming to the nation.[12] Postwar counterculture coded youth rebellion instead as anti-conformist. *Knute*'s story arc moves from immigrant to "all-American"—a homogenizing pattern repeated in other biopics so much that it became a generic formula. In these ways the film exemplifies the assimilationist character of Hollywood cinema before the 1960s.

The democratic challenge for assimilation is determining how the common ground is set, and who sets the neutral standard. The previous example of the business suit makes evident the tacit disadvantage of women and other bodies that cannot conform to a supposedly universal standard. Racial and ethnic minorities present a deeper challenge for democratic assimilation because skin color and hair cannot be shielded from public view, as a "color-blind" ethic would require.

Color-blindism poses two problems. First, it ignores the social fact that primordial group characteristics are always favored, as Alexander explains. Like a social default, the founding fathers set standard American identity as Anglo-European and male. A high-minded theory is not sufficient to correct the tribal instinct favoring the primordial. Incorporating Martin Luther King Jr. as a modern founding father points toward one solution to the primordial origin of white privilege in the United States. An equivalent weight of diverse leaders and founders would be necessary to correct inequality and achieve a truly color-blind culture.[13]

Second, color-blindism demands that ethnic culture be shielded from public life. To assimilate to standard American identity, no African-American, Native American, or other culture can be celebrated. Such a denial of public honor to ethnic cultures amounts to public shame. If Anglo-American culture becomes a tacit standard, that privilege oppresses minorities and renders the majority blind to that privilege. Or, if European-American ethnic cultures were equally excluded, such erasure of all community and culture also appears utopian and inhumane. Indeed, the alienated individual has been identified as a root problem of modern distress and of totalitarian social movements. Given that humans need to identify with a social group, assimilation poses the problem of primordial social privilege and the problem of society itself for the individual.

Multiculturalism

Whereas assimilation incorporates through sameness, multiculturalism paradoxically asserts that what everyone has in common is their difference. Rather than melting away foreign characteristics, multiculturalism preserves and even purifies the particular qualities of different groups. Multiculturalism appeared in the 1970s as a new understanding of pluralism supported by communitarian philosophers.[14] *Difference* serves as the perfect bridge among various groups because it promotes recognition of others as equals and expands understanding of particular life experiences and cultures.[15] For this reason, minorities have favored multiculturalism for both public recognition of their culture and protection from assimilation.[16] "This new mode of incorporation remains partial, tentative, and highly contested," Alexander admits, "but it provides a framework for solidarity that is dramatically different from those that had been available before."[17] With multiculturalism, the feeling of solidarity derives from a mutual embrace of difference.

Multicultural incorporation involves critique of one's own value system. Charles Taylor describes a "fusion of horizons," citing Gadamer. "We learn to move in a broader horizon," Taylor explains, "within which what we have formerly taken for granted as the background to valuation can be situated as one possibility alongside the different background of the formerly unfamiliar culture."[18] Mutual respect and recognition cannot occur without changing the horizon of values. It is significant that values themselves do not directly change; the encounter with unfamiliar values throws into question both backgrounds, initiating a critical process. In reading such a philosophical description, it is clear that multicultural solidarity is a particularly ethereal kind of feeling, and an ephemeral one. Incorporation becomes an ongoing process, not a bond anchored by fixed qualities.

Three potential limitations to multicultural incorporation stand out: ethereality, relativism, and individualism. First, from a pragmatic point of view, such high-minded solidarity appears weaker than forms based on sameness. The ethereal bond of difference borders on separation; this bond may be more easily dissolved, or it may hide other minorities within the minority (such as a gay minority within a religious minority).[19] Second, the fusion of horizons risks making all values relative. Although clearly useful for expanding a liberal circle of sympathy, incorporating a group with reactionary values would entail a compromise of progressive ones. Lastly, from a purely theoretical point of view, pure difference breaks down every group into atomized individuals. Unless sameness stabilizes some level of social grouping, then each minority group fragments into smaller minorities within it, all the way down to the unique person. At this limit of individualism, modern assimilation merges with multiculturalism. Given these limitations, multiculturalism cannot be thought of as a panacea to the challenges of social incorporation.

How multiculturalism works through cinema is a matter of debate. Hollywood was once considered the epitome of assimilation, along with other mass media in the culture industry; from that point of view, avant-garde and independent cinemas fit with multiculturalism. Yet if the latter are defined by opposition, it is not clear how they would be incorporative. Moreover, Hollywood has evidently made efforts to represent cultural difference. To the political right, those efforts have gone too far; to the left, they have not gone far enough. *White Men Can't Jump* offers a case study. Yet a binary approach to incorporation as either assimilation or multiculturalism will not be sufficient.

Hyphenation

Hyphenation appears midway on the spectrum between assimilation and multiculturalism, but it involves more than a balance of sameness and difference. In its strong form, hyphenation changes the core social identity to create a new hybrid. Ralph Waldo Emerson envisioned this intense process through the metaphor of brass, an alloy that synthesizes pure metals into a new compound. He writes[20]:

> By the melting and inter-mixture of silver and gold and other metals a new compound more precious than any, called Corinthian Brass, was formed; so in this Continent,—asylum of all nations,—the energy of Irish, Germans, Swedes, Poles, and Cossacks, and all the European tribes,—of the Africans, and of the Polynesians,—will construct a new race, a new religion, a new State, a new literature.

Emerson concludes this passage by quoting Charles Fourier's naturalist principle: "*La Nature aime les croisements* (Nature delights in hybrids)." Emerson appears to respond to the United States Constitution's call "to form a more perfect Union" on a social and cultural level.[21] Unlike assimilation and multiculturalism, strong hyphenation subjects everyone to change, including the formerly primordial group.

Hyphenation emphasizes ethnicity, especially when perceived on a generational timeline. Rather than denigrate non-primordial qualities as foreign, ethnic qualities are tolerated in public life (though not necessarily valued equally). Horace Kallen famously illustrated his idea of hyphenation with the metaphor of harmony—a less violent image than Emerson's metallurgy. Kallen likens each ethnic group to an instrument in a symphony that has a "specific timbre and tonality." Arguing against strong assimilation, Kallen writes, "What do we will to make of the United States—a unison, singing the old Anglo-Saxon theme 'America,' the America of the New England school, or a harmony, in which that theme shall be dominant, perhaps, among others, but one among many, not the only one?"[22] Kallen's acceptance of Anglo dominance also illustrates the drawback to hyphenation. In its weaker forms, minorities remain secondary and the dominant tune little changed.

Heating the fire is therefore necessary for hyphenation. This mode suits strong and progressive institutions in a republic to overcome the inertia of primordial domination. In addition, political theorists of migration have recognized the necessity of incorporating outsiders to counteract a natural tendency to nativist entrenchment, corruption, and oligarchy.[23] The underlying challenge for this mode is having solidarity with clear ideals to keep the furnace of change well lit.

Two examples of hyphenation in Hollywood films inform our case study. First, consider *Knute Rockne: All American* again. A spectacular scene of a Roman Catholic Mass in an ornate church recognizes Catholicism as part of the new normal, reflecting an early twentieth-century shift from the primordial national identity of Protestantism to a "Judeo-Christian" fusion.[24] Although young Knute chastises his father for not "talking American," Norwegian identity is more than tolerated. The film's title highlights Knute's ethnic name beside a universal, as if they were connected with a hyphen.[25] Thus within one film we can find multiple modes of incorporation at work, which agrees with Alexander's understanding of the actual process.

Elsewhere, *The Godfather* (1972) marked a new phase for Hollywood. Italian-American Francis Ford Coppola directed an almost exclusively Italian-American cast. Ethnic minorities, previously marginalized, had become primary characters as well as the featured talent behind the camera. Since the controversy over *The Birth of a Nation*, Hollywood had avoided discussing whiteness or "race" in accordance with a color-blind ethic, as Richard Dyer points out.[26] Color-blindism made whiteness socially invisible while characters of color remained marked as different by marginal roles or by the issue of race whenever nonwhites took center stage. Greg Garrett traces Hollywood's progress toward multiculturalism and mainstream minority filmmakers through the pivotal success of *The Godfather*.[27] *White Men Can't Jump* marks another step in that direction. Although a white male hero anchors the narrative and therefore plays a dominant chord by default (to employ Kallen's metaphor), Shelton's film amalgamates a diverse national identity through a satire of whiteness and a recognition of African-American culture.

A White Man in a Black World

Set in a Los Angeles world of street basketball that is predominantly Black, *White Men Can't Jump* draws attention to the protagonist's whiteness in an unprecedented way. Celestino Deleyto describes the film as having "a racial scenario practically unknown in mainstream comedy."[28] The film's title itself violates color-blind neutrality by focusing our attention on whiteness through a negative stereotype. By showcasing black culture and making whiteness an explicit object of attention, the film demonstrates hyphenation and multicultural modes of incorporation.

White Men Can't Jump signals American Blackness from the first sounds played over the 20th Century Fox logo. J. D. Connor expounds upon the boutique studio logo as a representation of a company's utopian ambitions.[29] In this case a jazz-funk version replaces the traditional brass fanfare with syncopated horns and an electric bass line. This funk fanfare combines with the icon of the traditionally white movie industry to announce a new hybrid Hollywood culture.

The opening scenes depict Venice Beach as a Black world. The credits montage centers on the Venice Beach Boys, an African-American a cappella group (with a cheeky Southern California name) who perform on the boardwalk in the early morning. Figure 5.3 shows them in a medium shot. Meanwhile a black weightlifter flexes in the background of the Gospel/Jazz singers, while a black skateboarder passes before him. Their quaint throwback tune suggests a pacific coastal atmosphere that subverts tropes of black urban aggressiveness. As the white protagonist strolls in, he bounces his basketball against a street mural that mirrors the black characters in the motion-picture-postcard boardwalk, captured in Figure 5.4. It should be said that Shelton creates a dream image of Venice Beach, which actually remains one of the whitest sections of Los Angeles. In her study of contemporary films set in L.A., Deleyto describes Shelton's "fictional Angeleno society dominated by black men and

Figures 5.3–5.4 The movie opens in a predominantly black Los Angeles indicated by the Venice Beach Boys singing a cappella and a mural of black figures set against one goofy white outsider.

women ... truly fantastic."[30] Hollywood films usually whitewash the city, reflecting a deep-seated European dream of a White promised land.[31] Rather than assimilate blacks into a white Venice Beach, this imaginative setting does just the opposite. It naturalizes the blackness of southern California. One might criticize the film's fantastical manipulation but accept its comedic play and progressive dream of a non-white cultural standard.

Next, the first basketball scene establishes the blacktop court as a distinctively Black cultural space. All the players are black. Plate 13 shows colorful tops that denote various Black icons: the album art of South African musician Miriam Makeba, Malcolm X in a Nation of Islam cap, and a Michael Jordan Chicago Bulls jersey. Sidney Deane

(Wesley Snipes) stands out in Nike Air Flight Lite sneakers that also evoke the NBA's predominantly black stars.[32] Meanwhile, his cycling cap seems totally displaced from its predominantly white European athletes; he has appropriated its flamboyance and functional little bill for the sun-drenched court. After Sidney blocks a shot, he talks trash by ironically mimicking Muhammad Ali: "I don't mean to brag, but I am the greatest!"[33] Just as Ali broke with the white norm of modesty, Sidney's sartorial stylishness also denotes black culture.

The court serves as a stage for performing masculine aggression and skill. More trash talk with serious intent suddenly stops play but quickly sublimates into playful "yo mama" jokes between players. "Yo mama's so fat," says one player, "she broke her leg and gravy poured out." The context of a verbal game mitigates some of the jokes' machismo in a way comparable to the exaggerated performance of physicality in *Slap Shot* (1977), discussed in chapter 3. Here improvisation stands forth as a characteristically Black skill present in music, the joke battle, and basketball. Aaron Baker remarks that "the Sidney Dean character in *White Men* plays a Jordan-inspired brand of ball in his playground games, supremely confident as he improvises ... and creates distinctly stylized moves."[34] In the opening scene Sidney and the others perform in front of beach babes, chiseled weightlifters, and the white protagonist on the bench, all seen in cutaways at a distance. The court acts as a social center that is defined as Black from head to toe, with lighter-skinned spectators relegated to the margins. Open aggression and stylized performance present a Black masculinity at odds with the Victorian modesty and frankness that characterizes basketball in educational settings.

White Men Can't Jump follows Black independent cinema in its authentic representation of vernacular life and in its satire of racial stereotypes. Aside from the fantastical Black location of Venice Beach, the film's other basketball scenes are set in actual Black neighborhoods in Los Angeles, on authentic street basketball courts in South Central, Watts, Lafayette Park, and Crenshaw. What's more, Deleyto remarks upon the uncommonly sunny representation of these Black places, in contrast to stereotypical portrayals of shadowy black ghettos.[35] Such genuine admiration reflects the integration of key black creative figures in the production. Victoria Thomas assembled the diverse cast, Francine Jamison-Tanchuck designed the costumes, Stephanie Cozart Burton and Sterfon Demings led makeup and hair, and Kokayi Ampah managed locations. Camera assistant Sabrina Simmons was the only Black female union camerawoman in the industry at the time.[36]

Furthermore, the film's satire of racial types adopts a mode that Mark Reid recognized in Spike Lee's films of the late 1980s. "The satiric hybrid minstrelsy narrative form," as Reid calls it, involves a "dualistic process" that objectifies characters while implicitly criticizing binary and essentialist thinking.[37] Deleyto agrees that "the comic framework allows spectators the sufficient distance to recognize both the stereotypes and the ideological work that the film is doing with them."[38] *White Men Can't Jump* trusts its viewers to see beyond racial stereotypes in order to appreciate its play with them.

Street basketball became widely represented as vernacular African-American culture in this era. Rick Telander's book *Heaven Is a Playground* (M. Evans, 1976) and Darcy Frey's *The Last Shot: City Streets, Basketball Dreams* (Houghton Mifflin, 1994) exemplify the subject in sportswriting, alongside Steve James's widely regarded documentary about street players in Chicago, *Hoop Dreams* (1994). The American dream evidently serves as their common theme; the narrator usually takes a white outsider's point of view and chronicles the migration of young men out of a Black city neighborhood and their attempts to assimilate into mainstream white culture.[39] *White Men Can't Jump* reverses that scenario with a white protagonist who migrates to Black Los Angeles to pursue his dream, suggesting that Black neighborhoods and street courts are the more authentic locus of the sport.[40]

The opening scenes also accentuate this Black world by introducing the white protagonist as a fish out of water. During the credits sequence, Billy (Woody Harrelson) struts into the neighborhood like a wannabe, white outsider. He approaches the Venice Beach Boys and praises them so effusively that they gape awkwardly. Billy says reassuringly, "Keep singing guys. My old man was a preacher. I love this shit." He then asks about local Black basketball legends as if he were a teenager from Compton. His interlocutors remain agape. This subtle exchange, relayed through close-ups, indicates that Billy is seemingly ignorant of his foreign origin and that his folksy familiarity is out of place. Writer-director Ron Shelton, a white college athlete from Santa Barbara, seems to wink self-deprecatingly at his own outside perspective in this humorous moment. If Billy does not use the gentle language of a preacher's son, he certainly expresses enthusiasm for African-American culture. Having a laugh at this White wannabe type certainly breaks with Hollywood's older mode of assimilation.

Billy both continues and subverts the tradition of comic ethnic yokel characters. Historically, the fully assimilated Anglo protagonists bore no ethnicity while non-Anglo types such as the Swede or the black "Coon" were tolerated on the margins as objects for satire.[41] By reimagining the world as fundamentally Black and making the Anglo character an ethnic outsider Shelton's film inverts Hollywood's assimilationist White tradition.

In its general admiration for a distinctive Black American culture, *White Men Can't Jump* exemplifies multiculturalism, yet its overall hyphenation sets the movie apart from the Black film wave. The fantasy of a fundamentally Black Los Angeles and the reorientation of the American dream around white incorporation into Black America point toward a new hybrid vision of national culture. The drama that unfolds explores the complications of that new harmony.

Unhealthy Competition

In Horatio Alger's kind of American dream, the hero succeeds by competing against others and proving his worth. He may benefit from a little luck, but he enters a world that justly rewards him. A vision of sports as a sphere of pure competition and as a means for color-blind assimilation is closely tied to that version of the American dream. Billy initially follows this classic pattern. Upon arriving in Los Angeles he competes and wins, to the surprise of the locals. However, his plans go awry by the end of the first act. Deception escalates the conflict between Billy and Sidney. Through this dramatic action Shelton's film criticizes the political economic theory of liberalism and the social theory of color-blind assimilation that both center on pure competition. This section spotlights a critical aspect of *White Man Can't Jump* that previous critics have not fully appreciated.

Sham Neutrality

The protagonist's white yokel character turns out to be a ruse, at least as far as his basketball skills are concerned. He profits on basketball wagers against black locals who underestimate him. Read in the context of U.S. race relations, Billy's hustle is an allegory for the sham neutrality of color-blindism, meritocracy, and assimilation. It demonstrates how competition brews racial conflict rather than social equality.

The first basketball scene in Venice culminates in a showdown between Billy and Sidney with explicit racial connotations. In the middle of the all-black game a score dispute erupts. Sidney turns away from the court to single out Billy, the white spectator. "Chump!" Sidney addresses him. "What's the score?" Sidney assumes that the neutral white observer will not favor either side. "I don't know," Billy replies, disappointing his interlocutor and confirming his doltish character. Sidney escalates the situation by addressing him in the mock voice of a proper female elementary schoolteacher: "Okay, Billy. Can you count to ten? What is the score, Billy?" Wesley Snipes's performance of this mask contrasts the artifice of White culture with the authentic Black ball court. The mockery goes a step further when the other teams invite Billy to substitute for an injured player. As the white outsider begins stretching his limbs before coming on court Sidney comically mimes his Jane Fonda–like routine—to the delight of onlookers. Sidney teases the "foreigner," as he calls him, and pokes fun at the naïveté and institutional conformity of White culture.

Indeed, Woody Harrelson exemplifies the naïveté and foolishness of a chump through his goofy costume, airhead expression, and star persona. His only notable prior role was a Midwestern yokel on the sitcom *Cheers*. Placing Harrelson's bumpkin in a Black world now makes the normative white American male a visible "Other" in an unprecedented way for a mainstream genre movie. The white man is a "chump."

Yet Billy Hoyle is not as naïve as he first appears. After leading his team to victory, he baits Sidney into a three-point contest for all the money in their wallets. Taking for granted his advantage, Sidney accepts the bet. As they prepare to shoot, the symbolic stakes are raised further when a new camera angle reveals a large American flag behind the basket, shown in Figure 5.5. Each amazingly makes four shots in a row. Then, before their fifth and final shots, Hoyle reveals his disguise:

BILLY. The thing is, you guys look at me, you see the backwards hat, and you say, 'This guy's a chump.'
OTHER PLAYER. A fucking geek.
BILLY. What you don't realize is ... I must be doing it for a reason.

Billy sinks his shot. He is actually a college-level player disguised as what he calls a "slow, white, geeky chump." His last name *Hoyle*, a playing card brand, alludes to the mind games of poker. Furthermore, to make his opponent nervous before the final shot Billy whispers in his ear, "Sidney, I've hustled a hell of a lot better players than you before." Figure 5.6 captures this cruel moment. Suddenly aware that he is being conned by a skilled hustler disguised as a bumpkin, Sidney tenses up, misses his shot, and loses.

Billy dons a mask of "the chump," the epitome of White innocence, to con the Black players. Figure 5.7 gives a portrait of this character. Sidney recognizes the brilliance of the ruse and teams up with Billy to hustle at other Black neighborhood courts in subsequent scenes. They act out a scenario: Sidney arrives at a court separately and boasts that he can win a high-stakes game of two-on-two with any partner. The opponents inevitably choose Billy, who sticks out like a sore thumb, and the talented duo wins. Their hustle exploits two incorrect assumptions: that Billy is an innocent yokel and that white men can't play basketball well.

Billy's mask of innocence becomes an allegory for the sham neutrality of color-blindism and the hidden privilege of whiteness. Clifford Geertz has shown how negotiating the conditions for competition, especially gambling, has a ritual dimension that involves the social status of participants.[42] Behind the wagering and schemes of these characters lies a deeper reflection on race and society in the United States.

By the 1980s, color-blind policy had become accepted on the political right and criticized by the left. At midcentury, liberals had promoted this neutral ethic as a correction to racially discriminatory public systems. But now they observed conservatives wielding the principle of neutrality to attack affirmative action and other programs helpful to minorities. The ideal of color-blind treatment of individuals that had once warranted reform was now invoked to undercut progressive policy. Multiculturalists made clear how denying recognition to minority cultures caused real harm; although racist ideology had created the social divisions that cultivated racial minorities, assimilation is no neutral repair. Moreover, evidence of racial inequality exposed the neutrality of the justice system to be a sham.[43] The critical race theory movement denounced color-blind policy, assimilation, and individualism as arms of a White supremacist ideology that masquerades as universalistic.[44] Differentiating neutral policy in theory from its application in practice had become a serious point of contention.

In the terms of political philosophy, sham neutrality and hidden privilege are rooted in the tyranny of the majority. The rule of law demands that all citizens are

Figures 5.5–5.6 The U.S. flag framed behind the hoop adds symbolism to a shooting contest in which the white outsider deceives the black Angeleno. Billy whispers in Sidney's ear to unsettle him.

treated equally—this principle distinguishes the republic from monarchy or despotism, which are ruled by hereditary privilege and by force. In theory, laws in a republic treat all citizens impartially or neutrally, without bias. However, if the lawmakers represent some but not all of the people, the supposedly neutral law favors the privileged group. Anyone within that group experiences impartial treatment, while marginal groups lack the privilege of equal treatment. In the United States the claim of impartial rule is challenged by minorities arguing that neutral treatment is limited to a White majority and does not extend to all citizens. The tyranny of the majority creates a sham neutrality. Persuading the majority of the problem poses a challenge because rule already appears impartial to them, and any correction appears partial to minorities. The deeper problem here is that rule by majority

Figure 5.7 To con the local Black players, Billy (Woody Harrelson) dons the mask of an innocent White man whose idealism is signaled by a hippyish, rainbow tie-dye hat.

representation does not align automatically with rule impartial to all citizens; the emergence of any majority creates a natural inertia. Correcting the tyranny of the majority requires knowledge that rule is truly impartial and persuading everyone to adopt a new policy.

This opening scenario would set Billy up to be a great hero for the political right and a villain for the left. By abusing the local Blacks he teaches them the color-blind lesson about racial prejudice. Although some might seize upon this interpretation, the film's subsequent action will favor a leftist perspective: Billy embodies the sham neutrality and phony innocence of Whites. The conflict escalates and prompts critical reflection on color-blind ideology, leading to a positive change that recuperates Billy as a hero.

Men's Rules

Sidney double-crosses Billy, raising the question of competition in society generally. When they take their chump hustle to a court in Crenshaw, Billy stakes all his previous winnings on the game. But Sidney does not play well, and they lose. "You got hustled," Gloria (Rosie Perez) realizes when Billy later explains how he lost the couple's nest egg. Sidney had collaborated with the other team to split the winnings; he deceived Billy by pretending that the game was played fairly. Incensed, Gloria wants to confront Sidney.

GLORIA. I'm going back to that house and getting my money back.
BILLY. No, honey, no. A man cannot ask for the money back.
GLORIA. He lives in the jungle, right?

BILLY. No, honey, we can't. They don't let white people in the Crenshaw district. But I don't know about Puerto Ricans. It's a reverse discrimination thing.

GLORIA. We dropped off Sidney on the corner of Crenshaw and Washington.

BILLY. Honey, you don't understand. Men understand how these things work. .... Let me explain. *Men's rules are very simple. If you win, you win. If you lose, you lose.* You don't ask for the money back.

GLORIA. Why not?

BILLY. It's not part of the rules.

Note how Billy's code of ethics links masculinity to pure competition, and how race comes into the picture. The dialogue reveals two potential contradictions in the ethic of pure competition. First, Billy's prejudicial view of the Black ghetto at night scares him away, contradicting the color-blind ethic of pure competition. Second, his fear suggests that race rivalry accompanies individual competition through the old racist principle of survival of the fittest. No-nonsense Gloria will lead her silly man to Sidney's apartment with these issues in the air.

Perhaps surprisingly, Sidney adheres to the same code and refuses to return the money. He reminds Billy that "what goes around comes around." It was Billy who had hustled Sidney when they first met, preying upon his prejudice of the White chump. Now Sidney has preyed on Billy's assumption of the loyal Black sidekick (and of the menacing Black ghetto). "Look, man, it goes like this," Sidney explains. "You either smoke, or you get smoked. And you got smoked!"

BILLY. I trusted you. There are rules to hustling, there's an ethics involved.

SIDNEY. That you wouldn't know anything about.

BILLY. I never shook anyone's hand and stabbed him in the back.

SIDNEY. The Indians shook hands with the Pilgrims, and look who got fucked.

Kant would laugh at Billy's notion of "an ethics" here because hustling is by nature deceptive and exploitative. If "men's rules" imply an idealistic field of fair play, Sidney takes the realist view of a struggle for power. The game behind the basketball game is a ruthless survival of the fittest. He implicitly compares Billy to a Pilgrim—a seemingly innocent European-American who migrates west, exploiting native people of color. Sidney evidently had race in mind, as well as individual revenge, when he decided to double-cross Billy. (The car scene in which the color-blind white hero insists that he can *hear* Jimi Hendrix immediately precedes Sidney's betrayal.) Rather than help the white outsider exploit other local blacks, Sidney arranges for Billy's comeuppance. The symmetry of this sequence demonstrates how competition does not naturally incorporate individuals upon a neutral common ground. Bad faith inevitably puts the opponents at loggerheads and also entrenches racial division.

Classical liberal economics revolve around what John Kenneth Galbraith calls "the competitive model." Developed in the seventeenth and eighteenth centuries and culminating in Say's law, the theory of self-regulating competition derives from an agricultural market in which numerous small producers participate.[45] Transposed from market economics to politics, that liberal theory posits a small, impartial state that mediates among various interest groups who have competing conceptions of the good life. Liberalism flourished in the twentieth-century to counteract the specter of totalitarian states and in concert with color-blind assimilation. "A neutralist liberal approach," Iseult Honohan explains, "also supported limiting the scope of the state to matters which do not interfere with the privacy and freedom of individuals."[46] For instance, John Rawls extended the mathematical logic of economics to his *Theory of Justice* (1971). At the kernel of his theory is an "original position" in which one adopts a veil of impartiality to judge fairly. This ideal position abstracts the individual from his self-interest, like a referee who floats above the competition, and aligns with the color-blind ethic of individual antiracism. Neutrality is evidently crucial to philosophies of the small state and of justice based exclusively on the individual.

However, Gilded Age monopolies, the Great Depression of the 1930s, and persistent racial inequality revealed major flaws in the competitive model. John Maynard Keynes and Galbraith show that oligarchy and depression are normal outcomes of free market policy that must be corrected by state intervention.[47] Meanwhile, communitarian philosophers denied the possibility of a neutral state because any policy represents some "specific conception of the human good" that cannot be impartial; they likewise criticized Rawls's utopian abstraction of the individual from all social contexts.[48] Rather than balance power evenly, pure competition leads to privileged classes whose self-interest works against a level playing field. The classical liberal focus on economic self-interest exacerbates these problems by weakening the communal solidarity and civil society necessary to democratic state intervention.

In a poetic speech, Gloria pokes fun at the competitive model. "I got a different set of rules," she declares to Billy:

GLORIA. Sometimes when you win, you really lose.
Sometimes when you lose, you really win.
Sometimes when you win or lose, you actually tie.
Sometimes when you tie, you actually win or lose.

"Winning and losing is one big organic globule from which one extracts what one needs," she concludes. Her counter-principles challenge the notion that the meaning of competition can be stabilized like a logical machine; the rhetorical curlicues also resemble the writing of Gertrude Stein.[49] Gloria does not detail an alternative theory, but the film's most astute and successful character points beyond competition to a more holistic picture.

Gloria temporarily resolves the men's conflict by having Billy and Sidney register for a tournament that does not involve wagers. While this prevents them from deceiving one another, Billy adopts a new mask that illustrates another problem with the competitive model.

Escalating Conflict

Two other basketball scenes emphasize how competition escalates conflict and inhibits social incorporation. Sidney and Billy's first try at the chump hustle ends in violence. Sidney unknowingly wagers against an ex-con who naively chooses Billy to partner with Sidney. When the duo prevails with ease the ex-con, Raymond, senses that he has been deceived. "These motherfuckers set us up," he steams, then pulls out a knife as shown in Figure 5.8. To calm him, Sidney lies that he has never met the "goofy white boy" before. But Billy gets scared and breaks character, confirming the ruse. Raymond (Marques Johnson) becomes more incensed. "I'm going to my car, get my gun, and shoot everybody's ass," he declares. People run in every direction and gunshots are heard as Billy, Sidney, and Gloria speed away in their car. Although Raymond is a character of comic excess, he is rightly provoked by his opponents' dishonesty. His violent reaction illustrates the extreme result of interaction based on competition.

Raymond's reaction also suggests that violence in Black neighborhoods stems from social injustice. An earlier moment characterizes him as a mercurial personality, not the racist stereotype of an aggressive predator.[50] To stake the game, the ex-con hilariously attempts to rob a corner store, is recognized, then sells his gun to the owner as protection against others "a lot crazier than me" in the neighborhood. The owner sees the fool behind the mask and only offers two-hundred and fifty dollars, prompting Raymond to say, "Now you're robbing me!" A lyric rapped over the game montage points to the deeper cause of violence: "In this dog-eat-dog world, you know I'm going to get mine."[51] The scene thus invites one to understand liberalism's competitive model and social inequality as the cause of violence more generally. Raymond

Figure 5.8 Raymond (Marques Johnson) appears charmingly foolish as an ex-con, but his violent reaction to being hustled illustrates the ugly endpoint of human competition.

represents an underclass exploited by competition, driven to violence, then stigmatized as a criminal with independent moral failings.

Elsewhere, the corporate-sponsored basketball tournament in which Billy and Sidney compete adds to the criticism of color-blind assimilation. Shelton begins by satirizing the whiteness of bureaucratic corporate culture from a local point of view; then, Billy incites conflict through explicitly racist trash talk that transgresses the norms of white civility.

In the first case, Billy's mask of innocence represents the neutral ideal of individual judgment; now the corporate organizers represent the neutral procedure of bureaucracy. Meanwhile activists of various stripes saw their enemy as a liberal establishment who exerted central authority, top-down, over "the system" they controlled. They saw in supposedly neutral procedures an inhuman instrumentality, and bureaucracy that served a technocratic elite foremost. Big government and big business all appeared complicit. The corporate technocrats depicted in the charity tournament scene of *White Men Can't Jump* portray the face of that system.

The tournament scene opens upon Lafayette Park looking as artificially blissful as Disneyland. Figure 5.9 depicts a crane shot that lifts up from the Venice Beach Boys singing and a Harlem Globetrotter–type performer to a panorama of bustling Americana topped off by a colorful grandstand and an emoji-like logo of an interracial handshake. Editors Paul Seydor and Kimberly Ray signal irony through a hyperbolically quick transition from the previous scene's heated argument in Sidney's apartment to the utopian park. A loudspeaker then announces the event and its purpose in a white voice:

ANNOUNCER. Welcome to the first annual Two-on-Two for Brotherhood Basketball Tournament, also known as the TTBBT, sponsored by a coalition of American corporations, in the spirit of promoting brotherhood among us all.

"That's bullshit," comments one black spectator to another, in a cutaway. A low angle shot illustrates the conformist corporate hierarchy on the pyramid-shaped grandstand portrayed in Figure 5.10. A heavyset white announcer in a suit presides over officials in logoed polo shirts and hostesses in skimpy swimsuits—with a perfectly diverse mix of employees. Their uniforms contrast with the vivid personal styles of the attendees, including one who wears a Public Enemy T-shirt. The executive's geeky glasses and his awkward TTBBT acronym poke fun at the procedural character of bureaucracy.

Overall, Shelton mocks white culture and its pretense of unity and equality through such hyperbolic contrasts. From a leftist point of view, the corporate hierarchy on stage illustrates sham neutrality in another place. If Billy's mask of innocence represented color-blindness on a personal level, the corporate tournament represents the institutional appearance of equality. The economic power of big business inherently contradicts corporate social responsibility. From a rightist point of view, the TTBBT corporate artifice satirizes liberal idealism and political correctness. For either point

Figures 5.9–5.10 The corporate tournament is staged at a hyperbolically blissful Lafayette Park. The executive atop the grandstand contrasts with a man wearing a Public Enemy t-shirt in the front row, thus pointing to the white-dominated power structure behind the ostensibly egalitarian event.

of view, however, skepticism of civic institutions (and their total absence from the film otherwise) falls back upon libertarianism. Such ideological contradiction is typical of liberal multiculturalism and will be discussed further in the chapter on *Ali*. The reason that the sincerity of the corporate motivations comes into question is that businesses are understood as essentially competitive economic ventures. The idea that these outsiders could have a genuinely benevolent interest in this local community is a great send-up of phony civic involvement.

Next, Billy disrupts the fairytale atmosphere with explicitly racist trash talk. Upon arrival he loudly heckles two black players and mocks their hair—a distinctive racial

Plate 1 Rocky symbolically embraces the city that he has paraded across in his training. The character, his pose, his jog, and the montage become icons for the collective effervescence of Philadelphia and Bicentennial America.

Plate 2 *Rocky* (1976) concludes on a freeze frame, a technique made famous by François Truffaut's *The 400 Blows* (1959). Despite losing the fight, the rosy embrace creates an icon for common people's hopefulness and solidarity.

Plate 3 The poster image for the Bicentennial Super Battle pastiches the Great Seal of the United States. Apollo Creed stands before the Liberty Bell in flag-pattern shorts, crowned by a golden eagle holding a banner that bears his name.

Plate 4 Now in an Uncle Sam costume that recalls a World War I military recruitment campaign, Creed pretends to recruit his opponent Rocky.

Plate 5 The reddish brown ducts and vest suggest the impending rust belt. The local steel mill's closure is the backdrop to the dramatic action in *Slap Shot* (1977).

Plate 6 The austere sign and medically green light suggest that the state anesthetizes its provincial citizen consumers with the store's only product, alcohol.

Plate 7 Framed like a comic strip, the Hanson brothers are childish goons who cheer and brawl without reserve.

Plate 8 Wearing a pastel pantsuit in her chic country villa, hockey team owner Anita McCambridge (Kathryn Walker) represents a new elite driven by purely financial logic.

Plate 9–10 Children at the Bicentennial parade, accompanied by Maxine Nightingale's song "Right Back Where We Started From," convey an optimistic revolutionary spirit.

Plate 11 The protagonist playing catch with his father in a childhood flashback sequence added by the filmmakers to their novel adaptation of *The Natural*.

Plate 12 The opening shot of *The Natural* (1984) blends Edward Hopper's emptiness with Norman Rockwell's quaintness to introduce its common-man hero.

Plate 13 *White Men Can't Jump* (1992) opens at the Venice Beach basketball courts. The players' tops feature Black icons Miriam Makeba, Malcolm X, Nelson Mandela, and Michael Jordan.

Plate 14 In *A League of Their Own* (1992) the recruits enter the verdant field through a tunnel that symbolizes the birth of the women's league and their personal rebirth.

Plate 15 The widescreen aspect ratio gathers multiple characters within the frame as they sing the league anthem. Bras, a pinkish hue, and a bashful boy in blue emphasize the locker room as a space for women.

Plate 16 Staged like a soldier's departure for war with the flag waving goodbye, Marla's journey to the city is coded as a national quest, battle, and sacrifice. The metallic train symbolizes the progress of women's liberation.

Plate 17 The bright sun, teal wall, and television antennas depicted in this early moment from *Ali* (2001) pay tribute to director Michael Mann's *Miami Vice* (1984–1989).

Plate 18 The mirror represents Ali's reflective conscience and his dyslexia as it corrects the reversed text of the Miami gym window.

Plate 19 In Ali's first title bout against Sonny Liston low angles diminish the spectators and elevate the boxers upon a cosmic backdrop.

Plate 20 On his 1964 trip to Ghana, the dawn symbolizes Ali's blossoming consciousness as well as the era of African independence.

Plate 21 Zairean and American flags surround Ali in the hubbub after his 1974 victory over George Foreman, marking the high point of the film.

and cultural characteristic. "Hey chump," Billy says. "Yeah, you, potato head. . . . You got that big *Z* in your 'fro, man. Are you the black Zorro?" The opponent retorts by comparing Billy to Opie Taylor, the innocent white son from *The Andy Griffith Show*. "You and your Cream-of-Wheat man," he calls Billy and Sidney, "take your ass back to Mayberry." The 1960s sitcom was set in the idyllic, white, and fictional North Carolina town of Mayberry. He casts Sidney as the icon of a mass-produced breakfast food, a happy black chef comparable to Aunt Jemima. So this retort insults Billy as a racist and Sidney as an Uncle Tom–like sidekick. Sidney even pulls Billy aside and complains, "You're embarrassing me."

In confidence, Billy explains to Sidney that his trash talking is a mere mask, a cynical strategy to discombobulate their opponents. Billy reasons that most players perform poorly when angry; Sidney is one exception. Thus making them all angry with racist trash talk plays to his team's advantage. Here Billy employs the competitive logic of a hustler, similar to the innocent white chump mask he wore on the street court. In the opposite environment of a white corporate tournament, Billy dons the opposite mask to upset his opponents. When he sees one miss a shot, with the ball clanking off the backboard like a brick, Billy heckles: "Let's gather up all these bricks and let's build a shelter for the homeless, so that maybe your mother has a place to live." The racist assumption here is that all blacks are homeless. Truly angered now, the opponents aggressively reply, "Fuck you!" When the two teams finally face off, they push and shove so aggressively that the corporate organizer says, "Stop them before we lose our sponsors!" With their opponents consternated by the trash talking, Billy and Sidney win the tournament and collect $5,000. The aggressively angry losers scare the corporate organizers, who literally flee. "Let's pay them and get the hell out of here," they say. Billy's racist trash talk effectively ruins the feel-good unity the corporations aimed to create, and the tournament ends in animosity.

Billy is transgressing two social norms. First, he is wearing a Black mask in a White environment. He brings street basketball's vernacular trash talking to a respectable corporate event. Whereas his chump character brought the Whiteness of school basketball to the streets, he now chafes against the straight-faced referees and organizers who are trying to stage a puff piece for local news cameras.[52] Where the white corporate types expect all the Black players to wear a White mask to assimilate, Billy spites them by adopting a Black mask in resistance, reclaiming the atmosphere of the street basketball court. He even starts throwing trick passes reminiscent of Sidney's improvisational style, highlighted in a montage. He repeats, "I'm in the zone," suggesting that his trash talk and spectacular athletic play go hand-in-hand. He performs a kind of multicultural hero, except that he is white.

Second, Billy's (feigned) racism is especially provocative in the Black neighborhood. Truly embarrassing for Sydney, Billy foolishly undercuts his multicultural heroism. On the street courts he might be instantly and justly challenged, but the tournament puts the onus on the corporate organizers. They are not prepared to act, and thus they enable Billy's racism.

The corporate tournament scene creates a more complex and multicultural way to criticize assimilation than showcasing the oppression of individuals. For instance, the hair cutting scene in *Full Metal Jacket* (Stanley Kubrick, 1987) portrays the liberal establishment as tyrants that turn individual men into machines, traumatically conforming their bodies.[53] In *White Men Can't Jump*, rather than acting too strongly, the conformist institution reacts too weakly. The idealist do-gooders and their color-blind ideal do little to solve the practical problems of poverty and racial animosity.

More importantly, the scene's racist trash talk demonstrates another problem with color-blind neutrality. Competition inevitably escalates conflict and cannot be excused as neutral. Billy feigns racism to gain a competitive edge; according to "men's rules," racial jokes are fair game if they go both ways. However, this ostensibly neutral principle goes wrong in two ways. Jokes are only harmless among friends and equals. Without a relationship of trust and solidarity, the effect of racist public speech is undetermined. Regardless of the speaker's intention, the hearer can be harmed. In addition to that general uncertainty, social inequality destroys the symmetry of racist jokes. History situates each group in a different context of privilege, so punches never land equally hard. When Billy's trash talk is read from this perspective, the foolish protagonist demonstrates the escalation of racial conflict caused by the competitive model and its false symmetry.

Yet Billy's trash talk could be interpreted as an endorsement of racist jokes freed from political correctness. This scene risks the same reactionary appeal as his hustle in the opening scene. If the protagonist's actions are considered implicitly admirable, this scene reads as Billy teaching another antiracist lesson, this time by telling racist jokes. That idea is evidently absurd, but the fact that the hero's action leads to winning creates an ambiguity.

Subsequent action clarifies the wrongness of Billy's racist talk. On the ride home from their victory, Billy's arrogance boils over to an argument with Sidney. The white hero bets all his winnings that he can dunk, promptly fails, then hands over his money and pride to Sidney. Once again, Billy's competitiveness breaks his pocketbook and his friendship in the end. Sidney does not come out ahead, either. In the following scene his apartment is robbed of his winnings and more. His wife expresses her anger at neighbors whom she believes know the culprit but will not speak to the police. This sequence implies that Sidney's black opponents—Raymond and the men in the tournament—exact their revenge upon him. All these bad consequences reply to Billy's racist talk. Such an outcome fits the form of satire, in which the hero's actions are ridiculed more often than admired.

Through the motifs of exploitation and conflict, Shelton's plot points to a cycle of poverty and violence. In contrast to Alger's American dream scenario of individual financial growth and assimilation, *White Men Can't Jump* illustrates how the competitive model of classical liberal economics leads to deception rather than fairness, and to racial tension rather than incorporation.

Friendship Is Priceless

Rather than victory, riches, and marriage, Shelton's film finds its happy ending in friendship. The hero's modest fate relative to his non-white companions translates to a hyphenation and multiculturalism. In particular, one final basketball victory comes at the cost of Billy's relationship with Gloria and thus insists upon the limits of competition. Through an emphasis on friendship *White Men Can't Jump* underlines the solidarity of civil society as a part of the American dream more important than financial earning.

This Is Jeopardy!

One character does win a fortune—Gloria. But Shelton cleverly avoids promoting Horatio Alger's American dream. The film first represents the improbability and foolishness of her plan to become a contestant on the game show *Jeopardy!* Then, her opportunity and success are represented so fantastically that the satire reinforces criticism of social inequality. The help of a friend will also underline the importance of affirmative action policy.

Gloria (Rosie Perez) first appears in her and Billy's dire hotel room, studying trivia. With the ludicrous hope of becoming a *Jeopardy!* contestant, she waits months for a call back to try out for the show, to no avail. In the meantime she does nothing but study trivia, even bringing an almanac to read on the sidelines during one of Billy and Sidney's basketball games, as depicted in Figure 5.11. She naively believes that

Figure 5.11 Gloria (Rosie Perez) studies trivia during a game in a poor neighborhood, portraying an absurd dedication to the unlikely dream of becoming a game show contestant.

she will have equal opportunity and that a perfectly meritocratic system will reward her talent. In reality, the best opportunities come through privileged personal connections that a near-penniless Newyorican migrant to L.A. does not have. She and Billy face a true jeopardy of poverty, crippled by debt to a loan shark. But the evidently cerebral Gloria knows no outlet for her intellect other than far-fetched hope in a television trivia show.

With the Gloria character, Shelton satirizes the improbable dream of wealth that fascinates the working classes, similar to the lottery. Her dire circumstances illustrate the reality of social inequality. Winning the lottery or a game show are terrible solutions to the problem of poverty—they are truly trivial. Gloria's dream epitomizes the cruel deception of capitalism. If she were a character in a naturalist novel or an art film Gloria would suffer an awful fate.

To arrive at the comedy's happy ending, Shelton will send Gloria to success on the game show under excessively fantastical circumstances. That excess maintains the satire of white privilege and an unfair economic system. Her dreams will come true but we are not meant to indulge in them.

Jeopardy! does not randomly call her in. A basketball friend of Sidney's works security on the television studio lot, and Billy asks him to give Gloria entry, as a favor. To persuade this friend-of-a-friend Billy must make a three-quarter-court hook shot—a nearly impossible feat. Thanks to an obvious edit, he sinks it. This little wink says that only in Hollywood fantasy is anyone so lucky. Thus, Gloria's opportunity does not come through any neutral, meritocratic process, but through the inside connection of a friend.

On the show, the puertorriqueña stands out wildly in the stodgy White atmosphere (Figure 5.12). The announcer introduces Gloria Clemente as a "former disco queen" from Brooklyn, in between an English teacher and a rocket scientist! Their hyperbolic pedigree, Anglo names, and conservative dress highlight the privilege of the middle-aged white men. This scene parodies the quiz shows of the 1950s that rigged the contest to favor contests preferred by sponsors; in particular, Ivy league English professor Charles Van Doren epitomized the white elite complicit in the fraud. Congress took interest and held televised hearings precisely because the public was scandalized by the show's disregard for the neutral principle of meritocracy.[54] Shelton's scenario allegorically restores fair play by giving Gloria special access. This reverse rigging of the system represents affirmative action.

Circumstances again swing fantastically in Gloria's favor when the trivia categories are revealed. They play to her strengths, especially "Foods That Start with 'Q' "—a subject we witnessed her studying in an earlier scene, as if by chance. Quince, quiche, and quahog vault her to success, capped off by a montage sequence. Gloria clearly has a talent for trivia, but her miraculous luck dispels the myth of meritocracy that sports and trivia contests often represent.

Gloria's star turn also deconstructs an ethnic stereotype. Usually relegated to marginal roles, this ethnic side character here takes center stage and achieves the dream typically reserved for the male hero. Rather than serving as the butt of ethnic jokes as

Figure 5.12 Gloria the newyoriqueña, introduced as a "former disco queen" and dressed in sequins and hoop earrings, is juxtaposed with a rocket scientist and an English teacher who typify America's White male elite.

a naïve outsider, Gloria confirms an intelligence already demonstrated in her deduction that Billy was hustled and in her challenge to "men's rules." Angharad Valdivia observes that Rosie Perez "thickens, complicates, and deconstructs her own stereotypical representation" as a loud, working-class Latina.[55] Her character serves as a canvas for the migrant's unrealistic dream of fortune; Perez's savvy performance and Shelton's satire attempt to both acknowledge certain problems of social inequality and create a character who circumvents received wisdom. In this ambiguity lies a form of hyphenation that incorporates the Hispanic, Puerto Rican–American character into the fold while setting her Anglo-American opponents as the objects of ridicule.

The Big Game

Billy and Sidney's final basketball game also complicates classical tropes. Their victory comes at the cost of Billy's relationship with Gloria. Rather than centering the drama around a conflict between sporting opponents, the hero's obsession with competition becomes the main obstacle to overcome.

Flush with game show winnings, Gloria gives Billy two thousand dollars on the condition that he buy a suit and get a regular job. Unsurprisingly, he takes her gift and immediately chooses to risk it on a street basketball game with Sidney. Gloria makes an ultimatum that Billy ignores. He and Sidney win the game, but Gloria has already left him, dampening the perfect outcome that the hero had expected. "How can that be?" Billy asks himself, flummoxed. He recalls Gloria's "organic globule" speech, *Sometimes when you win, you really lose . . . or tie*, but he cannot make sense of it.

This outcome reinforces the limits of competition. Gloria's ultimatum suggests that she recognizes how hustling basketball appeals to Billy's pride and love of risk, which incur the cycle of poverty. She also recognizes that her own success in the trivia contest came through luck and is not sustainable in the long run. By not yielding to Billy's desire, Gloria embodies the ideal of an independent woman and points to a feminist critique of liberalism. The phrase *men's rules* underlines the patriarchal and individualist qualities of competition, while her alternative *organic globule* suggests interdependence. Although the loose ending will not insist on a feminist message, the plot departs from the cliché of individual male triumph. To a greater extent than *Rocky* or *Slap Shot*, Shelton's film ultimately separates romantic love from the athletic contest.

Meanwhile, Billy and Sidney's final friendship also reconfigures the interracial buddy dynamic. From *The Defiant Ones* (1958) and continuing through *Green Book* (2018), buddy movies consistently center the action around the white hero's quest for self, aided by a selfless black sidekick. Although they idealize equality, such asymmetry points to assimilation's implicitly Anglo-American basis.[56] We have already noted how Sidney breaks this pattern when he double-crosses Billy and when he wins the bet that Billy can't dunk. But the big game seems to restore Billy to the dominant role. Like a good sidekick, Sidney arranges a game against the two local legends that Billy raved about in the opening credits sequence. This time it is honest competition with no deception. At the climax of a close affair, Sidney lobs an alley-oop pass that Billy dunks, in slow motion, to seal victory. This moment proves Billy's basketball skill, proves that white men can jump, and the big payday reverses his prior losses. If the plot ended here it would conform to the old pattern of the white hero's quest for self and dominance, with Sidney's alley-oop pass exemplifying his subordination.

However, the ending brings Billy back down to earth. First, he becomes upset when he realizes Gloria has left him and he turns to Sidney:

SIDNEY. Brother, I only have four words for you: 'Listen to the woman.'
BILLY. I tried to listen to the woman, you're the one who talked me out of it!
SIDNEY. I didn't have to talk to you very long. I presented you with an option, and you
    took it. You shouldn't listen to me, you should've listened to her.
BILLY. I shouldn't have listened to you then, and I'm supposed to listen to you now?
SIDNEY. Yeah, I'm just trying to give you advice.
BILLY. Who am I supposed to listen to?
SIDNEY. You're a grown man, you're supposed to figure that out for yourself.

Billy stares at him speechless for a moment in close up, then walks out. It angers Billy to learn that Sidney had his own motivations for recruiting him to the game. The black buddy did not selflessly guide the white hero to the promised land; he let Billy make a bad decision, and then tells him not to expect easy guidance. Shelton has created a pyrrhic victory for the hero.

If true victory conforms to assimilation and white dominance, Shelton's alternative has elements of multiculturalism and hyphenation. In the next scene the loan sharks arrive to purloin all of Billy's money. The Stucci brothers are Italian-American and speak with heavy accents. To settle his debt he must pose for a photo pretending he has been beaten to death—a symbolic emasculation. "No hard feelings, Billy boy?" one Stucci says. "It's all about respect," he continues, "you understand?"

"I respect you guys," Billy replies. The exchange aligns the white hero's financial debt to a cultural debt that he has finally repaid. A keyword for multiculturalism, *respect* signifies mutual recognition of social difference as a bond of incorporation.

The last scene restores Billy and Sidney's friendship but sets the Black man in the dominant position. Billy confesses that Gloria is not coming back, then he asks Sidney for a job in his construction firm. The hero ends up broke and dumped, but he is consoled by self-awareness, by a friendship with Sidney, and by Gloria's sage advice to abandon hustling for a regular job. "Now you're starting to hear the music," Sidney says. "I can hear Jimi now?" Billy replies. "No, that's not what I said," Sidney scoffs. "You can't hear Jimi...." Their voices fade away as the credits roll. Concluding the drama at this point is significant. Sidney does not yield, but they continue to amicably joust. A friendship that maintains difference and the subordination of White privilege almost qualifies as multicultural, but Billy's obstinate ignorance still falls short. On one level, that Billy remains a fool is a comedic trope. In the context of social incorporation, the mixed ending and the film overall are best described as hyphenation. Although the drama centers on a white protagonist, its satire of this jester-figure and elevation of minority characters creates a hybrid alternative to the classical Hollywood model of the white victor.

Outcomes for the three main characters all emphasize friendship over money. Gloria does win big, but under circumstances too far-fetched for sincere belief in the old myth of the immigrant's rise to the top in America. She recognizes her luck and advises her boyfriend to find a regular job rather than spending lavishly. Billy's choice of one more wager and game over Gloria's sage counsel breaks up any romantic and complete happy ending. Although Billy and Sidney prevail, it merely covers their earlier losses, and they end up turning toward regular work. Broke, dumped, and only a smidgen less foolish, the white hero is worse off than the other characters in the end. He and Sidney are too tough to dwell upon the sentiment but their principal gain is fraternal companionship.

Conclusion

A concluding vision of friendship and stability may seem too modest for the American dream. But the association of that dream with wealth is too narrow. Cultural historian Lawrence Samuel traces the dream to colonial America and highlights its fluctuating contours: equal opportunity, hope and change, owning a home, simple wealth, or being one's own boss. He articulates the through lines as "the devout belief that tomorrow can and will be better than today" and the belief in "perpetual progress."[57] Common hope for a better life does not require fame and fortune, although everyone certainly fantasizes about those things. Carol Graham's sociological study observes varying attitudes toward the American dream but finds that "people who believed in their future would work hard and invest in the future."[58] Shelton's film illustrates a development of the dream from simple wealth to freedom from economic distress. Billy, Sidney, and Gloria all fantasize about gaining wealth through gambling or a game show prize. Their focus on fantastic wealth and their misfortunes suggest the problem of stifling poverty that offers no reasonable hope for improvement. Personal gain entails losses by others. The dramatic development of friendship and cooperation in *White Men Can't Jump* points toward collective action, while Gloria's miraculous opportunity suggests the need for outside stimulus to overcome poverty. Rather than awarding Billy and Sidney wealth, they recover hope in honest work.

Shifting from a myth of freedom as personal wealth to freedom from poverty reorients attention from pure economics to civil society. Classical liberalism ignores civil society by superimposing an openly competitive market upon all of public life. Even social incorporation comes to be seen as assimilation to a market society, blind to non-economic elements of culture. The state has a minimal role as a neutral arbiter; it does not resolve conflict but merely restores balance to the totalizing conflict of the marketplace. Democracy is reduced to equal participation in the market. But this supposed freedom to participate is a necessity. The only true freedom from necessity is fantastic wealth, which is inherently unequal. Hence the problem with the Alger-esque American dream is not simply that it aims for too much wealth or that it is too individualistic. The total focus on economics betrays the civic aspects of freedom and democracy.

By contrast, the classical Greek understanding of freedom from economic necessity restores democracy to the sphere of civic life. Equal participation in representative government and representing the will of all the people equally stand forth as the higher objective than material abundance or imperial power. I discuss these issues raised by Hannah Arendt in the introduction to this book.

Shelton's film does not engage in politics directly. No officials from government or any other institutions appear except for the corporate charity. Their absence and the mockery of that one institution align with liberal political philosophy despite the film's other criticisms of liberalism and of bogus corporate charity.

Through the drama's sustained critique of pure competition and emphasis on cultural difference, *White Men Can't Jump* does communicate progressive ideas. At no point does it become blind to race or ethnicity, not even in the final moment of friendship. The heroes' competitive pursuit of victory is shown to cultivate deception, escalate conflict, and leave them worse off. More of a buffoon than an epic hero, Billy does not model normative conduct; thus, his misadventures compose a fairly complex satire of whiteness. Ultimately, the theme of solidarity and the alternative modes of hyphenation and multiculturalism develop a progressive politics. With a white hero surrounded by a mixed cast, Shelton's film does not go as far as Black cinema in counteracting the tyranny of the majority on screen (and behind the camera), but it does take a step beyond previous interracial buddy movies and two steps beyond studio-era Hollywood. In regard to these alternatives to assimilation, the 1992 film seems to point toward subsequent buddy movies designed around non-white heroes, such as *Rush Hour* (1998), *Shanghai Noon* (2000), and *Remember the Titans* (2000).[59] Denzel Washington's prolific work in the 1990s may best represent how the social nature and character of Hollywood's crossover stars were changing.[60]

Previous critics focused on the white male protagonist and identified longstanding, conservative patterns of interracial buddy films. This chapter has revealed several ways that Shelton's film works against conservative ideology: an admiration for Black culture as different, a satire of whiteness, and a dramatic conflict between community and masculine competition. Its comic ambiguity diverges from the didacticism of mainstream message movies and of avant-garde political cinema, such as that put forth by Spike Lee. Instead, Shelton's dynamic comedy attempts hyphenation that upsets the core identity of neutral white liberalism into a more colorful and more closely woven tapestry.

However, *White Men Can't Jump* has one major regressive element: Shelton centers the story's dynamism on a white protagonist, which represents a clear continuity with old Hollywood. Character identity is a fundamental aspect of story design, and this studio project maintains a traditional identity at its center. If representation in Hollywood were truly equal, one might not reproach this particular film, but the reality in the 1990s was far from diverse. White male heroes, created by white male directors, writers, and producers, reflect the privileged identity of Euro-American men in culture broadly. These discursive structures mirror sociopolitical structures that can be described by inequality, privilege, advantage, class, racism, injustice, and the tyranny of the majority. Progressives agree that an unjust social structure, developed and entrenched historically, is the reason why Hollywood, one of the nation's primary media institutions, lacks diversity. And they agree that minorities taking more prominent roles will help correct that unjust social structure and that denying this problem under the guise of color-blindness entrenches inequality further by not recognizing minority culture or underprivileged minorities.

Nonetheless, the role of Hollywood has its limits. Shelton's film was still on the marquee in the spring of 1992 when four white officers were acquitted of brutalizing Rodney King, which set off riots across Los Angeles. No fabulous performance then or now can easily repair severe violations of civic solidarity. In the big scheme of things, the effort of *White Men Can't Jump* to incorporate ethnic groups in the United States is merely one part of a complex civic-social fabric.

6

A League of Their Own (1992)

Egalitarian Women and Sideline Men

"Are you crying?" demands manager Jimmy Duggan (Tom Hanks), depicted in Figure 6.1. "There's no crying in baseball!"[1]

Right-fielder Evelyn (Bitty Schram) tears up because Jimmy has berated her for making an error that lost their team the lead. And now he is berating her for not taking his criticism "like a man" in front of the whole team and the crowd behind the dugout, who appear in the background of the medium close-up.

"Roger Hornsby, my manager, called me a talking pile of pig shit … on the day my parents came from Michigan to see me play the game," Jimmy tells Evelyn, who tries to respond through her sobs. But he continues, "Did I cry? No, because there's no crying in baseball. There's no crying in baseball! No crying!"

This comedic scene riff on "crying" has become the most memorable moment of Penny Marshall's 1992 movie *A League of Their Own*. But its significance has not been well articulated. Obviously, this hothead's brutal frankness goes too far. "Perhaps you chastised her too vehemently," intervenes the umpire, causing Jimmy to insult him and be ejected. The simple shot and reverse shot pattern shown in Figures 6.1 and 6.2 draws a sharp contrast between the egomaniacal coach and the innocent player—and every other sensible person around them. Situating his character and this scene within the larger dramatic arc, it is clear that Tom Hanks satirizes a tough-guy type of American masculinity.

Coach Jimmy Duggan demonstrates the pathology of pure competitiveness—a core principle for certain interpretations of the American dream. Introduced as an alcoholic former player, Jimmy serves as a comic sideshow in the first act. Hanks' clownish performance makes the tall tales about Duggan believable: that the drunkard started a hotel fire and leapt from a floor high enough to break his knee and end his playing career; and that as a minor league coach he sold off team equipment for booze money, which led to his being fired. Recounting these episodes in conversation with his prospective employer, magnate Mr. Harvey, Jimmy laughs about it under a flippant shrug. He's pure id—boyishly jovial in what should be a serious moment, then hell's fury over a minor error in a minor game. More than a satire of alcoholism, his drunkenness reveals the destructiveness of the hard-charging American man.

Over the course of the drama Jimmy will reform into a better man. Rather than dominating everywhere or lounging apathetically, he begins to give support on the sideline through encouragement and constructive criticism. As manager he adopts

Hollywood Sports Movies and the American Dream. Grant Wiedenfeld, Oxford University Press. © Oxford University Press 2022.
DOI: 10.1093/oso/9780197624920.003.0006

Figure 6.1–6.2 Fans and other players watch manager Jimmy Duggan (Tom Hanks) harangue a player, putting an ugly masculinity on full display. A reverse angle portrays innocent Evelyn (Bitty Schram) like Little Red Riding Hood before the wolf.

a limited and consistent role, making strategic decisions. Dottie, the hero, befriends him and hands him a soda pop at one point, inducing him to lay off the booze. When one player receives a telegram that her husband was killed in action, Jimmy consoles her by letting her cry in his arms. Tellingly, Evelyn will repeat her fielding error in the championship game, but he holds back his ire and coaxes a smile from her; this positive approach pays dividends when she makes the right play in the end. Without performing a crucial action, Jimmy becomes a minor but valued hero on the team, the Rockford Peaches. As a secondary character he models the reform of masculinity that shifts the meaning of sports from dominance to solidarity.

When the Rockford Peaches lose the final game on a close play, no one cries or screams. Jimmy, who fumed earlier over a minor error, accepts the result with equanimity. Rather than berating Dottie (Geena Davis) for losing the game, he is shown in Figure 6.3 standing beside her, taking in the scene with a sigh. Deep focus situates them with the people in the crowd, dispelling the individual despair that one might feel in this losing moment. Penny Marshall's drama sets up a stark contrast from the winning-is-everything mentality that has characterized men's sports and American

Figure 6.3 Reformed from a paradigm of dominance to one of solidarity, Jimmy accepts defeat with equanimity beside team leader Dottie (Geena Davis). Their attitude matches that of the crowd shown behind them.

masculinity since the late nineteenth century. Rather than a ruthless, individual survival of the fittest, which surely does not allow crying in baseball, the Peaches promote solidarity above all. Reading their story as an allegory for political values, *A League of Their Own* champions the democratic virtue of equality through its progressive gender politics.

Nonetheless, the movie's protagonist, Dottie, is no model feminist. She is reluctant to play professionally at first, and eventually decides to quit baseball and become a housewife when her husband returns from the war. In her study of women's sports movies, Viridiana Lieberman lambastes the film for "projecting patriarchal ideologies through the story of a female athlete hero, Dottie, who chooses to forego her career."[2] The filmmakers composed her character from a half dozen actual players, so they were free to design or select a more liberal heroine. And though one might defend Dottie's choice to be a homemaker as feminist, according to a doctrine of individual freedom, the moderate character surely suited the commercial logic of Hollywood producers seeking a broad appeal to middle America in 1992, especially to older viewers who had lived through that era and had made similar compromises. For Lieberman and other critics, the conservative traits of Dottie characterize the film overall as conservative.[3]

However, those critics have overlooked another feminist theme—collectivity.[4] By centering the story on moderate Dottie, Marshall's drama appeals to a broad coalition of women, much like the communal association movement in 1990s feminism. This chapter asserts that *A League of Their Own* expresses a more democratic vision of the American dream. Its emphasis on solidarity is evident in the diversity of the team, the satire of competitive men and haughty women, wartime patriotism, and the emphasis on sisterhood. Montesquieu will provide a useful lens for reflecting on the tension between participation and competition that underlies the meaning of sports in the national imaginary.

Aristocratic Competition and Democratic Participation

The film's subject, women's sports, has a democratic premise. Although the exclusion of men involves unequal access, that division renders more equal participation. Ideally democratic participation would mix all participants and be blind to sex and gender difference. However, the physical nature of athletics cannot be blind to the general difference between male and female bodies that makes equal participation and fair competition difficult to achieve. Greater size and muscle mass, on average, give men an advantage in most activities. Only in ultra-distance sports does a general parity exist among men and women, owing to the superior muscle endurance of women. Other kinds of divisions in sports also aim at equal participation and fair competition: age divisions, weight classes in combat sports, skill levels such as colored belts in martial arts, or parasports organized for a variety of disabilities. Restricting competition to special divisions renders participation more democratic. In contrast, open competition eliminates all but the best.[5] In other words, equal access and universal rules do not necessarily translate to equal participation or equal opportunity.[6] In this sense, there is a democratic virtue to women's sports that *A League of Their Own* celebrates in its subject and, as I will show later, in its story design.

In general, women's sports challenge the conception of the American dream as pure meritocracy. This section introduces Montesquieu's political theory to distinguish the aristocratic nature of competition from the democratic nature of equal participation. In this sense, meritocracy is a euphemism for aristocracy, and that revelation demands a careful reconsideration of the American dream.

In *The Spirit of the Laws* (1748) Montesquieu posits three principles in political life: equality, honor, and fear. Each principle corresponds to a form of government: republic, monarchy, and despot.[7] "Virtue, in a republic, is the love of one's country, that is, the love of equality," he writes, "as honor is the spring which gives motion to monarchy."[8] The ideal republic is a democracy in which the people are equally sovereign. The other two forms both concentrate authority in a single ruler, but the monarch abides by fixed rules (that the nobility enforce) whereas the despot rules by his own will or capriciousness. Monarchy thus mediates between the republic's rule of law and despotism's severe hierarchy.[9] Between the democratic republic and monarchy Montesquieu also adds the aristocratic republic as an intermediary form that privileges an elite set of representatives. It is that tension between democratic and aristocratic republics that concerns the political character of the United States.

The term *aristocracy* has become synonymous with *nobility*, but the old distinction is useful to recover. For the ancient Greeks, aristocracy means simply rule by the best—the *aristoi*. Aristotle viewed this form of government by the few positively, in contrast to oligarchs that privilege their own interests above the betterment of all. But the caste concept of noble birth overshadowed that distinction and confused the meaning.[10] The fact that ennoblement had become openly sold in the French kingdom surely led Montesquieu to concentrate on the systemic aspect of monarchy more than the mystique of superior bloodlines.[11] Marx and Engels make clear that the transition from feudalism to capitalism did not eliminate social hierarchies. More equal access to markets does not entail a more equal distribution of value, as Piketty and others have confirmed.[12] The American revolution rejected monarchy's hereditary nobility but maintained racial and gender caste distinctions as well as the original aristocratic values of talent and ambition.

Montesquieu brings into view a tension between inclusivity and ambition that persists in American culture, especially in sports, that will frame interpretation of *A League of Their Own*. Ambition accompanies honor, at the behest of equality. "Ambition is pernicious in a republic," he warns, "but in a monarchy it has some good effects; it gives life to that government."[13] Striving to win, to be the best, and to earn recognition reflect the basic aristo-monarchical tendency of social distinction.

The cultivation of ambition and honor therefore constitutes a non-democratic element in sports. "High performance athletics," Gerald Early declares, "is perhaps the most theatrical and emotional form of ritualized honor that we have left in the world."[14] Aside from the spectacle of the contest itself, these rituals include victory ceremonies, records, and judging and comparing performance that culminate in awards. The modern origin of organized sports in elite schools and the Olympic movement fit the aristo-monarchical profile perfectly.[15]

Honor, privilege, and ambition are likewise central to the classical liberal political economy. The principle of selecting the best candidate for the job corresponds to *aristos* in the most basic sense. One may have equal opportunity to apply, but the ultimate rule of selection by merit is not egalitarian. Montesquieu contrasts monarchy's emphasis on choosing the best to democracy's employment of random selection. For instance, jury duty and conscription exemplify a democratic mode that can be traced to the drawing of lots among ancient Athenian citizens. In general, the monarchical ethic of competition dominates in sports and free-market enterprise. Even voting for public officials and legislation follows this ethic. A liberal system can be just according to aristocratic principles yet undemocratic, while oligarchy transgresses the principle of merit. For Montesquieu, good monarchy demands a just order to the competitive system.[16] The free market may have equal access and may aim at an ideal harmony, but it lacks the equal distribution or equal negotiating power implied by pure democracy. Liberal systems based on fair competition have the selective character of monarchy.

Meritocracy, a term coined satirically in the mid-twentieth century, has become a euphemism for *aristocracy* in its original sense of rule by the best.[17] Daniel Markovits describes *The Meritocracy Trap* as "a mechanism for the concentration and dynastic transmission of wealth and privilege across generations."[18] He points to the danger of oligarchy that lurks in the liberal, competitive order of the United States, effectively recreating a social class of hereditary nobility who rule as an oligarchy.

Racism and sexism stand out as caste features of oligarchy. Indeed, the word *privilege* is poignant way to describe the historically established social advantage of whites, males, and others.[19] Color-blind policies that forbid discrimination erode caste distinction but do not correct for past gains or demolish social hierarchy itself. In fact, color-blind policy would restore a monarchical system of pure competition and merit.

Affirmative action goes a step further by disrupting competitive selection. The outrage that affirmative action causes for some can be well understood as an offense to monarchy's honor code and the culture of excellence. Democracy removes everyone from a privileged station by eliminating social hierarchy altogether. Democratic honor consists in recognition without social privilege—a distinction articulated by Hannah Arendt that I discuss further in the next chapter.

This brief philosophical reflection clarifies the complex character of the United States' national identity. Although founded in revolt against a hereditary nobility, aristo-monarchical elements persist in the culture of competition and excellence (that can have positive attributes) as well as the residues of imperial caste systems. Egalitarian elements appear in civil rights and in some public services. Montesquieu provides a theoretical lens to analyze the political qualities of sports represented on screen.

Honoring women's sports therefore challenges the primacy of aristocratic ambition in American culture. Like the participation trophy, *A League of Their Own* venerates women as equal participants in a historic national sport. Decried by right-wing champions of the competitive model, the participation trophy in children's sports emerged from democratic activism against the Vietnam War.[20] The movement for non-competitive games emphasized inclusive participation, solidarity, and play over winning.[21] Although Penny Marshall's film does not abandon the culture of excellence entirely—it admires the talent and competitiveness of the women players—the film stands out for its insistence on democratic themes of solidarity and inclusion.

Equal Yet Diverse Participation

Professional screenwriters Lowell Ganz and Babaloo Mendel developed the *League of Their Own* scenario from articles and a documentary by Kim Wilson and Kelly Candaele, whose mother played in the All-American Girls Professional Baseball League (AAGPBL). The drama has a simple flashback structure. A frame story of the hero Dottie's visit to the league's Hall of Fame induction event contains a flashback story of her single season in the league in 1943. A work of historical fiction, the screenwriters describe Dottie as an artistic invention composited from several historical players while certain details correspond to actual events and persons. This section demonstrates how the dramatic arcs of the frame and container story place greater emphasis on the democratic values of participation, inclusion, and diversity than the aristocratic ethos of individual achievement through competition.

In the frame story, Dottie's reluctance serves a dramatic purpose that has been mis-read as antifeminist. The movie opens upon elder Dottie packing her bags to visit the National Baseball Hall of Fame in Cooperstown, New York (we later learn), where the AAGPBL will be inducted. Yet Dottie hesitates, and her daughter must convince her to go. "I'm not really part of it," Dottie pleads. "It was never that important to me ... just something that I did." She is indifferent to seeing her sister Kit there, too. Her refusal to accept the "call to adventure" is a fundamental step in the hero's myth-ical journey that Campbell and Murdock have theorized.[22]

In fact, Dottie's refusal and eventual acceptance underline the sacred civic impor-tance of the league. "When are you going to realize how special it was, how much it all meant?" her daughter insists. A Carole King ballad then takes over the soundtrack with sentimental lyrics: "Now and forever / you are a part of me / and the memory cuts like a knife...."[23] The earnest music indicates that the daughter has won the argument. (The love song also adds a lesbian undertone.) Functioning like the ancient Greek chorus, the non-diegetic music expresses Dottie's inner feeling, which the narrator approves for the audience.[24] This scene establishes the principal themes of the drama as remembrance of the league and the hero's participation. Dottie will not receive any individual honor, and the fact that she only played one season makes her hesitant to attend the ceremony. But daughter and soundtrack insist that her participation car-ries utmost importance, which implies the values of equality and civic engagement.

Dottie warms to the egalitarian theme in the second part of the scene, which also indicates the problem of gender inequality. As mother and daughter prepare to drive off to Cooperstown, Dottie pauses in the driveway where her grandsons are playing basketball. Figure 6.4 depicts their encounter. She advises the older brother to be gen-erous and the younger one to be ruthless. The different advice she gives to each of her grandsons serves to level the playing field. Meanwhile, two neighbor girls perched behind the hoop watch the boys play. The passivity of the girls, who do not participate

Figure 6.4 The hero attempts to level the playing field between her grandsons by advising each. The girls watching in the background indicate a gender inequality—a touch of suspense for the drama overall.

in sports, subtly indicates a problem in the initial environment and echo Dottie's reluctance. Furthermore, the grandsons' sibling rivalry mirrors the conflict between
Dottie and her sister Kit that will be introduced in the next scene. Dottie represents
a more conservative character who prefers the passive and conventional role of wife
and mother, whereas her sister Kit represents a spark plug drawn to sports and urban
life. The drama develops a response to these problems, and the girls suggest its feminist import for the future.

The choice of a modest hero sets up a pedagogical scenario that underlines the
values of participation. As a composite character invented on the margins of history,
the point of comparison for Dottie is Walter Scott's Waverley. Kathryn Sutherland
explains that Scott's hero, caught up in events beyond his comprehension, "earns our
compassion not because he is heroic (he is not) but because in him we see represented
what we understand to be our own condition of helplessness and moral inadequacy.
Waverley refines our historical intelligence through the failures and education of his
own."[25] Although Scott's politics were monarchist, his literary model of the marginal
hero is applied to a democratic republican cause in *League*.[26] As the narrator flashes
back to her 1943 memory, Dottie will move from the margins to the center of the action, and then back to the margins again. The work does not honor an outstanding
individual and thus avoids the aristocratic tendency that a biopic of a feminist leader
or other ideal woman would carry.[27] In memorializing a more ordinary participant
with origins as an agricultural laborer, Marshall's film aims to gather a broad and popular audience. Dottie thus serves as a proxy for moderate and conservative viewers to
acknowledge the women's movement.

The formation of the team, covered in the first act of the 1943 story, celebrates
democratic participation and diversity. The heroines act to include women with diverse characteristics and talents, while hard-headed men, who would exclude certain
women, stand forth as minor antagonists.

Dottie insists upon her sister's inclusion by selflessly refusing to participate alone.
A scout (Jon Lovitz) recruits Dottie in rural Willamette, Oregon. He attends a soft-
ball game featuring the Lukash Dairy team and its two sisters, who are employees.
Kit strikes out by swinging at high pitches, demonstrating her youthful indiscipline
as a shortcoming. After Dottie's hit wins the game, the scout only extends an offer to
Dottie, who politely declines. "I'm married, I'm happy, it's what I want. Let's not confuse things," she says. But the eager Kit (Lori Petty) first persuades the scout to take
her too, if Dottie goes. Petty's verve reveals an ambition in the younger sister that
cannot be satisfied as a Tess of the d'Urbervilles-type dairymaid. Then Kit persuades
the hero with a call to adventure: "Just so you can say you once did something—something special."[28] They catch the train in a flurry of excitement. Dottie has two reasons
to go along—to support her sister, and for the glory of public action. Those reasons
correspond to the liberal democratic political values of the women's movement—solidarity and independence.

Then Dottie and Kit together insist upon the inclusion of the next recruit, who
tests the scout's beauty standard. They stop in Fort Collins, Colorado, to watch

Marla Hooch (Megan Cavanagh) whack pitches from both sides of the plate. When Lovitz's character rudely rejects her for her homeliness, Kit is stunned. "You ain't taking her because she ain't pretty?" she asks, making crystal clear the situation. Marla's father (Eddie Jones) then adds his own confession, "I raised her like I would a boy. I didn't know any better. She loves to play." The sisters boycott until the scout yields, and Marla boards the train following a heartfelt goodbye to her father. This scene illustrates the double standard that male authorities place upon women. Kit was first rejected purely based on performance, and now Marla is rejected for her appearance. In this way the script neatly stages the denigration of women's sports as inferior performance only suited for ogling at. In addition, although Marla is not a transgendered character, her father's comment expresses sympathy for non-binary identity. The inclusion of both players illustrates the inclusiveness of the team.

The Chicago tryout also emphasizes inclusion, despite being an event designed to select the best players. Plate 14 depicts a dolly shot through the tunnel into the field. The tunnel intimates the feeling of passing through a gateway into an enlightened sanctuary. Wrigley Field is shown with women arrayed across it, performing drills. Marshall underlines democratic inclusion by framing groups of women, rather than dramatizing the individual competition for selection. Marshall introduces Mae (Madonna) and Doris (Rosie O'Donnell), who horse around and wisecrack in exaggerated New York accents. "They got over a hundred girls here, so some of youse will have to go home," Mae warns Kit, Dottie, and Marla. Their ethnic difference adds satire that lightens the atmosphere of competition. When they eventually befriend each other, they symbolize the melting pot of urban and rural America, or of eastern, central, and western regions.

Given that sixty-four of the hundred-odd players present are ultimately included in the league, the selection ratio is not severely competitive. The scene climaxes with the players finding their names on posted lists, in no particular order. It implies a random and democratic allocation, rather than an aristocratic process that would establish a firm hierarchy. None of the excluded players are even shown. One woman who lingers before the lists turns out to be illiterate, and another player (Ann Cusack) helps her find her team. Rather than emphasize the honor of selection and shame of being cut, Marshall uses this moment to underline women's lack of education and the progressive civic role that sports can play (exemplified by Title IX, a federal civil rights law passed in 1972). When Kit exclaims, "I'm a Rockford Peach!" it certainly does not mimic the esteem Lou Gehrig boasts in playing for the Yankees in *Pride of the Yankees*. Has anyone ever celebrated Rockford, Illinois, so joyously on screen? Kit's enthusiasm highlights the importance of inclusion and solidarity for their own sake, regardless of social distinction.

A league anthem exemplifies the themes of inclusion, solidarity, and diversity. It appears after a crisis divides the sisters onto opposing teams. Kit feuds with Dottie and is traded from Rockford to the Racine team, but the other players downplay the split. One consoles Kit by reaffirming their friendship and shared membership in the league. In the next scene players gather in the locker room before a game, shown in Plate 15, and sing the league anthem in unison:[29]

> We are the members of, the All-American League
> We come from cities, near and far
> We've got Canadians, Irish ones, and Swedes
> We're all for one, we're one for all
> We're All-American

Cinematographer Miroslav Ondricek utilizes the widescreen aspect ratio to include multiple figures at a medium distance, something not possible in the old Hollywood frame. The dressing room scene makes a subtle reference to *Grease* (1978) (and other post-war musicals that pioneered widescreen visual style), underlining the importance of women-only spaces as sites of liberation and solidarity. As the viewer's eye pans across the Rockford team, the song invites reflection on their diversity. It includes rural Westerners, urban New Yorkers, and a former Miss Georgia. To this regional diversity is added various lifestyles, from Evelyn the single mother to wives and widows, as well as sexually liberated Mae (Madonna) and her companion Doris (Rosie O'Donnell), whose lesbianism is implied.

Although its diversity does not extend beyond white ethnicities, the film acknowledges its lack of women of color with a surprising scene midseason. A black spectator picks up a stray baseball during warmups and hurls it across the field so hard and so accurately that Kit and Dottie reveal their awe and respect in medium-closeups. The unnamed black woman nods with a gorgeous expression, depicted in Figure 6.5, that mixes pride, respect, resentment, and perhaps mild condescension. Framed against a chain-link fence with a gate partially open, Marshall's mise-en-scène makes a crystal-clear symbol for the barrier of segregation that was beginning to crack. This one scene

Figure 6.5 A black woman demonstrates her awesome throwing skill, framed before other blacks and a fence that symbolizes segregation. With this offhand moment Marshall's film acknowledges an unequal focus on whites.

only amounts to a small gesture, but it nevertheless goes further than *The Natural*, set in the same era, where people of color are invisible. Marshall's film suggests that the barriers of segregation and discrimination are the next horizon for achieving truly all-American inclusivity.

The film's celebration of diversity is more significant than the actual diversity of its cast. The differences among all the players are viewed positively; none of the players has to be assimilated by eliminating some difference, nor is anyone excluded. In fact, the film satirizes high-society femininity as a bad mode of assimilation that will be detailed later. According to Jeffrey Alexander's theory of social incorporation, Marshall's drama exemplifies the mode of hyphenation that fuses a new whole while preserving some difference.[30] *League* fits within the broader pattern of team sports movies from *The Longest Yard* (1974) to *The Mighty Ducks* (1992) and *Remember the Titans* (2000) that promote sports (and sports movies) as a means of progressive national integration. Reflecting the growing multiculturalism of the 1990s, *League* neither takes diversity for granted nor remains completely blind to color.

Sideline Men

A related aspect of diversity in the film is its men. The male characters in *League* have not received much attention from critics. Of course, there is no obligation for a women's sports movie or for its critics to have much to do with men or to deal with the social problems of masculinity. Yet a closer look at these minor characters in *League* testifies to the film's strongly democratic and republican values. All through *League* the male characters have distinctly limited roles that complement the leadership of women. They model progressive masculinity in a way that I label *sideline men*.

Men's studies scholar Anthony Synnott observes that equality is not a part of most conceptions of masculinity. The subtitle of his study, *Rethinking Men: Heroes, Villains, and Victims* identifies the three dominant paradigms for thinking about manhood.[31] Synnott notes the stark inequality in status and power distribution among men, who appear both hegemonic and in crisis depending on which men are under consideration. What is striking about those three paradigms is their antipathy to democratic participation. The heroic leader and his villain counterpart exemplify aristocracy and monarchy, while victims take no positive political role at all. These types each involve dominance—the good dominance of the hero, the bad dominating villain, and the dominated victim.

The sideline man does model egalitarian support through collectivity and non-dominance. The key conceptual differences of sideline men from other paradigms are diversity, the relationship to a group, and non-dominance. Participation varies among men (and among women), not following a cookie-cutter view of equality. Instead of male action in isolation, the sideline man's action contributes to the group. He is not necessarily a sensitive and utterly passive New Age man; in supporting women the sideline man may bravely act to protect their autonomy from other agents.[32] Participation, in the literal sense of playing a part in a whole, implies non-dominance. A key word for republican theories of freedom developed by Quentin Skinner and Philip Pettit, *non-dominance* contrasts to the liberal conception of freedom as non-interference.[33] Liberal autonomy, self-mastery, and the pursuit of victory through competition are conceived as dominance over anything that would interfere with individual will. Meanwhile, non-domination shifts emphasis to the collective and to participation. In this way sideline men represent a civic republican alternative to classical liberal and neoliberal masculinities.

The range of male characters in *League* illustrates different kinds of sideline men. Tom Hanks's club manager Jimmy Duggan is first sidelined by drunkenness, not by egalitarian principles. He is introduced as a broken down and desperate former Cubs star who permanently injured his leg, we learn, by jumping from a hotel where he'd started a fire while inebriated. Penny Marshall and Hanks gleefully satirize his incompetent management as he dozes off on the bench and scratches his balls. The team is startled when he has not prepared a lineup, prompting the women to take action themselves, led by Dottie. "How hard can it be to make a lineup?" she asks rhetorically, cutting through passive anxieties with action. If Jimmy's self-destructive drinking and disdain for women's sports represent classical American masculinity, *League*'s plot implies that women rise from the ashes of male-led calamity.

Jimmy's recuperation involves restricting his role as manager. When he first sobers up and takes interest in the game, he overly asserts himself, illustrated by a scene in which Dottie and Jimmy send conflicting signs to Marla at bat. Dottie relaxes her control to let him try out his strategy, to swing away rather than bunt, which is proven correct. But the plot does not highlight his contribution as crucial to team success. He simply plays the part of the manager correctly and pleasantly. The reformed Jimmy is not ruled by the drive to win, either. He downplays ambition to win the league and accepts defeat gracefully, as was shown in Figure 6.3. He evolves from a shameful masculinity to a model for public conduct.[34]

And while sober Jimmy has taken some control of the team, he remains subordinate to Dottie. At a crucial point he defers to Dottie when deciding whether to let Kit continue to pitch; Dottie's decision causes a rift between the sisters. Then, when Dottie leaves the team and returns for the final game, Jimmy is entirely on the sideline of the action. Surprised to discover her in uniform, Jimmy says half-mockingly, "Hold it! Who said you could play? Alice has been catching for us the last six games." Marshall makes light of his threat to take control, and so does Dottie. He quickly relents sheepishly, "Well, you're already dressed. . . . I don't care." The joke is that Dottie is obviously the team leader. Jimmy contrasts with the strong coach characters, almost authoritarian, of Gene Hackman in *Hoosiers* (1986), Denzel Washington in *Remember the Titans* (2000), and others. (Those controlling coaches are also driven by democratic values, but they represent institutions that prohibit the dominance of private enterprise and of White Americans.[35]) The gender dynamic in *League* demands that a progressive male coach take a sideline role in the drama rather than play the heroic protagonist. Hanks's comedic sideshow complements the dramatic lead of the heroines. Duggan represents an active agent in a limited, participatory role.

AAGPBL director Ira Lowenstein, played by David Strathairn, models a more passive agent in a position of authority. A parody newsreel introduces him as a "Harvey's promotional whiz kid" who is entrusted with building the league. Although he appears villainous when he first presents skimpy uniforms at the tryout, Lowenstein's character develops into a humane mediator between conservative owner and progressive players.[36] He meekly offers explanations for league policies and concerns, inviting action by the players. For instance, at one point in the second act he reveals a crisis to the Rockford team: the league does not have sufficient ticket sales and revenue to survive, and their last hope is the presence of national media at the game that day. Dottie responds by making a catch while doing the splits, which captures the attention of a *Life* magazine photographer. This moment sparks a montage of promotions and plays that revitalize the league. Lowenstein's character does not direct his own initiative to avert the crisis; he simply presents the situation to the women who take action. The revitalizing montage therefore implies credit to the players for saving the league. A few scenes later, Mr. Harvey appears at a game and congratulates his whiz kid for the robust crowd, but Lowenstein replies, "To be perfectly honest, the girls deserve most of the credit."

The administrator's strongest action comes in support of the players. When Mr. Harvey says that he plans to dissolve the league when men return from war, Lowenstein gives a speech lauding the women's effort and dedication: "We told them it was their patriotic duty to get out and go to work. When the men come back, they're sent to the kitchen?" Critical of a return to the old gender norms, Lowenstein demands to take over the league from Harvey and to prove its viability as a business. Strathairn's emotional delivery signals that his motivation is not entrepreneurship but rather his admiration for and solidarity with the women players.

Within the drama overall, Lowenstein's character serves an important function. His role orients the central conflict around the league's survival. That collective concern involves everyone more democratically than a drama centered on team rivalry or individual players. Marshall and her screenwriters give the coach and administrator secondary roles that complement the women as the central agents in a group struggle to build a league. The league's success folds into the patriotic aim of World War II as a crisis of democracy, with the sideline men here mirroring women's contributions to the war effort.

A few men appear as ardent fans and supporters of the players. Marla's father (Eddie Jones) arranges her tryout and encourages his reluctant daughter to pursue her love of baseball. The widower refuses her offer to stay home and support him domestically. Later, the players earn a host of male admirers and fans. A sly visit to a roadhouse dance introduces Marla to a man who becomes her spouse. (She leaves the team for a honeymoon, but promises to return next year.) Darla, Kit, and Mae also discover men enamored with them, first at the roadhouse and then in the stands. The simplicity of these male characters mirrors mother, wife, and girlfriend types in male-centered dramas who create an aura around the heroes.

Other male characters are notably unremarkable. Marshall and her screenwriters keep the male characters on the sidelines of the drama. For instance, the father of Kit and Dottie never utters a word. He is only glimpsed as human furniture in two cutaways, parked beside the radio in his parlor. Dottie's husband (Bill Pullman) only utters a few lines. During the climactic final game one brief cutaway, captured in Figure 6.6, reveals him in the stands cheering, "That's my wife!" He likewise refrains from pressuring her decisions onscreen. Rather than designing a conflict between the players and these men, the film's writers and director have the men recede into the background, with women making autonomous choices. Jon Lovitz's scout character is one exceptionally important male agent, but he quickly departs at the end of the first act, with no further consequence. The majority of the men in the movie are cheerleaders.

A feminist critic might argue that any male characters detract from the autonomy of women characters. That logic holds true in the absolute, but the progressive aspects of sideline men merit acknowledgment nevertheless. Sideline men represent a modest correction to Hollywood's historical male dominance that substitutes better models for men. *League* makes a moderate alternative to an all-women cast that might have a more radical impact on male viewers but would risk excluding them entirely. In their non-dominance and solidarity with women, Marshall's sideline men represent a progressive masculinity that takes a step toward gender equality within the genre and within mainstream American cinema.

Meanwhile, another naysayer might criticize the subordination of male dramatic roles in *League* as not strictly equal to the women's. As with color-blindism, this way of thinking misconstrues democracy as individual striving for dominance in a zero-sum game. Montesquieu makes clear the aristocratic-monarchical character of such neutral liberalism. Moreover, demanding symmetrical roles for men and women ignores the history of inequality and offers no compensation for past injustice.

Figure 6.6 Dottie's husband (Bill Pullman) admires her from the stands. Framed at medium distance and surrounded by women extras, Marshall situates him in the collective background; his uniform hints that a good solider for democracy supports women.

Privilege accrued into cultural tradition is not necessarily corrected by blindness or superficial symmetry. Sideline men who practice non-dominance serve a democratic good by counteracting male privilege.

League promotes women and democracy through its various sideline men. Male coaches, owners, and boyfriends are present but never major dramatic agents or causes for conflict.

Satire of Aristocracy

Meanwhile, Marshall satirizes aristocratic men and women. Two classes of characters appear in a negative light: male war profiteers and "society" women. Both earn ridicule for betraying the democratic spirit, with the men criticized for their selfishness and the women for their conformity. Whereas Jimmy and Ira develop from an initially negative portrait into positive sideline men, these minor villains remain flat.

League owner Mr. Harvey is portrayed as a profit-minded tycoon. A "Moviescope News" parody newsreel initiates the flashback to 1943. A segment on the AAGPBL explains that major league owners discuss the problem of suspending professional baseball during the war. Figure 6.7 frames the neoclassical exterior of "Harvey Mansion" with limousines, and Figure 6.8 reveals crystal glasses around the table inside. The men share a happy toast in the midst of war, then Marshall cuts to rural Oregon. The class contrast highlighted by production designer Bill Groom compares to *A Corner in Wheat* (D. W. Griffith, 1909). Marshall's satirical montage implies that Mr. Harvey, the wealthy aristocrat, decides to launch the women's league in order to recuperate revenue from their fixed assets, namely the stadiums, while the men's league is suspended. His intention to dissolve the league after one year, revealed in a later scene, positions Mr. Harvey as an antagonist without any serious interest in the women's cause of gender equality.

Another sly critique links Harvey's product, candy bars, to an opiate of the masses. His character is altered from Wrigley the Chicago Cubs owner and gum manufacturer, to chocolate bars, a pastiche of Hershey. The newsreel introduces the "candy bar king" posing with his eponymous "Harvey Bar." A later scene reveals player Evelyn's obese and hyperactive child Stilwell smothered in chocolate and wreaking havoc. Only the promise of more Harvey bars can win his obedience. This subtle allegory derides the aristocrat's unhealthy, exploitative enterprise and even suggests that the sugary junk food is doping the masses. Marshall's implied narrator does not go so far as to reject capitalism outright but certainly takes aim at the selfish qualities of one tycoon.

Marshall's drama ridicules a middle-class war profiteer more directly. In the first act, the train departure scene from Oregon begins with an unnamed businessman sitting across from the scout (Jon Lovitz) in the Streamliner lounge car, as depicted in Figure 6.9. The chipper white vacuum salesman (David Franks) chatters on about the windfall that the war has brought him: "In the Pacific Northwest, my territory, we

Figures 6.7–6.8 A mock newsreel introduces league owner Mr. Harvey as an aristocratic tycoon, illustrated by a symmetrical façade and toasts with crystal glasses.

Figure 6.9 The plush Streamliner lounge highlights the evilness of a fighting-age vacuum salesman who boasts of profits doubled during the war.

have increased sales 106 percent in a twelve-month period. And this with a war on!" Lovitz groans and rolls his eyes. If those expressions of disgust were not enough, the scout stands up to change seats and insults the man: "If I had your job, I'd kill myself." The no-nonsense Lovitz trivializes the salesman's commercial accomplishments. (The scout slowly evolves from antagonist into a more sympathetic character.) In the context of the war, such prideful profiteering offends a collective driven by sacrifice for the national cause. The fact that the salesman appears to be a younger man of fighting age makes his self-satisfaction profane. With both anticapitalist and nationalist implications, this swipe at the salesman comes from a democratic ethos. Marshall satirizes Mr. Harvey and the salesman by scoffing at their special privileges.

Meanwhile, women aristocrats who appear in *League* antagonize the heroines through a hegemonic norm for femininity. First, Marshall presents a radio commentator named Miss Maida Gillespie (Laurel Cronin) to whom Dottie and Kit's parents listen. Figure 6.10 then depicts the studio where Miss Maida broadcasts the program. Designer Cynthia Flynt costumes her in a modest floral print dress, hat, wire-rimmed glasses, and pearls that all signal a bygone Victorian era, much like Mrs. Bates in *Psycho*. In a grating, hifalutin tone she speaks out against the creation of the girls' league. Three similarly dressed women sit behind her and nod along, framed across the widescreen aspect. None wear their hair down. These proper ladies await with their own texts to pontificate on whatever subject, together representing a regime of assimilation. Their grayness and bookishness contrasts with the athletic and diverse players. Marshall inserts a second Miss Maida program on the verge of the league's debut, further decrying women's sports as "the masculinization of women" and a "disgusting example of sexual confusion." Such a caricature aims to make Victorian norms appear archaic. The contrast between the working-class women and the bookish ladies also implies that the older gender norms were aristocratic. Miss Maida must hold tremendous national influence through her radio program if the

Figure 6.10 As she reads a socially conservative attack on the women's league, Miss Maida (Laurel Cronin) is flanked by others dressed in floral print, pearls, and hats that suggest a retrograde and oppressively conformist Victorian Era.

folks in rural Oregon listen to it. WMGM, a station in New York City indicated on the microphone, was owned by the same company as Metro-Goldwyn-Meyer film studios. Here lies a special privilege of media power and knowledge. Miss Maida does not exude wealth but rather cultural superiority.

"Charm" school adds another set of wealthy and conformist women to the satire. Directly following Maida's second radio program comes a long montage of the players at etiquette school, accompanied by a different radio voice explaining that all the girls in the league have been enrolled. The sequence implies that Lowenstein came up with etiquette school as a public relations strategy to appease and counter Miss Maida. Marshall plays the charm school montage as comedy, ridiculing its normative conception of femininity. Performed as an ensemble, the women walk through a mansion with books balanced on their heads for posture—a great send-up of bookishness as more posturing, as captured in Figure 6.11. They sit at long tables to practice sipping tea with delicate arm and lip movements, over and over, on command, to the point that they resemble robots. "And sip, [place the cup] down, don't slurp; and sip ..." drones the school mistress (Ellie Weingardt). Showing everyone perform these petty tasks in unison underlines the conformist and assimilationist character of Victorian femininity. The headmistress'domineering voice and presence, with an assistant at her side, reveals how servile the women are; and Weingardt's cartoonish performance makes her aristocratic posturing appear ridiculous. Overall, the charm school scene presents a stark contrast with the baseball players' diversity, independence, and athleticism.

The etiquette school scene culminates in a critical beauty assessment. The headmistress walks down the line evaluating them individually, recommending new clothes and hair for one, an eyebrow trim for another, and wholly approving of a few that include Dottie. Marla stands at the end of the line, and the sight of her repulses the mistress. Rather than make recommendations for improvement she snidely calls for "a lot of night games." While the petty tasks of posture and tea sipping may have been

Figure 6.11 A headmistress (Ellie Weingardt) directs the players at "charm" school like a drill sergeant. This ridiculous posture exercise suggests a femininity that consists in conformity and posturing, in contrast to their athleticism.

universal, this evaluation makes clear that the headmistress' conception of beauty is exclusive and aristocratic. Recall that Montesquieu characterizes any selection by criteria as aristocratic. Performance in sport certainly has an aristocratic element as well, but Marshall emphasizes team solidarity in contrast to the harsh judgment of individual appearance at charm school.

Homely Marla serves as the butt of jokes three times but blossoms later in the film. Viridiana Lieberman is right to criticize these kinds of jokes as antithetical to the feminist principles touted elsewhere in the film.[37] Nevertheless, these jokes are made through somewhat despicable characters: the headmistress, the newsreel narrator, and Lovitz's heavyset scout. Moreover, Lieberman overlooks a subtle critique made through Marla. Megan Cavanagh performs Marla's ugliness by hunching her back and contorting her face into dumbfounded looks, exemplified by Figure 6.12. Her face appears pretty when married, and she looks athletic at play, never obese. Cavanagh's expressionistic contortions imply that Marla's ugliness is mere timidity that can be alleviated. It is significant that etiquette school fails to achieve any change, but rejects her severely. Her character will instead change during the roadhouse scene, where Dottie discovers her drunk onstage and singing to the man who will later marry her. This sequence suggests that the good company of her teammates, success in her occupation, and a liberal social environment allow Marla's confidence to develop. In this way Marla's character orients beauty around personality ultimately, not the superficial and rigid physical attributes valued at charm school. Having Marla married to a man is a somewhat conservative character arc, but it is notable that Marshall does not grant marriage arcs to Madonna's character Mae or to the Miss Georgia character, both of whom represent the attractive opposite to Marla. Charm school is never validated as a step to marriage or to any other achievement. Marshall thereby breaks the old formula of feminine beauty and gentility, girlishness and marriage. The team's diverse types of women and athletic bodies

Figure 6.12 Megan Cavanagh performs a hunched posture to imply that Marla's ugliness is mere timidity. The good company of her teammates and a liberal social environment grow her confidence, whereas charm school exacerbates her self-consciousness.

begin to self-consciously challenge conventional discourses, anticipating the effects that women's soccer and basketball would have in the late 1990s.[38]

Although the film is rather mute on normative femininity for 1992, the range of women characters it admires is clearly progressive for 1943. Within the historical 1943 setting Marshall unfolds a comedic contrast between the aristocratic old ways and the progressive sporting women. Such contrasts are not out of character with Hollywood films of that era, exemplified by Bette Davis's makeover in *Now, Voyager* (1942) from a Victorian old maid to a cosmopolitan jet-setter. That film's indication of a shift away from the Boston Brahmin is amplified by Marshall's satire. The context of the war will subordinate the individual, especially the wealthy elite, to the importance of the nation as a collective.

Solidarity in 1943

A League of Their Own highlights the 1943 setting, on the U.S. home front during World War II, to reinforce its democratic principles. Like *The Natural*, Penny Marshall's film is nostalgic for the civic solidarity of the Franklin Roosevelt era. But the women's subject has a more progressive effect by counteracting the chauvinist tradition. Through the theme of patriotism, understood foremost as national solidarity, the film promotes expanded public roles for women and criticizes aristocracy.

Ubiquitous American flags and wartime posters code the women's league as a sacred part of the national effort. Production designer Bill Groom and Art Director Tim Galvin fly a flag in the background of the Oregon ballpark where the story begins. Framed beside the celebration over Dottie's game-winning hit in Figure 6.13, this shot points to American women's effort to overall victory. Its quaint touch offers a new version for American nostalgia, in contrast to old Hollywood filmmakers such as John Ford who show flags above frontier churches—an image that signifies manifest destiny and American imperialism. *League* gives us the church of baseball instead (a phrase popularized by *Bull Durham* [Ron Shelton, 1988]), imagining women's sports as a venerable civic institution.

A war bond poster underlines the liberation that the war offered for women. Kit (Lori Petty) hangs her head after a disappointing strikeout. In the background cinematographer Miroslav Ondricek gives a glimpse of a poster whose subtitle reads, "There's no way like the American Way," beside a Norman Rockwell-esque image of a girl outdoors and her mother peering over her from the doorframe, as shown in Figure 6.14. The advertisement seems to suggest that the rambunctious girl aids the war effort. This scene foreshadows Kit's appeal to leave the country for the city, where she will find success and autonomy.

Later, the scene of Marla's departure compares the players to conscripts entering military service. Marla Hooch (Megan Cavanagh) and her father (Eddie Jones) share a sentimental goodbye at the train station in Fort Collins. When the train pulls away, Ondricek frames the U.S. flag prominently over their goodbye waves, as illustrated by

Figure 6.13 In Oregon, Dottie's game-winning hit is celebrated by a flag in center field that implies women's sports represent the American dream of equality.

Figure 6.14 A billboard suggests that "the American Way" is for girls to go outside and play despite their mothers' reluctance—a liberation message that Kit (Lori Petty) will live out.

Plate 16 and Figure 6.15 in shot/reverse shot. With a melodramatic sentiment underscored by Hans Zimmer's music, the weight of their sentiment compares to parents sending a son off to war, perhaps never to return. In making this parallel Marshall suggests the readiness of women to contribute to national service. Marla's superior athleticism even implies women's capacity to serve in the military. Or, read another way, the parallel made by this scene suggests that the city is a kind of battlefield for women who have left the domestic sphere of home. Zimmer's musical score does not give a feeling of sacrifice so much as adventure and coming of age—traditional themes of romance.

The station scene draws an allegory for modernizing the nation through gender equality. She offers to stay home to care for her widower father, but he insists that she go: "Marla, nothing's ever going to happen here. You have to go where things happen."

Figures 6.15 Staged like a soldier's departure for war with the flag waving goodbye, Marla's journey to the city is coded as a national quest, battle, and sacrifice. The wood and brick station symbolizes an era before women's liberation.

He reiterates the theme that progress begins in the city. Another war poster inside the station reads, "Is *your* trip necessary?" Marshall's plot suggests that the players' trip is indeed necessary—if not necessary to the war effort directly, it is necessary to the cause of women's liberation and equality. Both themes resonate with the film's mythical structure as an epic journey.[39] Marla waves through the glass and stainless steel Streamliner train that represents modernity; she looks back upon her father standing on brick in front of a timber station building, whose materials represent a past age.

Does *League* overstate the importance of women's baseball to the nation? Surely the general importance of gender equality cannot be overstated, but one might claim that the players were not building war materials like Rosie the Riveter, nor were they on the front lines battling fascism—the league was primarily entertainment. In fact, the film's subject is not the war. Patriotic themes lie mostly in the background, although I have foregrounded them here. If the home front merits depiction on screen at all—compare this subject to scores of action-packed war movies—then one cannot object to this picture. It celebrates the liberal democratic ideals that motivated the United States in the conflict.

The theme of civic duty clarifies the importance of the home front. The concept of duty understands one's effort as part of a greater whole. From an egalitarian point of view, no person can do more than their own duty. While individual capacities for different tasks may not be equal, duty itself is allocated equally, and fulfilling that duty merits equal respect. *League* highlights the theme of duty in two specific ways.

A poster in the Racine announcer's booth speaks to the allocation of tasks. Seen over the shoulder of the announcer in Figure 6.16, the banner reads "Find your war job," and beside the image of a smiling woman is a quotation: "'I've found the job where I fit best!'" The ad communicates the idea of different talents making their contribution to an organic whole. (Marx's slogan "From each according to his ability, to each according to his needs" shares the same organic principle but applies it to

Figure 6.16 A poster behind the announcer reads "Find your war job" with a testimonial quotation, "I've found the job where I fit best." It communicates the egalitarian character of civic duty.

a broader ideology of political economy.) In the context of women's baseball, this poster implies that these women are best suited for the job of entertainment, that this entertainment constitutes a duty within the overall war effort, and that the best place for women is not necessarily in the home.

A national anthem scene before the final World Series game drives home the civic importance of the league. The anthem is staged and performed in a dutiful manner. Long shots from several angles, including Figure 6.17 view from the stands, depict the teams arrayed along each base line, with a singer at home plate. The V stands for both victory and vagina/vulva, superimposing the war for gender equality onto the world war. Such a geometric formation also portrays patriotism as a duty and the nation as a structure composed of many parts. Cutaways to the crowd reply with rows of reverent spectators, some in uniform. Players and crowd all look outward to the flag-pole in center field, and symbolically beyond Racine field. An opera singer evidently performs the task well-suited to her talent; she is the only figure depicted in close-up during the song. Maudlin music or close-ups of teary-eyed players might have over-stated the seriousness of the occasion, or shifted attention away from the collective to the individual. Her upbeat performance characterizes the baseball game as a simple yet important part of the overall effort.

Including the anthem scene gives a sense of the film's own patriotism. It could easily have been cut out, without affecting the plot. Through this civic ritual Marshall says that the film is performing a patriotic duty by remembering the women's league and its importance to American heritage and identity. The drama does not overstate the league's importance, as if it were a crucial episode in national history or in the civil rights struggle. It simply holds importance for what it was, and for how it exempli-fied the feminist and democratic theme of gender equality. Consider how attempts to rank the historical importance of the league, relative to other actions during the war or during the struggle for women's rights, would follow an aristocratic-monarchical

Figure 6.17 A long shot highlights the collective, with players arrayed in the shape of a V for the singing of the national anthem.

logic whereby each distinction must be measured against every other distinction. Such analysis is useful for certain inquiries but does not serve the affirmative purpose of civic ritual, a matter outlined in this book's introduction. The film refrains from comparing the baseball players to soldiers or to suffragettes. The flags, war posters, anthem, and remembrance of relatively minor efforts affirm national solidarity and equality broadly.

The Feminism of Dottie and Kit

Through the conflict between Dottie and Kit, *League* expresses the value of independent women, yet the epilogue at the Hall of Fame asserts collectivity's greater importance for feminism. Lieberman interprets the championship game's climax as a regressively feminine sacrifice by the hero that parallels her retirement to domestic life. A closer look at this scene and a broader view of the conflict's dramatic arc point to a competitive showdown won fatefully by Kit that communicates a more progressive meaning. Marshall nonetheless opts for a scenario laced with ambivalence.

The championship game circles back to the conflict that began the flashback to underline Kit's growth. In rural Oregon Kit had failed to make a winning hit because she was cowed by Dottie's advice:

DOTTIE. Sis, don't swing at that high pitch.
KIT. I can hit it.
DOTTIE. You can't.

The high pitch symbolizes Kit's high ambition to leave Oregon for independent life in the city, while Dottie is content there. "No high ones," repeats the older sister. "I like the high ones!" replies Kit before striking out on a high fastball that Kit nevertheless perceives as "right down the middle." Dottie's advice was correct, but Kit complains, "You got me so crazy" that she became to hesitant to swing. The scenario thus establishes a general conflict between Dottie's maternal protection and Kit's ambition. The married sister also advises her to date a man Kit considers "one step up from dating pigs." Dottie replies, half-jokingly, "but an important step." Dottie eventually realizes Kit's frustration and yields to her desire to join the league. This early scene establishes the high fastball as an aspiration to independence for Kit.

The early scene also shows the younger sister's dependence on Dottie, whom she blames for her shortcoming. An angrier confrontation occurs later. When Kit struggles, Duggan defers to Dottie, who decides to replace her with a fresh pitcher. Like a brat, the younger Kit overreacts to what she perceives as a betrayal. The loyalty she expects corresponds to a dependent relationship. Their row and split onto opposing teams breaks this bond but cultivates their independence.

When the sisters meet in the championship games on opposing teams, Kit triumphs, reversing her earlier failure. When Kit comes up to bat, Dottie mercilessly instructs the pitcher to attack her sister's weakness. "High fastballs—she can't hit 'em, can't lay off 'em," Dottie whispers matter-of-factly. Clearly, Dottie is not in the subordinate feminine mentality of sacrificing her own chance at victory for her sister's. Just prior, Dottie hit a pitch and scored a run to take the lead, all at Kit's expense. The younger sister's tears do not affect Dottie's competitive mindset. Kit misses twice, but on her third and final chance she wallops the ball to the outfield, which ties the score.

More surprisingly, Kit dashes to home plate to win. Dottie plays the position of catcher who must protect home plate in this situation—symbolic of her domestic tendency. Kit's direct attack therefore represents a final breakthrough to independence. As they collide Dottie drops the ball, resulting in victory for Kit and her Racine team. Dottie's look of surprise and then fear at Kit's aggression, captured in Figures 6.18 through 6.20, testify to their unrestrained competition. Editors Adam Bernardi and George Bowers cut quickly to transmit Dottie's surprise, then show the climactic collision in slow motion. The ball appears to trickle slowly out of Dottie's hand, which some interpret as her intentional defeat. But the whole sequence has established her purely competitive motivation. The close insert of her hand releasing the ball underlines the fateful change that occurs with Kit besting her older sister. Their parental relationship ends here. Kit's unexpected play is a fine example of action according to Arendt's philosophy of *la vita activa*, which will be discussed in the next chapter.

A postgame scene confirms Kit's independence. As the champion, she signs a baseball for a girl and encourages her while Dottie merely observes. When they meet, Dottie says, "You did what you had to do. You just beat me. You wanted it more than me." Dottie then invites her to drive back to Oregon, but Kit declines. She will instead join her teammates in finding jobs, then playing next season. In developing from dependent youngster to autonomous champion and citizen unbound by family obligation, Kit exemplifies the individual rights tradition of feminism. One can also read in this outcome a symbolic passing of the baton from Dottie's older generation, content as homemaker, to the younger generation of her sister who seeks the life of an urban professional.

Figures 6.18–6.20 Geena Davis expresses surprise at Kit's ambitious hit of a high fastball, and then the aggression on Lori Petty's face strikes fear in her. Their collision demonstrates the achievement of individual autonomy and competition in sport.

Why did Marshall and the screenwriters center the story on Dottie rather than Kit? Although the older sister is more conservative in her preference for domestic, rural life, orienting the story around Dottie emphasizes collectivity.[40] Important to the re-publican and socialist tradition of feminism, collectivity is amplified in three ways by Dottie.

Rather than center all heroic action around Dottie, another character takes the spotlight. Concentration around one character would tend to the liberalist conflict of the individual against society, or even to solipsism. Distributing the heroism among Kit and Dottie conveys the theme of sisterhood. Although the climax represents their independence from family bondage, the dramatic structure underlines a more egalitarian bond that balances independence with solidarity. One can even see a certain independence in Dottie's choice to become a homemaker. Her husband never exhibits pressure, nor is she obligated to establish a home for Kit. Highlighting the solidarity between sisters who chose different paths implies a broad political coalition of women.

Second, Dottie's defeat deflects attention away from the aristocratic-monarchical value of victory. In the postgame sequence, Dottie commiserates with Jimmy, Mae, Kit, and others. Rather than an ashamed individual who stalks off and bides revenge, the heroine's even keel shifts the importance to the collective. When Kit tries to persuade her sister to stay on another season, Dottie does not waver but tells her sincerely, "I'll miss the girls, and I'll miss you." Marshall thereby directs sentiment away from the honor of dominance to their equal worth as women in a shared endeavor. Moreover, Marshall is careful to avoid portraying Dottie's desire to live with her husband as subordination. He returns from the war with a limp and a cane; he speaks softly and rarely. His character implies that Dottie will have a dominant role in the household. Her insistence on duty elsewhere (she had told her sister after the championship, "You did what you had to do") does imply that Dottie's domestic role participates in the broader collective of the nation, although Marshall does not dwell on the matter.

Third, the ambivalent outcome of the championship suspends the emotional apogee for the Hall of Fame induction. Unlike *The Natural*, which concludes upon a golden image of Roy Hobbs back on the farm, *League* never represents Dottie's return to Oregon.[41] The destination for the happy ending is the ceremony of remembrance for the league that gathers everyone together again. The frame story sets forth one overarching objective for the hero: to recognize the deeper importance of the league. The flashback begins when Dottie gazes pensively upon the Cooperstown field where the AAGPBL veterans are playing, and the flashback ends with her old teammates recognizing her. Their ritual reunion is egalitarian through and through, presenting a panorama of players without rank. But their mutual recognition as individuals exemplifies the basic political quality of public life (the next chapter, on *Ali*, will elaborate upon this point). The epilogue's Hall of Fame induction scene neatly mirrors the act of remembrance carried out by the film itself.

The film's dual focus on Kit and Dottie expresses the collective aspect of feminism. Scholars recognize three currents of feminism: individualist, evangelical, and collectivist.[42] Penny Marshall evidently aims at a broad coalition by emphasizing the collective while balancing Kit's individualism with Dottie's evangelical desire to be a wife. The lens of Montesquieu's theory clarifies an aristocratic quality of individualism that complicates narrow understandings of feminism. It is noteworthy that the film does not center on women's conflict with men but emphasizes women's collective initiative and solidarity. While certainly more moderate than avant-garde feminist cinema or radically independent characters, the feminist qualities of Penny Marshall's film have not been fully appreciated.

Conclusion

When analyzed according to Montesquieu's political theory, it becomes evident that *A League of Their Own* champions the egalitarian virtue of women's collective achievement over the aristocratic-monarchical virtue of individual distinction. The drama revolves around the formation and survival of a league that represents solidarity among diverse and independent women as well as men who support them from the sidelines of the action. The main obstacles and antagonists are rooted in the monarchical principle of honor: aristocratic society women and patronizing men who resist women in these new gender roles.

Penny Marshall's film exemplifies the focus on communal association within the women's movement in the 1990s, a period referred to (tendentiously) as the "third wave." Historians have identified a first wave that focused on suffrage and other policy reforms that peaked in the 1910s, a second wave of mass member organizations who drove to radically change all social institutions that peaked in the 1960s and 1970s, and a third wave or contemporary period where action persisted through communal association and micropolitical expression with an emphasis on intersections with other minority social movements. The emphasis on collectivity in *League* compares to the rise of women's self-help groups in the 1980s and 1990s.[43] Rather than focus on the accomplishment of a particular legal or policy reform, Marshall's film asserts the primary importance of the community of women formed within the league, with its moderate hero Dottie exemplifying a broad coalition.

League also represents the continuity of consciousness-raising within the women's movement. The wave metaphor has been criticized for overlooking actions beyond bureaucratic organizations led by middle-class white women. Laura K. Nelson demonstrates that women activists have always striven to raise consciousness, especially through storytelling that makes the personal political (and vice versa).[44] As a history film that aims to draw a connection from the 1990s to the 1940s, *League* partakes in a similar effort to see continuity across periods. From this angle, *League* looks forward to a continued focus on civic organizations in the twenty-first century. Although the movie only makes the slightest of nods to women of color and to queer communities, its communal spirit and egalitarian virtue does align with contemporary feminism.

For the politics of Hollywood in general, the mere existence of a women's sports subject represents progress toward democratic representation. The still-limited number and variety of women in sports movies (and of women's involvement in movies generally) reflects a traditional designation of sports as a male domain and the persistent regime of male domination. Philosophers of multiculturalism have shown that withholding recognition to minorities causes harm by effectively denying public access and civic worth.[45] Because sports have become a sacred part of civic life in the United States, critics who diminish women's sports (or para-athletes and other closed divisions) discourage participation and devalue their citizenship across the board. The public visibility of women's sports as a subject for a major Hollywood movie thus emphasizes the equality of women as a minority group generally. Its communal spirit and the progressive model of masculinity offered by its sideline men do represent significant departures from a tradition centered on individual honor. *A League of Their Own* reorients the American dream around equal participation and solidarity.

Yet *League*'s modest hero is not the only means to express a democratic politics. *Ali* has a more classical hero who nevertheless challenges the older American paradigm by presenting its hero as a people's champion.

7

Ali (2001)

Actions of the People's Champion

"The man you've all been waiting for," announces a Black American voice over the title screen, "Mr. Sam Cooke!"[1] The pioneering musician steps to the microphone before a crowded club in the film's first image, Figure 7.1. As Cooke begins his opening number a cut takes us to a deserted city street where the young hero jogs down the center line, his head covered by his gray hoodie, silent. Another cut flashes back to Ali's childhood on a segregated bus, then jumps forward to Ali at a Malcolm X sermon, now to witness heavyweight champion Sonny Liston walloping another man in the ring, and now meeting Bundini, the poetic cornerman; scenes of Ali's training and the concert alternate with these memories continually. Cooke performs a medley that lays down the soundtrack for the whirlwind sequence, all without Ali uttering a word.

With this deceptive opening gesture and virtuosic montage, director Michael Mann veers away from convention. The man the film's audience anticipates is Muhammad Ali (played by Will Smith), not Sam Cooke. Moreover, this is not the Ali whom everyone knows spoke as fast as he punched, in lyric combinations that rap with characteristic wit and humor or cut with critical jabs and slug with transcendent devotion, always surrounded by others. Mann instead gives us the shadow of that Ali: alone on the streets and in the gym; lost in his thoughts and in his body; a negative space filled by Black experience.[2] With this creative introduction the hero becomes a prism for the social and historical context of 1960s America.

Two years prior to the film's release, Gerald Early warned that hagiography could lead to Ali "being diminished as a public figure and a black man of some illustrious complexity."[3] If the 1960s white mainstream had underestimated Ali's athletic talent and political seriousness, the 1990s mainstream was overcorrecting and creating a problem of "overestimation."[4] Early echoes James Baldwin and Frantz Fanon, who showed that oversimplified representations of Blacks, even if positive, reflect a preconception of racial simplicity. Frantz Fanon criticized assimilation through "white masks" that dehumanize blacks: "The colonized is elevated above his jungle status in proportion to his adoption of the mother country's cultural standards. He becomes whiter as he renounces his blackness, his jungle."[5] Assimilation not only forfeits Black culture; the white mask belongs to a middle-class society beset by "intellectual alienation"—"rigidified in predetermined forms, forbidding all evolution."[6] To liberate consciousness Fanon calls for critical recognition of social and economic realities.[7]

Hollywood Sports Movies and the American Dream. Grant Wiedenfeld, Oxford University Press. © Oxford University Press 2022.
DOI: 10.1093/oso/9780197624920.003.0007

JAMIE FOXX

Figure 7.1 *Ali* opens upon the silhouette of Sam Cooke (David Elliott), where one would expect to see the title character.

This line of criticism rightly demands portrayals of the full range of black personalities, experiences, and humanity. Elevating Ali as an icon risks creating a kind of white mask that hides such complexity.[8]

Academic critics have lauded Mann's *Ali* for avoiding the oversimplification that plagues typical Hollywood representations of Black Americans and popular biography generally. Andrew Pepper praises Mann and Will Smith, who "rescue Ali from universal sainthood and insert him back, as a complex and contradictory figure, into the social and historical context that made him."[9] Grant Farred agrees that "Smith's Ali is a textured, conflicted and unquestionably intelligent protagonist; in terms of complexity of representation, Smith's Ali provides a sharp contrast to Gast's 'real' Ali in *When We Were Kings*," the 1996 documentary.[10] David Rodríguez-Ruíz even compares Mann's Ali to a philosopher given how critically the film questions "our beliefs about the nature of patriotism, brotherhood, and other concepts that shape the social order."[11] These critics credit the filmmakers for reimagining the Hollywood biopic as an art film or Black indie film that represents Ali in his multifaceted social reality and mimics the critical dimension of his political engagement. The unconventional opening illustrates these qualities.

However, praise of complexity raises three interrelated problems that the aforementioned critics do not fully address. First, their postmodern emphases on radical difference and resistance disregards the normative qualities of democracy and culture. Although difference is important to destroying rigid forms of thinking and social organization, absolute difference atomizes all social forms and knowledge. Resistance is also dear to reactionaries who invoke liberal philosophy's concept of freedom as non-interference, also known as negative freedom.[12] Does *Ali* play to the anarchist and machismo tendencies of U.S. counterculture, or does its hero maintain certain normative civic values?

Second, does Ali's complexity negate the goodness he represents as a hero? A complex personality is not necessarily admirable; the sociopath is extremely complex, after all (*The Stranger* of Albert Camus comes to mind, or the antiheroes of *Taxi Driver* [1976], *Fight Club* [1999], and *Joker* [2019]). More needs to be said about how the biopic holds Ali's many parts into a whole that represents the good without forfeiting his uniqueness or cultural difference.

Third, how does the film relate Muhammad Ali's greatness as an athlete to his greatness as a political figure? Ali has been a flashpoint for an ongoing popular debate over the relationship of sports to politics, reignited by police killings of African-Americans that drew responses from Colin Kaepernick and other athletes around the Black Lives Matter movement. To say that athletic fame establishes a platform for public speech subordinates sports to politics. Conversely, to elevate Ali's athletic feats as inspiring symbols, as Vincent Gaine and others do, short-changes Ali's specific politics and disregards the egalitarian virtue of speech.[13] More critical attention is needed on how *Ali* understands the meaning of sports for the United States.

This chapter argues that *Ali*'s Ali coheres around his growing consciousness of the struggle for liberation that culminates in his 1974 victory in the ring. Hannah Arendt's philosophy of action articulates the fundamentally political quality of athletics and explains how a unique individual can represent different people and general ideas. I will analyze three crucial montage sequences and two remarkably realist fight sequences that develop the picture of a multilayered people's champion—at once Black, African, and American—rooted in the democratic ethos of multicultural liberalism.

Miami Montage

Ali opens with a montage sequence that unfolds the complex social tensions of the United States in the early 1960s. Departing from the rosy picture of youth that opens the conventional biopic, the artistic montage associates Ali with the struggle for racial justice and social change while aligning Sonny Liston, opponent in his first championship fight, with the old regime.

Midcentury sports biopics often began with an all-American boy playing on a sandlot. That idealized image of a level playing field then supports the hero's smooth assimilation into American life. For instance, *The Jackie Robinson Story* (1950) opens with the boy hero strolling to an unsegregated sandlot as a white narrator tells the audience in voiceover, "It is the story of an American boy, in a dream that is truly American."[14] The commonplace sandlot underlines the conformity to one "all-American" identity. These biopics' titles make evident the common mold their heroes represent: *Knute Rockne: All-American* (1940), *Jim Thorpe: All-American* (1951), *The Babe Ruth Story* (1948), *The Jackie Robinson Story* (1950), and *The Joe Louis Story* (1953).[15] Michael Oriard describes the dime-novel hero Frank Merriwell as the aptly named model for a straightforward, optimistic, and well-meaning man of action.[16] The simple and taciturn heroes of these biopics contributed to the assimilationist culture of postbellum America.

In addition to assimilation, the idealized sandlot promotes the political ideology of neutral liberalism. Based on the principle of equal competition in a free market, the neutral state manages public affairs like a referee and scorekeeper in an ongoing contest of competing interests. The sandlot's level playing field spawns a hero whose talent undoubtedly merits success and attention. Furthermore, the scene of childhood innocence allegorizes political theorist John Rawls's notion of an original position—an ideal setting in which judgment transcends cultural bias by identifying with the individual actor.[17] In these midcentury films the sandlot represents the old liberal image of a nation undivided by class or cultural difference.

Ali will come closer to noir boxing films that present the origin of the hero's violent tendencies as an innocent reaction to external forces. For instance, *Champion* (1949) flashes back to a boxcar fight against ten men during the Great Depression. The hero (Kirk Douglas) thus represents a common struggle for basic necessities and for dignity.[18] *Ali* also throws the innocent hero into an antagonistic social environment. However, Mann and Roth add an emphasis on cultural difference and, more surprisingly, they never depict Ali's origin as a boxer.

Ali's title sequence introduces the hero in the contested world of 1964, underlining his Blackness and his youthful rebellion. Sequence editor Kristopher Kasper begins by alternating between images of Cooke's concert and Ali training across town in Miami, where the Liston fight was held. Then a second theme weaves in flashbacks to adolescent Ali on a segregated bus and to first contacts with Malcolm X and Bundini. A third theme flashes images of Liston in the ring against a previous opponent. What anchors this dizzying montage—a vogue in 1990s American cinema—are two social conflicts: one racial and the other generational.[19]

An image of white cops who harass the hero testifies to everyday racial oppression. While Sam Cooke (David Elliott) performs at the Hampton House, a Black haven off white Miami Beach, Ali jogs through the city's deserted night streets, alone. Emmanuel Lubezki's cinematography compares the two like Kara Walker cut-outs: Cooke's silhouette before the stage lights (Figure 7.2) and Ali in light gray against the black night sky (Figure 7.3). A police cruiser with red lights pulsing pulls up behind the jogger. One cop leans out the window and yells, "What are you running from, boy?"[20] The dramatic irony is obvious: he is running from white cops who harass him for simply running freely in public. Will Smith looks resolutely forward, unperturbed by the sirens buzzing over his shoulder as Cooke's buoyant accompaniment conveys Black solidarity and strength. Alternating chiaroscuros contrast a safe Black space to hostile White streets.

The death of Trayvon Martin and the Black Lives Matter movement have given new significance to Figure 7.3's image of a black hero jogging at night in a gray hooded sweatshirt. In 2012, Martin, a black Miami teenager, wore a gray hoodie pulled up against the rain as he walked to a relative's house from the store, unfamiliar with their neighborhood. A light-skinned suburbanite felt alarmed seeing the dark-skinned stranger, whom he chased down and shot dead. His exoneration on a self-defense claim fueled an uproar. The Black Lives Matter movement grew in response

Figure 7.2 Sam Cooke silhouetted on stage at the Hampton House, a Black Miami nightclub and hotel.

Figure 7.3 Ali jogs the Miami streets in a gray hoodie that now recalls Trayvon Martin.

to Martin's death and a series of other cases of police brutality. Costume designer Marlene Stewart's look for *Ali* now appears sadly prophetic and underscores Mann's effort to depict racial tension in a contemporary style.[21]

The dangers of the color line are reinforced by a flashback to the young hero on a segregated bus depicted in Figure 7.4. An older passenger thrusts a front-page image of Emmett Till's mangled head at the young Ali, who recoils. Ali was actually closer to Till's age and was stunned to face this violent threat simply for being black. "I felt a deep kinship to him when I learned he was born the same year and day I was," Ali wrote.[22] Mann emphasizes Ali's vulnerability and disillusionment with a pubescent protagonist in this flashback. The unruffled postures of the older passengers also suggest a certain complacency with the racist status quo—the second conflict in the sequence.

Images of Ali's father and of Sonny Liston characterize an older generation of Black men who do not actively resist racism and therefore represent the internalization of

Figure 7.4 On a segregated bus, young Ali is frightened when he sees a newspaper story of Emmett Till's brutal lynching. The other passengers, unfazed, appear complacent.

Figure 7.5 Reigning champion Sonny Liston, seen from an intimidating frontal view to represent the fear in Ali's imagination before their fight.

systemic injustice. Mann represents reigning heavyweight champion Sonny Liston as a bull. We witness him aggressively knock out another black opponent and then confront Ali ringside. Liston's voice rises above Cooke's music to warn, "I'm gonna bust you up—beat your ass like I was your daddy." Before this paternalistic brute, seen from a frontal point-of-view shot in Figure 7.5, Ali initially stands back doe-eyed, like the young Ali on the bus. Liston's bullying points toward an alternative response to racial oppression: violence internalized by Blacks as patriarchy.[23]

Meanwhile Cassius Clay Sr. (Giancarlo Esposito) appears painting a white Jesus and later smiling subserviently before the Louisville Sponsorship Group, a set of white patrons who managed Ali early in his career. Photographs of prize racehorses on their office wall suggest a certain racism in their sponsorship of Ali.[24] These images portray Clay Sr. as an Uncle Tom type, loyal to the white peers. While a conventional biopic might stage whites unjustly treating Ali to motivate his boxing, such a direct approach would oversimplify racism as individual moral prejudice (and oversimplify sport as a moral contest). Smith instead performs a subtle discomfort that sets Ali apart from the older Black men. By framing a Black generational conflict in addition to a racial one, the film points toward a view of racism as a social structure.

The appearance of Malcolm X crystallizes the racial and generational conflicts. Mann and Lubezki introduce him through more play with chiaroscuro, cutting from an image of a white Jesus in a Black church to the black Muslim minister against a stark white wall. Malcolm X (Mario Van Peebles) calls upon a black congregation to resist White injustice and to "carry yourselves ... in a proud, Afro-American way." The audience includes Ali, who stands against the back wall, patiently listening. This posture accentuates the environment of critical thought. Malcolm X's voice is heard above Sam Cooke's continuing medley, both now folding into one expression of a younger generation's Black pride. Anna Dzenis describes the title sequence as a "celebration of Black culture."[25] This part of the montage emphasizes Ali's budding consciousness as a young Black Muslim facing an old, White, Christian establishment.

Finally, the introduction of Drew "Bundini" Brown brings a prophetic dimension to the origin sequence. Played by Jamie Foxx, the corner man and "motivator" wears a Star of David chain to indicate his Jewish faith, complicating the Christianity–Islam conflict traced earlier in the sequence. Bundini introduces himself to Ali as a divine emissary: "Now Shorty done sent me here to work for you." Ali decodes this reference in one fight anecdote in his 1975 autobiography:

"Shorty" is Bundini's name for God. And during the whole [fight] ... Bundini is screaming, "Shorty's watching! In the living room! On TV in the living room! He's watching you!"[26]

Bundini's curious picture of God is evoked by Mann and Lubeszki, who frame Foxx between a television and a rooftop antenna. The bright Florida sun and teal wall shown in Plate 17 also pay subtle tribute to the television series *Miami Vice* (NBC, 1984–1989), Mann's breakthrough work.[27]

More importantly, the antennae reflect upon media as an instrument of social change. The whole sequence showcases communication technology, from Sam Cooke's microphone and the Emmett Till headline in the newspaper to Howard Bingham's camera. Cinema itself is invoked in a more creative way through a slow-motion flicker effect. In the middle of the sequence, after Bundini's appearance, Mann and Lubezki cut to Ali punching a speed bag, depicted in Figure 7.6. Through a speed ramping technique they slow the bag's motion until it flickers across the screen like a projector shutter. Figures 7.7 and 7.8 illustrate how the speed bag imitates the basic mechanism of the celluloid motion picture. Ali's direct gaze, filmed from behind the bag he punches, implicates us viewers as active participants in a world that merges with ours. Just as the punching bag imitates an opponent for solitary training, the rapid montage jabs at our brains to elicit our social consciousness. The reflected view

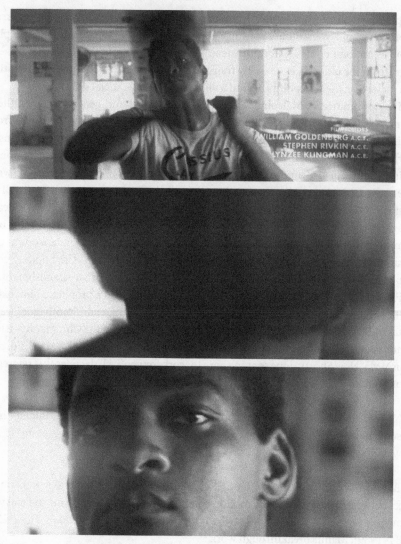

Figures 7.6–7.8 Ali, then still known as Cassius Clay, training with a speed bag at the 5th Street Gym in Miami. The background light, mirror, and flickering bag call to mind the mechanism of the motion picture camera (and the mechanism of thought à la Vertov's *Man with a Movie Camera*).

in Plate 18 also indicates Ali's self-understanding. It is no surprise that Mann cites the influence of Soviet montage masters Dziga Vertov and Sergei Eisenstein.[28] In connecting media technology to consciousness and social change the sequence evokes leftist thought.[29]

A parallel stylistic influence of Ali's 1975 autobiography *The Greatest: My Own Story* has not been remarked. Edited by Toni Morrison and written from interviews with Nation of Islam (NOI) scribe Richard Durham, the book is organized like a collage that jumps freely around different points in the subject's life. This style of digressions recalls oral storytelling and infuses the hero with a collective memory of the past. During Morrison's stint as an editor at Random House she took a particular interest in affirming African-American heritage, exemplified by *The Black Book* (also published in 1975). In the same vein (if not to the same degree) the opening montage in *Ali* emphasizes Black culture in its difference and diversity. Through his muteness the sequence represents Blackness as a relational component of Ali's life and persona rather than an inner essence. The young hero who cannot fit into the older all-American mold serves as a proxy for the viewer to discover a convoluted world.

As an origin scene, the bravura opening sequence represents Ali as a young Black pioneer for a multicultural America. "In a few moments we know this movie is talking about boxing, civil rights, and popular culture in America," says Adrian Wootton.[30] By presenting an uncharacteristically quiet Ali, Mann's film shifts attention from a singular personality to a hero who acts like a sponge for his environment. Ali is portrayed as a product of, and prophetic response too, the generational and racial conflicts of midcentury America. He tests White hegemony on the streets and confronts the power of Black complacency to thus become the vehicle for Malcolm X's words, Sam Cooke's music, and Emmett Till's soul. Because such a complex montage demands an active viewer to weave together all these audiovisual threads in the absence of dialogue, the sequence accentuates the cerebral aspect of multiculturalism. In this way the montage invites non-Blacks to relate to the hero through critical understanding.

Liston Fight

Surprisingly, the origin scene omits Ali's background in the ring. He is only seen in training, as if the imminent Liston fight would be his first-ever competition. But that suspense does not subordinate sports to politics. The heady opening montage sets the stage for a showcase of the boxers' phenomenal experience in the ring.

This section argues that the Ali-Liston fight scene represents the champion athlete's special kind of political action. An absence of dialogue maintains the observational style of the opening sequence, but now Mann abandons the freewheeling montage that had painted the social backdrop. Realist sound design and camerawork convey the feeling of bodies fighting, in real time, for over ten minutes. This focus on pure sport will elevate Ali as a heroic representative in a way that preserves difference, in contrast with conformist modes of political representation based on common qualities.

First, the 1964 fight scene reveals Ali's distinctive, improvisational fighting style.[31] Whereas his opponent, Sonny Liston, slugged with raw, overpowering strength, Ali boxed in an unconventional way that depended on quick body movements and unpredictable combinations. "Float like a butterfly, sting like a bee" was more than a just a witty verbal jab; it expresses the principle behind Ali's unique way of boxing. Jan Philipp Reemtsma explains that Ali's "style is organized around his goal of quick combinations of hits, without favoring one particular punch or favoring one lead hand over the other."[32] Given that unexpected punches produce knockouts more frequently than simply heavy blows, the improvisational element of Ali's style made him supremely dangerous. His unstable stances also exposed him to danger that required boldness, deft footwork, and exceptionally quick head movements to evade threats.

Improvisation has been an important element of African-American culture, epitomized by jazz music. Ali pioneered an unconventional and subtle technique that only connoisseurs of the sweet science could well appreciate. Before downing Liston, many considered his evasive dancing and rapid combinations as glib as his verbal boasting. But unlike a decorative improvisation, such as a stylish dunk by Michael Jordan, Ali's syncopated moves serve the purpose of parrying or of brutal attack.[33] His style is at once individual, characteristically Black, and indisputably effective.

Mann's coverage of the fight scene recognizes Ali's exceptional skill and courage from up close. A sound design centered on Ali's body anchors the scene. No dialogue or musical score interrupts the suspenseful silence that fills the ring; only distant background noise makes the presence of an audience felt. Close sounds of the boxers' heaving breaths and smacking bodies take center stage. At certain moments Ali's respiration sounds so near that it gives the impression of his internal perception. Mann and his sound editors Gregory King, Darren King, and Yann Delpeuch focus attention on the boxers' bodies. Moreover, the environmental soundscape endures the fight's five full rounds. Without conventional cuts to compress the time of action, the scene's duration can feel like an eternity. Mann asks viewers to dwell in the dangerous and intimate space of the ring for over ten minutes, with little more than grunts to cling to.

Lubezki's camera likewise floats in the immediate, phenomenal space of the boxers. Spot lighting and low angles set the athletes apart from the spectators hidden in the black background, like a cosmic gigantomachia illustrated in Plate 19. A Steadicam dances around the ring continuously, much nearer to the boxers than in Rocky. Then, at key moments, rapid montage of video images (Mann's visual signature) mimics the complex action unfolding. Each burst sequence begins with a closeup of Ali's white boots dancing rapidly in preparation, as depicted in Figure 7.9. Shot with a fisheye lens without stabilization, the shaky video closeups disorient the viewer from the arena space. Figures 7.10, 7.11 and 7.12 illustrate how bodies and gloves crowd out normal reference points and smother the frame, as if the boxers wore body cameras. Lubezki's color palette and blur also resemble Bellows' Stag at Sharkey's, illustrated in Figure 7.13, with more vibrancy than the opening scene of Rocky (compare to Figures 2.3 and 2.4).[34] In these heightened moments the low-definition video images register a palpability and an authenticity. The alternation between stabilized dancing and video bursts mimics Ali's floating butterfly and stinging bee. The fight accelerates in combination punches, then pauses in the clutch. The action thus becomes the physiological rhythm of boxing.

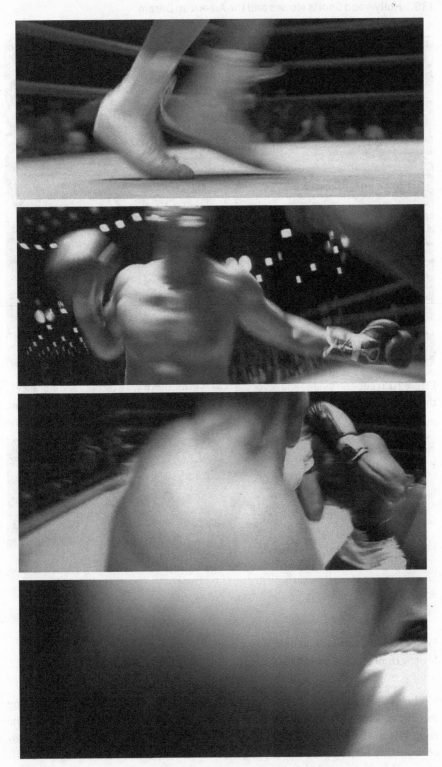

Figures 7.9–7.12 Burst sequences represent quick movements of the sweet science. Lubezki's special video cameras create a modernist style of instability.

Figure 7.13 Lubezki's video images of the boxers in motion have a tactility and vibrancy that compare to the George Bellows brushwork in *Stag at Sharkey's* (1909). Public domain.

Figure 7.14 Broadcast announcer Howard Cosell (Jon Voigt) is half-obscured and his fleeting comments heard at half-volume, destabilizing the viewer's position in the scene.

The muffled sounds and handheld camerawork portray Ali as a blur. The looping camera and rapid cuts avoid showing images of the stable background outside the ring. When Mann does cut away from the whirling center, the spectators are half-obscured by boxer limbs and ropes in the frame. A shot of Howard Cosell's half-obscured face, depicted in Figure 7.14, is mirrored by hearing his radio commentary at half-volume and distorted. Even the corner men are half-muted, relegated to the background. We are not permitted to watch the fight from a stable position outside the ring and must instead roll with the dancing bodies. Only in scenes set underwater or depicting inebriation does one typically find such accent on breath and impression of instability. Lubezki never dwells on any pose until the fight's ending.

Ali's focus on athletics stands out within a film genre that typically subordinates physical play to dominant moral themes. The "big event" usually illustrates more general conflicts through the sport, favoring drama over athletics. For instance, the cartoonish slugs in *Rocky IV* add to ubiquitous flags and anthem music that represent the Cold War rivalry.[35] Stallone always pays more attention to sentiment than to sport. Even *Raging Bull* uses boxing to illustrate the protagonist's violent machismo and self-destruction in the film noir tradition of *Body and Soul* and *Champion*. Because pure athletics is inarticulate and thus comprehensible only to devotees of the sport, conventional Hollywood filmmakers add clear dramatic signals to supplement the action.[36] In boxing films, dialogue presses into the ring via announcers, voiceover narration, or a focus on conversation in the corners between rounds.[37] For instance, both *Rocky* and *Raging Bull* rely on ringside commentators to narrate the boxing in voiceover, following the conventions of television broadcasting. Their stable dramatic structure portrays the hero as a more static, sculptural icon; the creative cinematography of Garrett Brown and Michael Chapman adds detail and emphasis like a reality effect.[38] They exchange the duration of television broadcast for spectacular sequencing. Although cinema's high-definition imagery may purport to be more realistic than television, most movies lack the duration necessary to appreciate embodied athletic interaction. In their own ways, both *Rocky* and *Raging Bull* assimilate boxing to stable dramatic structures. Conventional narration, music, and decoupage bind athletic play under unambiguous and broadly accessible meaning.

In contrast, Mann's athletic realism dwells in the boxers' perspective, embodied and in flux. The action plays out in real time with few cutaways, captured by mobile cameras and microphones significantly nearer than in normal broadcasts. Only Moby's synthesizer score of minimalistic chords (also a stylistic signature of Mann) departs from strict realism to organize the fight into three periods of poise, crisis, and joy. But the athletic contest itself is held in the foreground. In fact, Mann aimed to reenact the fight as accurately as possible. He insisted that Will Smith threw actual punches with his opponents, who were played by legitimate boxers.[39] Smith's slimmer body and inexperience therefore authenticate Ali's underdog status in the Liston fight.

More importantly, Mann's realism demonstrates how Ali outperforms Liston as a boxer, pure and simple. The phenomenalist approach to the fight scene also manifests Ali's distinctiveness. Mann does not suggest that Ali prevailed because he had better political opinions or a nicer personality. No particular inner motivation surges up and overwhelms the opponent as often happens with Rocky Balboa. The dramatic conflicts of civil rights and generational change set up by the title sequence remain in the background of the boxing contest. The realist style ushers another kind of political quality into the foreground.

Sports as Public Action

Athletic competition has a fundamentally political quality that has been obscured by narrow conceptions of the political. Hannah Arendt reminds us that that word's root is *polis*—the city or public space. In the classical sense of the word, our political nature developed from living among equals in a realm unbound by necessity. "The rise of the city-state meant that man received 'besides his private life a sort of second life [outside the home], his *bios politikos*,'" writes Arendt, quoting Werner Jaeger.[40] She explains:

> The foundation of the *polis* was preceded by the destruction of all organized units resting on kinship, such as the *phratria* and the *phylē*. Of all the activities necessary and present in human communities, only two were deemed to be political and to constitute what Aristotle called the *bios politikos*, namely action (*praxis*) and speech (*lexis*), out of which rises the realm of human affairs (*ta tōn anthrōpōn pragmata*, as Plato used to call it) from which everything merely necessary or useful is strictly excluded.[41]

From this perspective, *freedom* and *civic* connote a shared public realm and affairs beyond bodily or household necessities. Arendt challenges conceptions of politics confined to economic affairs, legislation, or private opinion.[42] In that classical sense sports, usually public and by no means a necessity, are fundamentally political.

That deeper political nature involves a dynamic mode of representation. The athletic champion represents his people without forfeiting individual difference. Arendt develops a concept of political action as a spontaneous intervention that distinguishes an individual agent within the public arena. Defined classically as a great deed or a great speech, the public recognizes the actor's unique being. That interrelation resolves the tension between individual and collective. Arendt describes action as "the actualization of the human condition of plurality, that is, of living as a distinct and unique being among equals." The public space is egalitarian while the spontaneous intervention is unique. Arendt writes:

> In acting and speaking, men show who they are, reveal actively their unique personal identities and thus make their appearance in the human world, while their physical identities appear without any activity of their own in the unique shape of the body and sound of the voice. This disclosure of the 'who' in contradistinction to 'what' somebody is—his qualities, gifts, talents, and shortcomings, which he may display or hide—is implicit in everything somebody says and does.[43]

In contrast to a homogeneous relationship through common qualities, action and speech elevate representation to a unique being comprised of multiple attributes who is recognized by all. The people are equal in their presence in civic space, but do not possess equal qualities.

Furthermore, by recognizing the uniqueness of the body as a key part of public identity Arendt is not blind to the racial components of social life. Racism involves judgment of "'what' somebody is" but ignores the complexity of who they are. Blindness to color (race) suppresses judgment of race but creates another problem in denying public recognition to the sociocultural and physical components of a person, still missing the whole person.[44] Arendt's focus on action recognizes the individual in their multiplicity. The agent is not subordinated to a social quality like their race or disability, nor are these aspects of their being refused public recognition. Ali epitomizes Arendt's picture of representation as a unique individual who insisted upon his identity as a Black American athlete. Mann's film likewise insists on Ali's Black American identity through the opening montage, but lets the athletic action stand on its own.

It is also important to note that Arendt's approach to individual recognition does not dissolve the collective. Action is relational. The greatness of the action stems from the agent initiating something spontaneously. She calls this initiative *natality*, which defines the human condition in tandem with plurality. The greatness of the actor is shared by everyone present because it depends on a spontaneous moment experienced collectively, rather than some innate attribute possessed by an individual. Arendt's relational conception of action understands how an athletic champion is recognized as an individual who may represent a minority group but must represent all the public who are equally present.

In sports, the champion demands recognition from everyone on the playing field as well as spectators. The arena of sports has the essential political qualities of publicness and spontaneity. On the day of competition the champion is recognized as one among the many. Even other participants can be recognized for great performance; the champion's recognition is simply given. Individual distinction need not be achieved through dominating all others, but through initiating action. In fact, sport's artificial contests multiply occasions for distinction, which accounts for their ritual importance in ancient Greece. Sports may have universal rules but their fundamental form of representation is not conformist.

This section has shown how the Ali-Liston fight scene represents Ali's boxing as an independent action. The opening montage, which established the hero as a young Black American motivated by social change, now merely accentuates the unique initiative of the people's champion. The plot will develop by representing the spontaneity and boldness of other actions: his press conference declaration, "I don't have to be what you want me to be. I'm free to be what I want"[45]; his controversial statement on the Vietnam War, "I ain't got no quarrel with them Viet Cong. Ain't no Viet Cong ever called me nigger"[46]; his conscientious objection to the draft; and finally his 1974 victory against George Foreman. What holds together all these actions, I argue, are Ali the person, the arc of his growing consciousness, and the theme of multicultural liberalism.

The second half of the chapter will examine two montage sequences that precede the Foreman-Ali fight. Symmetrical to the opening montage, they explore the complexity of African heritage and frame the hero as a liberator from oppressive institutions.

Accra Montage

Following the championship bout, a montage sequence depicts Ali's 1964 trip to Ghana. It represents the hero discovering himself as an icon for larger Black and anti-imperial traditions. Interestingly, the sequence complicates essentialist notions of Africanness by describing a certain alienation experienced by Ali. Through these introspective moments the film also reflects upon its own political importance as a memorial.

A scene on the airplane crossing the Atlantic manifests the deeper context of Black America's relationship to Africa.[47] A flight attendant welcomes the new champion to the cockpit and the pilots invite him to sit down. Warm light pours into the airplane's port side, depicted in Plate 20. Surprised to find all the pilots and crew to be black, Ali quips, "Where I grew up, they barely let black folks drive buses." In demonstrating admiration for his African hosts, this people's champion establishes a human equality and solidarity among them. This line of dialogue, apparently invented by the film-makers, also calls to mind Marcus Garvey and his Black Star Line.

In 1919 Marcus Garvey established the Black Star Line Steamship Corporation. Named in counterpart to the White Star Line, the leading transatlantic shipping company (best known for the Titanic), Garvey sought a Black-owned, Black-oper-ated rival that would open new routes to Africa and consequently new opportunities for Blacks.[48] Through the Harlem-based United Negro Improvement Association he raised money from thousands of inspired individuals. The Pan-Africanism that blos-somed in Garvey's time would bloom even larger with the wave of decolonization after 1945 in tandem with Black organizations that included the Nation of Islam. The brief airplane scene and Ghana's black star monuments therefore portray Ali as a suc-cessor to Garvey's project.

The montage sequence of Ali's majestic arrival in Ghana communicates his de-veloping consciousness of a complex African heritage. The sequence compresses a motorcade through Accra, Ghana, that was filmed on location.[49] As with the title se-quence, a mute Ali soaks up the social environment. Wide shots of crowds lining the streets make evident a new public that embraces the champion, as shown in Figure 7.15. He rides perched atop a convertible white limousine, just two years after John F. Kennedy's assassination, to indicate his total trust of the Ghanian people. But Will Smith does not pander to them like a politician. Mann cuts to the telephoto view of Figure 7.16 to show Ali looking humbly upon the crowd as if astonished by his own popularity in this foreign place.

Salif Keita's song "Papa" (1999) underlines Ali's new sense of self and a certain al-ienation. Like Sam Cooke's medley in the opening montage, the non-diegetic mu-sical score implies an inner soundtrack that connects the hero to the people. Yet the

Figure 7.15 The film replicates Ali's motorcade through Accra and shows him riding exposed atop a convertible with no fear, two years after President Kennedy's assassination in Dallas.

Figure 7.16 Will Smith expresses Ali's bewilderment at his awesome reception abroad.

lyrics Keita sings in Bambara, untranslated, cannot be read as Ali's inner voice. On the one hand, Keita's music suggests a communal voice from deep within as Ali discovers his African heritage. Keita, as a musician who emigrated from Mali to Europe and blended his traditional folk music with pop to find success in world music, clearly represents a Pan-African voice for Mann. A purist might criticize the anachronistic use of 1990s music. Here Mann breaks his own practice of using contemporary covers of period music. Nonetheless, this anachronism creates another effect.

On the other hand, Keita's voice introduces a foreignness that signals Ali's alienation from himself. The non-diegetic music constructs another self from outside the American hero, symbolizing his emergence as a global icon. A series of closeups of Ali's silent face indicate a critical reassessment of his African heritage. The quizzical look seen in Figure 7.16 does not show a person who feels at home; it suggests the double strangeness of being abroad and being loved by strangers. Whereas the celebration directly after the Liston fight and in Harlem was depicted as natural, this parade involves a measure of artifice.

Further exchanges of gazes reflect upon the Black American's relationship to contemporary Africans. At first Mann shows people along the streets who cheer in admiration for his procession. But the sequence concludes with Ali observing locals on the sidewalk who go about their normal business. Figure 7.17 showcases these Accrans, who do not appear to be actors or extras paid to cheer the motorcade. Lubezki's camera maintains an egalitarian eye-level and even uses slow motion to reflect Ali's appreciation of the passersby. Their everydayness indicates a fellowship grounded in human recognition, not celebrity worship. By alternating with Ali's visage in shallow focus, seen in Figure 7.18, Mann also hints at the hero's sense of estrangement.[50] The accompanying music echoes this tension between belonging and being outside. In this way the scene avoids promoting the simplistic notion of a Black racial essence.[51]

Meanwhile at the center of the montage stand two monuments that convey Ali's consciousness of becoming a political icon. The motorcade first pulls up to

Figures 7.17–7.18 Ali observes passersby with a shallow focus that suggests his estrangement and fascination. Filmed on location from a car, these locals do not appear to be actors.

Independence Square, a seaside complex that consists of an arch flanked by stands. As the cars approach, Lubezki's onboard camera racks the focus to the empty grandstand in the background. Figure 7.19 illustrates the crowd blurred in the foreground. This shift in focus highlights the grandstand as a social infrastructure, and suggests the political power of sports. Then, as the parade stops in the middle of the square, Lubezki takes up a static view, depicted in Figure 7.20. An axis runs from the ceremonial flame in the foreground, to Ali in mid-ground, to an arch crowned by a black star in the background. Here Mann stages a ceremonial pause in the otherwise mobile images of the motorcade montage. On a complex built for iconicity a crowd gathers around Ali like a king ascending a sacred throne. No explanation for the site's significance is given, as if the captivating visual composition speaks for itself.

Astute viewers would recognize Independence Square (also known as Black Star Square), constructed under Kwame Nkrumah upon declaring Ghana an independent republic in 1957. The scene of Ali's 1964 visit recalls early optimism for the socialist, anti-imperial regime.[52] North American viewers might also see in the flame and

Figures 7.19–7.20 Attention shifts from the people to Ghana's independence monuments midway through the sequence to suggest Ali's enlarged awareness of political power.

Figures 7.21–7.22 The sequence culminates in low-angle shots of Ali gazing at Black Star Gate, underscoring a prophetic dimension of anti-colonial political movements.

stadium a harbinger for Ali lighting the Olympic flame at the 1996 opening ceremony, a paramount moment of international fame and of national redemption.

The sequence climaxes at Black Star Gate to portray Ali as a kind of messiah. The actual motorcade would have first passed the triumphal arch before arriving at the square. Mann's intentional rearrangement in editing constructs a formal pattern that rises from people in the streets to grandstands and finally up to the celestial black star. Lubezki moves the camera closer with low angles that reverently frame Ali and the icon against the sky, as depicted in Figures 7.21 and 7.22. Several eye-line matches of Ali gazing at the monumental black star imply his recognition of a divine, anti-colonial mission on behalf of oppressed and African peoples.

Drama as Memorial for Action

The Ghana montage does two things for the work overall. First, it bridges the two main actions that structure the drama. This pivotal sequence recognizes the global public of Ali's 1964 victory while establishing a background for the climactic action of the 1974 fight in Zaire. The parade through Accra serves the plot by indicating Ali's growing awareness of African peoples and of himself as an icon; the sequence dwells in the estrangement involved in this new awareness. Will Smith's pensive face also suspends the moment of glory with the people until the climactic fight in Zaire.

Second, this interlude provides a meta-dramatic moment to reflect upon the nature of memorial. The deep reflection of Ali's quiet face and of Keita's introspective ballad mirror the massive monuments and crowds around them. Black Star Gate and Square of course celebrate African independence from White European colonial powers. A montage sequence is itself a formalized ritual of cinematic style that, like those architectural memorials, communicates without dialogue and across linguistic borders.

However, the biopic differs from the Black Star monuments in one key respect. The film memorializes Ali while Ghana's leader Kwame Nkrumah is not featured in the independence memorials. They symbolize democracy and Pan-Africanism abstractly, with concrete gathering spaces for the people. Arendt, who criticized Marx (and classical liberals) for overlooking the individual agent, would favor the biographical drama as a memorial for action.

Arendt understands artwork primarily as public remembrance for action. More than mere adulation or legitimation, memorials achieve the action. Initiated by an individual agent amid the flux of the present, only in retrospect is the action recognized; and only in perpetual remembering does its important intervention endure amid the ongoing flux of the present. "Because of its inherent tendency to disclose the agent together with the act, action needs for its full appearance the shining brightness we once called glory, and which is only possible in the public realm," writes Arendt.[53] To describe the aim of action as immortal fame implies an act that merits everlasting admiration.[54] Arendt conceives of art as a form of work that constructs a world. Connoting something like *culture*, a world shapes public life across time. Recognizing the agent who initiated the action suits a democratic polity in which all individuals are equally present and potential actors.

Drama is the key memorial for Arendt. Deriving from the Greek δράω (*dran*), the word *drama* literally means "to act." Arendt explains that, in Homer, *hero* referred to any free man who participated in the Trojan enterprise; more generally, it referred to "any person about whom a story can be told."[55] While no story can capture the totality of meaning because actions occur in the complex web of human relationships, one story can "isolate the agent who set the whole process into motion" and reveal "the living essence of the person as it shows itself in the flux of action and speech."[56] Arendt distinguishes the agent who initiates action from a total author who takes all the credit. Arendt's evidently Aristotelian view of drama centers on a plot that reenacts one action, initiated by one hero. But whereas Aristotle lauds fiction for representing universal truths, Arendt favors historical subjects.[57] A proper biographical drama, for instance, recognizes a unique individual and situates their spontaneous initiative within a specific context. By nature drama is a public ritual that relates the actor to the people.[58]

Ali's reflective visit to the Black Star memorials during the Accra montage clearly identifies him as a successor to the Pan-African movement and its anti-colonial, democratic values. Smith's somber expressions indicate the weight of that struggle for Ali (and for Smith taking on that role); they also suggest Ali's growing awareness of himself as a public figure. Bundini and Malcolm X were shown guiding him through public appearances up to this point, but in this scene he will break out upon his own path. The parade lacks glory for Ali because he has yet to fully comprehend his place in this wider world. A subsequent montage sequence set in Zaire will develop his feeling of estrangement into a political theme, setting the stakes for the final fight.

Kinshasa Montage

A montage sequence in Kinshasa, Zaire, frames Ali's 1974 championship as a democratic action against imperial oppression. After the film opens with the 1964 title, a series of corrupt leaders and institutions challenge the hero: the NOI, CIA, boxing commissioners, the US military, and now Zaire's dictator, Mobutu. This section reflects critically on the danger of ethnic nationalism and describes how the montage portrays Ali as a popular folk hero in contrast to those despotic rulers.

Mann and Roth establish two central antagonists as counterpoints to Ali: Nation of Islam (NOI) prophet Elijah Muhammad and Mobutu Sese Seko, dictator of Zaire (a country now known again as Congo). Production designer John Myhre stages both leaders in prim formal quarters that indicate class pretension: plastic-covered couches for the petty bourgeois cleric seen in Figure 7.23 and an opulent salon for the autocrat in Figure 7.24. Lubezki's wide-angle lens makes the rooms' capaciousness and décor dominate both scenes to underline their vain materialism. Furthermore, the villains barely speak and are performed with coldness by Albert Hall and Malick Bowens, respectively. Nameless U.S. government agents serve as go-betweens who suggest the leaders' corruption. That ugly picture of conspiracy reduces these official representatives to puppets and opportunists. The Black antagonists also complicate naïve notions of Pan-African renaissance. If the riddle of the hero is how one individual can represent all of a people, the despot offers a nightmare solution—he imposes his will on his subjects while feigning solidarity. Mann showcases hypocrisy as didactically as Ousmane Sembène does in *Xala* (1975). Elijah Muhammad and Mobutu therefore serve as doppelgängers to Ali (and to Malcolm X, presented as a martyr figure through his death early in the film).[59]

To convey Ali's authentic popularity, a montage sequence stages Ali jogging through the footpaths of a Kinshasa neighborhood just before the 1974 fight. The scene begins with him running down a wide avenue behind a vehicle escort, then following children who duck down a side footpath. A matrix of official billboards on the avenue are juxtaposed with artisanal murals on the houses. One billboard, depicted in Figure 7.25, sets an iconic image of Mobutu beside a political slogan: "Un seul chef, Un seul peuple, Une seule nation (*one leader, one people, one nation*)." When Ali

Figure 7.23 Nation of Islam leader Elijah Muhammad (Albert Hall) framed behind a plastic-covered couch to suggest his sanctimoniousness, coldness, and cupidity.

Figure 7.24 Dictator Mobutu (Malik Bowens) framed behind a CIA agent and an opulent table, in wide angle, to characterize Zaire's leader as a decadent stooge.

arrives deep inside the neighborhood, he discovers murals that depict him as a giant who punches tanks and fighter jets, as seen in Figure 7.26.[60] The official propaganda of Mobutu contrasts with Ali's presence in vernacular spaces.

Ali was known for interacting with people very openly, and his biographers saw the attention of the people and mutual respect that Ali developed with everyone, especially children and elders, as a source of his charisma.[61] Dozens of non-actors in this sequence, shown in Figures 7.27 to 7.32, authenticate the hero as a popular representative. Children surround Will Smith as he runs down the official avenue, and they lead him through a gap in the billboards along a footpath to the favela shown. Then he exchanges looks with the local women who appear to have been drawn outside by the curious commotion. A young man in a yellow tank top pretends to challenge the boxer and smiles warmly. Children crowd around and lift up the hero's arms, symbolizing the people who motivate the pugilist. An old man follows him with a radio (a

Figures 7.25–7.26 Mobutu's propaganda billboards on the main road contrast with vernacular murals of Ali as liberator. A favela in Maputo, Mozambique, stands in for Kinshasa, Zaire, with production design led by John Myhre.

symbol for the media through which they came to know the global icon). Lubezki's mobile, stabilized camera captures the locals over Ali's shoulder in moments that look unscripted. When the crowd gathers around the murals, their faces fill the frame with Smith in close up, testifying to their actual proximity. Smith's encounters with locals in Mozambique pay tribute to Ali's closeness with the people. The hero's mute gaze around the favela suggests an awareness that the people see him as an honest liberator in contrast to the distant dictator.

Slow-motion imagery and African music signal Ali's expanding consciousness. In the first half of the montage, Salif Keita's upbeat tune "Bolon" conveys a populist joy through flutes and tambourines over guitars. Then a slow-motion, medium close-up of Ali transitions to a more pensive second part. Keita's grandiose, yearning ballad "Tomorrow" has a simple English refrain, the title, that functions as a cultural bridge. As in the Ghana montage, Keita's music implies that Ali's inner conscience has been inspired by the African people who admire him. Although these connections could point to a common racial essence, the impoverished setting and the refrain

Figures 7.27–7.32 Ali (Will Smith) jogs through a favela where Lubezki's handheld camera captures interactions that appear unscripted.

Figures 7.27–7.32 Continued.

"tomorrow" draw attention toward a universal struggle against oppression and hope for a better future.

The locals and the music in this sequence contrast Ali, as an authentic champion of the people, to Mobutu. The people who guide and surround Ali in the streets suggest that they inspire his action, so that his eventual triumph will represent them rather than his individual will to power. Keita's soundtrack parallels this suggestion like the chorus in ancient Greek drama. Arendt notes that "universal meaning is revealed by the chorus," not by the individual actor.[62] Keita's music and the local interactions thus accentuate the contrast between the popular Ali and the despot present only on billboards.

This jogging sequence evokes the training montage trope from the *Rocky* franchise. In the same way that Rocky's jog through Philadelphia symbolizes the hero's representation of the city, so does Ali's. But *Ali* goes a step further. The jog of the foreigner through an unfamiliar shantytown signifies Ali's representation of the disenfranchised around the globe, not merely his hometown. In both films the drama climaxes with the training montage because the hero gains full understanding of his importance to the people and vice versa.

In designing the paramount dramatic moment as a montage, these sports movies renounce a poetic tradition focused on great words. A speech or dialogue usually articulates the special synthesis at the heart of the work. Muting the characters for music and images risks coming off as a hokey and facile gesture—indeed, some montage sequences in the *Rocky* sequels and its knock-offs are downright trite and rightly parodied. The deeper influence for the montage sequence is, of course, the Soviet avant-garde, who saw the new medium of cinema as a means to communicate across linguistic barriers and unite the people of the world in a socialist project of revolution.[63] In this vein *Ali*'s preference for montage over speech matches the multilingual context of Zaire. This scene's montage of music, faces, and looks suggests that Ali's people have now expanded from Black Americans to Kinshasa locals and the oppressed everywhere, framing the upcoming fight before a global public.

Yet the lack of speech also reflects a liberal suspicion of rule by law and policy, as if deferring to individual judgment. *Ali* represents most all institutions as conspiratorial powers, especially the CIA. No state agencies are represented positively, such as legislators or courts; the Supreme Court decision that exonerates Ali is communicated by Howard Cosell, a journalist, in conversation. In this way Mann's drama fosters libertarian and populist distrust of the state.[64] However, the film's skepticism never extends to sport. Like *Rocky*, *Ali* stands apart from midcentury boxing films dominated by gambler and gangster villains. The absence of any corrupting influence from sport in the film recuperates a measure of faith in republican institutions.

The Kinshasa montage builds upon the African heritage established in the Ghana sequence. A strangeness remains in his relationship to the people, but Ali grasps his meaning as an icon for liberation from poverty and oppression. Just as the opening montage established a multicultural background to the Liston fight, the African montages paint a backdrop of liberal democracy around the Foreman fight.

Foreman Fight

In close conversation with Ali at one point in the film's second act, Howard Cosell (Jon Voigt) tells Ali, "All they are is political," comparing him to H. Rap Brown and Stokely Carmichael. "You're the heavyweight champion of the world." Cosell underlines the fact that, unlike most verbal arguments, sporting contests produce an undisputed victor. Whereas politicians and actors adopt an artifice to persuade an audience, the champion athlete earns their public standing more transparently.[65] Mann and Roth foreground Ali the athlete by opening and closing the film with his 1964 and 1974 championships. But they neither subordinate social issues nor let them dominate the sporting action—each is embedded in a larger action of the hero coming to consciousness and taking initiative on behalf of the people.

Ali famously employed a "rope-a-dope" stratagem to defeat reigning champion and heavy favorite George Foreman. Similar to Liston, the younger Foreman was a hulk who fought with a powerful and aggressive style. But rather than attempt to evade and surprise the bigger opponent, an approach he attempted in the first round, the older Ali settled into a defensive posture and allowed Foreman to wallop his body. This shift in strategy was unplanned and confused Ali's own corner. He even taunted young George to strike harder while leaning back against the ropes to deflect the brunt of the blows. Foreman eventually tired. Ali then sprung back with a surprising combination that knocked Foreman out. Already described by others at length, Ali's defensive strategy exemplifies endurance and savvy to defeat a powerful opponent. Its spontaneous invention also complements the physical improvisation of his youthful style. This stunning action again led to recognition of Ali's unique greatness in the ring. Mann stages the fight almost as quietly as the first Liston fight scene and in real time to showcase Ali's initiative as a boxer.

Outside the ring, Mann frames the Foreman fight scene with anti-imperialist symbolism. Because Foreman is not developed as a character he can be seen to symbolize the bullies CIA and Mobutu. Before the fight, long shots reveal the actual crowd of tens of thousands gathered at Machava Stadium in Mozambique.[66] Massive posters erect the image of Mobutu above the stadium, as shown in Figure 7.33. The beating Ali purposely endures from Foreman therefore mirrors the oppression that the people endure under the despot and the war to control Zaire. Furthermore, earlier scenes that associated Mobutu with the CIA suggest that Ali's true political opponent is an imperialism driven by White Americans and Europeans before them. The biopic thus portrays Ali as a representative for all people oppressed by imperial power. The hero's perseverance conveys their enduring struggle and their hope for liberation. Mann scholar Mark Wildermuth describes this moment as "the rarest of rarities in Mann's world, a moment of justice."[67]

A reprise of Keita's song at the fight's conclusion reinforces the democratic theme. At the pinnacle moment when Ali knocks out Foreman, the sound of "Tomorrow" fades in and initiates a mini-montage of post-fight celebration, recalling the Kinshasa jogging sequence. Rain pours down. Will Smith expresses Ali's relief and joy by dancing through the entourage that fills the ring, embracing everyone except profiteer Don King (Mykelti Williamson), whom he snubs. Large flags of the United

Figure 7.33 A poster of Mobutu towers above a crowded national stadium that was replicated on location in Mozambique. The autocratic ruler of Zaire offered $5 million to host the 1974 fight, apparently to promote his regime.

Figures 7.34 Mann concludes the scene with a freeze frame of Ali posing before the stadium crowd. The boxing icon eclipses a Mobutu poster in the distance.

States and Zaire, seen in Plate 21, wave through the crowd. Ali then moves to pose at the ropes, where he raises his hands in triumph before the massive crowd. Figure 7.34 shows the freeze-frame that concludes the film, with the hero facing the people and the Mobutu poster obscured in the background. As a picture of the American dream, this image emphasizes his commitment to common people and a faith in a righteous destiny.

The combination of flags complicates the imperialistic association of flag and victory. For instance, *Rocky IV* (Stallone, 1985) embraces the role of a Cold War propaganda vehicle by staging the villain surrounded by Soviet flags and wrapping the hero in Old Glory. One might have expected Mann to downplay two emblems that he has associated with antagonists Mobutu and the CIA up to this point. Surprisingly, the flags accompany Ali and shine brighter than they did in historical footage. With the American stars and stripes waving alongside Zaire's green banner with circular yellow MPR emblem, we cannot read any conflict between the two nations; nor does Ali represent one nation as a folk leader.[68] Instead, Ali's iconic pose before various flags and world music seems to supplant imperialism with an internationalism.[69] The moment recalls a hope for democracy and peace born in the Accra and Kinshasa montage sequences.

A certain melancholy nevertheless dampens this ecstatic moment. The more somber chords of "Tomorrow" sigh for a dream ever on the horizon. The final freeze-frame also suggests death or an irreversible passing of time, adding a sense of fleetingness to the happy moment. Historically informed viewers will think of Mobutu's long reign as dictator, Ali's unrealized political ambitions, and the boxer's severe physical decline due to Parkinson's syndrome.[70]

With a tragic undertone to its happy ending, *Ali* creates a new kind of victory plot. In the 1970s, *Rocky*, *The Bad News Bears*, and *The Longest Yard* embraced the honorable loss, which resonated with the debacle of Vietnam and the promise of revitalization. By the 1980s, full-throated comedic joy began to pulse through the genre, to the point of cliché in *Rocky IV* or later in *The Mighty Ducks*. The unbridled happy ending even appeared in civil rights history sports films *The Hurricane* and *Remember the Titans*, which can convey the message that equal rights have been definitively achieved. In contrast, *Ali* accompanies its victory with a measure of skepticism. The historical drama therefore honors the hero's action while reinforcing the call for ongoing effort.

Conclusion

The film *Ali* represents its hero as a champion of democracy in two ways. The championship bouts that bookend the film are depicted in a realist style to emphasize the egalitarian play of sport and to highlight Ali's unique style and action. In this way sports illustrate Arendt's model for political action in which democratic freedom is achieved in the singular action performed by a citizen-hero, who simultaneously represents to the polis the rule of law, the solidarity of the collective, and his unique individual being.

The drama composes a higher action—Ali's becoming conscious of himself as the people's champion—from the two sporting actions and other events during the decade between the fights. Following the creative tradition of the Soviet avant-garde, three montage sequences embed the hero in his socio-historical contexts to sow symbolic links with peoples who struggle against imperial dominance. The drama follows Ali's experience of colonial empire's residues at home and abroad, and his growing consciousness of his own meaningfulness as representative of an African-American minority and an underprivileged global majority. Through this composite action the biopic praises the higher good of democracy while portraying the complexity of Ali's person and environment.

Ali thus represents an American dream of progress toward democracy. The political ethos of multicultural liberalism informs the artistic effort to balance emphasis among the uniquely great individual, his ethnic identity, and a belief in universal equality. The biopic affirms minority identity and righteous dissent as quintessentially American. Previous critics overlooked the libertarian character that lurks in the negative representation of states and other civic institutions, but correctly recognized the film's portrayal of a complex subject. If Hollywood movies show us the heart of the American people, the development from *Rocky* to *Ali* is revealing.

8

Conclusion

Five Issues

Our story began with Muhammad Ali's triumphant 1974 reception at the nation's capital but his ambivalent reception at the nation's popular temple—the movies. By the time he died, in June 2016, that ambivalence had long faded away. Several best-selling biographies, at least a dozen documentaries, and Michael Mann's grand biopic had memorialized the living legend. President George W. Bush had awarded him the Medal of Freedom in 2005, at a ceremony depicted in Figure 8.1.[1] For his funeral, President Barack Obama made a special statement that concluded, "Muhammad Ali was America. He will always be America."[2] A photo of relics in the White House, reprinted in Figure 8.2, accompanied the written tribute. Ali's immortal fame testifies to the gradual acceptance of multiculturalism in the United States.

However, any simple notion of progress is challenged by the backlash to NFL star Colin Kaepernick's not standing for the national anthem in 2016. His demonstration joined with the Black Lives Matter movement in protesting a series of outrageous killings by police beside racial inequality in the United States generally.[3] When Kaepernick first addressed the media he said, "This country stands for freedom, liberty, and justice *for all*. And it's not happening for all right now."[4] He was careful to mention that "I have great respect for the men and women that have fought for this country. I have family, I have friends that have gone and fought for this country." Former Green Beret and NFL athlete Nate Boyer even persuaded Kaepernick to kneel as a posture of respect.

But the political right would not be satisfied by any form of dissent. Donald Trump, first as a candidate and then as president, led vehement criticism of kneeling that enflamed tensions further. Tweets shown in Figure 8.3 demonstrate his vituperative rhetoric.

Athletes sympathetic to Kaepernick and his cause subsequently refused to visit Trump in the White House, led by NBA champion Stephen Curry and FIFA World Cup winner Megan Rapinoe.[5] It all resembled the controversy that followed the raised black fists of Olympians John Carlos and Tommie Smith in 1968, or that had followed Ali's objection to conscription during the Vietnam War in 1966. Hollywood studios certainly did not rush to produce a Kaepernick biopic in the 2010s. Had no real change occurred in the United States since the 1960s, after all?

Hollywood Sports Movies and the American Dream. Grant Wiedenfeld, Oxford University Press. © Oxford University Press 2022.
DOI: 10.1093/oso/9780197624920.003.0008

Figure 8.1 George W. Bush embraces Muhammad Ali upon awarding him the Presidential Medal of Freedom in 2005. Ali's fingers coil as a result of Parkinson's disease. Courtesy George W. Bush Library.

This study has led us to five interwoven conclusions about the political character of the United States since 1976. Progress toward democracy was neither automatic, linear, nor complete, but some development is evident.

1. Multiculturalism

The sports movies examined in this study testify to the gradual acceptance of multiculturalism in America. The minority athlete's struggle for recognition and equality became a staple theme by the 1990s, culminating in *Ali* (2001). Hollywood in general developed to a stage that Greg Garrett calls "casual multiculturalism" in which the reality of racial difference is taken for granted.[6] The year 1996 seems to mark the crossing of that threshold for sports movies. *Space Jam* hit it big with Michael Jordan, Cuba Gooding Jr. won an Academy Award for Best Supporting Actor in *Jerry Maguire* (1996), and Whoopi Goldberg starred in the coach comedy *Eddie*. Denzel Washington vehicles *He Got Game* (1998), *The Hurricane* (1999), and *Remember the*

Figure 8.2 A White House "Photo of the Day" staged this reflexive tribute to Muhammad Ali just after his death. Photo by Pete Souza. Courtesy Barack Obama Presidential Library.

Titans (2000) testify to regular, major roles for Blacks in American sports movies subsequently. The Black heroes of *42* (2013) and *Race* (2016), Jackie Robinson and Jesse Owens, are now cut from the Ali mold.

Kaepernick's demonstration caused controversy, but the historical precedents of Ali and others were immediately mentioned by everyone. Although demonized on the right, the black athlete's revolt was defended by a large chorus and endorsed by Nike.[7] If Hollywood has not yet lionized Kaepernick, it has not vilified him either. His vilification is surely harder to imagine now than a panegyric on screen. The lack of support from league owners and commissioners underlined a lack of diversity in the sport's upper echelons—the final frontier for progress.

Casual multiculturalism fittingly describes the Rocky sequel *Creed* (2015) and the Latino subjects of *Goal!* (2005) and *McFarland, USA* (2015). The lesbian hero of *Battle of the Sexes* (2017) widens the circle a smidgen further. In these dramas the minority hero's success is now meaningful as cultural pride, whereas midcentury biopics had framed success as assimilation that melted away cultural difference. If having mainstream minority filmmakers and representation of all minorities on screen would represent a truly multicultural nation, then that horizon has surely grown nearer since 1976.

Religion has become more explicit on screen within the paradigm of multiculturalism, challenging its association with the progressive left. Ali was a pioneer in this regard as well. The Jackie Robinson played by Chadwick Boseman in *42*, for instance, is a Christian hero on par with the inspired member of the Nation of Islam memorialized by *The Greatest*. A shift appears to be underway from the implicitly Christian but muted public sphere of the early twentieth century to more explicit but varied religious (and atheist) discourse.[8]

2. Community

Multiculturalism also implies the value of community. Our study demonstrates an emphasis on community since 1976 that contradicts the ideology of American individualism which has preoccupied other critics. A turn away from self-interest and toward community is pivotal in *Rocky*, *The Natural*, and *A League of Their Own*. Meanwhile, *Slap Shot* and *White Men Can't Jump* criticize economic competition. And *Ali's* individual heroism is defined by his representation of the people above all. These films express the deeper motivation of democratic social movements that challenge the ideal of a hard masculine atom driven by a singular purpose.

Kaepernick was clearly motivated by the needs of the Black community and ended up sacrificing his football career. Even backlash against his individual demonstration appealed to communal solidarity. Trump's threat to "fire" dissenters implies that their protest is disloyal and selfish. Seeing the controversy through the lens of community reveals conflicts between justice and tradition, between social subgroup and nation, and between one minority group and another. Both left and right evidently take issue with liberalism, though with different priorities.

The dramatic form of comedy suits the sports movie's focus on community. From Rocky to Ali, this study has shown how the individual hero of the sports movie represents the collective and how the happiness they find reimagines a more democratic political ideal. "The point is not that such-and-such was done on earth," Joseph Campbell explains. "The point is that, before such-and-such could be done on earth, this other, more important, primary thing had to be brought to pass within the labyrinth that we all know and visit in our dreams."[9] Fiction affirms the American dream of democracy, in our case. Hollywood's sports movies reconfigure the nation's political imaginary after the 1960s toward a more inclusive and communal ideal.

A League of Their Own stands out as a truly great memorial to the community of women in sports. The cinematic ode to the collective achievement of historically marginal people exemplifies Arendt's classical definition of great words that elucidate great actions. Among many sports history films produced since the 1980s, this major Hollywood production recognized the women athletes of the All-American Girls Professional Baseball League (AAGPBL) on an unprecedented and grand scale. The story credits the players as a collective whose athletic skills and dedication made the league a significant endeavor, while also heeding individual and social differences. Directed by Penny Marshall, the film reflects the movement for greater representation of women in the industry generally.[10]

This study of democratic community in sports movies indicates progressive development after 1976. The importance of solidarity, equality, and inclusivity contrasts with the individualism and conservative social order valued in earlier periods, although further study is necessary to confirm that comparison.[11]

3. Imperial Legacy

Trump's criticisms of Kaepernick are also rooted in an imperial character that clashes with democratic values. Honor, the central value in monarchy according to Montesquieu, appears in three aspects of the controversy. First, Trump speaks of ambition, competition, and rank in the economic sphere as matters of honor. The tweet shown in Figure 8.3 criticizes NFL players as employees who dishonor their rank, whom he therefore calls to be "fired." For him, the honor code of employment extends to the passive anthem ceremony. Second, Trump also criticizes Kaepernick for disrespecting the military through dissent. Honor is reflected in the military's paradigmatic hierarchy, in the notion of blood sacrifice, and in the ancient identification of nobility as a warrior caste. Individual dissent thus threatens the priority the military

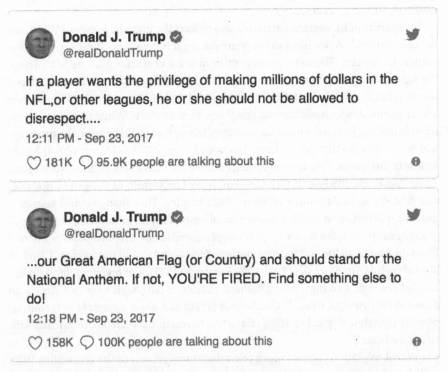

Donald J. Trump ✓
@realDonaldTrump

If a player wants the privilege of making millions of dollars in the NFL, or other leagues, he or she should not be allowed to disrespect....

12:11 PM - Sep 23, 2017

♡ 181K ♡ 95.9K people are talking about this

Donald J. Trump ✓
@realDonaldTrump

...our Great American Flag (or Country) and should stand for the National Anthem. If not, YOU'RE FIRED. Find something else to do!

12:18 PM - Sep 23, 2017

♡ 158K ♡ 100K people are talking about this

Figure 8.3 After a right-wing white person drove over protesters in Charlottesville, Virginia, another round of anthem demonstrations took place and solicited this response from President Trump, which uses a catch phrase from his reality television show.

claims in national life and the hierarchical social order more broadly. Third, the social honor of Whiteness is latent in discounting the cause of Black lives. The racial caste system of European colonies persists like a residue in America, as Isabel Wilkerson makes clear.[12] In a democracy intent on repairing its racist history, minority causes would merit extra attention. Trump's criticism of Kaepernick acutely contrasts the economic, military, and racial aspects of empire with the democratic priorities of inclusion, tolerance for cultural difference, social justice, and common welfare.[13] Indeed, Trump's campaign slogan "Make America Great Again" can be said to epitomize the imperial priority of greatness.

In our study, the nation's imperial legacy is illustrated by the backward pattern of multiculturalism's growth in Hollywood sports movies. Diversity develops on screen according to an imperial logic of privilege rather than a logic of justice. The minority theme is first represented sympathetically by European-American types—the working-class Italian, the rural white man in the city, and white women in wartime— while Black characters only ascend from opponent to teammate and finally to hero after 1996. That counterintuitive pattern reflects the tension between an imperial social structure and a democratic movement.[14] The broad acceptance of multiculturalism entailed White segments of society reassessing themselves as minorities with competing interests. The flow of democracy collides against the stones of imperial tradition, whirling in eddies.

The sparsity of immigrant narratives also reflects the imperial legacy of White settler colonialism.[15] A few films in the genre during this period do, however, challenge nativist tendencies. The most prominent immigrant character must be Mr. Miyagi, the Japanese-American mentor of *The Karate Kid* (1984). Although his stereotyped role is subordinated to an Italian-American lead with a blond girlfriend, the heroes are set against Anglo-American villains.[16] Some sensitivity to White racism is also evident in making Drago the über-Caucasian villain of *Rocky IV*; however, the prototypical Soviet enemies that persist from *American Flyers* (1985) to *Miracle* (2004) hardly welcome foreigners. One no longer finds immigrant characters such as Norwegian-American Knute Rockne or German-American Lou Gehrig in the genre, nor does one find the assimilationism of their 1940s biopics. That change could suggest a growing nativism, or it could indicate a racial basis of assimilation that is subsiding.

One can also detect a turn away from imperial expansion in sports movies' internal focus on American life and in some positive representations of the foreign. Films set abroad such as *Mr. Baseball* (1992), *Cool Runnings* (1993), and *Invictus* (2009) resolve conflict through a recognition of cultural difference (although they cast American actors in the principal roles).[17] *Caddyshack* (1980) and *Major League* (1989) contrast positive (but stereotypical) foreign characters to reactionary Anglo-Americans, satirizing the latter.[18]

Internal migration appears more often than immigration in the genre after 1976, with foreignness serving as a metaphor for cultural difference in *White Men Can't Jump*, as detailed earlier. Unlike the western's explicitly imperial backdrop of manifest destiny, sports movies are not rooted in a myth that concerns the land or cultural dominance. The primarily internal focus of sports movies and their growing pluralism indicates a complicated dilution of the nation's imperial legacy.

More generally, sports movies in our study perform a delicate balance between ambition and equality. Ambition is a counterpart to honor in Montesquieu's theory, fundamentally distinct from equality and fear as the principles behind monarchy, democracy, and despotism, respectively.[19] Our six dramas formulate various combinations of the competing values: equal respect despite defeat (*Rocky*), solidarity in victory without honor (*Slap Shot*), victory honorable in its egalitarian goal (*The Natural, Ali*), and egalitarian friendship without victory (*White Men Can't Jump, A League of Their Own*). The films demonstrate a democratic movement away from the pure love of victory; however, the drive for excellence never disappears—ambition is taken for granted among all athlete characters. As leaders graced with talent, Roy Hobbs and *Ali*'s Ali in particular model the genuine aristocrat's selfless sacrifice for one's people. Where pure democracy might subsume the individual and reduce all effort to mere duty, Hollywood sports movies balance equality with an individual ambition to excel. That balance corresponds to democratic and aristocratic republics in Montesquieu's theory. He might understand the United States as an evolving compromise between the two.

Overall, the democratic progress visible after 1976 comes against the background of an ambivalent imperial legacy. A competitive field with universal rules is a monarchical form of organization, in Montesquieu's sense. It offers more democratic access than hereditary nobility, but never equal outcomes. The spoils of victory contradict equal participation in authority. The rags-to-riches plot and the honor of winning above all exemplify that imperial tradition. In theory, a culture of excellence can serve good ends that complement American democracy if civil society is emphasized and merit is truly judged through action. The sports movies under study move in this direction by putting more emphasis on the humanist values of solidarity, recognition, and initiative than on individual victory. Yet the tendency to caste and privilege, which corrupts the lofty ideal of pure merit with class dominance or despotism, accompanies ambition and excellence like a shadow.

4. Liberalism

The tilting balance of democratic and imperial values during this period still hangs upon the beam and pillar of liberal political philosophy, defined by limited government and individual rights.[20] Neither the acceptance of multiculturalism nor the renewed accent on community has eclipsed the individual's importance, which is evident in the anthem controversy and in the films.

Consider how Kaepernick's demonstration was framed as individual free speech, even by critics. His dissent was not coordinated with any organization. Only through the attention of the mass media did his action spread. In this way Kaepernick reflects the Black Lives Matter movement's eschewal of top-down institutional organization that it considered a root problem of social injustice. Horkheimer and Adorno's principle that all structures serve oppression informs that view. The proliferation of personal charitable foundations among athletes, including Kaepernick, also represents a liberal approach to public action. No one is hailing tax payment as the responsible contribution of a good citizen and the proper means to confront social problems, as a civic republican might do.

In governing by Twitter, Trump takes a more radical liberal step. He disregards bureaus and concentrates state power around himself, as if reducing public affairs to public opinion. The intimidating tone expressed in all-capital letters raises the specter of the despot who rules by fear and by fiat, violating even aristocratic codes of civility. His tweets amount to counter-protest outside the law and thus point toward the storming of the Capitol in 2021. While that extreme may not characterize the period as a whole, the underlying logic of individual autonomy (even with regard to truth itself being a matter of individual conviction) remains a major feature of the nation's ethos.

In sports movies, the absence of public officials and heroic speeches reflects America's liberal political basis. Among the six films we studied, the only positive public officials who appear are a newsreel Franklin Roosevelt and a few soldiers in the margins of A League of Their Own. Meanwhile, the antagonistic cops and federal agents in Ali make a strongly negative impression of the state. More importantly, none of the heroes in these six movies ascend to a position of authority or ally with institutions.[21] While these films all showcase populist heroes battling plutocrats and thus implicitly criticizing capitalism, no countervailing institutions or policies accompany them.[22] That absence may imply that the injustices of capitalism should be solved through individual moral judgment—a patently liberal approach.

A dearth of heroic speeches reflects a decline of civic virtue in contemporary American liberalism. Even characters who are not public officials can represent public policy through dramatic speech. No film in this study culminates in a monologue as a Frank Capra picture would have. They instead conclude with songs and picturesque imagery. While I have highlighted potential support for institutions in the architecture of the Rocky steps, The Natural's implicit call for a farm bill, or the general faith in the integrity of sporting competition, the lack of concrete officials or words indicates a competing liberal current. Exceptions in the genre are films with coaches as protagonists, notably Nick Nolte in Blue Chips (1994) and Samuel L. Jackson in Coach Carter (2005), that revive the climactic monologue. Fittingly, those films center on public schools.[23]

Accelerated by national scandals over the Vietnam War and surveillance at Watergate, the declining faith in civic institutions is a significant regression from midcentury that has received less attention from film critics. Political theorists from Arendt to Jan-Werner Müller underline the importance of civic institutions and the threat posed by radical movements (lately under the banner of "populism").[24] Sports movies affirm a collective spirit that constitutes the basis for republican government, but the themes of multiculturalism and community do not seem to translate into any foundational policy changes since the 1960s. The absence of public office in this comedic Hollywood genre may indicate the precarity of democratic reform.[25]

5. Civil Religion

Kaepernick's dissent from public etiquette sparked a firestorm. Despite American culture's ubiquitous romantic refrains to break the mold and embrace personal freedom, his opponents drew the line at a ceremony they consider sacrosanct. Had Kaepernick criticized racism and injustice in a poem, few would have claimed the same offense. Feelings about ceremonies and icons evidently hold sacred importance for the nation. Modern society may live in a disenchanted world dominated by markets and competing interests, but that disenchantment only amplifies the stakes for meaning in the few places the transcendent is evoked and performed publicly. My premise that civil religion is a necessary part of democracy challenges the dominant critical tradition and recuperates an important role for popular movies.

Philip Gorski asserts that oligarchy and the culture wars in the United States have caused the decay of the nation's defining myth—the American dream. He depicts civil religion in America as a middle ground between radical secularism and religious nationalism. That vital center of "prophetic republicanism" combines a philosophy of an enlightened republic with the prophetic vision of communal evolution.[26] Gorski writes:

> The secular Left champions a version of American history that is true but uninspiring, a tale of victims without any heroes, while the Religious Right prefers one that is inspiring but untrue, a tale of heroes that leaves out the victims. Obviously what is needed is a version that is true *and* inspiring, one that includes the victims as well as the heroes and is critical but hopeful.[27]

Kaepernick's evolution from sitting to kneeling finds that middle ground, in my eyes. Idly ignoring the ceremony abandons the prophetic dream of democracy while standing proudly ignores the historical and contemporary injustice minorities face in the country. Kneeling reverently combines shame for the sins the nation has committed against itself with the hope of redemption and progress.

But such a compromise demands wide adoption to be significant. Tolerating individual dissent cannot satisfy the need for meaning that transcends the individual (at least for a formal ceremony designed to display unity, unlike a festival). While critics of kneeling are right that solemnity has less strength than the feeling of pride, the real weakness is in disunity. Finding unity within difference is the deeper challenge. There is no holiday of national mourning for slavery or injustice. Until that shame is fully incorporated into the nation's story and into the American dream, not only through ceremonies but in the feelings people feel about the transcendent meaning of the nation, it cannot realize the dream of equality.

The sports movies we have examined do begin to repair the dream of a righteous republic that Gorski describes. They introduce minority heroes and victims, with a critical view of oligarchy countered by a more hopeful picture of community life and collective action. Prophetic hope is strongest in *Rocky* and *The Natural*, while the republican themes of community and civic virtue are key to *Slap Shot* and *White Men Can't Jump*; both currents appear equally strong in *A League of Their Own* and *Ali*. These films are neither explicitly Christian nor atheistic. *Bull Durham* (1988) best expresses the genre's civil religion in this period when narrator-protagonist Annie extols "the church of baseball" as her preferred national tradition.

The sacred feeling of civil religion is also evident in the richness of these Hollywood sports movies as artworks. Their intricate construction amounts to more than mere commercial products. Ideological formulae do not capture the unique qualities and coherence evident in *Rocky*'s carnivalesque inversions, the zany realism of *Slap Shot*, *The Natural*'s self-conscious fairy tale, the hyphenated satire of *White Men Can't Jump*, *A League of Their Own*'s collectivist structure, and *Ali*'s pivotal montage sequences. As a low but vital part of American society's practice of civil religion, Hollywood sports movies have more to say than any one book could contain.

To come full circle in closing, Muhammad Ali speaks to the American dream of a righteous republic in a statement he made on an official visit to the Soviet Union as an envoy for President Carter. Aware that his compliment of Brezhnev's peaceful welcome could be misconstrued as unpatriotic, Ali praised his home country in a way that did not excuse its imperfections. "I love America," he declared. "I love the food in America, the TV, the movies, the highways and cars, the flag, and the president. And I also love the truth."[28]

Notes

Chapter 1

1. Shirley Povich, "Ali to Get Red Carpet Tour Today," *Washington Post*, December 10, 1974, D1, D7, ProQuest Historical Newspapers.
2. Dave Brady, "Ali Hits It Off with President, Says He'd Like Job," *Washington Post*, December 11, 1974, E1, E9, ProQuest Historical Newspapers.
3. In 1974 Toni Morrison also edited a scrapbook-like anthology titled *The Black Book* which won a National Book Award. It presents a wide range of historical black experience with a richness and cultural consciousness similar to Ali's autobiography. The Nation of Islam (NOI) adopted mainstream reforms following Elijah Muhammad's death in early 1975, seemingly in parallel with Ali's public redemption. A longtime writer for the NOI, Richard Durham, co-authored the autobiography. In the 1980s Louis Farrakhan led a splinter group that reclaimed the NOI name while the reform wing, led by Elijah's son, Warith Deen Mohammad, took the name American Muslim Mission and eventually the American Society of Muslims.
4. Thomas Cripps argues that the success of Wolper Productions' television adaptation of *Roots* was driven more by the scarcity of Black subjects in the medium than the cultural integrity of the work. See Thomas Cripps, *Black Film as Genre* (Bloomington, IN: Indiana University Press, 1993), chapter 2, https://publish.iupress.indiana.edu/projects/black-film-as-genre.
5. One reviewer predicted, "*The Greatest*, like the new Muhammad Ali candy bar, will most certainly do tremendous box office." But his disparaging appraisal of the film's quality proved more apt. The movie did so poorly at the box office that figures are scarcely documented. D. G., review of *The Greatest*, *Cinéaste* 8, no. 2 (1977): 60.
6. Given that public discourse about a genre signals its salience, Sarris's article is significant. Andrew Sarris, "Why Sports Movies Don't Work," *Film Comment* 16, no. 6 (Nov./Dec. 1980): 49–53. Scholars well versed in pragmatics remind us that genre ultimately exists in the expectations of the culture and not in the texts themselves. See Rick Altman, *Film/Genre* (London: BFI, 1999), and see Jason Mittell, *Genre and Television: From Cop Shows to Cartoons in American Culture* (New York: Routledge, 2004).
7. Gunn was an outspoken critic of racism in Hollywood. Nicholas Forster, "'Improvisational Jamming': The Process and Production of *Personal Problems*," *Metrograph Edition*, March 29, 2018. http://metrograph.com/edition/article/58/improvisational-jamming-the-proc ess-and-production-of-personal-problems. See also the two notes after next.
8. In June 1985, *Washington Post* columnist Richard Cohen criticized the reactionary element common to *Rambo* and Reagan's intervention in Nicaragua. A month later, during a hostage crisis in Lebanon, Reagan said, "Boy, I'm glad I saw *Rambo* last night. Now I know what to do next." Stallone's appearance at a state dinner later that year confirmed the proximity of the two figures. In fact, they had lived in the same "dependably Republican" Pacific Palisades neighborhood since 1980. Richard Cohen, "Next: Rambo Goes to Nicaragua?," *Washington Post*, June 4, 1985, A17; Bernard Weinraub, "Reagan Hails

Move," *New York Times*, July 1, 1985, A1; Jacqueline Trescott and Donnie Radcliffe, "White House Starscape: Stallone, Welch and Fox Brighten Reagan's Dinner for Singapore's Lee," *Washington Post*, October 9, 1985, B1; Lou Cannon, "Reagan Promises to Heal and Unify," *Washington Post*, November 5, 1980, A17.

9. The lack of representation on television first sparked protest. See Ed Guerrero, *Framing Blackness: The African American Image in Film* (Philadelphia: Temple University Press, 1993), 120.

10. "After being fired off of *The Greatest*, Gunn was convinced that the Ali biopic could very well be the last black-focused film made in Hollywood," writes Keith Corson in *Trying to Get Over: African-American Directors after Blaxploitation, 1977–1986* (University of Texas Press, 2016), 8. Bill Gunn wrote a veiled account of his experience as a screenwriter in Hollywood in his novel *Rhinestone Sharecropping* (New York: I. Reed Books, 1981).

11. Pippin states, "The great Hollywood Westerns present in a recognizably mythic form dimensions of an American self-understanding of great relevance to the question of the nature of the political in the American imaginary." The sports movie trades the mythic past and quasi-divine heroes for the myth of the American dream expressed in more ordinary settings. Robert B. Pippin, *Hollywood Westerns and American Myth: The Importance of Howard Hawks and John Ford for Political Philosophy* (New Haven, CT: Yale University Press, 2012), 141.

12. Science fiction and fantasy genres replaced the western, as many have pointed out, because the mythic settings avoid the explicit racism and settler colonialism of an Old West where the Indian and the Mexican typically played foil to the White Euro settler protagonists. Yet a setting of space and alien villains may convey the same caste-like social dynamic in a more hidden way. For instance, see Robert T. Tally, Jr., "Let Us Now Praise Famous Orcs: Simple Humanity in Tolkien's Inhuman Creatures," *Mythlore* 29, no. 1/2 (Fall/Winter 2010): 17–28, https://dc.swosu.edu/mythlore/vol29/iss1/3.

13. The genre is not the primary object of my study. On that subject, see the bibliography in Bruce Babington, *The Sports Film: Games People Play*, Short Cuts (New York: Wallflower, 2014). Other studies of the genre will also be cited later in this chapter and in following chapters where relevant.

14. Seán Crosson, *Sport and Film* (London: Routledge, 2013), 66.

15. Jameson argues that mass culture manipulates the public through a mechanism "which strategically arouses fantasy content within careful symbolic containment structures which defuse it, gratifying intolerable, unrealizable, properly imperishable desires only to the degree to which they can again be laid to rest." His theory of this utopian character develops the Frankfurt School theory discussed later in this chapter. Frederic Jameson, "Reification and Utopia in Mass Culture," *Social Text* 1 (1979): 141.

16. Baker also directs criticism at the NBA and cites Henry Louis Gates Jr.'s *New Yorker* essay "Net Worth," published June 1, 1998. Quotation from Stuart Hall, "What Is This 'Black' in Black Popular Culture?," in *Black Popular Culture*, ed. Gina Dent (Seattle: Bay Press, 1992), 23. Aaron Baker, *Contesting Identities: Sports in American Film* (Urbana: University of Illinois Press, 2003), 13, 30–31.

17. Robin Wood, *Hollywood from Vietnam to Reagan*, rev. ed. (1986; New York: Columbia University Press, 2003), 211.

18. See Martin Jay, *The Dialectical Imagination: A History of the Frankfurt School and the Institute of Social Research, 1923–1950* (Berkeley: University of California Press, 1996);

and Phil Slater, *Origin and Significance of the Frankfurt School: A Marxist Perspective* (London: Routledge, 2020).

19. Habermas argues that modernity has corroded the private sphere of family life, whose autonomy cultivated free debate over literature and politics; consumer culture obviates critical discussion by favoring spectacle. In a chapter entitled "From a Culture-Debating to a Culture-Consuming Public" Habermas writes, "Radio, film, and television by degrees reduce to a minimum the distance that a reader is forced to maintain toward the printed letter—a distance that required the privacy of the appropriation as much as it made possible the publicity of a rational-critical exchange about what had been read." Jürgen Habermas, *The Structural Transformation of the Public Sphere*, trans. Thomas Burger and Frederick Lawrence (Cambridge, MA: MIT Press, 1991), 170.

20. The original 1968 editorial reads, "*Tout film est politique*, dans la mesure où déterminé par l'idéologie donnée qui le fabrique." Jean-Louis Comolli and Jean Narboni, "Cinéma/Idéologie/Critique (I)," *Cahiers du Cinéma*, no. 216 (October 1969): 12. On its influential English publication and for a new translation, see Jean-Louis Comolli, *Cinema against Spectacle: Technique and Ideology Revisited*, trans. and ed. Daniel Fairfax (Amsterdam: Amsterdam University Press, 2015), 253, http://library.oapen.org/handle/20.500.12657/32378. The 1971 English translation reads, "*Every film is political*, inasmuch as it is determined by the ideology which produces it." Jean-Luc [*sic*] Comolli and Paul [*sic*] Narboni, "Cinema/Ideology/Criticism," trans. Susan Bennett, *Screen* 12, no. 1 (Spring 1971): 30, https://doi.org/10.1093/screen/12.1.27.

21. Theodor Adorno, "Culture Industry Reconsidered," trans. Anson G. Rabinbach, *New German Critique*, no. 6 (Autumn 1975): 14.

22. Felski illustrates the paradoxical quality of an anti-normative norm and a dogma of skepticism that define dialectical critique. She calls for a wider range of affective styles and modes of argument but cautions against a retreat to belletrism. Rita Felski, *The Limits of Critique* (University of Chicago Press, 2015). One origin point for this wave was Bruno Latour, "Why Has Critique Run out of Steam? From Matters of Fact to Matters of Concern," *Critical Inquiry* 30, no. 2 (Winter 2004): 225–248, https://doi.org/10.1086/421123.

23. "The scholarly turn, for all its explicit politicization, has left us with a discipline of cultural analysis alone," North writes. "It ought to be clear that analyzing culture through a political lens only takes one so far; a coherent body of techniques and methods by which to change that culture would be something else entirely." His solution appears to be to extend the scholarly method from analysis to application. While I agree that contemplative practice of scholarship is a crucial limitation, I argue that an overly narrow conception of the political is a more fundamental issue. Joseph North, *Literary Criticism: A Concise Political History* (Cambridge, MA: Harvard University Press, 2017), 12.

24. See Bruce Robbins, "Fashion Conscious Phenomenon," review of *Critique and Postcritique*, ed. Elizabeth S. Anker and Rita Felski, in *American Book Review* 38, no. 5 (July/August 2017): 5–6, https://doi.org/10.1353/abr.2017.0078. See also Felski, *Limits of Critique*, 12.

25. Known as neoformalism or the Wisconsin School, their challenge to *Screen* theory seemed enflamed by the culture wars of the 1980s and 1990s. See Noël Carroll, *Mystifying Movies: Fads and Fallacies in Contemporary Film Theory* (New York: Columbia University Press, 1988) and David Bordwell and Noël Carroll, eds., *Post-Theory: Reconstructing Film Studies* (Madison: University of Wisconsin Press, 1996).

26. Villa contrasts Arendt's general approach to totalitarianism with Adorno's more particular, causal and historical narrative. Dana Villa, "Genealogies of Total Domination: Arendt, Adorno, and Auschwitz," in "Arendt, Adorno, New York, and Los Angeles," special issue, *New German Critique* 100 (Winter 2007): 1–45, https://www.jstor.org/stable/27669

186. Prager summarizes the competing political sociologies: "Where Durkheim sees democracy influencing all social spheres, Weber identifies democracy as a narrow enclave of social life." Jeffrey Prager, "Moral Integration and Political Inclusion: A Comparison of Durkheim's and Weber's Theories of Democracy," in "Durkheim Lives!," special issue, *Social Forces* 59, no. 4 (June 1981): 920, https://doi.org/10.2307/2577974.

27. Adorno, "Culture Industry Reconsidered," 19.

28. Adorno, 19.

29. They employ *culture* in the sense of fine art and letters. Franz Boas's appropriation of the term in anthropology and its ubiquitous application hence obscured the older sense. "In our drafts we spoke of *mass culture*," Adorno explains. "We replaced that expression with *culture industry* in order to exclude from the outset the interpretation agreeable to its advocates: that it is a matter of something like a culture that arises spontaneously from the masses themselves, the contemporary form of popular art." Adorno, 12.

30. The critical theorists lament the decline of classical tragedy: "Tragedy is leveled down to the threat to destroy anyone who does not conform, whereas its paradoxical meaning once lay in hopeless resistance to mythical threat." The postmodern critics echo Nietzsche, who advocated for wild Dionysian energy against the Apollonian order in *The Birth of Tragedy*. They transpose his picture to the instrumental economic order that rules the culture industry. Max Horkheimer and Theodor W. Adorno, *Dialectic of Enlightenment*, trans. Edmund Jephcott (1944; Stanford, CA: Stanford University Press, 2002), 122.

31. Horkheimer and Adorno, 95, 106, 129.

32. Horkheimer and Adorno, 100.

33. With a whiff of misogyny Horkheimer and Adorno summarize the basic "recipe" of mass drama: "The housewife's description of the recipe for drama as 'getting into trouble and out again' encompasses the whole of mass culture." Horkheimer and Adorno, 123.

34. Horkheimer and Adorno, 109.

35. Noël Carroll dismantles Adorno's claim that formula inhibits the free play of the viewer's imagination, pointing first to the conventional forms of the sonnet or the sonata rondo. Adorno mistakenly relies on Kant's analysis of *free beauty*. It concentrates on the viewer's response, especially to nature, and is therefore ill-suited for Adorno's judgment of all art objects. Carroll instead employs Kant's account of *dependent beauty* to analyze what he terms *mass art*. The American philosopher shows that artworks specifically designed for mass access may have familiar structures (crucial for their mass accessibility) but that these conventions do not preclude finer forms of play. Noël Carroll, *A Philosophy of Mass Art* (New York: Oxford University Press, 1998), 104–106, 174.

36. Foucault contrasts biopower to sovereign power exercised through law. See Michel Foucault, *Il faut défendre la société: cours au Collège de France, 1975–1976* ["Society Must Be Defended": Lectures at the Collège de France, 1975–1976] (Paris: Seuil, 1997).

37. Horkheimer and Adorno, *Dialectic of Enlightenment*, 16.

38. Horkheimer and Adorno, 17. Lest their philosophy be considered exclusively Jewish, recall that iconoclasm is central to the Enlightenment. For instance, Bacon described the scientific quest for truth as a courageous struggle against "idols of the human mind." Quoted

in Charles Taylor, *Hegel* (Cambridge: Cambridge University Press, 1975), 4. See also Martin Jay, *Downcast Eyes: The Denigration of Vision in Twentieth-Century French Thought* (Berkeley: University of California Press, 1993).

39. Horkheimer and Adorno, 18. Note that the kind of restraint that merely contemplates the difference between image and truth is nowhere to be found in their vehement criticism of the culture industry.

40. In the introductory chapter to *Hegel*, Charles Taylor describes this Romantic current centered on Herder and Fichte, and shows how Hegel combines their expressive theory with Kant's moral autonomy.

41. Pippin explains how Adorno's theory is weakened by his misunderstanding of Hegel. Both thinkers nonetheless agree that art embodies spirit's self-negation. Pippin is also sympathetic to "the genuine and distinctive aesthetic autonomy that Adorno is rightly worried about in an age of consumption frenzy and the culture industry." Robert B. Pippin, "Adorno, Aesthetic Negativity, and the Problem of Idealism," in *Philosophy by Other Means: The Arts in Philosophy and Philosophy in the Arts* (Chicago: University of Chicago Press, 2021), 158.

42. Hannah Arendt, *The Human Condition* (Chicago: University of Chicago Press, 1958), 7.

43. Arendt's statement suggests that pure autonomy is meaningless because it does not involve communication. Arendt, 4.

44. Arendt, 8.

45. Hannah Arendt, *On Revolution* (London: Faber and Faber, 1963), 116.

46. It appears to me that the higher human endeavors of pleasure, contemplation, and action correspond to beauty, truth, and goodness. Adorno exemplifies the dominant focus of modernist esthetics, on truth and contemplation, owing to the subjectivity of pleasure and to moral authority's intolerance for free play.

47. Arendt might seem to support a "great man" approach to history, criticized for its antidemocratic and sexist bent. Yet she distinguishes the action and the agent who initiates it from an actor totally responsible for authoring an event. For further discussion of this distinction, see the chapter on *Ali*.

48. She also notes that Marx and Nietzsche reverse the hierarchal order by elevating labor. Although labor, work, and action together comprise *la vita activa* in her system, I will use the term as a synonym for action to insist on the contrast with contemplation. Arendt, *Human Condition*, 17.

49. Patterson shows that the very conception of freedom developed in contradistinction to slavery, notably in Ancient Greece, and he shows how different practices of slavery correspond to these three types of freedom. Orlando Patterson, *Freedom: Freedom in the Making of Western Culture* (New York: Basic, 1991), 3.

50. Quentin Skinner and Philip Pettit developed the theory of non-domination. Other guiding principles of republicanism include popular sovereignty, the common good, civic virtue, widespread political participation, and deliberation. Karma Nabulsi and Stuart White, eds., *Radical Republicanism: Recovering the Tradition's Popular Heritage* (New York: Oxford University Press, 2020), 2.

51. Among political philosophers since the 1940s, *liberalism* had come to denote primarily a negative conception of freedom as non-interference and minimalist models of the state as a neutral instrument amid competing interests. For a detailed history see Helena Rosenblatt, *The Lost History of Liberalism: From Ancient Rome to the Twenty-First Century* (Princeton, NJ: Princeton University Press, 2019).

52. Arendt, *On Revolution*, 115.

53. Philip Gorski confirms this rather civic sense of the word *happiness* among the founding fathers. Philip Gorski, *American Covenant: A History of Civil Religion from the Puritans to the Present* (Princeton, NJ: Princeton University Press, 2017), 145.

54. *Happiness* derives from *hap*, which connotes luck, chance, and fortune—corresponding to the spontaneous character of natality underlined by Arendt. *New Oxford American Dictionary* (New York: Oxford University Press, 2017), s.v. "happiness."

55. Charles Louis de Secondat, Baron de Montesquieu, *The Complete Works of M. de Montesquieu*, vol. 1, *The Spirit of Laws*, unnamed translator (London: T. Evans, 1777), ch. 3, 53. https://oll.libertyfund.org/titles/montesquieu-complete-works-vol-1-the-spirit-of-laws.

56. The philosophies of Hannah Arendt and Charles Taylor sparked a revival of the republican tradition in late the twentieth century. See Iseult Honohan, *Civic Republicanism* (London: Routledge, 2002).

57. See §6, "The Rise of the Social," in Arendt, *Human Condition*, 38–49.

58. Taylor, *Hegel*, 541.

59. Critique must traverse from autonomous contemplation to public speech or deed to become significant. For a statistical approach to the state as a neutral median among competing interests, critique moves the needle no differently than any particular claim to a bigger slice of the pie. The civic republican approach to the public sphere through meaning, rather than as a mathematical system, envisions how righteous criticism can change the public state of affairs generally. See the later section of this chapter, on the civil sphere, for further discussion.

60. *The Human Condition* opens with a surprising criticism of space exploration occasioned by Sputnik's launch. She reminds us that science adopts a position of observation from infinite distance to contemplate the cosmos as a mechanical system ruled by necessary laws. Abandoning the earth jeopardizes human freedom, predicated on the earth's fulfillment of our animal needs and on the free potential of people to gather. Perhaps the future invention of fantastical spaceships and life-support systems we see in the movies will prove Arendt wrong. In any case, she is right to caution against a scientific worldview that already abandons the earth.

61. On Marx's Romantic heritage see Taylor, *Hegel*, 548.

62. On the social sciences see Ian Hacking, *The Taming of Chance* (Cambridge, UK: Cambridge University Press, 1990), the final chapter of which covers American philosopher and scientist Charles Peirce, who posits the reality of chance in nature and in logic. I will develop these ideas and their implications for contemporary criticism in a future work.

63. Critical theory's name indicates a political engagement beyond what the Frankfurt School perceived as traditional philosophy's focus on abstractions and positivism's uncritical faith in instrumental thought and empirical science.

64. Wilhelm von Humboldt, *The Limits of State Action*, ed. J. W. Burrow (Cambridge: Cambridge University Press, 1969), 19. See also W. H. Bruford, *The German Tradition of Self-Cultivation: "Bildung" from Humboldt to Thomas Mann* (Cambridge: Cambridge University Press, 1975). I thank Aleksandar Stevic for bringing this background to my attention.

65. See Taylor, *Hegel*, 537.

66. Horkheimer and Adorno, *Dialectic of Enlightenment*, 105.

67. Georg Wilhelm Friedrich Hegel, *The Phenomenology of the Spirit*, trans. James B. Baillie, in *The Philosophy of Hegel*, ed. Carl J. Friendrich (New York: Modern Library, 1954), 399.

68. Hegel, *Phenomenology*, 402.

69. Hegel, 403.

70. Adorno misunderstands "pure thinking" in Hegel to mean always conceiving of a world structured by substances and properties. Pippin clarifies that pure thinking only applies to formal logic and that Hegel's approach to empirical thinking does account for experience. Pippin, "Adorno," 154.

71. See Pippin, 144.

72. A strong case for the importance of pleasure to democratic politics, based on an idea of ecstatic ritual derived from Durkheim, is made by Barbara Ehrenreich, *Dancing in the Streets: A History of Collective Joy* (New York: Holt, 2007).

73. Heidegger and Dewey revive the esthetics of nature with their interest in earth and in experience. Arendt would seem to follow in their line, although she does not debate the question of art.

74. Taylor notes the influence of Protestantism and Pietism on German Idealism, especially in reaction to the disenchanted character of the French Enlightenment and the 1789 revolution. Taylor, *Hegel*, 11.

75. Arendt, *Human Condition*, 15.

76. Arendt distinguishes the deathly state of eternity from immortality, the human goal of *vita activa*, that is carried out through cultural memory. She describes immortality as "deathless life on earth." Arendt, 18, 20.

77. European Christians also associate divinity with the color white, even as an invisible clarity. See Richard Dyer, "White Death," in *White* (London: Routledge, 1997), 207–223.

78. Horkheimer and Adorno, *Dialectic of Enlightenment*, 18.

79. Although Horkheimer and Adorno describe dialectic as conflict and resistance, in line with Hegel's combat metaphor for self-consciousness, I have not found that physical struggle serves as anything more than a metaphor in their understanding of dialectic. In contrast, their contemporary Siegfried Kracauer explored the externality and sensation of movies as a means to social change. He sees democratic potential in the "cult of distraction" offered by mass entertainment. Alexander Kluge, Oskar Negt, and Miriam Hansen develop this line of thinking further. Siegfried Kracauer, *The Mass Ornament: Weimar Essays*, ed. Thomas Y. Levin (Cambridge, MA: Harvard University Press, 1995).

80. Of course I do not mean to imply that critique is fundamentally European. In fact, the ideal of contemplation that informed Plato's philosopher-king presumably originated in Ancient Egypt. See Ian Rutherford, ed., *Greco-Egyptian Interactions: Literature, Translation, and Culture, 500 BCE–300 CE* (London: Oxford University Press, 2016).

81. In fact, critical race theory supports the idea that critique itself is not necessarily neutral. The movement criticizes laws that purport to be neutral, abstract, and color-blind yet are used to racist ends. For further consideration see the discussion of "sham neutrality" in the chapter on *White Men Can't Jump*. Racism and antiracism are also discussed at various points throughout the study. Kimberlé Crenshaw et al., eds., *Critical Race Theory: The Key Writings That Formed the Movement* (New York: The New Press, 1995).

82. Horkheimer and Adorno, *Dialectic of Enlightenment*, 17–18.

83. They write, "With the concept of determinate negation Hegel gave prominence to an element which distinguishes enlightenment from the positivist decay to which he consigned

it. However, by finally postulating the known result of the whole process of negation, totality in the system and in history, as the absolute, he violated the prohibition and himself succumbed to mythology." Positivism was a nineteenth-century intellectual movement led by Auguste Comte, among others. Hegel points out that things themselves are riven with contradictions when considered closely. Dialectic is a logical process for resolving those conflicts, in part. More radically, he posits that contradiction is constitutive of the absolute, so the movement and process of dialectic are interminable. Horkheimer and Adorno, 18.

84. Compare the anarchist tendency in critical theory to the overlap between left and right in Foucault. See Daniel Zamora and Michael C. Behrent, eds., *Foucault and Neoliberalism* (Cambridge, UK: Polity Press, 2016). For another example of how libertarian politics and critical theory converge, see the "story of the bohemian cultural style's trajectory from adversarial to hegemonic" told by Thomas Frank, *The Conquest of Cool: Business Culture, Counterculture, and the Rise of Hip Consumerism* (Chicago: University of Chicago, 1998), 8.

85. Charles Peirce criticizes Cartesian doubt from an interesting perspective. See Robert G. Meyers, "Peirce on Cartesian Doubt," *Transactions of the Charles S. Peirce Society* 3, no. 1 (1967): 13–23, http://www.jstor.org/stable/40319490.

86. At its vulgar limit such engagement merely raises awareness about politics without taking action. When contemplated from the fathoms of pure critique, ideology and counter-ideology seem to differ primarily in their esthetic qualities.

87. The parallel development of statistics and new means of social control illustrates how non-order can become another kind of order. Unlike stochastic movement in physical systems, humans respond to the perception of a norm that always orders a group. Hacking, *Taming of Chance*, 2.

88. Arendt illustrates the danger of ideology replacing the actual world as a ground for truth in a critique of totalitarianism that spans both Nazi and Bolshevik movements. Hannah Arendt, *The Origins of Totalitarianism* (New York: Harcourt, Brace, 1951), 407.

89. Because one must hold their judgment up against a community sense, this epistemology avoids the subjective private condition of contemplation. Conservative inertia is overcome through what Arendt calls action. Consider Peirce's development of Kantian critical philosophy and the "old Scotch" philosophy of common sense to create a doctrine of critical common sense distinguished by the principle that indubitable beliefs are vague. Charles Sanders Peirce, "Survey of Pragmaticism," in *Collected Papers of Charles Sanders Peirce*, ed. Charles Hartshorne and Paul Weiss (Cambridge, MA: Belknap Press of Harvard University Press, 1965), vol. 5, para. 505–525. Hereafter short references to page numbers in this edition are given on this model: *CP* 5.505–525.

90. Louis Althusser's description of ideological state apparatuses expands upon this idea of control, as hinted at by Jephcott's translation here. Horkheimer and Adorno, *Dialectic of Enlightenment*, 98.

91. Horkheimer and Adorno, 94.

92. Core sectors of heavy manufacturing, energy, and finance drive the system: "Compared to them the culture monopolies are weak and dependent." Horkheimer and Adorno, 96.

93. Marx recognizes that work creates a surplus value, but the owner class profits more in the labor market as the larger players have an advantage in any market. For a liberal perspective see John Kenneth Galbraith, *American Capitalism: The Concept of Countervailing*

Power, in *The Affluent Society and Other Writings, 1952–1967* (New York: Library of America, 2010). See also Thomas Piketty, *Capital in the Twenty-First Century*, trans. Arthur Goldhammer (2013; Cambridge, MA: Harvard University Press, 2014).

94. For a social history see Garth Jowett, *Film: The Democratic Art* (Boston: Little, Brown and Co., 1976).

95. See Max Horkheimer, "Society and Reason," lecture 1, Max Horkheimer Archive, Frankfurt, quoted in James Schmidt, "The 'Eclipse of Reason' and the End of the Frankfurt School in America," *New German Critique* 100 (Winter 2007): 63, https://www.jstor.org/stable/27669187.

96. They develop this picture from Marx and Engels's description of the German ideology. Horkheimer and Adorno, *Dialectic of Enlightenment*, 117.

97. They reflect on how the star collapses the distinction between ideal and commoner, a duality later remarked upon in Richard Dyer, *Stars* (London: British Film Institute, 1979). Horkheimer and Adorno, 135–136.

98. Horkheimer and Adorno, 120.

99. Arendt, *Human Condition*, 42.

100. Horkheimer and Adorno seem to share Max Weber's view of democracy as a narrow enclave of resistance. Weber believes "democracy can only impede individual subordination to the collective and coercive structures of modern life," as Prager describes it. He labels Weber's a "formal theory" of democracy that resembles, to me, neutral liberalism's theory of the state as a mediator among various forces. These views contrast with Durkheim's broader view of democracy that surfaces in the competing political theories of Arendt, Alexander, and the civic republicans discussed in the next section. Prager, "Moral Integration," 920.

101. Camus's motto for affirmative negation is "Je me révolte, donc nous sommes." He revises Descartes's motto "I think, therefore I am" into "I revolt, therefore we are." It implies a positive, collective thrust of humanity upon which dialectic negation is predicated. Albert Camus, *L'Homme révolté* (Paris: Gallimard, 1951).

102. Jeffrey C. Alexander, *The Civil Sphere* (New York: Oxford University Press, 2006), 4.

103. Prager describes how Durkheim "sees in democracy a dynamic political force that can produce a society of free individuals morally regulated through the state." He situates both Weber and Durkheim in the liberal tradition, but I want to highlight the latter's republican emphasis on the collective and the state. One wonders if Durkheim reflects the context of France's third republic in contrast to the constitutional monarchy of Prussia and the more federated German Empire where Weber resided. Prager, "Moral Integration," 920.

104. Alexander, *Civil Sphere*, 3.

105. A conservative tendency to favor "primordial" qualities restrains change. Jeffrey Alexander, *The Dark Side of Modernity* (Cambridge, UK: Polity, 2013), 126.

106. Alexander, *Dark Side*, 114.

107. Here Arendt seems to diverge sharply from Foucault and others who insist on material control as the source of power. Arendt, *Human Condition*, 200.

108. Arendt explicates Montesquieu and Kant here, and later explains totalitarianism as precisely a lack of principle of action, and of freedom, because the movement of Nature or History predominates. She sees ideology as the substitute for a principle of action. Hannah Arendt, "On the Nature of Totalitarianism: An Essay in Understanding," in *Essays in Understanding: 1930–1954* (New York: Harcourt Brace, 1994), 335.

109. Montesquieu, *De l'esprit des lois* [The Spirit of the Laws], in vol. 2 of *Œuvres complètes*, ed. Roger Caillois (1748; Paris: Bibliothèque de la Pléiade, 1951).

110. Arendt explains that the totalitarian regime must stalk "potential enemies" once overt opposition has been eliminated. "Simply because of their capacity to think, human beings are suspects by definition, and this suspicion cannot be diverted by exemplary behavior, for the human capacity to think is also a capacity to change one's mind," she writes. "Mutual suspicion, therefore, permeates all social relationships in totalitarian countries and creates an all-pervasive atmosphere even outside the special purview of the secret police." She details how the official government becomes a façade in totalitarian regimes, whose ambition is global domination. The nucleus of power resides with the secret police and the leader, not in state bureaucracy. This picture contradicts libertarian images of the slippery slope from the social welfare state to Big Brother. Arendt, *Origins of Totalitarianism*, 401, 407.

111. To understand power and the world as appearance challenges the intuitive grasp of both as matter. But consider that the matter of people gathering is always mediated by appearance. Given that one cannot physically touch more than a few people simultaneously, only through vision, sound, and language does the presence of a crowd appear to us. The public realm itself therefore has a virtual quality that accounts for symbolic power. For instance, the effervescence of the hero seems to collapse the crowd's power onto one charismatic figure. Arendt, *Human Condition*, 200.

112. Alexander, *Civil Sphere*, 4.

113. Polls merely grasp at the reality of public opinion (in the full understanding of *reality*) Ehrat explains. And reports on polls feed back into the chorus of the news media, of course. Johannes Ehrat, *Power of Scandal: Semiotic and Pragmatic in Mass Media* (Toronto: University of Toronto Press, 2011), ix.

114. Max Weber describes charisma as an extraordinary quality with social resonance: "a certain quality of an individual personality by virtue of which he is set apart from ordinary men and treated as endowed with supernatural, superhuman, or at least specifically exceptional qualities." Max Weber, *On Charisma and Institution Building: Selected Papers*, ed. S. N. Eisenstadt (Chicago: University of Chicago Press, 1968), xviii, 329.

115. The nature of reality was a matter of intense debate between scholastic logicians, realists, and nominalists, which Charles Peirce explains through the question "Are universals real?" From an idealist and phenomenalist point of view, matter must also be experienced through appearance (sensation), but its reality is immanent. Charles S. Peirce, "Fraser's *The Works of George Berkeley*," in *The Essential Peirce*, vol. 1, *Selected Philosophical Writings (1867–1893)*, ed. Nathan Houser and Christian Kloesel (Bloomington, IN: Indiana University Press, 1992), 88.

116. Nietzsche's reflection that people need illusion also seems to support the view that common appearances form the basis of the public sphere, in a way. But Nietzsche sets art's illusion in opposition to truth in *The Birth of Tragedy*. Postmodern critics follow this binary logic in emphasizing art's function as negation and counter-enlightenment. Peirce avoids the binary of fact and fiction by arguing that possibility is a mode of being prior to the actuality of truth and falseness. Contingent knowledge converges with truth in the final opinion. See Peirce, "The Doctrine of Necessity Examined," *CP* 6.35–65.

117. Carey attributes the ritual view to the Chicago School, and similarities can also be seen with continental theorists such as Niklas Luhmann. The origins of the Chicago

School were in German sociology, so this parallel is not surprising. James W. Carey, *Communication as Culture: Essays on Media and Society* (New York: Routledge, 1992), 19.

118. Dialectic throws universality into question. Richard Rushton debates Michael Shapiro whose 1999 book *Cinematic Political Thought* uses Deleuze's concept of "uncommon sense." Rushton shows how postmodern theorists such as Althusser and Deleuze reject Kant's notion of common sense in an effort to imagine society without a subject. Rushton counters that "universalism is a goal worth aspiring to and that any politics worthy of being called a politics will stake a claim for the universality of its propositions." He argues that the deconstruction of subjectivity benefits primarily billionaires who are not likely revolutionaries, and he calls for an egalitarian collective centered on a subject: "To believe in one's subjectivity, even if that might entail being deceived about one's status as a subject, is a risk worth taking … for film studies and for democratic politics." Richard Rushton, *The Politics of Hollywood Cinema: Popular Film and Contemporary Political Theory* (New York: Palgrave, 2013), 6, 15.

119. She elaborates, "The objectivity of the world—its object- or thing-character—and the human condition supplement each other; because human existence is conditioned existence, it would be impossible without things, and things would be a heap of unrelated articles, a non-world, if they were not the conditioners of human existence." Arendt, *Human Condition*, 9.

120. Social movements also legitimize their competing authority through public opinion. Alexander details how twentieth-century social movements dramatize their urgent conflicts, such as Mao Zedong and the Chinese Communist Party's staging of economic exploitation or Martin Luther King Jr. and the Southern Christian Leadership Conference's nonviolent protests that put white racism on stage. Jeffrey Alexander, *The Drama of Social Life* (Cambridge: Polity, 2017).

121. Fraser proposes "transnational public powers" that would give teeth to opinion beyond national borders, effectively creating a level of institutions above the nation-state. But she admits that the nation-state endures, so a practical approach to democracy cannot ignore it. Nancy Fraser, "Transnationalizing the Public Sphere: On the Legitimacy and Efficacy of Public Opinion in a Post-Westphalian World," *Theory, Culture and Society* 24, no. 4 (2007): 7–8, emphasis in original.

122. Robert Bellah, "Civil Religion in America," *Daedalus* 96, no. 1 (Winter 1967): 1–21.

123. Even the paradoxical quality of liberal acceptance must be reciprocated to engender solidarity. Such apparent openness is conditional upon the other's reciprocal openness. If not reciprocated, a boundary is asserted by the other according to their primordial qualities, whereupon liberal acceptance transforms into mere subordination. Alexander describes multiculturalism as a pure form of reciprocal acceptance of the other's difference. See Alexander, *Civil Sphere*, 4.

124. Max Weber also supports the idea that charisma is not detached from the routine aspects of civic institutions. See S. N. Eisenstadt, introduction to *On Charisma*, by Max Weber, ix; and see Michael Billig, *Banal Nationalism* (London: Sage, 1995), 12–13.

125. One might also see an Augustinian tradition here. Recall his definition: "A people is an assemblage of reasonable beings bound together by a common agreement as to the objects of their love." Aurelius Augustine, *The City of God*, vol. 2, trans. Marcus Dods (Edinburgh, 1871; Project Gutenberg, 2014), bk. 19, ch. 24, https://www.gutenberg.org/files/45305/45305-h/45305-h.htm#Page_340. See Alexander, *Civil Sphere*, 450.

126. Alexander, *Drama*, 3.

127. Alexander's perspective should not be mistaken for religious proselytizing. The nature of religion is the complex matter in question here. Compare his Durkheimian picture of the civil religion to Charles Taylor's call for discovering a good that transcends human flourishing. Taylor's critique of modernity's "immanent frame" challenges the Enlightenment from a different angle than Horkheimer and Adorno, whose dialectic operates from within that frame. Charles Taylor, *A Secular Age* (Cambridge, MA: Harvard University Press, 2007), 5, 15–16.

128. Religion is a fundamental antagonist for Horkheimer and Adorno. They describe the Enlightenment project of demystification as criticism that annihilates myth. They do acknowledge that this process of annihilation nonetheless generates new myths and so constitutes an unending dialectical process. From the perspective of civil religion, critique constitutes (paradoxically) a key ritual for secular life. Horkheimer and Adorno, 7.

129. Gorski, *American Covenant*, 17.

130. See Lawrence R. Samuel, *The American Dream: A Cultural History* (Syracuse, NY: Syracuse University Press, 2012), and Carol Graham, *Happiness for All? Unequal Hopes and Lives in Pursuit of the American Dream* (Princeton, NJ: Princeton University Press, 2017).

131. Consider how the dream of public happiness has a grander recognition for individual action than economic exchange. An action significant to a community can be celebrated by everyone. The choice to pursue work is merely a matter of personal freedom; even compensation is treated as a private matter.

132. Jack Balkin develops an approach to constitutional law as an evolving project. By affirming the democratic ideal and revisable nature that established law in the United States, Balkin opens a progressive potential between revolution and retrogression. Jack M. Balkin, *Living Originalism* (Cambridge, MA: Harvard University Press, 2014).

133. The international dimension of the American dream is a complex matter not taken up here. But I dispute the claim that the American dream, as a symptom of nationalism, is necessarily imperialistic. Caspar Hirschi differentiates nationalism from imperialism. He locates the former's origin in Europe during the late middle ages where "multipolar" nations saw each other as peers, in contrast to older empires that egoistically considered themselves the only legitimate state. Caspar Hirschi, *The Origins of Nationalism: An Alternative History from Ancient Rome to Early Modern Germany* (Cambridge: Cambridge University Press, 2012).

134. Mark Dyerson, *Making the American Team: Sport, Culture, and the Olympic Experience* (Urbana: University of Illinois Press, 1998), 13, 2, respectively.

135. The chapter on *A League of Their Own* that follows will elaborate on the tensions between aristocracy and democracy in American culture. Montesquieu, *De l'esprit des lois*, 227.

136. "The Star-Spangled Banner" was first played during the World Series in 1918 and only sparingly until the 1940s, it appears. See Jonathan Fraser Light, *The Cultural Encyclopedia of Baseball* (Jefferson, NC: McFarland, 2005).

137. Although ritual evokes mystical cosmology and control, especially for Marxists, it is not too strong a term for a certain understanding of religion. Alexander prefers the term *performance* to *ritual* because it captures "the pragmatics, conflicts, fragmentations, and competing institutional powers that mark contemporary social life." He distinguishes rituals as more rare performances that fuse spectators with performers, fully melding the world of imagination with that of actuality. Alexander, *Drama*, 3.

138. Alexander agrees with Adorno that mass entertainment has replaced high culture in its regulative function and colonized popular folklore. Nevertheless, he does not see mass media as necessarily antidemocratic. The difference is that Adorno considers the conformist logic of the economic sphere to irreparably corrupt the aesthetic and cultural functions of culture industry. Alexander, *Civil Sphere*, 75, 78.

139. Aristotle, *Poetics*, 1451a36–1451b10. When he writes, "Poetry utters universal truths, history particular statements," the universal truth can be understood as a sacred ideal that unites a civil sphere. The objective nature of truth as both ultimate aim and actuality is a recurring theme in the philosophy of Charles Peirce. Aristotle, *Poetics*, trans. Anthony Kenny (New York: Oxford University Press, 2013), 28.

140. Reconsider Habermas's history of an epochal shift from a culture-debating literary public to a culture-consuming object of the culture industry. It is not a change in material medium from print that fosters free thought to spectacle that precludes it; instead, it is the culture of debate that gives print public life. From this perspective the erosion of the public sphere is the cause rather than the effect of mass alienation, and the material factors are better found in the architectural change of the theater (Wagner's and Zola's darkness—accompanied by sacred silence—and the reduction of lobbies) and in suburbanization, although the obscure environments of the back row of seats or the drive-in car seat bred their own subversion of that alienation. Adorno's condescension might erect a higher barrier to debate than spectacle. There is a danger of technological determinism in criticism of the culture industry.

141. Oral poetry is better thought of as a script than as concrete words; the oral information can be widely shared. Haun Saussy explains: "What is passed on and learned from poet to poet, if this is seen as occurring, is not the poem itself, a determinate series of words from beginning to end, but rather a recipe or a strategy for making a poem that will answer to such-and-such a description. Conversely, no particular rendition of a poem exhausts the possibilities of the poem's tradition." Haun Saussy, *The Ethnography of Rhythm: Orality and Its Technologies* (New York: Fordham University Press, 2016), 72.

142. Repetition does not eliminate playful difference for another reason that Gertrude Stein describes as the movement of living itself. In "Portraits and Repetition" she makes the case that pure repetition does not exist because people are living, so even the experience of the same artwork changes from moment to moment. "Is there repetition or is there insistence. I am inclined to believe there is no such thing as repetition," she declares. Her view contradicts the culture industry argument that formulas stupefy the audience, and it underlines the living variation of drama in the public sphere. Gertrude Stein, "Portraits and Repetition," in *Lectures in America* (New York: Random House, 1935), 166.

143. Stein also suggests that genre be understood as insistence rather than repetition of a formula. "Think about all the detective stories everybody reads. The kind of crime is the same, and the idea of the story is very often the same." Stein, "Portraits," 167.

144. Rancière focuses on the contradictory dimension between figuration and de-figuration. This kind of hermeneutics and his edification of exceptional films and filmmakers does not contradict the general idea of a culture industry, however. Jacques Rancière, *La Fable cinématographique* (Paris: Seuil, 2001).

145. See Philip Rosen, ed., *Narrative, Apparatus, Ideology: A Film Theory Reader* (New York: Columbia University Press, 1986).

146. Hall adheres to critical theory in assuming that the culture industry communicates a dominant code that represents hegemonic class interests—a point I disagree with. His revindication of the spectator's agency does support my approach to the civic screen and the civil sphere. Stuart Hall, "Encoding/Decoding," in *Culture, Media, Language* ed. Stuart Hall et al. (London: Hutchinson, 1980).

147. Joseph Campbell, *The Hero with a Thousand Faces* (Princeton, NJ: Princeton University Press, 1992), 28.

148. "There is a general distinction between fictions in which the hero becomes isolated from his society, and fictions in which he is incorporated into it. This distinction is expressed by the words 'tragic' and 'comic' when they refer to aspects of plot in general and not simply to forms of drama." Northrop Frye, *Anatomy of Criticism: Four Essays* (1957; New York: Atheneum, 1968), 35, 43.

149. MacDowell points out that the cliché of the dumb happy ending is an invention of critics more than the films themselves. James MacDowell, *Happy Endings in Hollywood Cinema: Cliché, Convention and the Final Couple* (Edinburgh: Edinburgh University Press, 2013), 191.

150. Horkheimer and Adorno, *Dialectic of Enlightenment*, 116–117. Critics at *Screen* argued further that the industry's social control extends to narrative form itself; for instance, Mulvey connects the protagonist's objective to the male desire for sexual dominance in sadism and the fetish. Laura Mulvey, "Visual Pleasure and Narrative Cinema," *Screen* 16, no. 3 (Autumn 1975): 6–18, https://doi.org/10.1093/screen/16.3.6.

151. In her pioneering study of Hollywood sports movies, Tudor argues that the sports hero is antithetical to multiculturalism. Drawing upon the theory of Althusser, Roland Barthes, and Richard Dyer, she claims that the traditional hero model corresponds to Joseph Campbell's theory. In my view, her approach shares Horkheimer and Adorno's overemphasis on autonomy. Deborah V. Tudor, *Hollywood's Vision of Team Sports: Heroes, Race, and Gender* (New York: Garland, 1997), 182.

152. Frye interprets Aristotle, who describes the relationship between hero and spectator in the more brute terms of social status or class. Relative power of action involves more subtle comparison and a more abstract theory. Frye, *Anatomy of Criticism*.

153. A leftist political motivation similar to the Frankfurt School led theorists of "Third Cinema" to stress the participation of viewers in filmmaking and the anti-colonial aspect of media. They recognize the political relationship of representation on screen to forms of government. "We have not gone deeply enough into developing a revolutionary theater, architecture, medicine, psychology, and cinema; into developing a culture *by and for us*," write Fernando Solanas and Octavio Getino in "Toward a Third Cinema," *Cinéaste* 4, no. 3 (Winter 1970–71): 2, http://www.jstor.org/stable/41685716.

154. The cycle of superhero movies that has dominated the American blockbuster scene in the 2000s appears to be a sign of despotism and monarchy if we compare these movies' heroes to myth and romance. However, the movies address the spectator as if they too had superpowers. Marvel's Avengers series, for instance, incorporates the viewer into the elite team. These fantasies therefore complicate the simple conclusion that demigod heroes correspond to authoritarian political meaning.

155. For an in-depth discussion of the hero's agency, which Arendt distinguishes from total authorship of an action, see the chapter on *Ali* (2001).

156. Arendt, *Human Condition*, 180.

157. Aaron Baker, as we have alluded to earlier, argues that conventional dramatic form is part of a conservative regime that includes racial hierarchy. Baker, *Contesting Identities*, 30. Manthia Diawara, for instance, argues that the Black spectator must resist the representation of conventional form. Manthia Diawara, "Black Spectatorship: Problems of Identification and Resistance," *Screen* 29, no. 4 (Autumn 1988): 66–79, https://doi.org/10.1093/screen/29.4.66.

158. Following Schleiermacher, Charles Peirce understands logic as a "normative science" alongside ethics and esthetics. Ethics ultimately assures the rightness of logical thought, through ideals of conduct predicated on the ultimate good, or *summum bonum*. The source of the good, in turn, is esthetics. Normative conceptions of the good arise out of play in the realm of pure possibility. There is no ultimate authority for what is good in itself—the admirable asserts itself. Peirce criticizes the Germans who invented the word *esthetics* for limiting the conception to taste and excluding emotion; he considers esthetics a matter of feeling more broadly conceived, centered on sentiment and *agape*. See Peirce, Introduction to "Basis of Pragmatism," *CP* 1.574. Peirce's philosophy seems to agree with Kant on the transcendent quality of esthetic judgment, if it arrives at that conclusion in another way. Arendt explored a similar interpretation of Kant that privileged the faculty of the imagination as the ultimate source of categories and appearance. See Jim Josefson, *Hannah Arendt's Aesthetic Politics: Freedom and the Beautiful* (New York: Palgrave, 2019).

159. A critical focus on the values represented in drama involves a virtue ethics rather than a consequentialist approach to moral judgment. Critics point out that consequentialism depends upon specifying the good and the bad *prior* to judging a particular act, and therefore tends to *a priori* judgment. Larry Alexander and Michael Moore, "Deontological Ethics," in *The Stanford Encyclopedia of Philosophy* (Winter 2016 edition), ed. Edward N. Zalta, https://plato.stanford.edu/archives/win2016/entries/ethics-deontological/.

160. Horkheimer and Adorno's extreme skepticism of the capitalist system might be taken as a mere rhetorical posture. Gunster argues that "their work consciously employed exaggeration as a technique to bring into bold relief the hidden authoritarian tendencies" of liberal capitalism, and that subsequent critics err in taking their description as empirical. Shane Gunster, "Revisiting the Culture Industry Thesis: Mass Culture and the Commodity Form," *Cultural Critique* 45 (Spring 2000): 41, http://www.jstor.org/stable/1354367.

Chapter 2

1. Sylvester Stallone, interviewed by Gary Arnold, "The 'Rocky' Road to the Big Time," *Washington Post*, November 24, 1976, B9.

2. Stallone, "The 'Rocky' Road," B9.

3. New primary delegate rules, introduced in the wake of the 1968 Democratic National Convention fiasco, allowed Carter's grassroots campaign to succeed in unprecedented fashion. "The people of this country want a fresh face, not one associated with a long series of mistakes made at the White House and on Capitol Hill," Carter would say. Quoted in Julian E. Zelizer, "How Jimmy Carter Revolutionized the Iowa Caucuses," *The Atlantic*, January 25, 2016.

4. Black American voters proved crucial to his campaign. Carter would not initiate any major civil rights measure, but he enforced existing ones much more strongly than his Republican predecessors. Scholars assessing his civil rights record note his exemplary

appointment of minorities to public employment and the judiciary, as well as the First Lady Rosalynn Carter's support of the Equal Rights Amendment. However, the issue of civil rights was not a high priority during his tenure. Carter, quoted in *President Carter* (Washington: Congressional Quarterly, April 1977), 6. See also Hugh Davis Graham, "Civil Rights Policy in the Carter Era," in *The Carter Presidency: Policy Choices in the Post–New Deal Era*, ed. Gary M. Fink and Hugh Davis Graham (Lawrence: University Press of Kansas, 1998), 202–223.

5. Judging by Carter's appointment of Paul Volcker as Federal Reserve chairman, prudence was indeed the solution that was called for. Volcker's policies initially exacerbated an economic downturn that would sink Carter's reelection campaign, but ultimately bore fruit in the mid-1980s. See Kate Davidson and Sudeep Reddy, "Paul Volcker, Who Guided U.S. Monetary Policy and Finance for Nearly Three Decades, Is Dead," *Wall Street Journal*, December 9, 2019, https://www.wsj.com/articles/paul-volcker-who-guided-u-s-monet ary-policy-and-finance-for-nearly-three-decades-is-dead-11575901675.

6. Known for his folksy ways, Carter began his inaugural address, "As my high school teacher, Miss Julia Coleman, used to say, 'We must adjust to changing times and still hold to unchanging principles.'" Jimmy Carter, Inaugural address, https://www.jimmycarter library.gov/assets/documents/speeches/inaugadd.phtml.

7. Carter's tenor here so exemplifies the concept of civil religion—a secular faith in the nation—that he might well have read Robert Bellah's 1967 article on the subject. Jimmy Carter, "Energy and National Goals: Address to the Nation," July 15, 1979; also known as the Malaise or Crisis of Confidence speech; https://www.jimmycarterlibrary.gov/assets/documents/speeches/energy-crisis.phtml.

8. Sylvester Stallone, interview with Judy Klemesrud, "'Rocky Isn't Based on Me,' Says Stallone, 'But We Both Went the Distance,'" *New York Times*, November 28, 1976, 111 [17, 48]; https://search.proquest.com/docview/122970864.

9. Unlike the big budget productions of *Jaws* (1975) and *Star Wars* (1977), *Rocky* did not adapt a best-seller or debut innovative special effects. Chartoff and Winkler produced the film on a modest $1 million budget for United Artists. See Chris Nashawaty, "How 'Rocky' Nabbed Best Picture," *Entertainment Weekly*, February 19, 2002, http://ew.com/article/2002/02/19/how-rocky-nabbed-best-picture/.

10. Stallone goes on to lament how barriers to opportunity led many to "turn to drink" or, in his case, to fight. Stallone, "'Rocky Isn't Based on Me,'" 17.

11. Gene Siskel gave three stars to the "nice little fantasy picture," and *New Yorker* critic Pauline Kael was charmed by *Rocky's* "innocence." Gene Siskel, review of *Rocky*, *Chicago Tribune*, December 21, 1976, A7; Pauline Kael, "Stallone and Stahr," review of *Rocky*, *The New Yorker*, November 29, 1976, 154.

12. *Rocky* won Best Picture over *All the President's Men*, *Taxi Driver*, *Bound for Glory*, and *Network*. Decades later Steven Soderbergh looked back on this award as the moment Hollywood reverted from New Wave experimentation to feel-good entertainment. Steven Soderbergh, interviewed by Rick Lyman, "Follow the Muse: Inspiration to Balance Lofty and Light," *New York Times*, February 21, 2001, E14.

13. In another 1976 interview Stallone elaborated on his defense of Hollywood idealism: "The world might be a crappy place, but it's the only place we've got, so my attitude is, why not fake it? I want to create an illusion, but I'm convinced it's a necessary illusion." That notion of a necessary illusion compares to Plato's noble lie that motivates people to care for their city. Carter's call to revive faith in America, seemingly based on no reason but

the goodness of faith itself, likewise resembles Plato's noble lie. See Stallone, " 'Rocky' Road," B9.

14. Stallone, " 'Rocky Isn't Based on Me,' " 48.

15. Jimmy Carter, personal correspondence, Carter Presidential Library, Staff Secretary Collection, Folder 2/20/77, Container 8.

16. On Jane Fonda's career and star image, see Richard Dyer, *Stars* (London: BFI, 1992), 77.

17. See Larry Powell and Tom Garrett, *The Films of John G. Avildsen: Rocky, The Karate Kid, and Other Underdogs*, with a foreword by Jean Bodon (Jefferson, NC: McFarland, 2014), 67, 79.

18. It is not clear precisely to which "anti-" groups and issues he refers, indicating that moderation is his guiding principle. Stallone, " 'Rocky Isn't Based on Me,' " 48.

19. Listing all criticism on the film, the franchise, and Stallone is a bibliographic project on its own. See these key early essays: Daniel J. Leab, "The Blue Collar Ethnic in Bicentennial America: Rocky (1976)," in *American History/American Film: Interpreting the Hollywood Image*, ed. John E. O'Connor and Martin A. Jackson (New York: Ungar, 1979), 257–272; and see Peter Biskind and Barbara Ehrenreich, "Machismo and Hollywood's Working Class," in *American Media and Mass Culture: Left Perspectives* (Berkeley: University of California Press, 1987), 201–215. Previously published under the same title in *Socialist Review* 10, no. 2–3 (1980): 109–130.

20. For an overview of the conservative masculinity that Rocky invokes, see Clay Motley, "Fighting for Manhood: Rocky and Turn-of-the-Century Antimodernism," in *All-Stars and Movie Stars: Sports in Film and History*, ed. Ron Briley et al. (Lexington: University Press of Kentucky, 2008), 199–217.

21. On white resentment in this era, see Matthew Frye Jacobson, *Roots Too: White Ethnic Revival in Post–Civil Rights America* (Cambridge, MA: Harvard University Press, 2006).

22. For a recent iteration of this argument, see Séan Crosson, *Sport and Film* (London: Routledge, 2013), 93.

23. In particular, see Robin Wood, *Hollywood from Vietnam to Reagan* (New York: Columbia University Press, 1986), 162. See also Andrew Britton, "Blissing Out: The Politics of Reaganite Entertainment," *Movie* 31/32 (1986): 1–42; reprinted in *Britton on Film: The Complete Film Criticism of Andrew Britton*, ed. Barry Keith Grant (Detroit: Wayne State University Press, 2009), 99.

24. Thomas Elsaesser, "The Pathos of Failure: American Films in the 1970s: Notes on the Unmotivated Hero," in *The Last Great American Picture Show*, ed. Thomas Elsaesser et al. (Amsterdam University Press, 2004): 279–292. Previously published under the same title, in *Monogram* 6 (1975): 13–19.

25. Elsaesser, 283.

26. Elsaesser, 280.

27. Elsaesser's political analysis predates *Rocky*'s release. Although Webb confirms that *Rocky*'s opening act exemplifies the unmotivated hero, he perceives the second half of the film as a reversion to the classical tradition. In my view, Webb oversimplifies the second part and echoes the judgment of previous critics. See Lawrence Webb, *The Cinema of Urban Crisis: Seventies Film and the Reinvention of the City* (Amsterdam: Amsterdam University Press, 2014), 60.

28. George Bellows, *Stag at Sharkey's*, 1909, oil on canvas, 36 × 48 in. (92 × 122 cm), Cleveland Museum of Art, http://www.clevelandart.org/art/1133.1922.

29. All transcriptions by author. *Rocky*, directed by John G. Avildsen, performance and screenplay by Sylvester Stallone (1976; Beverly Hills: Twentieth Century Fox Home Entertainment, 2015), Blu-Ray. The source for all figures in this chapter is Metro-Goldwyn-Meyer Studios except where otherwise noted.

30. The heckler recalls a cruel female fan in *The Harder They Fall* (1956) who calls a boxer carried out of the ring on a stretcher a "yellow dog." He falls into a coma and dies, exploited by his managers.

31. This moment also exemplifies meta-cinema, another element inherited from European new wave cinema that Elsaesser observes in pathos of failure narratives. Stallone's look at the camera implies that he is a pawn in the movie business. At this stage of his career he was still a bit player who could speak authentically to a viewing public of common people who also feel exploited by the establishment.

32. Michael Kimmell, *Manhood in America: A Cultural History* (New York: Free Press, 1996), 280.

33. Some members of the movement, notably Farrell, turned to oppose feminism by the 1990s. Warren Farrell, *The Liberated Man: Beyond Masculinity: Freeing Men and Their Relationships with Women* (New York: Random, 1974), 339.

34. Men's studies scholars today observe the same problems of isolation, exemplified by the far higher percentage of men who fall victim to suicide and homelessness. See Anthony Synnott, *Rethinking Men: Heroes, Villains, and Victims* (Farnham, UK: Ashgate, 2009).

35. Kael, "Stallone and Stahr," 154.

36. Kael, 154. Not everyone was convinced. One prominent critic scoffed at "an unconvincing actor imitating a lug," and compared Stallone's performance to "Rodney Dangerfield doing a nightclub monologue." He and Kael react to the same mask of toughness, but Canby seems to prefer an authentic tough. Vincent Canby, "Pure '30s Make-Believe," review of *Rocky*, *New York Times*, November 22, 1976, 63.

37. Jack Nichols, *Men's Liberation: A New Definition of Masculinity* (New York: Penguin, 1975), 56.

38. Kael, "Stallone and Stahr," 154.

39. Psychiatrist Harvey Kaye made a call to recognize the "masculine mystique" as a "major symptom of social madness" for which alternatives should be sought. Named in parallel to Betty Friedan's feminine mystique, Kaye diagnoses both soft femininity and hard masculinity as counterparts of the same system of conservative gender norms. See Harvey E. Kaye, *Male Survival: Masculinity without Myth* (New York: Grosset and Dunlap, 1974), 188.

40. Director Francis Ford Coppola is Talia Shire's brother, which adds an interesting angle to the bratty character he has her play in *The Godfather* (1972), and another angle to the Paulie character in *Rocky*.

41. By associating prudery with Paulie's other problems, *Rocky* compares to *Psycho* (Alfred Hitchcock, 1960). Norman Bates's more extreme pathologies are also attributed to Victorian prudishness.

42. Kael, "Stallone and Stahr," 154.

43. Stallone may not have read Farrell's study, but he seems to have either soaked up key ideas from men's liberation somehow or developed similar ideas in parallel. Farrell, *The Liberated Man*, 339.

44. Here I employ Montesquieu's triadic political theory that associates republics, monarchy, and despotism with the principles of equality, honor, and fear. Hollywood glamor would

align with the honor-based politics of monarchy and aristocracy. See the chapter on *A League of Their Own* for an in-depth discussion.

45. Obviously, a crossover marketing strategy is also involved in putting the couple's image on the poster, but that commercial ambition does not betray the egalitarian political character of the film.

46. Avildsen conceived of this moment. Powell and Garrett, *Films of John G. Avildsen*, 76.

47. "Cannon in the Morning" was a popular radio show from 1969 to 2004. See Larry Mendte, "Don Cannon, Philadelphia Radio Legend, Has Passed," *Philadelphia*, October 22, 2014, https://www.phillymag.com/news/2014/08/22/don-cannon-philadelphia-radio-legend-passed/.

48. *Cool Hand Luke*, directed by Stuart Rosenberg (Warner Bros., 1967).

49. Reading Railroad Bridge spans the Schuylkill River and was constructed in the 1850s. Compare this image to Sergei Eisenstein's *Battleship Potemkin* (1925) that features the archways of bridges and viaducts as symbols of collective strength.

50. One shot actually plays in reverse for the sake of continuity. Its curious rhythm adds to the ethereal quality of the music.

51. One "Fluffian" said that the only city Philadelphia can look down upon is Cleveland; everywhere else appears superior. Steve Rivele, personal conversation, May 11, 2019.

52. Other films have played upon the city's deep relationship to its sports teams, notably the Disney picture *Invincible* (2006) and David O. Russell's *Silver Linings Playbook* (2012), each of which involves the Eagles football team.

53. Frazier's corner threw in the towel just before the fifteenth and final round. Both fighters described their state as close to death at the end of the long bout. For instance, see Jan Philipp Reemtsma, *More than a Champion: The Style of Muhammad Ali*, trans. John E. Woods (New York: Knopf, 1998), 145.

54. The sequel *Rocky II*, with a larger budget, even repeats this ritual on a grander scale. Its training montage features a flock of children jogging alongside Balboa and culminates in a helicopter view of the joyous swarm cascading down Ben Franklin Parkway. Stallone clearly understood how meaningful his movie hero became for his city. In *Rocky III* (1982) he imagines Rocky retiring and accepting the city's gift of a bronze sculpture to be installed at the top of the museum steps. The sculpture from the movie would actually be installed there, then moved across the city under criticism by the museum board, but returned to an adjacent museum site under public pressure. In this case, life imitates art.

55. Rousseau waxes lyrical about a folk dance he witnessed as a boy in Geneva, led spontaneously and without central coordination by a local regiment quartered in the St. Gervais square. He concludes, "No, there is no pure joy, but that of the community; and the genuine sentiments of nature are felt only by the people." Jean-Jacques Rousseau, *A Letter from M. Rousseau of Geneva to M. d'Alembert of Paris, Concerning the Effects of Theatrical Entertainments on the Manners of Mankind* (London: J. Nourse, 1759), 187–188.

56. In ancient Greek theater the chorus mediated between the actors on stage, the public, and the gods above. Johannes Ehrat introduces a model for public opinion based on the chorus that I discuss further in the first chapter. See Johannes Ehrat, *Power of Scandal: Semiotic and Pragmatic in Mass Media* (Toronto: University of Toronto Press, 2011), 94.

57. Populism and progressivism developed cooperative and republican organizations in response to markets and economies of scale opened by new technologies. See Charles Postel, *The Populist Vision* (New York: Oxford University Press, 2007), 9–11.

58. The 1910s were the dawn of modern city planning, which was preceded by the City Beautiful movement and came under the banner of urban renewal at midcentury. See Jon A. Peterson, *The Birth of City Planning in the United States, 1840–1917* (Baltimore: Johns Hopkins University Press, 2003).

59. It is no wonder that one often hears Conti's "Gonna Fly Now" or the *Rocky III* theme "Eye of the Tiger" played along the course of road races even today. On the Progressive Era, see Mark Dyerson, *Making the American Team: Sport, Culture, and the Olympic Experience* (Champaign: University of Illinois Press, 1998).

60. See Leger Grindon, "Body and Soul: The Structure of Meaning in the Boxing Film Genre," *Cinema Journal* 35, no. 4 (1996): 54–69, https://doi.org/10.2307/1225717.

61. See Wolfgang Welsch, "Sport Viewed Aesthetically, and Even as Art?," in *The Aesthetics of Everyday Life*, ed. Andrew Light and Jonathan M. Smith (New York: Columbia University Press, 2005), 135–149.

62. Rocky's rebirth even constitutes a political action, in Hannah Arendt's sense of the term, because it is not driven by necessity and because it involves community. I discuss Arendt and political action in the chapter on *Ali*.

63. Scare quotes on "race" are useful in flagging the false premise of scientific racism. In American English *race* can refer to a sociocultural group as well as a genetic stock—distinguishing the two is an important component of antiracism. Henceforth *race* will appear without scare quotes, yet a critical awareness of the bad concept and of the word's ambiguity should be kept in mind.

64. For this study, formal terms for ethnicities such as *African-American* and *European-American* are capitalized and hyphenated, while informal terms of *black* and *white* usually remain in lower case. Alternating usage and capitalization reflects an actual fluidity of sociocultural distinction. A subsequent chapter on *White Men Can't Jump* discusses the significance of hyphenation as a mode of social incorporation.

65. Howard Sackler used the phrase satirically to title his biographical play of Jack Johnson (1967) and its film adaptation, *The Great White Hope* (1970), starring James Earl Jones. Also, Johnson's career and its racial controversy intersected with the rise of cinema as a mass medium. See Dan Streible, *Fight Pictures: A History of Boxing and Early Cinema* (Berkeley: University of California Press, 2008).

66. For instance, see Leab, "Blue Collar Ethnic": Biskind and Ehrenreich, "Machismo"; and Jacobson, *Roots Too*.

67. *Variety* reviewer A. D. Murphy does point out the competing messages in *Rocky*: "There are occasional flashes that the film may be patronizing the lower end of the blue-collar mentality, as much if not more than the characters who keep putting Rocky down on the screen. However, Avildsen is noted for creating such ambiguities." Ehrenreich observes the same ambiguity in *Saturday Night Fever* (1978). Murf [Arthur D. Murphy], "*Rocky* (Color): Potential Sleeper Unless Oversold," review of *Rocky, Variety*, November 10, 1976, 20; Biskind and Ehrenreich, "Machismo," 209–211.

68. As noted earlier, Elsaesser identifies the 1970s vigilante films of Clint Eastwood and Charles Bronson as conservative/Republican counterparts to the unmotivated hero. See Elsaesser, "Pathos of Failure."

69. See Stallone, "'Rocky Isn't Based on Me,'" 17.

70. Ali explained, "You're a citizen of the world when you're a Muslim; not just an American; not just a little integrator begging for a job." Evidently, at that time, he had still not

embraced liberal integration policy, although elsewhere in the article he praises President Ford. Dave Brady, "Sleepless Night Fails to Quiet 1st Ali Drill; Ali Eyes 'Black Kissinger' Role," *Washington Post*, April 17, 1976, C1, C9.

71. See Kevin Klose, "Ali in Moscow; 'All He (Brezhnev) Talked about Was Peace and Love of Humanity,'" *Washington Post*, June 20, 1978, A1, A7. See also Dorothy Gilliam, "Ali as a Presidential Envoy: Fighting in the Wrong Ring: Ali as a Diplomat: In the Wrong Ring," *Washington Post*, February 11, 1980, C1.

72. See Donald Janson, "Ali Leads 1,600 at a Rally in Trenton for Release of Carter from Prison," *New York Times*, October 18, 1975, 63.

73. Ali suffered from dyslexia and was always ashamed of his lack of education. See Gerald Early, "Three Facts Essential to Understanding Muhammad Ali," *Washington Post*, June 5, 2016, https://www.washingtonpost.com/opinions/three-facts-essential-to-unders tanding-muhammad-ali/2016/06/05/1bd85198-2b46-11e6-9de3-6e6e7a14000c_story. html?utm_term=.75f1666b7c7f.

74. For instance, at the press conference before the Jimmy Young fight, Ali said, "I know I play and clown ... but afterward; not now. There's a time to be serious." See Brady, "Sleepless Night," C1.

75. An earlier version of the script had Mick the Irish trainer an outright racist. Nashawaty, "How 'Rocky' Nabbed Best Picture."

76. Leah N. Gordon, *From Power to Prejudice: The Rise of Racial Individualism in Midcentury America* (Chicago: University of Chicago Press, 2015).

77. Madison prefigures critics of the white savior film that I discuss in a later chapter on *White Men Can't Jump*. Kelly J. Madison, "Legitimation Crisis and Containment: The 'Anti-Racist-White-Hero' Film," *Critical Studies in Media Communication* 16, no. 4 (December 1999): 399–416.

78. Joe Frazier, a Philadelphia native who has a cameo appearance in *Rocky*, was one such target of Ali's. See Early, "Three Facts."

79. Debate in the 1970s centered on race and gender in employment, then shifted to college admissions in the 1990s. For an overview, see "Affirmative Action," *Stanford Encyclopedia of Philosophy*, April 9, 2018, https://plato.stanford.edu/entries/affirmative-action/.

80. On this point, consider David Boonin's argument that there is a stronger moral obligation to prioritize racial minorities because pure performance criteria hold less moral weight. Indeed, abstracting performance to quantitative measurement has the same instrumental flaw as quotas. David Boonin, *Should Race Matter? Unusual Answers to the Usual Questions* (Cambridge: Cambridge University Press, 2011), 140, 200. For further discussion of how democracy relates to meritocracy/aristocracy, see the subsequent chapter on *A League of Their Own*.

81. For reactionary whites, the rise of black athletes threatened European social privilege and seemed to prove that whites needed affirmative action too. But given that Apollo is the race villain in this scenario, his fantastical wish fulfillment of affirmative action for whites would be totally confusing. One way to read the reversal is by saying that if the race roles were reversed, it would be clear that affirmative action is more American and democratic than pure merit. His action even suggests that artificially including whites in black-dominated sports is a good thing; if the same measure were carried out in white-dominated sports such as golf, swimming, hockey, and lacrosse, the logic would hold.

82. *Rocky* would be released in November 1976, so the film is set roughly one year prior. Its concluding scenes were actually filmed on location in January 1976, in sync with the story.

83. Stallone insisted on taking the lead role over more Anglo stars such as Robert Redford who could not have matched his authentic portrayal of the "Italian Stallion." See Powell and Garrett, *Films of John G. Avildsen*, 69.

84. Talia Shire's previous role in *The Godfather*, a film suffused with Italian-American talent, established a star persona that bled into Adrian here. Her brother, Paulie, is played by Burt Young, a stage name for Italian-American Richard Morea.

85. Racial "jokes" are justified by adherents of individualism. Such discourse obviously does not ignore race, but rather demotes all social forms to a level they consider inconsequential and safe for play. Apollo's nonchalance appears to speak on this level, but his endorsement of affirmative action again complicates the film's position.

86. Original plans for a centralized event were scuttled. See John Bodnar, *Remaking America: Public Memory, Commemoration, and Patriotism in the Twentieth Century* (Princeton, NJ: Princeton University Press, 1992); Tammy S. Gordon, *The Spirit of 1976: Commerce, Community, and the Politics of Commemoration* (Amherst: University of Massachusetts Press, 2013).

87. ARBA even established a proto-internet called BINET to access the catalog via computer terminal. American Revolution Bicentennial Administration (ARBA), *Comprehensive Calendar of Bicentennial Events*, 2 vols. (Washington, DC: U.S. Government Printing Office, June 1976), 2–130, appendix 3-3.

88. Older tales would melt away ethnic difference in the process of assimilation. Now these differences came to be celebrated and preserved, while putting cultural and national identities in question. See Jacobson, *Roots Too*; Joshua Glick, *Los Angeles Documentary and the Production of Public History, 1958–1977* (Berkeley: University of California Press, 2018), 153; and Hua Hsu, "The Asian American Canon Breakers," *New Yorker*, January 6, 2020, https://www.newyorker.com/magazine/2020/01/06/the-asian-american-canon-breakers.

89. See Amy Gutmann, ed., *Multiculturalism: Examining the Politics of Recognition*, expanded edition (Princeton, NJ: Princeton University Press, 1994).

90. To the extent that minority groups lack economic privilege, affirmative action also fulfills an economic-centered antiracist strategy which views inequality as the fundamental cause of racist social division. Whether carried out through a command economy or more liberal progressive measures, such an economic strategy also conflicts with an individualist worldview that attributes inequality to merit, not to any systemic force.

91. Charles Taylor, "The Politics of Recognition," in Gutmann, *Multiculturalism*, 67.

92. Without a major star to achieve grand success, the film needed some "novelty" to attract an audience. Stallone, "'Rocky' Road," B9.

93. Mikhail M. Bakhtin, *Rabelais and His World*, trans. Hélène Iswolsky (Cambridge, MA: MIT Press, 1968), 11.

94. Rita Reif, "Home Furnishings: Producers Get Set for Bicentennial," *New York Times*, October 14, 1974, https://www.nytimes.com/1974/10/14/archives/home-furnishings-producers-get-set-for-bicentennial-even-linens.html.

95. The People's Bicentennial Commission lobbied successfully against a centralized celebration but did not stop widespread commercial exploitation of the occasion. Planning had begun with Congress in 1966, and controversy erupted in 1974. See Bodnar, *Remaking America*, 231; see also Gordon, *The Spirit of 1976*.

96. Dr. King mentioned *The Ten Commandments'* inspiring story of Exodus in a 1957 Montgomery speech about decolonization in Ghana. See Dr. Martin Luther King, Jr., "The Birth of a New Nation," April 1957, audio recording, https://kinginstitute.stanford.edu/king-papers/documents/birth-new-nation-sermon-delivered-dexter-avenue-baptist-church. See also Charles Hillinger, "900,000 View Freedom Train; Bicentennial Spirit—U.S. Steaming at Full Throttle," *Los Angeles Times*, June 26, 1975, B1, 30–31; "Freedom Train Spans 200 Years of History," *New Pittsburgh Courier*, November 15, 1975, A6; "'Ten Commandments' Script on Freedom Train Journey," *Los Angeles Times*, July 3, 1975, A28.

97. In interviews timed for the release, Stallone told his own rags-to-riches story, which effectively became part of the marketing strategy. United Artists promoted the film so heavily that *Variety* headlined its review "Potential Sleeper Unless Oversold." The title sequence demonstrates this confidence with Conti's brass fanfare and scrolling letters that fill the entire screen. Vincent Canby described the film's debut in New York City as "absurdly oversold." See Murf, review of *Rocky*; Canby, "Pure '30s Make-Believe."

98. Nevertheless, *Rocky IV* does characterize the Russian villains as white supremacist, and the Americans as racially integrated.

99. As a young lifeguard in Wilmington, Delaware, Biden faced off against a black tough and they developed mutual respect; retelling the story apparently had the same effect. For an overview of the incident and controversy it provoked in 2019, see Chana Garcia, "Joe Biden's Black Pass," *The Root*, May 7, 2010, https://www.theroot.com/joe-bidens-black-pass-1790879439; and Tommy Christopher, "WATCH: Joe Biden Tells Story of Facing Down Razor-Wielding Gang Leader Named 'Corn Pop,'" *Mediaite*, September 14, 2019, https://www.mediaite.com/news/watch-joe-biden-tells-story-of-facing-down-razor-wielding-gang-leader-named-corn-pop/amp/.

100. Northrop Frye, *Anatomy of Criticism: Four Essays* (1957; New York: Atheneum, 1968), 43–44.

101. An important school of criticism considers the happy ending in general to be politically regressive and anti-democratic. The introduction addresses this matter in more depth.

102. Greg Garrett, *A Long, Long Way: Hollywood's Unfinished Journey from Racism to Reconciliation* (New York: Oxford University Press, 2020).

103. Following the postmodern school of thought and radical political position, Biskind and Ehrenreich criticize both cowboy and laborer-hero types as deceptive fantasy for the middle class. They therefore consider *Rocky* conservative because its happy ending does not emphasize Marxist class conflict and proletarian resistance. Biskind and Ehrenreich, "Machismo," 213.

104. Most critics preferred the tragic realism of *Raging Bull* for its critical attitude. However, Pam Cook argues that Scorsese's tragedy in fact honors toxic masculinity. Pam Cook, "Masculinity in Crisis?," *Screen* 23, no. 3–4 (Sep/Oct 1982): 39–46, https://doi.org/10.1093/screen/23.3-4.39.

105. Clémentine Tholas agrees that Rocky's tender heart defines his character more than any other trait, and her study of his development across a half-century shows "how Rocky's social, emotional, and physical fragility is increased throughout the series of films." Clémentine Tholas Disset, "From *Rocky* (1976) to *Creed* (2015): 'Musculinity' and Modesty," *InMedia* 6 (2017), http:// journals.openedition.org/inmedia/849.

106. For a reading of the political ambiguities in his 1980s work, see Stephen C. LeSueur and Dean Rehberger, "*Rocky IV, Rambo II,* and the Place of the Individual in Modern American Society," *Journal of American Culture* 11, no. 2 (1988): 25–33.

Chapter 3

1. All dialogue transcribed by author. *Slap Shot*, directed by George Roy Hill (1977; Universal City, CA: Universal Studios Home Entertainment, 2013), Blu-Ray. The source for all figures in this chapter is Universal Studios except where otherwise noted.

2. See Daniel Bell, *The Coming of Post-Industrial Society: A Venture in Social Forecasting* (New York: Basic Books, 1973); and Richard Florida, *The Rise of the Creative Class: And How It's Transforming Work, Leisure, Community and Everyday Life* (New York: Basic Books, 2004). Richard Florida hatched his idea in Cleveland, Ohio. Michael Dwyer has criticized the "creative class" project's implicit orientation to upper class fantasy. Michael Dwyer, "Steel City, Tinsel Town: Pittsburgh, Hollywood, and the Screening of the Creative Class" (presentation, Annual Conference of the Society of Cinema and Media Studies, Toronto, March 17, 2018).

3. Initial reviewers found the movie and its politics confusing, which helps account for its limited commercial success. For instance, see Gary Arnold, review of *Slap Shot*, *Washington Post*, April 1, 1977, B1.

4. Peter Biskind and Barbara Ehrenreich, "Machismo and Hollywood's Working Class," 1980, reprinted in *American Media and Mass Culture: Left Perspectives* (Berkeley: University of California Press, 1987), 201–215.

5. Derek Nystrom, *Hard Hats, Rednecks, and Macho Men: Class in 1970s American Cinema* (New York: Oxford University Press, 2009); John Bodnar, *Blue-Collar Hollywood: Liberalism, Democracy, and Working People in American Film* (Baltimore, MD: Johns Hopkins University Press, 2003).

6. John Lawlor, "Radical Satire and the Realistic Novel," in *Jonathan Swift: A Collection of Critical Essays*, ed. Claude Rawson (Englewood Cliffs, NJ: Prentice Hall, 1995), 16–28.

7. Frye also comments on the "ironical and equivocal context" of Chaplin's films. See Northrop Frye, *Anatomy of Criticism: Four Essays* (1957; New York: Atheneum, 1968), 34, 228.

8. Nancy Dowd, interview by Judy Klemesrud, "Author Says Her 'Slap Shot' Talk Is Realistic," *New York Times* (March 3, 1977), 28.

9. See Chloe E. Taft, *From Steel to Slots: Casino Capitalism in the Postindustrial City* (Cambridge, MA: Harvard University Press, 2016), 31, 212. See also Steven High, *Industrial Sunset: The Making of North America's Rust Belt, 1969–1984* (Toronto: University of Toronto Press, 2003), 124.

10. The Jets were temporarily revived as the Chiefs, named after the film. In 2010 the hockey team moved to Greenville, South Carolina, following the pattern of Rust Belt to Sun Belt. "Johnstown Jets," *Wikipedia*, last modified January 30, 2018, https://en.wikipedia.org/wiki/Johnstown_Jets; "History," Greenville Swamp Rabbits, accessed April 26, 2018, http://www.swamprabbits.com/history/.

11. See *Arbus, Friedlander, Winogrand: New Documents, 1967*, catalog of an exhibition curated by John Szarkowski (New York: Museum of Modern Art, 2017). On the concept of "world" see Eric Hayot, *On Literary Worlds* (New York: Oxford University Press, 2012). Johnstown has featured in several films, notably *All the Right Moves* (1983). See Michael Dwyer, "The Johnstown Landscape" (seminar paper presented at the SCMS Annual Conference, March 18, 2019).

12. For a landmark realist manifesto, see Émile Zola, "The Experimental Novel," in *The Experimental Novel and Other Essays*, trans. Belle M. Sherman (New York: Cassell, 1893), 1–57, https://archive.org/details/cu31924027248867/page/n13.

13. In this scene one might also find a reference to the 1790s Whiskey Rebellion, a populist resistance to federal taxation centered in western Pennsylvania. The anarchist culture of the Appalachian region makes this location choice for the film significant.

14. See Erich Auerbach, *Mimesis: The Representation of Reality in Western Literature*, trans. Willard R. Trask (Princeton, NJ: Princeton University Press, 1953), 554.

15. Dowd, interview by Judy Klemesrud, 28. On Newman's angry fans, see Shawn Levy, *Paul Newman: A Life* (London: Aurum, 2010), 385.

16. Gœthe's *Wilhelm Meister* is Bakhtin's model novelist in this regard. He notes how the realist coming-of-age tale develops from writers' interest in folklore, which is "saturated" with historical time. M. M. Bakhtin, "The Bildungsroman and Its Significance in the History of Realism (Toward a Historical Typology of the Novel)," in *Speech Genres and Other Late Essays*, ed. Caryl Emerson and Michael Holquist, trans. Vern W. McGee (Austin: University of Texas Press, 1987), 10–59, 52. Hayot names this realist quality "dynamism." Hayot, *Literary Worlds*, 80.

17. Christine Becker, "Paul Newman," in *New Constellations: Movie Stars of the 1960s*, ed. Pamela Robertson Wojcik (New Brunswick, NJ: Rutgers University Press, 2012), 15.

18. "New York Jets quarterback Joe Namath, wearing his long, white fur coat, watches from the sidelines as the Baltimore Colts defeat the Jets, 14–13, at New York's Shea Stadium on Nov. 14, 1971." Anonymous AP photo, "Jets Colts Namath," *AP Images*, 2003. http://www.apimages.com/metadata/Index/Associated-Press-Sports-New-York-United-States-/b92613caa1e5da11af9f0014c2589dfb/8/0.

19. Three major texts in this era were Kate Millet, *Sexual Politics* (Garden City, NY: Doubleday, 1970); Shulamith Firestone, *The Dialectic of Sex: The Case for Feminist Revolution* (New York: William Morrow, 1970); and Julia Kristeva, "The System and the Speaking Subject," *Times Literary Supplement* (October 12, 1973): 1249–1252.

20. For an overview of the history and competing currents of feminism, see Janet K. Boles and Diane Long Hoeveler, "Introduction," in *Historical Dictionary of Feminism* (Lanham, MD: Scarecrow, 1995), 1–20.

21. A *New York Times* writer described the movie as "the bawdiest, most obscenity-sprinkled major movie ever made." It was rated R and contained a warning in its advertisements, "Certain language may be too strong for children." Dowd, interview by Judy Klemesrud, 28.

22. One can deduce that the best version of Dowd's story would have Reg discovering his bisexuality. But that may have been too radical for Newman and for Hollywood at the time.

23. See Michael Warner, "Queer and Then," *The Chronicle of Higher Education* (January 1, 2012); https://www.chronicle.com/article/QueerThen-/130161.

24. James W. Carey, *Communication as Culture: Essays on Media and Society* (New York: Routledge, 1992).

25. Marc Feigen Fasteau, *The Male Machine* (New York: Delta, 1975); Jack Nichols, *Men's Liberation: A New Definition of Masculinity* (New York: Penguin, 1975).

26. Stewart Brand, quoted in *The New Games Book*, ed. Andrew Fluegelman (San Francisco: New Games Foundation/Headlands Press, 1976), 7–8.

27. Matt Weinstein and Joel Goodman, *Playfair: Everybody's Guide to Noncompetitive Play* (San Luis Obispo, CA: Impact, 1980), 22. See the "Resources" in that publication for information on DeKoven, who published *The Well Played Game* in 1978, and on Marta Harrison, whose Friends Peace Committee published *For the Fun of It!* in 1976. See also Terry Orlick, *The Cooperative Sports and Games Book: Challenge without Competition* (New York: Pantheon, 1978).

28. Such a distinction is controversial. For instance, Bly distinguishes the savage man from the wild man, whom he compares to a zen priest or shaman. Robert Bly, *Iron John: A Book about Men* (Reading, MA: Addison-Wesley, 1990), x.

29. See Weinstein and Goodman, *Playfair*, 22.

30. *Network*, performance by Peter Finch, screenplay by Paddy Chayefsky (Metro-Goldwyn-Mayer, 1976).

31. Theodore Roosevelt, "The Strenuous Life: Speech before the Hamilton Club, Chicago, April 10, 1899," in *The Strenuous Life: Essays and Addresses* (New York: Century, 1900), 3, 6; http://www.bartleby.com/58/1.html, published February 1998, accessed April 29, 2018; Michael Kimmel, *Manhood in America: A Cultural History* (New York: Free Press, 1996), 269–270.

32. Lily's character is too complex and underdeveloped, in my view. Her discontent seems to stem from both her feminist desire for an independent occupation and an aristocratic disdain for the steel town, as if she would be content as a genteel homemaker back east. By the end of the film she seems to lose her class pretense and embrace a certain freedom in her position, but her character does not represent a strong alternative to the team owner whom I discuss in the next section.

33. Wollen uses the term *nationalism* in a sense that I take to mean imperial expansion and arrogance. I distinguish that belligerent form of social identity from a reciprocal and multipolar form that Hirschi defines as nationalism. See Caspar Hirschi, *The Origins of Nationalism: An Alternative History from Ancient Rome to Early Modern Germany* (Cambridge: Cambridge University Press, 2012).

34. One wonders if Wollen's text (1969) influenced Hill and his screenwriters, especially David S. Ward, who wrote *The Sting* and later *Major League* (1989). Peter Wollen, "The Auteur Theory," in *Signs and Meaning in the Cinema*, 3rd ed. (Bloomington: Indiana University Press, 1972), 82.

35. Judith Butler, *Gender Trouble* (New York: Routledge, 2007), 200.

36. On subversion and the carnivalesque, see Mikhail Bakhtin, *Rabelais and His World*, trans. Helene Iswolsky (Cambridge, MA: MIT Press, 1968).

37. In a sense the Rust Belt was caused by a midcentury smelting design rendered obsolete in the late 1960s. New smelting technology was more efficient and profitable, but new mills were built elsewhere while older ones were slowly amortized. See High, *Industrial Sunset*.

38. *Wall Street*, screenplay by Oliver Stone and Stanley Weiser, performance by Michael Douglas (1987; 20th Century Fox).

39. See Manfred B. Steger and Ravi K. Roy, *Neoliberalism: A Very Short Introduction* (Oxford: Oxford University Press, 2010).

40. J. D. Connor fittingly uses Gecko's image to illustrate the cover of his critical study of the industry during late capitalism, *The Studios after the Studios: Neoclassical Hollywood (1970–2010)* (Stanford, CA: Stanford University Press, 2015), https://www.sup.org/books/title/?id=21461.

41. The introduction to this book discusses the Frankfurt School (The Institute for Social Research) in detail, specifically Horkheimer and Adorno's treatise *Dialectic of Enlightenment* (1947).

42. Team owners in *Major League* (1989) and *Any Given Sunday* (1999), as well as Barbara Streisand's role as a promoter in *The Main Event* (1979), compose the female owner type. Viridiana Lieberman, *Sports Heroines on Film: A Critical Study of Cinematic Women*

Athletes, Coaches and Owners (Jefferson, NC: McFarland, 2015), 151; ProQuest Ebook Central, docID 1863930.

43. Dowd, interview by Judy Klemesrud.

44. For a popular representation of Schlafly, see *Mrs. America*, created by Dahvi Waller, featuring Cate Blanchett, aired April 15, 2020, on FX and Hulu, https://www.fxnetworks.com/shows/mrs-america.

45. My reading disagrees sharply with Lieberman, who finds in Anita the epitome of the female owner type in the sports movie genre: "Placing a female in the position of owner in these films offers a distraction from the sometimes harsh truth of this profession: Owners don't see players as human beings, they see them as investments. Having a woman embody this notion is incredibly damaging. Instead of seeing her as a savvy businesswoman, these films choose to use her to embody the questionable practices of sports owners" (Lieberman, *Sports Heroines*, 150–151). Lieberman is correct that the hockey movie does not particularly admire Anita's savviness and success as an independent woman. However, she is on more dubious ground when she suggests that the film demeans her in a sexist way, and portrays all owners as "unmanly." In my view, the film asserts a Marxist class critique ahead of a concern for gender representation. Anita's cool financial calculation and flippant attitude is not strongly coded as feminine or unmanly; if anything, it is classically masculine stoicism.

46. See Stanley Cavell, *Pursuits of Happiness: The Hollywood Comedy of Remarriage* (Cambridge, MA: Harvard University Press, 1984).

47. "Right Back Where We Started From," written by Pierre Tubbs and J. Vincent Edwards, performed by Maxine Nightengale, *Right Back Where We Started From* (London: United Artists, 1975); Barbara Ehrenreich, *Dancing in the Streets: A History of Collective Joy* (New York: Holt, 2007).

48. Wollen, "Auteur Theory," 84.

49. Jeffrey C. Alexander, *The Civil Sphere* (New York: Oxford University Press, 2006), ix.

Chapter 4

1. All transcriptions by author. *The Natural*, directed by Barry Levinson, screenplay by Roger Towne and Phil Dusenberry, performed by Robert Redford (1984; Culver City, CA: Sony Pictures Home Entertainment, 2016), Blu-Ray. The source for all images in this chapter is Sony Pictures Home Entertainment unless otherwise noted.

2. Subsequent sports movies *Hoosiers* (1986), *Field of Dreams* (1989), and even *Forrest Gump* (1994) have also been widely interpreted by academics as tales for white, rural conservatives. See Ron Briley, *The Baseball Film in Postwar America: A Critical Study, 1948–1962* (Jefferson, NC: McFarland, 2011), 6; Ron Briley, "Basketball's Great White Hope and Ronald Reagan's America: *Hoosiers* (1986)." *Film and History: An Interdisciplinary Journal of Film and Television Studies* 35, no. 1 (2005): 12–19, https://doi.org/10.1353/flm.2005.0003; Alan Nadel, *Flatlining on the Field of Dreams: Cultural Narratives in the Films of President Reagan's America* (New Brunswick, NJ: Rutgers University Press, 1997), 51–53.

3. Good links 1980s baseball films to the midcentury biopic cycle, suggesting that their success myth expresses an ethos of happiness, virtue, and community that he classifies as conservative, in contrast to the liberal pursuit of individual fortune. See Howard Good, *Diamonds in the Dark: America, Baseball, and the Movies* (Lanham, MD: Scarecrow Press, 1997), pp. 195–198.

4. One case in Iowa is chronicled in the documentary *Troublesome Creek: A Midwestern*, dir. Steven Ascher and Jeanne Jordan (New York: Forensic Films, 1995), https://www.pbs.org/wgbh/americanexperience/films/trouble/.

5. In the early 1980s the American Agriculture Movement campaigned for "parity," the Marxist idea that commodity prices paid to farmers should equate to the prices paid by consumers. See Ward Sinclair, "Tractorcade Protest a Memory but Farmers' Anger Lingers on," *The Washington Post*, January 4, 1982. https://search.proquest.com/docview/147442727/; Angus Phillips, "2,000 Farmers Mount Protest Here: One-Time 'Tractorcade' Group Bears White Crosses for Failed Farms," *The Washington Post*, March 5, 1985. https://search.proquest.com/docview/138717714/.

6. In 1977, 1978, and 1979, "Tractorcades" to the Capitol had captured public attention and produced a response from the Carter administration. They revived 1930s activism in these new patterns and became known as the AAM under Reagan. See Gay Cook, "A Fat Crop Year, but Tractorcade Is Coming Back," *The Washington Post (1974–Current File)*, December 14, 1978, https://search.proquest.com/docview/146946309/; Seth S. King, "Farmers Rally Quietly in Capital, in a Contrast to '79: Paritycade Replaces Tractorcade," *New York Times*, February 19, 1980, https://search.proquest.com/docview/121323863.

7. Gilbert C. Fite, *American Farmers: The New Minority*, Minorities in Modern America, series ed. Warren F. Kimball and David E. Harrell, Jr. (Bloomington: Indiana University Press, 1981), 202; Mark Friedberger, *Farm Families and Change in 20th-Century America* (Lexington: University Press of Kentucky, 1988), 195; Neil Young, "An Open Letter by Neil Young," *USA Today* (September 20, 1985), 9A; "Farm Aid: A Concert for America," featuring Timothy Hutton, aired September 22, 1985, on Gaylord Syndicom/Nashville Network, youtube.com/watch?v=-9Jfbd1w_1c, 0:56:00.

8. "Food Security Act of 1985," *Public Law 99-198*. https://www.govinfo.gov/content/pkg/STATUTE-99/pdf/STATUTE-99-Pg1354.pdf.

9. In 1907 Major League Baseball officially adopted a fanciful history: that Abner Doubleday founded the game in a field near Cooperstown, New York, in 1839. That legend and its sacred site aimed to market the game as uniquely American, echoing impressions of an agrarian and frontier past. In fact, nineteenth-century historian Henry Chadwick had recognized the *urban* origin of the game. Evolved from the British game rounders, a three-stick version became known as "town ball" because it was played in towns, and was later known as "the New York game" when the modern rules were adopted across New York City after 1850. See Benjamin G. Rader, *Baseball: A History of America's Game* (Urbana: University of Illinois Press, 1992).

10. D. W. Griffith's 1909 short film *A Corner in Wheat* was based on the scenario in Frank Norris's naturalist stories and novels on the subject of monopolies that exploit small farmers, notably *The Octopus* (1901) and *The Pit* (1903).

11. G. Edward White, *The Eastern Establishment and the Western Experience: The West of Frederic Remington, Theodore Roosevelt, and Owen Wister* (New Haven, CT: Yale University Press, 1968).

12. Pop sells the club in exchange for a lifetime contract to manage the team; Judge "Goodwill Banner" aims to wear down Pop's motivation to manage by inducing losses however he can. Bernard Malamud, *The Natural* (New York: Perennial Classics, 2000), 82.

13. Richard J. Wiedenfeld, personal interview, June 23, 2018; see Joseph F. Wall, "The Iowa Farmer in Crisis, 1920–1936," *The Annals of Iowa*, no. 47 (1983): 124. http://ir.uiowa.edu/annals-of-iowa/vol47/iss2/5.

14. M. Elizabeth Sanders, *Roots of Reform: Farmers, Workers, and the American State, 1877–1917* (Chicago: University of Chicago Press, 1999); Charles Postel, *The Populist Vision* (New York: Oxford University Press, 2007).

15. John Kenneth Galbraith, *American Capitalism: The Concept of Countervailing Power*, in *The Affluent Society and Other Writings, 1952–1967* (1952; New York: Library of America, 2010), 136.

16. Latham Hunter, "'What's *Natural* About It?': A Baseball Movie as Introduction to Key Concepts in Cultural Studies," *Film and History: An Interdisciplinary Journal of Film and Television Studies* 35, no. 2 (2005): 73–74.

17. Within film history, this shot has a retro feel owing to its frontality, a characteristic of early cinema underlined by film historian Tom Gunning. For example, compare this image to the rail stations depicted in *The Great Train Robbery* (Edwin S. Porter, 1903) and *The Lonedale Operator* (D. W. Griffith, 1911).

18. Will Kymlicka, *Liberalism, Community, and Culture* (Oxford: Oxford University Press, 1989).

19. Charles Taylor, "The Politics of Recognition," in *Multiculturalism: Examining the Politics of Recognition*, expanded edition, ed. Amy Gutmann (Princeton, NJ: Princeton University Press, 1994), 25–74.

20. The Civil Rights Act of 1964 prohibits discrimination on the basis of race, color, religion, sex or national origin in employment; age, disability, and genetic information were added to this list by laws passed in 1967, 1990, and 2008. African-American leadership in the civil rights movement and the centrality of slavery in American history have effectively made racial discrimination the standard to which all discrimination is compared in the United States.

21. For an appreciation of the evangelical left, see David R. Swartz, *Moral Minority: The Evangelical Left in an Age of Conservatism* (Philadelphia: University of Pennsylvania Press, 2012). By contrast, Richard Hofstadter exemplifies rural America's bad reputation. See his denigration of the yeoman farmer, *The Age of Reform* (1955), and his vulgar characterization of populism in *The Paranoid Style in American Politics* (1964).

22. A host of details in Malamud's novel suggest the Dodgers. See Harley Henry, "'Them Dodgers Is My Gallant Knights': Fiction as History in 'The Natural' (1952)." *Journal of Sport History* 19, no. 2 (1992): 110–129.

23. Malamud, *The Natural*, 126.

24. The homage is described in Grant Wiedenfeld, "Multicultural American Heroes: Reading the Obama-Era Biopics of Jackie Robinson and Jesse Owens through the Lens of American Civil Religion," in *Sport, Film and National Culture*, ed. Seán Crosson (Milton Park, UK: Routledge, 2020), 48–63, https://doi.org/10.4324/9780429327018-5.

25. Julie Lobalzo Wright, "The All-American Golden Boy: Robert Redford, Blond Hair and Masculinity in Hollywood," *Celebrity Studies* 7, no. 1 (2016): 69–82, https://doi.org/10.1080/19392397.2016.1104895.

26. Bird's character is based on a real incident in Chicago. From a feminist point of view, her story represents the nightmare of patriarchy in several ways. See Bob Goldsborough, "Chicago Woman Was Real-Life Stalker from 'The Natural,'" *Chicago Tribune*, March 14, 2013, http://articles.chicagotribune.com/2013-03-14/news/ct-spt-0315-steinhagen-eddie-waitkus-20130315_1_chicago-woman-ruth-ann-steinhagen-eddie-waitkus.

27. For an overview, see Helen Hanson and Catherine O'Rawe, eds., *The Femme Fatale: Images, Histories, Contexts* (London: Palgrave, 2010); https://doi.org//10.1057/9780230282018.

28. Malamud, *The Natural*, 192.

29. Malamud, 149, 207.

30. This book's introduction analyzes the general criticism of Hollywood fantasy through a detailed analysis of the "culture industry" concept from Max Horkheimer and Theodor W. Adorno, *Dialectic of Enlightenment*, trans. Edmund Jephcott (1944; Stanford, CA: Stanford University Press, 2002), 122.

31. "Avant qu'il y eût des lois faites, il y avoit des rapports de justice possible. Dire qu'il n'y a rien de juste ni d'injuste que ce qu'ordonnent ou défendent les lois positives, c'est dire qu'avant qu'on eût tracé le cercle, tous les rayons n'étoient pas égaux." Montesquieu, *De l'esprit des lois* (Paris: Gallimard, 1951), 233 [I.1]; unnamed trans. (Glasgow: David Niven, 1793), 2; https://books.google.com/books/about/The_Spirit_of_Laws.html?id=5zZJA AAAMAAJ.

32. Montesquieu's view of the possible offers a strong challenge to the existentialist credo that existence precedes essence. For further discussion of metaphysics, fiction, and their politic stakes, see the introduction to this book.

33. My straightforward moral judgment of the hero's action emphasizes drama. In this way my critical approach diverges from modernism, a movement which separated a work's artistic form from its moral content—epitomized in American literature by *Lolita* and in Hollywood cinema by *The Birth of a Nation*. Without exploring the question of the nature of art, this study has political meaning as its primary focus.

34. Northrop Frye, *Anatomy of Criticism: Four Essays* (1957; New York: Atheneum, 1968), 44.

35. Frye, *Anatomy*, 33.

36. Jonathan Fraser Light, *The Cultural Encyclopedia of Baseball* (Jefferson, NC: McFarland, 2005).

37. Michael Mandelbaum, *The Meaning of Sports: Why Americans Watch Baseball, Football, and Basketball and What They See When They Do* (New York: Public Affairs, 2004), 20.

38. Douglas A. Noverr, "The Ballpark: Out of the Shadows and Indistinct Background and into the Heart of the Baseball Film," in *Beyond the Stars: Studies in American Popular Film*, vol. 4, ed. Paul Loukides and Linda K. Fuller (Bowling Green, OH: Bowling Green University Popular Press, 1993), 172–182.

39. Brian Helgeland's Jackie Robinson biopic, *42* (2013), borrows the stadium tunnel staging to express a more explicitly evangelical Christian trope of being born again.

40. Malamud, *The Natural*, 208.

41. See Ronald Beiner, *Civil Religion: A Dialogue in the History of Political Philosophy* (Cambridge: Cambridge University Press, 2010), https://doi.org/10.1017/CBO978051 1763144.

42. See the introduction to this book for further discussion of Alexander's cultural sociology. For a bibliography, see Craig A. Forney, *The Holy Trinity of American Sports: Civil Religion in Football, Baseball, and Basketball* (Macon, GA: Mercer University Press, 2007). Forney applies Ninian Smart's theory of worldviews to analyze how sports shape national life through six dimensions: ritual, myth, doctrine, ethics, social life, and experience.

43. For an application of Raymond Williams's cultural materialism to the novel, see Glenn Hendler, *Public Sentiments: Structures of Feeling in Nineteenth-Century American Literature* (Chapel Hill: University of North Carolina Press, 2003). Note how his subtitle agrees with Jeffrey Alexander's view that "structures of feeling" constitute what he calls *The Civil Sphere* (New York: Oxford University Press, 2006). For a study that links sentiment

in the nineteenth-century novel to the Hollywood cinema of Frank Capra, and also chal-
lenges the characterization of modernism as amoral, which I have invoked here, see James
Chandler, *An Archaeology of Sympathy: The Sentimental Mode in Literature and Cinema*
(Chicago, IL: University of Chicago Press, 2013).

44. Katharina Bonzel suggests that sports movies set in rural America such as *Hoosiers* (1986)
decouple their "small town-ness" from the actual small town "in order to open up access to
the American dream across boundaries of place and race." See Katharina Bonzel, *National
Pastimes: Cinema, Sports, and Nation* (Lincoln: University of Nebraska Press, 2020), 21.

45. See Stephen Prince, *A New Pot of Gold: Hollywood under the Electronic Rainbow, 1980–1989*
(New York: Scribner's, 2000); Stephen Prince, ed., *American Cinema of the 1980s: Themes
and Variations* (New Brunswick, NJ: Rutgers University Press, 2007).

Chapter 5

1. All transcriptions by author. *White Men Can't Jump*, written and directed by Ron Shelton,
performed by Woody Harrelson, Wesley Snipes, and Rosie Perez (1992; Beverly Hills,
CA: Twentieth Century Fox Home Entertainment, 2012), Blu-Ray. The source for all figures in this chapter is Twentieth Century Fox Film except where otherwise noted.

2. In *Jerry Maguire* (1996), Marcee Tidwell (Regina King) says offhandedly in conversation,
"I went to see this so-called 'black film' the other day. . . . Twenty minutes of coming attrac-
tions. All black films and all violent. Brothers shooting brothers." Although critics generally highlight the progressive aspects of new Black cinema (especially authorship) in some
respects old stereotypes were reinforced.

3. Karl Ferris designed the cover for Reprise Record's U.S. release of the 1967 album. Shelton's
characters have an audiocassette version in the car. See Sean Egan, *Jimi Hendrix and the
Making of "Are You Experienced"* (London: Askill, 2014), 175.

4. Ed Guerrero's 1993 study frames the new Black wave in a longer history of African-
American cinema, observing in the relationship of mainstream to minority culture "the
dialectical push of Hollywood's cultural construction and domination of the black image
and the pull of an insistent black social consciousness and political activism that has re-
cently generated waves of black-focused and independent films into commercial cinema's trajectory." Ed Guerrero, *Framing Blackness: The African American Image in Film*
(Philadelphia: Temple University Press, 1993), 3.

5. Baker echoes Henry Louis Gates Jr.'s criticism of Michael Jordan. "Crossover" marketing
campaigns such as "Be Like Mike" or Jordan's Hollywood vehicle *Space Jam* (Joe Pytka,
1996) constitute new forms of assimilation. "They incorporate the difference, yet are still
strongly bound by formal and thematic conventions that have been used for decades to
privilege the values of whiteness." Aaron Baker, *Contesting Identities: Sports in American
Film* (Urbana: University of Illinois Press, 2003), 31. See also Gitanjali Maharaj, "Talking
Trash: Late Capitalism, Black (Re)Productivity, and Professional Basketball," *Social Text*
15, no. 1 (Spring 1997): 97–110.

6. Baker, *Contesting Identities*, 25.

7. Thomas DiPiero explains that white masculinity is characterized by invisibility and alien-
ation, so that a white man tends to see himself as an individual without any racial identity.
Thomas DiPiero, *White Men Aren't* (Durham, NC: Duke University Press, 2002), 9, 211.
The Oriental monk or a noble Indian serve a similar subordinate function elsewhere in

American popular culture. See Edward Saïd, *Orientalism* (New York: Pantheon, 1978); and see Jane Naomi Iwamura, "The Oriental Monk in American Popular Culture," in *Religion and Popular Culture in America*, ed. Jeffrey Mahan and Bruce Forbes (Berkeley: University of California Press, 2000), 25–43.

8. For criticism of ostensibly antiracist works that reinforce the superiority of whiteness, see Kelly J. Madison, "Legitimation Crisis and Containment: The 'Anti-Racist-White-Hero' Film," *Critical Studies in Media Communication* 16, no. 4 (December 1999): 399–416; and Matthew Hughey, *The White Savior Film* (Philadelphia: Temple University Press, 2014).

9. Jeffrey C. Alexander, *The Civil Sphere* (New York: Oxford University Press, 2006), 425–457.

10. Zangwill dedicated his play to Teddy Roosevelt, who advocated for monocultural policies (such as English language-only America) and criticized hyphenated ethnic identities. This fact confirms my placement of Zangwill here, although Alexander highlights other texts by the Jewish writer that speak more to hyphenation.

11. Habermas explains how the medieval public sphere took root in the ostentatious dress and formal speaking codes of aristocrats, locating publicity in their persons. I am extending his insight to the modern suit, which would correspond to the bourgeois public sphere in his scheme. The French republic's ban on religious dress in public schools, referred to by their secular principle of *laïcité*, is another relevant example of assimilation.

12. Given that *Knute Rockne: All-American* (1940) continued to play after the United States entered World War II, such a rebel/conformist mindset appealed to young men who sought adventure in war but whose parents might have objected. But the film was written and produced before the war, so the rebel/conformist mindset speaks to a more general spirit of modernity in which youth rebellion was yoked to a new society being created, rather than individual pursuits.

13. On this ground of tacit privilege Michael Rogin and others have argued that Hollywood and American culture remain ruled by White supremacy, despite the industry's disavowal of racism and increasing promotion of diversity. Michael Rogin, "Blackface, White Noise: The Jewish Jazz Singer Finds His Voice," *Critical Inquiry* 18, no. 3 (1992): 418; see also Ed Guerrero, *Framing Blackness: The African American Image in Film* (Philadelphia: Temple University Press, 1993).

14. The communitarian movement in philosophy arose as an attack on liberal individualism. Charles Taylor and others emphasize culture as the context in which the individual self must form, so that a citizen cannot be abstracted from a community like so many atoms. Some criticize this atomized view of human life as a fundamental flaw in liberalism, while Will Kymlicka and others defend the liberal tradition's compatibility with multiculturalism and dismiss the atomized view as a deviation. As a context for individual formation, particular cultures and their values have public importance for communitarianism as a key element in the realization of freedom.

15. If assimilation pretends that a core group's particular primordial qualities are universal, multiculturalism dispels such an illusion of the universal in favor of the particular. "In multiculturalism, the universal is particularized," says Alexander. Alexander, *Civil Sphere*, 450.

16. Amy Gutmann, Introduction to *Multiculturalism: Examining the Politics of Recognition*, expanded edition, ed. Amy Gutmann (Princeton, NJ: Princeton University Press, 1994), 11.

17. Alexander, *Civil Sphere*, 426.

18. Charles Taylor, "The Politics of Recognition," in Gutmann, *Multiculturalism*, 67.

19. For an overview, see Henry Louis Gates, Jr., "Beyond the Culture Wars: Identities in Dialogue," *Profession* (1993): 6–11, https://www.jstor.org/stable/25595500.

20. Corinth refers to the isthmus that connects mainland Greece with the Peloponnese, a symbolic natural bridge between the cultural regions of Athens and of Sparta. Ralph Waldo Emerson, *Essays and Poems of Emerson*, ed. Stuart Pratt Sherman (New York: Harcourt, Brace and Company, 1921), xxxiv; https://archive.org/details/essaysandpoemse00emerg oog/page/n40. See also Luther Luedtke, "Ralph Waldo Emerson Envisions the 'Smelting Pot," *MELUS* 6, no. 2 (Summer, 1979): 3–14.

21. Preamble to the *Constitution of the United States*.

22. Horace M. Kallen, "Democracy Versus the Melting Pot: A Study of American Nationality," *Nation*, February 25, 1915, http://www.expo98.msu.edu/people/kallen.htm.

23. See J. Matthew Hoye, "Neo-republicanism, Old Imperialism, and Migration Ethics," *Constellations* 24, no. 2 (2017): 157–159, https://doi.org/10.1111/1467-8675.12259.

24. Rockne's relationship with priests and his life at the University of Notre Dame are presented as normal, even admirable. One scene in the film offers a spectacular picture of a Roman Catholic Mass in an ornate church. Adult Knute is played by Pat O'Brien, whose Irish name immediately suggests a Catholic identity. O'Brien plays the hero straight, without demoting his Catholicism at all.

25. The original title has no punctuation and simply reads *Knute Rockne All American*, with the second half sometimes set apart as a subtitle.

26. Dyer argues that the position of whiteness as an implicit standard in an ostensibly neutral, color-blind world endows it with a power more subtle and perhaps greater than overt white supremacy. "This property of whiteness, to be everything and nothing, is the source of its representational power," writes Dyer. Because whiteness is "invisible" or unacknowledged in the narrative, it avoids association with any specific qualities and instead becomes so superlative that it comprehends all possible qualities. See Richard Dyer, "White," *Screen* 29, no. 4 (Autumn, 1988): 44–65, reprinted in *The Matter of Images: Essays on Representation*, 2nd ed. (London: Taylor and Francis, 2013), 127.

27. Ryan Coogler's *Black Panther* (2018) could be said to situate Blacks as the core social group and mark European-Americans as ethnic; to me, such a reversal constitutes strong hyphenation. Greg Garrett, *A Long, Long Way: Hollywood's Unfinished Journey from Racism to Reconciliation* (New York: Oxford University Press, 2020).

28. Celestino Deleyto, *From Tinseltown to Bordertown: Los Angeles on Film* (Detroit: Wayne State University Press, 2017), 52.

29. Connor decodes a superstructure for the industry's management and labor relations through the corporate logo, read as an allegory of the narrative contract. J. D. Connor, *The Studios after the Studios: Neoclassical Hollywood, 1970–2010* (Stanford, CA: Stanford University Press, 2015), 23.

30. Deleyto also interprets the fantastic view of black Venice Beach as a forecast of white flight from the city after the 1992 Rodney King riots, which occurred one month after the film's release. Deleyto, *Tinseltown to Bordertown*, 52.

31. See Daniel Bernardi, ed., *Classic Hollywood Classic Whiteness* (Minneapolis: University of Minnesota Press, 2001) and Daniel Bernardi, ed., *The Persistence of Whiteness: Race and Contemporary Hollywood Cinema* (London: Routledge, 2008). For more general history see Jason E. Pierce, *Making the White Man's West: Whiteness and the Creation of the American West* (Boulder: University Press of Colorado, 2016); and see Reginald Horsman,

Race and Manifest Destiny: The Origins of American Racial Anglo-Saxonism (Cambridge, MA: Harvard University Press, 1986).

32. See Brandon Elder, "A Complete Sneaker Guide to 'White Men Can't Jump,'" *Complex*, March 27, 2012, https://www.complex.com/sneakers/2012/03/a-complete-sneaker-guide-to-white-men-cant-jump/.

33. See Michael Oriard, "Muhammad Ali: The Hero in the Age of Mass Media," in *Muhammad Ali: The People's Champ*, ed. Elliott J. Gorn (Urbana: University of Illinois Press, 1995), 8.

34. Baker, *Contesting Identities*, 36.

35. Criticism of this mainstream tendency also appears in Hollywood. The cynical television producers in *Network* (Sidney Lumet, 1976) and *Nightcrawler* (Dan Gilroy, 2014) dramatize the depiction of violent ghettos as an appeal targeted to white suburbanites who hate and fear people of color.

36. See Alexis Krasilovsky, *Women Behind the Camera: Conversations with Camerawomen* (Westport, CT: Praeger, 1997), 173–183.

37. Mark A. Reid, *Redefining Black Film* (Berkeley: University of California Press, 1993), 136.

38. Deleyto, *Tinseltown to Bordertown*, 53.

39. See Todd Boyd, "True to the Game: Basketball as the Embodiment of Blackness in Contemporary Popular Culture," in *Am I Black Enough for You? Popular Culture from the 'Hood and Beyond* (Bloomington: Indiana University Press, 1997), 105–127.

40. Basketball culture has a complicated legacy. Progressive Era (1890–1920) reformers, namely James Naismith, invented basketball as an outreach effort to alleviate social problems of metropolis swelling with immigrants from Europe as well as the American South. Progressives likewise created urban parks and playgrounds where public courts still exist. Paradoxically, white flight to the suburbs created the conditions for street basketball to become distinctively Black. On the one hand, so-called "organized" basketball now represents the White legacy of those Progressive programs. On the other hand, Black street basketball maintains an individualist tradition of amateur sport that developed, ironically, in sylvan English boarding schools. The rural tradition imagined by *Hoosiers* (1986) compares to baseball's Cooperstown myth of rural origin; both sports were quintessentially urban but developed rural myths that resonated with older versions of the American dream and with whiteness. And yet, the coach in *Hoosiers* (Gene Hackman) is characterized as a progressive Easterner. On Progressive-Era parks, see Galen Cranz, *The Politics of Park Design: A History of Urban Parks in America* (Cambridge, MA: MIT Press, 1982).

41. On Black American ethnic types, see Donald Bogle, *Toms, Coons, Mulattoes, Mammies and Bucks: An Interpretative History of Blacks in American Films*, 5th ed. (1973; New York: Bloomsbury Academic, 2016).

42. Clifford Geertz, "Deep Play: Notes on the Balinese Cockfight," *Daedalus* 101, no. 1, Myth, Symbol, and Culture (Winter, 1972): 1–37, https://www.jstor.org/stable/20024056.

43. For one prominent study of inequality, see Michelle Alexander, *The New Jim Crow: Mass Incarceration in the Age of Colorblindness* (New York: The New Press, 2010).

44. A movement of leftist and minority activists, critical race theory discerned sham neutrality in U.S. history. Guided by a critical view of "law's role in the construction and maintenance of social domination and subordination," they acted in opposition to a longstanding "regime of white supremacy." If the social system is structured in a fundamentally unequal way, then a supposedly neutral, universal, or color-blind stance can inhibit reform and

perpetuate injustice. Cornel West, foreword to *Critical Race Theory: The Key Writings that Formed the Movement*, ed. Kimberlé Crenshaw et al. (New York: The New Press, 1995), xi.

45. The classical *liberal* school of political philosophy refers to policies now favored by American conservatives: a limited state, free market economy, and personal freedom. The development of modern liberalism under Keynes and the New Deal led *liberal* to connote an interventionist state, center-left policy, and social reform in American English. The terms *libertarian* and *neoliberalism* nonetheless preserve the classical, European connotation. Lexical confusion here may be inevitable, but I attempt to add the modifier *classical* or use synonyms for clarity.

46. Iseult Honohan, *Civic Republicanism* (London: Routledge, 2002), 119.

47. Galbraith explains that large industry and distribution favor oligarchy and depart from the self-regulation of the small agricultural model. The complexity of modernity also leads him to reject socialism's centralized planning, or "command economy," as a viable alternative. He recommends that the state cultivate "countervailing powers" such as regulated monetary policy, progressive income taxes, labor unions, or controlled markets that restrain the tendencies to oligarchy and to inflationary booms.

48. Pure individualism requires that social identity and culture be relegated to the private sphere, focusing public interaction on economic matters. Honohan, *Civic Republicanism*, 9.

49. Her repetitious rules reveal a stylistic trait of Shelton, whose previous work as a minimalist sculptor explored the play of meaning one form can create in different contexts. See Henry J. Seldis and William Wilson, "Art Walk: A Critical Guide to the Galleries," *Los Angeles Times*, February 11, 1977, part IV, p. 11; Linda Gross, "Film Showcase Screens Tonight," *Los Angeles Times*, February 3, 1978, part IV, p. 11. Thank you to Sunyoung Park at the MFAH-Houston's Hirsch Library for locating these articles.

50. Grant Farred explains that Hollywood sports movies had two dominant types for black athletes in the twentieth century: the Good Negro and the Bad N*gger. See Grant Farred, "When Kings Were (Anti-?)Colonials: Black Athletes in Film," in *Sport in Films*, ed. Emma Poulton and Martin Roderick (New York: Routledge, 2008), 124–136; Originally published in *Sport in Society* 11, no. 2–3 (2008): 240–252.

51. Keith Lewis, featured vocalist, "Jump for It," by Jesse Johnson, in *White Men Can't Jump*.

52. If trash talking has gradually come to be tolerated to a degree in U.S. sports culture, in 1992 it still chafed against the traditional norm of the modest athlete. See Michael Oriard, "Muhammad Ali."

53. Subsequent scenes extend this trauma of conformity to the mind, with one cadet's murder-suicide. While Kubrick's drama offers a caustic attack on strong assimilation, it does not necessarily criticize weak assimilation. His attack on institutional oppression takes root in the ideology of individual freedom, which is the very principle behind weak assimilation and color-blind neutrality.

54. The shows used methods such as choosing categories known to be in a contestant's repertoire, or more blatantly disclosing questions and answers in advance. The public reaction to their fraud revealed the symbolic significance of the game show in American society. See Kent Anderson, *Television Fraud: The History and Implications of the Quiz Show Scandals* (Westport, CT: Greenwood Press, 1978); *American Experience*, "The Quiz Show Scandals," directed by Michael Lawrence, aired January 6, 1992, on PBS, http://www.pbs.org/wgbh/amex/quizshow/index.html.

55. Angharad N. Valdivia, "Stereotype of Transgression? Rosie Perez in Hollywood Film," *Sociological Quarterly* 39, no. 3 (1998): 406, https://doi.org/10.1111/j.1533-8525.1998. tb00510.x.

56. Hernán Vera and Andrew Gordon, *Screen Saviors: Hollywood Fictions of Whiteness* (Lanham, MD: Rowman and Littlefield, 2003), 154.

57. Lawrence R. Samuel, *The American Dream: A Cultural History* (Syracuse, NY: Syracuse University Press, 2012), 6.

58. Carol Graham, *Happiness for All? Unequal Hopes and Lives in Pursuit of the American Dream* (Princeton, NJ: Princeton University Press, 2017), 73.

59. In the sports genre, the white coach/black athlete pairing continues to be a troublesome pattern, notably *Glory Road* (2006), *The Blind Side* (2009), *42* (2013), and *Race* (2016). Meanwhile the crime genre has seen mainstream success with two black buddies; *Ride Along* (2014) and *Central Intelligence* (2016) are two examples that pair Kevin Hart with Ice Cube and Dwayne "The Rock" Johnson, respectively.

60. "By the end of the 1990s, Washington had reconstructed key dimensions of black masculinity, revealing the narrowness of earlier images and disturbing the sacrosanct white male dominance of his contemporary times." Melvin Donaldson, "Denzel Washington: A Revisionist Black Masculinity," in *Pretty People: Movie Stars of the 1990s*, ed. Anna Everett (New Brunswick, NJ: Rutgers University Press, 2012), 65–84, http://www.jstor.org/stable/ j.ctt5hj8m7.7.

Chapter 6

1. All transcriptions by author. *A League of Their Own*, directed by Penny Marshall (1992; Culver City, CA: Sony Pictures Home Entertainment, 2016), Blu-Ray. Source for all images unless otherwise noted.

2. She judges the film "a profoundly unfeminist portrayal." Viridiana Lieberman, *Sport Heroines on Film: A Critical Study of Cinematic Women Athletes, Coaches, and Owners* (Jefferson, NC: McFarland, 2015), 48–49.

3. Aaron Baker agrees that Penny Marshall's film "ultimately discounts" liberal gender politics by "focusing on the more feminine main character Dottie" and on her "choice to give up baseball and dedicate herself to her husband and family." Aaron Baker, *Contesting Identities: Sports in American Film* (Urbana: University of Illinois Press, 2003), 78.

4. Following the film theory of Robert Ray, Aaron Baker claims that *League* adheres to the individualism of most sport history films because it focuses on only "two or three main characters." But Baker can't have it both ways: he calls for a more radically independent heroine as well as a dramatic focus on the collective. Baker, *Contesting Identities*, 10–11.

5. Subdivisions appear less democratic because they have smaller numbers; however, total quantity is less crucial than participation. Pure inclusivity in an enormous group is a weak form of participation; indeed, mass alienation is considered a severe political problem that fosters mob rule, despotism, and totalitarianism. Ramifying all persons into smaller groups increases active participation, and is therefore more democratic. Recall that Montesquieu says democratic republics are only possible in small towns, while larger territories tend toward hierarchical rule by a select few.

6. Nor does equal access equate to equal opportunity given that opportunity involves possibility and that possibility is not equal among individuals naturally different. Equal access

to competition still favors natural talent and oligarchic privilege. Leftist advocates of equal *results* make an argument based on the democratic principle of equal participation, especially with regard to standardized testing and access to education.

7. Although political scientists might consider Montesquieu's scheme a rather crude way to understand contemporary governments, his abstract relation of values to structures remains relevant generally—especially for analyzing objects of popular culture whose underlying political meaning happens on the abstract plane of values.

8. "La *vertu* dans la république est l'amour de la patrie, c'est-à-dire l'amour de l'égalité, comme l'*honneur* est le ressort qui fait mouvoir la monarchie." Note how distinguishing the term *vertu politique* (political virtue) from religious or moral virtue may imply a secular division of church from state. Montesquieu, *De l'esprit des lois*, in vol. 2 of *Œuvres complètes*, ed. Roger Caillois (1748; Paris: Bibliothèque de la Pléiade, 1951), 227; *The Spirit of Laws*, trans. Thomas Nugent (New York: The Colonial Press, 1899), xxxv, https://archive.org/details/spiritoflaws01montuoft.

9. Note how, like Aristotle, Montesquieu posits a mover behind each structure and abstracts all forms into triangular categories. A baron himself, one senses the French writer's admiration for the idea of a republic and his contempt for absolute monarchy as a form of despotism; moderate compromises that mitigate the despotic threats posed by mob rule and absolutism emerge as the most favorable in his theory. His understanding of despotism through fear also recalls Michael Moore's documentaries *Bowling for Columbine* (2002) and *Fahrenheit 9/11* (2004) that draw upon Barry Glassner, *The Culture of Fear: Why Americans Are Afraid of the Wrong Things*, 2nd ed. (1999; New York: Basic, 2010).

10. Aristotle begins the confusion by presuming that the wealthy and well-born have better characters. (Plato had a more ideal view of the aristocrat as monastic civil servants.) As American revolutionaries and others vilified "aristocracy," the confusion became complete. See William Doyle, *Aristocracy: A Very Short Introduction* (New York: Oxford University Press, 2010), 1–6.

11. Absolute monarchy led France to become an "open plutocracy" from the fifteenth through eighteenth centuries. The face of the nobility completely changed as new wealth bought the rights and privileges of nobility, which the monarch used to finance his growing state. Doyle, 17.

12. See the introduction to this book for further discussion. Thomas Piketty, *Capital in the Twenty-First Century*, trans. Arthur Goldhammer (2013; Cambridge, MA: Harvard University Press, 2014).

13. "L'ambition is pernicieuse dans une république. Elle a de bons effets dans la monarchie; elle donne la vie à ce gouvernement." Charles Louis de Secondat, Baron de Montesquieu, *The Spirit of Laws*, in *The Complete Works of M. de Montesquieu*, vol. 1, trans. unnamed (London: T. Evans, 1777), 7:33. https://oll.libertyfund.org/titles/montesquieu-complete-works-vol-1-the-spirit-of-laws.

14. Gerald L. Early, *A Level Playing Field: African American Athletes and the Republic of Sports* (Cambridge, MA: Harvard University Press, 2011), 3.

15. Consider England's Amateur Athletic Club, founded 1866. "The AAC formulated the first formal definition of an amateur athlete. It declared that working men, who were 'mechanics, artisans, or labourers' were de facto 'professionals.' They were, therefore, barred from all amateur contests, which were reserved for 'gentlemen'; that is, people who performed no labour for a living." David Young, "From Olympia 776 BC to Athens 2004: The

Origin and Authenticity of the Modern Olympic Games," in *Global Olympics: Historical and Sociological Studies of the Modern Games*, ed. Kevin Young and Kevin B. Wamsley (Amsterdam: Emerald Book Serials and Monographs, 2005), 10.

16. Montesquieu also clarifies that conflict without order amounts to mob rule and therefore corrupts the principle of democratic government. Ochlocracy comes closer to despotism. He diagnoses mob rule as either unequal belief in the polis or a people who refuse to be ruled by demanding extreme equality with the ruler, effectively doing everything themselves without order. Montesquieu, *Esprit des lois*, I.3: 349.

17. For background on Michael Young's dystopian satire, published in 1958, see David Civil and Joseph J. Himsworth, "Introduction: Meritocracy in Perspective. *The Rise of the Meritocracy* 60 Years On," *The Political Quarterly* 91(April–June 2020): 373–378, https://doi.org/10.1111/1467-923X.12839.

18. I disagree with Markovits's claim that meritocracy is a sham. It is perfectly true to the nature of aristocracy; however, claims to its having a democratic essence are false. Daniel Markovits, cover description of *The Meritocracy Trap: How America's Foundational Myth Feeds Inequality, Dismantles the Middle Class, and Devours the Elite* (New York: Penguin, 2019), https://www.penguinrandomhouse.com/books/548174/the-meritocracy-trap-by-daniel-markovits/.

19. Of course, denying the existence of privilege can also serve as a counterintuitive means to maintain the status quo. For the cynical oligarch, denial simply maintains his power and privilege. For devotees of meritocracy, denial is either a blindness to actual injustice (if there were no discrimination in a just system, demographic diversity would be evident at all ranks) or a confusion of democracy and monarchy.

20. For background and discussion of the competitive model that forms the basis for classical liberalism and the contemporary American conservative ideology of neoliberalism, see the previous chapter on *White Men Can't Jump*.

21. A brief description of this movement and some references are given in the chapter on *Slap Shot*.

22. Kris Vantornhout, "Film Analysis of *A League of Their Own*: Myths and Portrayals of Heroines in Sport" (master's thesis, San Jose State University, 1995), 79; https://doi.org/10.31979/etd.vw78-gydx; https://scholarworks.sjsu.edu/etd_theses/1190.

23. One can perceive a queer undertone in selecting Carole King's song "Now and Forever", which addresses a former lover, to memorialize the women's league.

24. The following chapter on *Ali* discusses the chorus as a model to understand the social power of media and of the soundtrack in cinema.

25. Sutherland co-edited the Oxford World's Classics 2015 edition of *Waverley* with Claire Lamont. Kathryn Sutherland, "Before *Wolf Hall*: How Sir Walter Scott Invented Historical Fiction," *OUPblog*, June 8, 2015, https://blog.oup.com/2015/06/sir-walter-scott-invented-historical-fiction/.

26. On the politics of Scott's *Waverley*, see Fiona Price, "The End of History? Scott, His Precursors and the Violent Past," in *Reinventing Liberty: Nation, Commerce and the British Historical Novel from Walpole to Scott* (Edinburgh: Edinburgh University Press, 2016), 170–206, http://www.jstor.org/stable/10.3366/j.ctt1bh2jss.9.

27. I do not mean to claim that biopics are necessarily aristocratic rather than democratic, merely that their individualist tendency must be weighed against egalitarian solidarity and judged on the particular work. See the following chapter on *Ali* for further discussion of biopics.

28. The verbiage of "do something special," repeated here and in the opening scene by Dottie's daughter, reflect the classical notion of political action that I discuss in the following chapter on *Ali*. The sisters' conflict contrasts private happiness with the public happiness of political action that the introduction to this book elaborates further.

29. The song's origin is never explained, and appears impromptu in the film. This official AAGPBL song is credited to Lavone Pepper Paire Davis, a star catcher in the league who later said, "We put our hearts and souls into the league. We thought it was our job to do our best, because we were the All-American girls. We felt like we were keeping up our country's morale." Quoted in Bill Francis, "League of Women Ballplayers," *National Baseball Hall of Fame*, https://baseballhall.org/discover-more/stories/baseball-history/league-of-women-ballplayers, accessed October 16, 2019.

30. For a discussion of social incorporation and Alexander's approach, see the previous chapter on *White Men Can't Jump*.

31. Anthony Synnott, *Rethinking Men: Heroes, Villains, and Victims* (Farnham, UK: Ashgate, 2009), 4.

32. Synnott remarks on the persistence of old stereotypes of masculinity, despite the ambition of a sensitive, New Age man paradigm to replace them. He observes the qualities of provision, protection, and bravery common to all definitions of men, but is careful to note that these qualities are not exclusively male. See Synnott, 50–52.

33. Philip Pettit, *Republicanism: A Theory of Freedom and Government* (Oxford: Clarendon Press, 1997); Quentin Skinner, *Liberty before Liberalism* (Cambridge: Cambridge University Press, 1998). https://doi.org/10.1017/CBO9781139171274.

34. Lieberman contends that Duggan's reformed masculinity doesn't extend beyond the sphere of women. It is true that no later scenes depict him in a men's world, where a more radical confrontation can be imagined; but one cannot conclude anything from that absence, in my view. His sideline conduct is framed with a mixed crowd in the background which I take to represent a public space rather than the exclusively women's spaces of the locker room, bus, or house. Lieberman, *Sport Heroines*, 46.

35. Even these authoritarian coaches defer to their players and associates at the climax of both dramas, which becomes the key to victory. The context of racial integration makes the democratic character of Washington's coach obvious. I contend that Hackman's character, a Northeasterner brought to a small Indiana burgh, creates an allegory for the democratic central authority of New Deal policies. The progressivism of *Hoosiers*' historical setting parallels *The Natural*. See the earlier chapter on that film for further discussion.

36. To support his argument that the film is ultimately conservative, Baker notes that the players complain about their short-skirt uniforms, but end up showcasing them throughout the film. While it is true that the filmmakers could have taken the liberty of historical drama to change the uniforms, significant and consistent criticism of the conservative gender regimes does appear, in my view, in the controversy around their adoption, in satire of the general controversy around masculinization, and in a later scene that highlights painful bruises caused by sliding without pants. Baker, *Contesting Identities*, 91.

37. Lieberman, *Sport Heroines*, 39.

38. See Daniela Baroffio-Bota and Sarah Banet-Weiser, "Women, Team Sports, and the WNBA: Playing Like a Girl," in *Handbook of Sports and Media*, ed. Arthur A. Raney and Jennings Bryant (Mahwah, NJ: Lawrence Erlbaum Associates, 2006), 485–500.

39. Vantornhout reflects that progress made for women during World War II happened quickly and easily within a context of security, whereas Title IX provoked fear that made change slow and difficult. See Vantornhout, "Film Analysis of *League*," 171.

40. Lieberman argues that the film invents fictional characters who are less feminist than the historical women for whom the league built a confidence to pursue professional lives. Namely, Dottie's decision to retire from baseball to domestic life contradicts the theme of women's liberation and empowerment. While I agree that Kit better exemplifies autonomy, the ambivalence around Dottie's decision (amplified by comparison with Kit, Marla, and others) has a realist quality that should not be overlooked. Lieberman, *Sport Heroines*, 37.

41. Comparison of Dottie to Roy Hobbs reveals a conflict between ambition and equality in both films. Both characters represent quintessentially American rural talents recruited to the big league in Chicago. However, their motivations and arcs are opposite. Hobbs begins with the highest ambition, to be the greatest there ever was, but his development of humility and solidarity ultimately extols an egalitarian virtue. Dottie, by contrast, begins her story with no ambition. She is content to work as a milkmaid, await her husband's return, and live a homemaker's life. She develops initiative that culminates at the Hall of Fame where her individual ambition is aggregated into the league's collective ambition.

42. The evangelical tradition developed in the temperance and anti-prostitution movements and assumes a fundamental difference between genders. I use the term *collectivist* to contrast republican and liberal political values rather than *socialist*—a freighted term that shifts emphasis to political economy. Janet K. Boles and Diane Long Hoeveler, "Introduction," in *Historical Dictionary of Feminism* (Lanham, MD: Scarecrow, 1995).

43. Noted in Laura K. Nelson, "Feminism Means More than a Changed World, It Means the Creation of a New Consciousness in Women: Feminism, Consciousness-Raising, and Continuity between the Waves," in *100 Years of the Nineteenth Amendment: An Appraisal of Women's Political Activism*, eds. Holly J. McCammon and Lee Ann Banaszak (New York: Oxford University Press, 2018), 187.

44. Nelson, 187.

45. On the harm done by not recognizing special aspects of identity, see Charles Taylor, "The Politics of Recognition," in *Multiculturalism: Examining the Politics of Recognition*, rev. ed., ed. Amy Gutmann (Princeton, NJ: Princeton University Press, 1994), 25–74.

Chapter 7

1. All transcriptions by author. *Ali*, directed by Michael Mann, performed by Will Smith, story by Gregory Allen Howard, screenplay by Stephen J. Rivele, Christopher Wilkinson, Michael Mann, and Eric Roth (2001; Munich: Universum Film, 2012), Blu-Ray. (The 2004 director's cut DVD and 2017 commemorative edition Blu-Ray slightly alter the theatrical release version of the film, especially the opening montage.) Source for all figures in this chapter is Sony Pictures Entertainment except where otherwise noted.

2. I capitalize *Black* and *White* to emphasize a distinct social group and culture, but I employ *African-American* and *European-American* to emphasize an ethnic part of a broader culture in formal and informal terms. I employ *white* and *black* to describe tones and colors. The earlier chapter on *White Men Can't Jump* discusses ethnicity as a "hyphenated mode" of social incorporation based on the cultural sociology of Jeffrey Alexander.) Alternating usage reflects an actual ambiguity. In some situations, such as this one, the terms may therefore be interchangeable.

3. Gerald Early, introduction to *A Muhammad Ali Reader* (New York: Ecco, 1998), vii.

4. Early was responding to Hauser's 1991 biography, a special appearance at the 1996 Atlanta Olympic Games, Gast's academy award-winning 1996 documentary, and Remnick's 1998 biography. Early also warns against overestimating Ali's analytical intelligence, judging that Ali "had the zealot's set of answers to life's questions." Early, vii, xvi.

5. Frantz Fanon, *Black Skin, White Masks*, trans. Charles Lam Markmann (London: Pluto Press, 2008), 9.

6. Fanon, 175.

7. Echoing Sartre, Fanon emphasizes individual consciousness above the crowd's fervor. He compares the crowd to an iron that heats iron "in order to shape it at once. I should prefer to warm man's body and leave him. We might reach this result: mankind retaining this fire through self-combustion." Fanon, 4.

8. To put this criticism another way, must every successful Black athlete be overburdened with representing his race, asks Grant Farred, while "the historical luxury of only 'personal' representation" is reserved for White subjects? Grant Farred, "When Kings Were (Anti-?)Colonials: Black Athletes in Film," in "Sport in Films," ed. Emma Poulton and Martin Roderick, special issue, *Sport in Society* 11, no. 2–3 (2008): 251. The article also appears in a monograph edition of the issue, *Sport in Films* (New York: Routledge, 2008), 124–136. See also Grant Farred, *What's My Name? Black Vernacular Intellectuals* (Minneapolis: University of Minnesota Press, 2003).

9. Andrew Pepper, "From Civil Rights to Black Nationalism: Hollywood v. Black America?," in *American History and Contemporary Hollywood Film*, by Trevor B. McCrisken and Andrew Pepper (New Brunswick: Rutgers University Press, 2005), 176, http://www.jstor.org/stable/10.3366/j.ctt1r21c6.11. Pepper takes responsibility for the chapter on page xii of the preface.

10. Farred asserts that Leon Gast's documentary fails to represent Ali as a "renegade and hero of the countercultural left" and that Gast represents Ali's opponent "George Foreman as an unreflective 'Uncle Tom abroad.' Or, to phrase it post-colonially, Foreman became a black American of the Fanonian 'Black Skins, White Masks' variety—the black American who was identified, despite his race, with the metropolis, with the US establishment, like some of the colonized subjects critiqued by Frantz Fanon in his book *Black Skin, White Masks*." Farred, "Black Athletes in Film," 242, 244.

11. David Rodríguez-Ruiz, "Mann's Biopics and the Methodology of Philosophy: *Ali* and *The Insider*," in *The Philosophy of Michael Mann*, eds. R. Barton Palmer et al. (Lexington: University Press of Kentucky, 2014), 244–245, http://www.jstor.org/stable/j.ctt5vkktc.18.

12. Despite multiculturalism's fundamental resistance to assimilation and individualism, overemphasis on resistance will curl round to assimilate every individual negatively—everyone is the same in their total difference. Consider Donald Trump's appeal to minorities, especially men, as a macho icon of countercultural resistance. People of color, provincials, and Christian nationalists resemble each other as cultural minorities to the extent that individual autonomy is emphasized. See Eric Levitz, "Men and Women Have Never Been More Politically Divided," *New York Magazine*, October 19, 2020, https://nymag.com/intelligencer/2020/10/2020-polls-gender-gap-women-voters-trump.html.

13. For instance, Vincent Gaine argues that Ali's social engagement lies in his consciously aiming to inspire others. It is not clear to me if that conscious aim is understood as a quality, an action, or something public. Vincent M. Gaine, *Existentialism and Social Engagement in the Films of Michael Mann* (London: Palgrave, 2011), 204. Elsewhere, as an admirer of Ali the activist, Grant Farred takes issue with memorials that prioritize athletics. He

argues that Leon Gast's biographical documentary *When We Were Kings* (1996) "renders Ali's political oppositionality incidental to his boxing, his splendid athleticism." Yet Farred also asserts that inspiration from accomplishment alone does not amount to strong social engagement and fails to distinguish Ali from other athletes. Farred, "Black Athletes in Film," 242.

14. *The Jackie Robinson Story*, directed by Alfred E. Green, screenplay by Arthur Mann and Lawrence Taylor (1950), 00:01:30, streaming video, https://tubitv.com/watch/461395/the_jackie_robinson_story_in_color.

15. *Pride of the Yankees* (1942) found its twin in a soldier biopic, *Pride of the Marines* (1945).

16. Michael Oriard, "Muhammad Ali: The Hero in the Age of Mass Media," in *Muhammad Ali: The People's Champ*, ed. Elliott J. Gorn (Urbana: University of Illinois Press, 1995), 8.

17. John Rawls, *A Theory of Justice* (Cambridge, MA: Belknap Press, 1971).

18. The tragic outcome of *Champion* will show his longing for excessive wealth and recognition but imply that his dream of achieving a better life is typical. *Jim Thorpe: All-American* (1951) is interesting in this regard because it combines an origin scene of running across the reservation with a school initiation scene in which bully jocks haze the callow newcomer and spark his less innocent interest in football.

19. Jonathan Rayner compares this opening montage to similar sequences in *Malcolm X* (1992), *JFK* (1994), and *When We Were Kings* (1996). Jonathan Rayner, *The Cinema of Michael Mann: Vice and Vindication*, Directors' Cuts (London: Wallflower, 2013), 149–151.

20. A similar line appears in *Forrest Gump* (1994), also written by Eric Roth. But in that film it plays as light comedy. Roth might be highlighting the divergent experiences of whites and blacks through that repetition. It is worth noting that the 2004 and 2017 video versions of *Ali* eliminate the cop's line. *Ali*, director's cut (Culver City, CA: Columbia Tristar Home Entertainment, 2004), DVD; *Ali*, commemorative edition (Culver City, CA: Sony Pictures Home Entertainment, 2017), Blu-Ray.

21. Hollywood films set in the past are often criticized for relegating racism to history. See Pepper, "Hollywood v. Black America?"

22. Till was in fact six months older than Ali. Muhammad Ali with Richard Durham, *The Greatest: My Own Story*, edited by Toni Morrison (1975; New York: Ballantine, 1976), 24

23. Lieberman's documentary biopic argues that Liston eventually adopted the public persona of a Black villain in reaction to his exclusion by the White mainstream, particularly after he first became champion and attempted to turn away from a disreputable past. *Sonny Liston: The Mysterious Life and Death of a Champion*, directed by Jeff Lieberman, aired 1995, on HBO.

24. The 2004 and 2017 video versions of *Ali* add these images of Ali and his father signing a contract with the Louisville Sponsorship Group (LSG). Ali's 1975 autobiography and 1977 film also feature Southern Whites who treat him like treasured property. Michael Ezra explains how the LSG legitimized Ali for the Euro-American mainstream but became a symbolic White enemy of his subsequent ownership group led by the Nation of Islam. Michael Ezra, *Muhammad Ali: The Making of an Icon* (Philadelphia: Temple University Press, 2009).

25. Anna Dzenis, "Impressionist Extraordinaire: Michael Mann's *Ali*," *Senses of Cinema* 19 (March 2002), http://sensesofcinema.com/2002/feature-articles/ali/.

26. A diminutive for people of diminutive stature, "Shorty" compares God to someone who is easily disregarded, but who sees you in passing and who you must reckon with ultimately.

At this moment in the book Ali describes the low point of his career that came in his first fight with Ken Norton. Ali, *The Greatest: My Own Story*, 5.

27. The series leads are a White and Black-Hispanic detective duo, resembling the Jewish and Muslim buddies here. Jamie Foxx later played the role of detective Ricardo Tubbs in Mann's film adaption, *Miami Vice* (New York: Universal, 2006).

28. Quoted in Anna Dzenis, "Michael Mann's Cinema of Images," *Screening the Past* 14 (September 2002), http://www.screeningthepast.com/2014/12/michael-manns-cinema-of-images/.

29. Although Marxism is typically associated with atheism, the religious left complicates that simple understanding. Mann and Roth's blending of religious figures with leftist themes is more easily understood through the context of American civil religion. This dimension of social life blends prophetic with radical secular traditions. For further discussion see the book's first chapter and Philip Gorski, *American Covenant: A History of Civil Religion from the Puritans to the Present* (Princeton, NJ: Princeton University Press, 2017).

30. Adrian Wootton, "The Big Hurt," *Sight and Sound* 12, no. 3 (March 2002): 16.

31. Rayner comments on the realism of Ali in the context of a debate over whether Mann's films adhere to the classical conventions of genre, or challenge them. The first chapter of this book challenges the postmodern equation of breaking convention with democratic political engagement. Rayner, *Cinema of Michael Mann*, 135–137.

32. Jan Philipp Reemtsma, *More Than a Champion: The Style of Muhammad Ali*, trans. John E. Woods (New York: Knopf, 1998), 122.

33. Recall from the chapter on *White Men Can't Jump* that Baker and Gates criticize White culture for showcasing improvisation while denigrating aggressive gangster elements of Black culture. Ali avoids that softening because he employs improvisation as an aggressive attacking strategy, within an anti-colonial project.

34. George Bellows, *Stag at Sharkey's*, 1909, oil on canvas, 36 × 48″ (92 × 122 cm), Cleveland Museum of Art, http://www.clevelandart.org/art/1133.1922.

35. An earlier chapter describes how *Rocky I* (1976) mixes class and race to stage its Philadelphia hero fighting for respect from the wider world.

36. Redundant signals are a conventional means to clarify dramatic action, especially character motivation. See David Bordwell, Janet Staiger, and Kristin Thompson, *The Classical Hollywood Cinema: Film Style and Mode of Production to 1960* (New York: Columbia University Press, 1987).

37. Aaron Baker criticizes *The Jackie Robinson Story* (1950) for a lack of narration during scenes that showcase the hero's distinctively Black style of running the bases. Given that voiceover narration dominates other parts of the film, I agree that its omission during and after certain athletic scenes denies recognition to Black American culture. But the lack of narration in *Ali* overall exemplifies how pure athleticism is best admired without narration, in my view. See Aaron Baker, *Contesting Identities: Sports in American Film* (Urbana: University of Illinois Press, 2003), 17–18.

38. Through his expressionistic style Scorsese pays more attention to violence than to athletics. *Raging Bull* adopts a different kind of realism that combines sociological observation with provocative brutality in the manner of Émile Zola. Cinematographer Michael Chapman films on artificially large boxing rings to create exaggerated impressions of the space. He also uses slow motion, speed ramping, and a smash zoom to make manifest Jake LaMotta's inner turmoil as he withstands punishment, statically. Scorsese famously

cuts away at the most brutal moment to show ringside spectators splattered with LaMotta's blood, then dwells on a close-up of blood dripping off a rope. If it were not in black and white, such gore would belong in horror and Grand Guignol. The stunningly beautiful cinematography counterbalances physicality in the same way as French realism. See Roland Barthes, "L'Effet de réel," *Communications* 11 (March 1968): 84–89.

39. Michael Bentt plays Sonny Liston, and Charles Shufford plays George Foreman. Michael Mann, "Commentary," *Ali*, director's cut (2004).

40. Hannah Arendt, *The Human Condition* (Chicago: University of Chicago Press, 1958), 24

41. Action, or *la vita activa*, is not the only aspect of life beyond necessity. Philosophy (*la vita contemplativa*) and pleasure (*la vita voluptuosa*), however, do not share action's public and egalitarian qualities. See the first chapter for further discussion of this point. Arendt, 24–25.

42. Arendt recalls that *oikia*, the root of *economy*, refers to the household. The common refrain that sports should be separate from politics depends on a narrow definition of politics as private matters of opinion; as many critics point out, there is nothing more clearly political than a national anthem. The real issue concerns competing political purposes: sports as a ritual of solidarity versus a forum for individual action. To say that national unity "shouldn't be political" pretends that the nation itself has no values that might sow division—a position either naïvely idealist or cynically nihilist.

43. Although I lean on the popular term *difference* that is dear to postmodernists, note that Arendt elevates action and speech from the mere difference of all things. "Otherness in its most abstract form is found only in the sheer multiplicity of inorganic objects, whereas all organic life already shows variations and distinctions, even between specimens of the same species. But only man can express this distinction and distinguish himself, and only he can communicate himself and not merely something—thirst or hunger, affection or hostility or fear. In man, otherness, which he shares with everything that is, and distinctness, which he shares with everything alive, become uniqueness, and human plurality is the paradoxical plurality of unique beings." Arendt, *Human Condition*, 176, 179.

44. In theory, liberalist assimilation destroys all sociocultural groups equally. But that project forfeits social justice by ignoring the past misdeeds of the domineering groups and by withholding compensation to the domineered. Assimilation's radical liquidation can only be justly led by minorities.

45. Mann and Roth transpose the famous press conference to a street scene in Harlem. Will Smith slightly alters the lines, but his delivery channels Ali's rhythm. Reporter Robert Lipsyte later described the 1964 press conference as "an athletic declaration of independence," underlining Ali's quintessential Americanness. The archetypal conflict of the individual with an unjust society—a romantic tradition rooted in Jean-Jacques Rousseau's autobiographical *Confessions* and his novel *Émile*—is a liberal theme common to Ali, Lipsyte, and Mann. Robert Lipsyte, "The Champion Speaks, but Softly: Clay Discusses His Future, Liston and Black Muslims," *New York Times*, February 27, 1964, 34; Robert Lipsyte, *An Accidental Sportswriter: A Memoir* (New York: HarperCollins, 2011), 69. In fact, Lipsyte would showcase Ali's declaration"I'm free to be what I want" in the headline of every subsequent feature story he wrote for the *Times* across Ali's career. Observe the headlines for Robert Lipsyte, "'I'm Free to Be Who I Want': The Name is Ali," *New York Times*, May 28, 1967, SM15; Lipsyte, "'Free to Be What I Want': In a Decade of Sports," *New York Times*, December 28, 1969, S3; Lipsyte, "'I Don't Have to Be What You Want Me to Be,' Says Muhammad Ali," *New York Times*, March 7, 1971, SM24.

46. The context of Ali's first line on the Viet Cong and attribution of the second have been a subject of controversy, especially for Lipsyte. See Stefan Fatsis, "'No Viet Cong Ever Called Me Nigger': The Story Behind the Famous Quote that Muhammad Ali Probably Never Said," *Slate*, June 8, 2016, https://slate.com/culture/2016/06/did-muhammad-ali-ever-say-no-viet-cong-ever-called-me-nigger.html.

47. This airplane episode actually occurred in 1974, but Mann and Roth shift it to ten years earlier. They also substitute an L-1011 cockpit for the actual DC-8. See the event documented in *When We Were Kings*, directed by Leon Gast (1996; Polygram, 2002). I thank Bobby Smiley for observing this detail. See also Thomas Hauser, *Muhammad Ali: His Life and Times* (New York: Simon & Schuster, 1991), 265–266.

48. The black star also has an association to Pan-Africanism through other related social and religious movements from the turn of the century, notably W. E. B. DuBois's 1911 historical pageant *The Star of Ethiopia*. On that play and context, see David Krasner, *A Beautiful Pageant: African American Theatre, Drama, and Performance in the Harlem Renaissance, 1910–1927* (New York: Palgrave Macmillan, 2002), https://doi.org/10.1007/978-1-137-06625-1. On Garvey, see Colin Grant, *Negro with a Hat: The Rise and Fall of Marcus Garvey* (New York: Oxford University Press, 2008); see also Adam Ewing, *The Age of Garvey: How a Jamaican Activist Created a Mass Movement and Changed Global Black Politics* (Princeton, NJ: Princeton University Press, 2014).

49. Mann and Roth probably draw this account from Hauser's biography, which underlines the importance of this Africa trip to Ali's growing consciousness of himself as a global icon. See Hauser, *Muhammad Ali*, 109–112.

50. In contrast, *When We Were Kings* depicts Ali at home in Zaire while George Foreman is estranged by the foreign surroundings. Mann and Roth's choice to estrange the hero complicates the drama.

51. Negritude and pan-Africanism were criticized for promoting an essential African identity that does not differ in kind from racist thought. Shifting the focus of Black unity to political action is exemplified by Nigerian writer Wole Soyinka's famous line: "A tiger does not proclaim his tigritude, he pounces." Soyinka is quoted in Janheinz Jahn, *A History of Neo-African Literature: Writing in Two Continents*, trans. Oliver Coburn and Ursula Lehrburger (London: Faber and Faber, 1968), 265. For an overview, see Bill Ashcroft, Gareth Griffiths, and Helen Tiffin, *The Empire Writes Back*, 2nd ed. (New York: Routledge, 2002). See also Reiland Rabaka, *The Négritude Movement: W. E. B. Dubois, Leon Damas, Aimé Césaire, Leopold Senghor, Frantz Fanon* (Lanham, MD: Lexington Books, 2015) and Patrice Nganang, "The Senghor Complex," trans. Cullen Goldblatt, in *Gods and Soldiers: The Penguin Anthology of Contemporary African Writing*, ed. Rob Spillmann (New York: Penguin, 2009), 87–104.

52. Nkrumah feared the CIA as a threat to his socialist-leaning but non-aligned regime, perhaps with reason. Before his assassination, Kennedy seemed to have favored a more supportive policy than the CIA. A 1966 military coup ousted Nkrumah. See Willard Scott Thompson, *Ghana's Foreign Policy, 1957–1966: Diplomacy Ideology, and the New State* (Princeton, NJ: Princeton University Press, 1969), 301; see also Mark O'Malley, "Ghana," in *Africana: The Encyclopedia of the African and African American Experience*, 2nd edition, ed. Anthony Appiah and Henry Louis Gates (New York: Oxford University Press, 2005), 789.

53. Arendt, *Human Condition*, 180.

54. Arendt insists on distinguishing eternity from immortality. Contemplation's object is an independent, changeless eternity, whereas political life concerns "deathless life on earth," that is to say, in the world. Arendt, 18.

55. She sees stories as "any series of events that together form a story with a unique meaning." Arendt, 185–186.

56. Arendt 181, 184.

57. Note the instrumental character behind Aristotle's preference for fiction. In representing the plausible, fiction maps the probable and necessary like a scientist's model. Arendt's preference for the historical subject parallels her emphasis on *la vita activa* over *la vita contemplativa*, which we discuss further in the next chapter. For a recent translation see Aristotle, *Poetics*, trans. Anthony Kenny (New York: Oxford University Press, 2013), 28 [§9, 1451a–b].

58. Arendt excludes private or anonymous deeds from action, giving as examples criminal feats and anonymous charity. They remain marginal because they sacrifice publicity to achieve some private end, whether necessity, pleasure, or spiritual fruit. However, one must admit that certain terrorist acts or vandalism may nevertheless qualify as "bad actions" in their intent to destroy a public. Not discussed by Arendt, the bad action is also remembered and shapes a world. See our discussion of Alexander in the next chapter.

59. A subplot around the military draft appears to exaggerate Ali's opposition to the Nation of Islam. NOI lawyer and manager Herbert Muhammad is shown hatching a deal with the Army, only for a rogue Ali to refuse any compromise. In reality, Ali and the NOI worked together closely to prepare the grounds for his defense as a conscientious objector through his status as a minister in the NOI. Hauser's biography confirms that Ali's decision to object was planned, with statements printed in advance. In skewing this account, Mann and Roth play up the theme of the liberal individual. See Hauser, *Muhammad Ali*, 170.

60. The filmmakers created these contrasting signs and murals and installed them on location in Mozambique. Mann pinpoints the location as Mavalane A, a favela adjacent to the international airport in Maputo, Mozambique. Michael Mann, "Commentary," *Ali*, director's cut (2001; Culver City, CA: Columbia Tristar Home Entertainment, 2004), DVD.

61. See Hauser, *Muhammad Ali*, 286–292.

62. Arendt, *Human Condition*, 187.

63. Mann acknowledges the Soviet's influence in Dzenis, "Michael Mann."

64. Mann appears to belong to the generation of 1960s and 1970s counterculture. Its libertarian aspect is evident in the heroes of *Shaft*, *Dirty Harry*, and *Serpico*. Consider that Arendt identifies the origin of totalitarianism in "the alienation of the masses from government." Hannah Arendt, *The Origins of Totalitarianism* (New York: Harcourt, Brace and Company, 1951), 256.

65. See Michael Mandelbaum, *The Meaning of Sports: Why Americans Watch Baseball, Football, and Basketball and What They See When They Do* (New York: Public Affairs, 2004), 14–15.

66. The production stirred up controversy when extras in Mozambique protested that they had not been properly compensated for their work on the film. Jon Jeter and Sharon Waxman, "'Ali' Extras Feel Sucker-Punched; Mozambicans Say Filmmakers Exploited Them for Work in Crowd Scenes," *Washington Post*, June 13, 2001, p. C1; *ProQuest Historical Newspapers*.

67. Mann's characteristic subject of isolated individuals struggling against powerful institutions usually ends tragically. Wildermuth interprets *Ali*'s ending as the individual triumph over nationalism. I contend that the ending represents triumph over imperialism, which I distinguish from nationalism. Mark E. Wildermuth, *Blood in the Moonlight: Michael Mann and Information Age Cinema* (Jefferson, NC: McFarland, 2005), 192.

68. Foreman famously waved the U.S. flag upon his gold medal victory at the 1968 Olympic Games in Mexico City. His gesture was perceived as a response to the provocative salute of sprinters Tommie Smith and John Carlos, whose raised fists (connoting the Black Power movement) had advocated for human rights during the 200-meter medal ceremony; Foreman thus represented a conservative reaction to the countercultural and radical Black activists. Mann's choice to swath Ali with the American flag here cuts through that binary and asserts Ali as the true representative of the nation.

69. While the 1974 fight occurred as the Vietnam War came to a close, the 2001 film was released in the period before 9/11. One might infer in this international image a positive picture of neoliberal globalization, although the demonization of the CIA disrupts that implied support for a *Pax Americana*.

70. President Carter sent Ali on several diplomatic missions to the USSR and to several African countries, but his political career did not materialize for various reasons. See Dorothy Gilliam, "Ali as a Presidential Envoy: Fighting in the Wrong Ring," *Washington Post*, February 11, 1980, C1.

Chapter 8

1. Michael Ezra credits Ali's wife Lonnie for guiding his legacy. Michael Ezra, *Muhammad Ali: The Making of an Icon* (Philadelphia: Temple University Press, 2009), 164.

2. Barack Obama, "Statement from President Barack Obama as Prepared for the Funeral of Muhammad Ali," *The White House* (blog), June 10, 2016, https://obamawhitehouse.archives.gov/blog/2016/06/10/president-obamas-tribute-muhammad-ali-he-will-always-be-america.

3. For an overview, see Mark Sandritter, "A Timeline of Colin Kaepernick's National Anthem Protest and the Athletes Who Joined Him," *SBNation*, September 25, 2017. https://www.sbnation.com/2016/9/11/12869726/colin-kaepernick-national-anthem-protest-seahawks-brandon-marshall-nfl.

4. Colin Kaepernick, transcript of media session, August 28, 2016, *NinersWire*, https://ninerswire.usatoday.com/2016/08/28/transcript-colin-kaepernick-addresses-sitting-during-national-anthem/. See also "Colin Kaepernick Explains Why He Sat During National Anthem," *NFL.com*, August 27, 2016. https://www.nfl.com/news/colin-kaepernick-explains-why-he-sat-during-national-anthem-0ap3000000691077.

5. Cork Gaines, "Championship Teams Visiting the White House Has Turned into a Mess—Here Is How Trump and the Teams Have Wrecked the Tradition," *Insider*, June 26, 2019, https://www.businessinsider.com/championship-teams-trump-white-house-2019-4.

6. Greg Garrett, *A Long, Long Way: Hollywood's Unfinished Journey from Racism to Reconciliation* (New York: Oxford University Press, 2020).

7. Kaepernick was mentored by the sociologist Harry Edwards, who penned *The Revolt of the Black Athlete* (New York: Free Press, 1970).

8. Radical secularism's libertarian tendency does surface in *White Men Can't Jump* and *Ali*, and hints of religious nationalism appear after 2001 in the evangelical Christian characters of *The Blind Side* (2009) and *42* (2013), but neither conquest narrative nor apocalyptic themes hold forth. On the liberal evangelical current in the mainstream genre, see Grant Wiedenfeld, "Multicultural American Heroes: Reading the Obama-Era Biopics of Jackie Robinson and Jesse Owens through the Lens of American Civil Religion," *Sport, Film and National Culture*, ed. Seán Crosson (Milton Park, UK: Routledge, 2020), 48–63, https://doi.org/10.4324/9780429327018-5. Christian cinema and its adoption of sports is a topic for future study. See Charlotte E. Howell, *Divine Programming: Negotiating Christianity in American Dramatic Television Production 1996–2016* (New York: Oxford University Press, 2020).

9. Joseph Campbell, *The Hero with a Thousand Faces*, 2nd ed. (Princeton, NJ: Princeton University Press, 1972), 29.

10. For historical background, see Maya Montañez Smukler, *Liberating Hollywood: Women Directors and the Feminist Reform of 1970s American Cinema* (New Brunswick, NJ: Rutgers University Press, 2018).

11. Our comparison is predicated on criticism of earlier eras that also follows the culture industry approach that we have questioned. Logic therefore demands a reexamination of Hollywood before 1976 from our civic humanist approach to support a conclusion of democratic progress. Furthermore, other genres and areas of popular culture may tell different stories.

12. The narrow understanding of racism as an individual prejudice or explicit rhetoric deflects criticism of a hierarchical social system. Meanwhile, at the opposite extreme, some consider racism the ultimate source of all social hierarchy and power. Such ideological framing has provocative rhetoric but risks either rejecting society itself as an inherent evil, which feeds back into individualism, or reinforcing racial conflict as inevitable. See Isabel Wilkerson, *Caste: The Origins of Our Discontent* (New York: Random, 2020).

13. Aside from the revolt of the Black athlete already mentioned, the achievements of space exploration during the crisis of poverty and race riots also exemplify the contrast—captured poetically in Gil Scott-Heron's "Whitey on the Moon," track 9 on *Small Talk at 125th and Lenox*, Flying Dutchman 10143, 1970, 33⅓ rpm, https://www.youtube.com/watch?v=goh2x_G0ct4.

14. The protocol of white privilege here might be compared to an archaic gift economy whereby the upper ranks have priority access. Marcel Mauss compares modern social welfare programs to "the old theme of 'noble expenditure'" in *The Gift: Forms and Functions of Exchange in Archaic Societies*, trans. Ian Gunnison (London: Cohen & West, 1966), 66, https://archive.org/details/giftformsfunctio00maus/page/66/mode/2up.

15. The nation's internal focus during this era can be interpreted as either persistently blind imperialism or a corrective withdrawal from imperialism after Vietnam. For an example of the former interpretation, see Scott Laderman and Tim Gruenewald, eds., *Imperial Benevolence: U.S. Foreign Policy and American Popular Culture since 9/11* (Berkeley: University of California Press, 2018).

16. On the racist aspect of Miyagi, see Jane Naomi Iwamura, "The Oriental Monk in American Popular Culture," in *Religion and Popular Culture in America*, eds. Jeffrey Mahan and Bruce Forbes (Berkeley: University of California Press, 2000), 25–43.

17. Another example: the heartless Italians of *Breaking Away* (1979) surprise the hero with their boyish villainy, but a French exchange student at the film's end redeems the image of Europe. Yet the question of Europe is grafted upon internal class conflict that centers the drama.

18. In *Caddyshack*, conservative Judge Smalls (Ted Knight) is set against nouveau-riche real estate developer Al Czervik (Rodney Dangerfield) who brings an enthusiastic Japanese entourage to the country club. In *Major League*, devout Christian Eddie Harris (Chelcie Ross) ridicules the voodoo practices of Afro-Caribbean slugger Pedro Cerrano (Dennis Haysbert) but drops Christ for Cerrano's gods later in the film.

19. See the chapter on *A League of Their Own* for a more detailed discussion of Montesquieu's *The Spirit of Laws*.

20. In her history of liberalism Helena Rosenblatt shows that John Dewey and Franklin D. Roosevelt employed *liberal* in a humanitarian sense that stressed generosity of mind and character and supported state intervention to emancipate individuals from arbitrary power and to protect people from plutocracy. She contrasts this progressive side of liberalism with free market economics and the limited state. Rather than oppose these two meanings of liberalism, this work contrasts civic republicanism with liberalism. Helena Rosenblatt, *The Lost History of Liberalism: From Ancient Rome to the Twenty-First Century* (Princeton, NJ: Princeton University Press, 2019), 260–262.

21. *Invictus* (2009) is a notable exception to the dearth of public officials; its drama involves the South African president allying with the national rugby team's captain. Protagonists of *Any Given Sunday* (1999), *High Flying Bird* (2019), and *National Champions* (2021) who end up leading a new team and advocating for player's unions, do represent countervailing powers. Yet if there is a lack of institutions represented positively, few bureaucrat villains appear in the genre outside of the NCAA investigator in *The Blind Side* (2009) and the CIA in *Ali*. The legal drama *The Hurricane* (1999) criticizes and redeems the justice system. For a background on the case and a proposal for reforming prosecutor authority, see Paul B. Wice, *Rubin 'Hurricane' Carter and the American Justice System* (New Brunswick, NJ: Rutgers University Press, 2000), 202.

22. Galbraith argues that market-based economies are not morally superior, but simply more pragmatic for modern scale and complexity than a command economy. His Keynesian solution of countervailing powers and progressive taxation aim to manage the vices of capitalism. John Kenneth Galbraith, *American Capitalism: The Concept of Countervailing Power*, in *The Affluent Society and Other Writings, 1952–1967* (New York: Library of America, 2010).

23. In addition, the minorities in *Hoosiers* (1986) are poor rural whites, in the same vein as *The Natural*; the coach played by Gene Hackman represents progressive standards introduced to a rural backwater (Jerry Goldsmith's musical score signals this modernization with synth chords). *Remember the Titans* (2000) and *Glory Road* (2006) also have influential coaches who shepherd the process of racial integration. The hero officials of these films affirm the worth of the public school as institutional agents of democracy.

24. Perplexingly, Müller dismisses Arendt's *Origins of Totalitarianism* as a historical study irrelevant to right-wing populism today. Yet his picture of the threat tracks very closely to Arendt's description of social movements that erode the state in favor of a select nation in opposition to it. Jan-Werner Müller, *Democracy Rules* (New York: Farrar, Straus and Giroux, 2021).

25. The American Disabilities Act of 1990 and the Supreme Court's same-sex marriage decision in *Obergefell v. Hodges* (2015) are two developments of multicultural policy that are represented figuratively in Hollywood sports movies by *Forrest Gump* (1994) and *Battle of the Sexes* (2017).

26. Gorski recalls Arthur Schlesinger's 1949 treatise *The Vital Center*, which has been criticized for leading liberalism's Cold War shift from positive state intervention to individual rights. Gorski adapts the idea to the contemporary United States in which a different set of centrifugal forces threaten the republic. Gorski, *American Covenant*, 223, 232. See also Rosenblatt, *Lost History of Liberalism*, 271.

27. Gorski, 228.

28. Muhammad Ali, quoted in Kevin Klose, "Ali in Moscow: 'All He [Brezhnev] Talked About Was Peace and Love of Humanity,'" *Washington Post*, June 20, 1978, A7.

Selected Bibliography

Adorno, Theodor. "Culture Industry Reconsidered." Translated by Anson G. Rabinbach, *New German Critique*, no. 6 (Autumn 1975): 12–19.

Alexander, Jeffrey C. *The Civil Sphere*. New York: Oxford University Press, 2006.

Alexander, Jeffrey C. *The Dark Side of Modernity*. Cambridge: Polity, 2013.

Alexander, Jeffrey C. *The Drama of Social Life*. Cambridge: Polity, 2017.

Ali, Muhammad, and Richard Durham. *The Greatest: My Own Story*. Edited by Toni Morrison. New York: Random, 1975.

Altman, Rick. *Film/Genre*. London: BFI, 1999.

Anderson, Benedict. *Imagined Communities: Reflections on the Origin and Spread of Nationalism*. London: Verso, 1983.

Arendt, Hannah. *The Human Condition*. Chicago: University of Chicago Press, 1958.

Arendt, Hannah. "On the Nature of Totalitarianism: An Essay in Understanding." In *Essays in Understanding: 1930–1954*, 328–360. New York: Harcourt Brace, 1994.

Arendt, Hannah. *On Revolution*. London: Faber and Faber, 1963.

Arendt, Hannah. *The Origins of Totalitarianism*. New York: Harcourt, Brace, 1951.

Aristotle. *Poetics*, translated by Anthony Kenny. New York: Oxford University Press, 2013.

Babington, Bruce. *The Sports Film: Games People Play*, Short Cuts. New York: Wallflower, 2014.

Baker, Aaron. *Contesting Identities: Sports in American Film*. Urbana: University of Illinois Press, 2003.

Bakhtin, Mikhail M. "The Bildungsroman and Its Significance in the History of Realism (Toward a Historical Typology of the Novel)." In *Speech Genres & Other Late Essays*, edited by Caryl Emerson and Michael Holquist, translated by Vern W. McGee, 10–59. Austin: University of Texas Press, 1987.

Bakhtin, Mikhail M. *Rabelais and His World*, translated by Hélène Iswolsky. Cambridge, MA: MIT Press, 1968.

Balkin, Jack M. *Living Originalism*. Cambridge, MA: Harvard University Press, 2014.

Becker, Christine. "Paul Newman." In *New Constellations: Movie Stars of the 1960s*, edited by Pamela Robertson Wojcik, 14–33. New Brunswick, NJ: Rutgers University Press, 2012.

Beiner, Ronald. *Civil Religion: A Dialogue in the History of Political Philosophy*. Cambridge: Cambridge University Press, 2010. https://doi.org/10.1017/CBO978051 1763144.

Bell, Daniel. *The Coming of Post-Industrial Society: A Venture in Social Forecasting*. New York: Basic Books, 1973.

Bellah, Robert. "Civil Religion in America." *Daedalus* 96, no. 1 (Winter 1967): 1–21.

Bernardi, Daniel, ed. *Classic Hollywood Classic Whiteness*. Minneapolis: University of Minnesota Press, 2001.

Bernardi, Daniel, ed. *The Persistence of Whiteness: Race and Contemporary Hollywood Cinema*. London: Routledge, 2008.

Billig, Michael. *Banal Nationalism*. London: Sage, 1995.

Biskind, Peter, and Barbara Ehrenreich. "Machismo and Hollywood's Working Class." In *American Media and Mass Culture: Left Perspectives*, 201–215. Berkeley: University of California Press, 1987.

Bly, Robert. *Iron John: A Book about Men*. Reading, MA: Addison-Wesley, 1990.

Bodnar, John. *Blue-Collar Hollywood: Liberalism, Democracy, and Working People in American Film*. Baltimore, MD: The Johns Hopkins University Press, 2003.

Bodnar, John. *Remaking America: Public Memory, Commemoration, and Patriotism in the Twentieth Century*. Princeton, NJ: Princeton University Press, 1992.

Bogle, Donald. *Toms, Coons, Mulattoes, Mammies and Bucks: An Interpretative History of Blacks in American Films*. 5th ed. New York: Bloomsbury Academic, 2016.

Boles Janet K., and Diane Long Hoeveler. "Introduction." In *Historical Dictionary of Feminism*, 1–20. Lanham, MD: Scarecrow, 1995.

Bonzel, Katharina. *National Pastimes: Cinema, Sports, and Nation*. Lincoln: University of Nebraska Press, 2020.

Boonin, David. *Should Race Matter? Unusual Answers to the Usual Questions*. Cambridge: Cambridge University Press, 2011.

Bordwell, David, and Noël Carroll, eds. *Post-Theory: Reconstructing Film Studies*. Madison: University of Wisconsin Press, 1996.

Bordwell, David, Janet Staiger, and Kristin Thompson. *The Classical Hollywood Cinema: Film Style and Mode of Production to 1960*. New York: Columbia University Press, 1987.

Boyd, Todd. *Am I Black Enough for You? Popular Culture from the 'Hood and Beyond*. Bloomington: Indiana University Press, 1997.

Briley, Ron. *The Baseball Film in Postwar America: A Critical Study, 1948–1962*. Jefferson, NC: McFarland, 2011.

Briley, Ron. "Basketball's Great White Hope and Ronald Reagan's America: Hoosiers (1986)." *Film & History: An Interdisciplinary Journal of Film and Television Studies* 35, no. 1 (2005): 12–19. https://doi.org/10.1353/flm.2005.0003.

Briley, Ron, Michael K. Schoenecke, and Deborah A. Carmichael, eds. *All-Stars and Movie Stars: Sports in Film and History*. Lexington: University Press of Kentucky, 2008. http://www.jstor.org/stable/j.ctt130hw2q.

Britton, Andrew. *Britton on Film: The Complete Film Criticism of Andrew Britton*. Edited by Barry Keith Grant. Detroit: Wayne State University Press, 2009.

Butler, Judith. *Gender Trouble*. New York: Routledge, 2007.

Campbell, Joseph. *The Hero with a Thousand Faces*. Princeton, NJ: Princeton University Press, 1992.

Carey, James W. *Communication as Culture: Essays on Media and Society*. New York: Routledge, 1992.

Carroll, Noël. *Mystifying Movies: Fads and Fallacies in Contemporary Film Theory*. New York: Columbia University Press, 1988.

Carroll, Noël. *A Philosophy of Mass Art*. New York: Oxford University Press, 1998.

Carter, James Earl. "Energy and National Goals: Address to the Nation." July 15, 1979. https://www.jimmycarterlibrary.gov/assets/documents/speeches/energy-crisis.phtml.

Cavell, Stanley. *Pursuits of Happiness: The Hollywood Comedy of Remarriage*. Cambridge, MA: Harvard University Press, 1984.

Chandler, James. *An Archaeology of Sympathy: The Sentimental Mode in Literature and Cinema*. Chicago: University of Chicago Press, 2013.

Comolli, Jean-Louis. *Cinema against Spectacle: Technique and Ideology Revisited*. Translated and edited by Daniel Fairfax. Amsterdam: Amsterdam University Press, 2015. http://library.oapen.org/handle/20.500.12657/32378.

Comolli, Jean-Louis, and Jean Narboni. "Cinéma/Idéologie/Critique (I)." *Cahiers du Cinéma*, October 1969, 11–15.

Connor, J. D. *The Studios after the Studios: Neoclassical Hollywood (1970–2010)*. Stanford, CA: Stanford University Press, 2015.

Cook, Pam. "Masculinity in Crisis?" *Screen* 23, no. 3–4 (Sep/Oct 1982): 39–46. https://doi.org/10.1093/screen/23.3-4.39.

Corson, Keith. *Trying to Get Over: African-American Directors after Blaxploitation, 1977–1986*. Austin: University of Texas Press, 2016.

Crenshaw, Kimberlé, Neil Gotanda, Gary Peller, and Kendall Thomas, eds. *Critical Race Theory: The Key Writings That Formed the Movement*. New York: The New Press, 1995.

Cripps, Thomas. *Black Film as Genre*. Bloomington: Indiana University Press, 1993. https://publish.iupress.indiana.edu/projects/black-film-as-genre.

Crosson, Séan. *Sport and Film*. London: Routledge, 2013.

Deleyto, Celestino. *From Tinseltown to Bordertown: Los Angeles on Film*. Detroit: Wayne State University Press, 2017.

Diawara, Manthia. "Black Spectatorship: Problems of Identification and Resistance." *Screen* 29, no. 4 (Autumn 1988): 66–79. https://doi.org/10.1093/screen/29.4.66.

DiPiero, Thomas. *White Men Aren't*. Durham, NC: Duke University Press, 2002.

Disset, Clémentine Tholas. "From Rocky (1976) to Creed (2015): 'Musculinity' and Modesty." *InMedia* 6 (2017). https://doi.org/10.4000/inmedia.849.

Doyle, William. *Aristocracy: A Very Short Introduction*. New York: Oxford University Press, 2010.

Dyer, Richard. *Stars*. London: British Film Institute, 1979.

Dyer, Richard. *White*. London: Routledge, 1997.

Dyerson, Mark. *Making the American Team: Sport, Culture, and the Olympic Experience*. Urbana: University of Illinois Press, 1998.

Dzenis, Anna. "Impressionist Extraordinaire: Michael Mann's *Ali*." *Senses of Cinema* 19 (March 2002). http://sensesofcinema.com/2002/feature-articles/ali/.

Dzenis, Anna. "Michael Mann's Cinema of Images." *Screening the Past* 14 (September 2002). http://www.screeningthepast.com/issue-14-first-release/michael-manns-cinema-of-images/.

Early, Gerald. *A Level Playing Field: African American Athletes and the Republic of Sports*. Cambridge, MA: Harvard University Press, 2011.

Early, Gerald. "Three Facts Essential to Understanding Muhammad Ali." *Washington Post*, June 5, 2016, Opinion.

Edwards, Harry. *The Revolt of the Black Athlete*. New York: Free Press, 1970.

Ehrat, Johannes. *Power of Scandal: Semiotic and Pragmatic in Mass Media*. Toronto: University of Toronto Press, 2011.

Ehrenreich, Barbara. *Dancing in the Streets: A History of Collective Joy*. New York: Holt, 2007.

Elsaesser, Thomas. "The Pathos of Failure: American Films in the 1970s: Notes on the Unmotivated Hero." In *The Last Great American Picture Show: New Hollywood Cinema in the 1970s*, edited by Noel King, Thomas Elsaesser, and Alexander Horwath, 279–292. Amsterdam: Amsterdam University Press, 2004. http://library.oapen.org/handle/20.500.12657/35116.

Emerson, Ralph Waldo. *Essays and Poems of Emerson*. Edited by Stuart Pratt Sherman. New York: Harcourt, Brace and Company, 1921. https://archive.org/details/essaysandpoemse00emergoog/.

Everett, Anna, ed. *Pretty People: Movie Stars of the 1990s*. New Brunswick, NJ: Rutgers University Press, 2012. http://www.jstor.org/stable/j.ctt5hj8m7.

Ezra, Michael. *Muhammad Ali: The Making of an Icon*. Philadelphia: Temple University Press, 2009.

Fanon, Frantz. *Black Skin, White Masks*. Translated by Charles Lam Markmann. London: Pluto Press, 2008.

Farred, Grant. "When Kings Were (Anti-?)Colonials: Black Athletes in Film." In *Sport in Films*, edited by Emma Poulton and Martin Roderick, 124–136. New York: Routledge, 2008.

Farrell, Warren. *The Liberated Man: Beyond Masculinity: Freeing Men and Their Relationships with Women*. New York: Random, 1974.

Fasteau, Marc Feigen. *The Male Machine*. New York: Delta, 1975.

Felski, Rita. *The Limits of Critique*. Chicago: University of Chicago Press, 2015.

Firestone, Shulamith. *The Dialectic of Sex: The Case for Feminist Revolution*. New York: William Morrow, 1970.

Fite, Gilbert C. *American Farmers: The New Minority*. Bloomington: Indiana University Press, 1981.

Florida, Richard. *The Rise of the Creative Class: And How It's Transforming Work, Leisure, Community and Everyday Life*. New York: Basic Books, 2004.

Fluegelman, Andrew, ed. *The New Games Book*. San Francisco: New Games Foundation, 1976.

Forney, Craig A. *The Holy Trinity of American Sports: Civil Religion in Football, Baseball, and Basketball*. Macon, GA: Mercer University Press, 2007.

Frank, Thomas. *The Conquest of Cool: Business Culture, Counterculture, and the Rise of Hip Consumerism*. Chicago: University of Chicago Press, 1998.

Fraser, Nancy. "Transnationalizing the Public Sphere: On the Legitimacy and Efficacy of Public Opinion in a Post-Westphalian World." *Theory, Culture & Society* 24, no. 4 (2007): 7–8.

Friedberger, Mark. *Farm Families and Change in 20th-Century America*. Lexington: University Press of Kentucky, 1988.

Frye, Northrop. *Anatomy of Criticism: Four Essays*. New York: Atheneum, 1968.

Gaine, Vincent M. *Existentialism and Social Engagement in the Films of Michael Mann*. London: Palgrave, 2011.

Galbraith, John Kenneth. *The Affluent Society and Other Writings, 1952–1967*. New York: Library of America, 2010.

Garrett, Greg. *A Long, Long Way: Hollywood's Unfinished Journey from Racism to Reconciliation*. New York: Oxford University Press, 2020.

Geertz, Clifford. "Deep Play: Notes on the Balinese Cockfight." *Daedalus* 101, no. 1, Myth, Symbol, and Culture (Winter, 1972): 1–37. https://www.jstor.org/stable/20024056.

Good, Howard. *Diamonds in the Dark: America, Baseball, and the Movies*. Lanham, MD: Scarecrow Press, 1997.

Gordon, Leah N. *From Power to Prejudice: The Rise of Racial Individualism in Midcentury America*. Chicago: University of Chicago Press, 2015.

Gordon, Tammy S. *The Spirit of 1976: Commerce, Community, and the Politics of Commemoration*. Amherst: University of Massachusetts Press, 2013.

Gorski, Philip. *American Covenant: A History of Civil Religion from the Puritans to the Present*. Princeton, NJ: Princeton University Press, 2017.

Graham, Carol. *Happiness for All? Unequal Hopes and Lives in Pursuit of the American Dream*. Princeton, NJ: Princeton University Press, 2017.

Grindon, Leger. "Body and Soul: The Structure of Meaning in the Boxing Film Genre." *Cinema Journal* 35, no. 4 (1996): 54–69. https://doi.org/10.2307/1225717.

Guerrero, Ed. *Framing Blackness: The African American Image in Film*. Philadelphia: Temple University Press, 1993.

Gunster, Shane. "Revisiting the Culture Industry Thesis: Mass Culture and the Commodity Form." *Cultural Critique* 45 (Spring 2000): 40–70. http://www.jstor.org/stable/1354367.

Gutmann, Amy, ed. *Multiculturalism: Examining the Politics of Recognition*. Princeton, NJ: Princeton University Press, 1994.

Habermas, Jürgen. *The Structural Transformation of the Public Sphere*, translated by Thomas Burger and Frederick Lawrence. Cambridge, MA: MIT Press, 1991.

Hanson, Helen, and Catherine O'Rawe, eds. *The Femme Fatale: Images, Histories, Contexts*. London: Palgrave, 2010. https://doi.org/10.1057/9780230282018.

Hauser, Thomas. *Muhammad Ali: His Life and Times*. New York: Simon & Schuster, 1991.

Hayot, Eric. *On Literary Worlds*. New York: Oxford University Press, 2012.

High, Steven. *Industrial Sunset: The Making of North America's Rust Belt, 1969–1984.* Toronto: University of Toronto Press, 2003.

Hirschi, Caspar. *The Origins of Nationalism: An Alternative History from Ancient Rome to Early Modern Germany.* Cambridge: Cambridge University Press, 2012.

Honohan, Iseult. *Civic Republicanism.* London: Routledge, 2002.

Horkheimer, Max, and Theodor W. Adorno. *Dialectic of Enlightenment,* translated by Edmund Jephcott. Stanford, CA: Stanford University Press, 2002.

Hoye, J. Matthew. "Neo-republicanism, Old Imperialism, and Migration Ethics." *Constellations* 24, no. 2 (2017): 157–159. https://doi.org/10.1111/1467-8675.12259.

Hughey, Matthew. *The White Savior Film.* Philadelphia: Temple University Press, 2014.

Hunter, Latham. "'What's *Natural* About It?': A Baseball Movie as Introduction to Key Concepts in Cultural Studies." *Film & History: An Interdisciplinary Journal of Film and Television Studies* 35, no. 2 (2005): 73–74.

Iwamura, Jane Naomi. "The Oriental Monk in American Popular Culture." In *Religion and Popular Culture in America,* edited by Jeffrey Mahan and Bruce Forbes, 25–43. Berkeley: University of California Press, 2000.

Jacobson, Matthew Frye. *Roots Too: White Ethnic Revival in Post–Civil Rights America.* Cambridge, MA: Harvard University Press, 2006.

Jameson, Frederic. "Reification and Utopia in Mass Culture." *Social Text* 1 (1979): 130–148. https://doi.org/10.2307/466409.

Jay, Martin. *The Dialectical Imagination: A History of the Frankfurt School and the Institute of Social Research, 1923–1950.* Berkeley: University of California Press, 1996.

Jowett, Garth. *Film: The Democratic Art.* Boston: Little, Brown and Co., 1976.

Kael, Pauline. "Stallone and Stahr." Review of *Rocky. The New Yorker,* November 29, 1976, 154, 157.

Kaepernick, Colin. "Transcript: Colin Kaepernick Addresses Sitting during National Anthem." *NinersWire,* August 28, 2016. https://ninerswire.usatoday.com/2016/08/28/transcript-colin-kaepernick-addresses-sitting-during-national-anthem/.

Kallen, Horace M. "Democracy versus the Melting Pot: A Study of American Nationality." *The Nation,* February 25, 1915. http://www.expo98.msu.edu/people/kallen.htm.

Kaye, Harvey E. *Male Survival: Masculinity without Myth.* New York: Grosset and Dunlap, 1974.

Kimmell, Michael. *Manhood in America: A Cultural History.* New York: Free Press, 1996.

Klose, Kevin. "Ali in Moscow: 'All He Talked about Was Peace and Love of Humanity.'" *Washington Post,* June 20, 1978. ProQuest Historical Newspapers.

Kracauer, Siegfried. *The Mass Ornament: Weimar Essays,* edited by Thomas Y. Levin. Cambridge, MA: Harvard University Press, 1995.

Kristeva, Julia. "The System and the Speaking Subject." *Times Literary Supplement* (October 12, 1973): 1249–1252.

Kymlicka, Will. *Liberalism, Community, and Culture.* Oxford: Oxford University Press, 1989.

Leab, Daniel J. "The Blue Collar Ethnic in Bicentennial America: *Rocky* (1976)." In *American History/American Film: Interpreting the Hollywood Image,* edited by John E. O'Connor and Martin A. Jackson, 257–272. New York: Ungar, 1979.

LeSueur, Stephen C., and Dean Rehberger. "*Rocky IV, Rambo II,* and the Place of the Individual in Modern American Society." *Journal of American Culture* 11, no. 2 (1988): 25–33.

Lieberman, Viridiana. *Sports Heroines on Film: A Critical Study of Cinematic Women Athletes, Coaches and Owners.* Jefferson, NC: McFarland, 2015.

Luedtke, Luther. "Ralph Waldo Emerson Envisions the 'Smelting Pot.'" *MELUS* 6, no. 2 (Summer, 1979): 3–14.

MacDowell, James. *Happy Endings in Hollywood Cinema: Cliché, Convention and the Final Couple.* Edinburgh: Edinburgh University Press, 2013.

Madison, Kelly J. "Legitimation Crisis and Containment: The 'Anti-Racist-White-Hero' Film." *Critical Studies in Media Communication* 16, no. 4 (December 1999): 399–416.

Maharaj, Gitanjali. "Talking Trash: Late Capitalism, Black (Re)Productivity, and Professional Basketball." *Social Text* 15, no. 1 (Spring 1997): 97–110.

Malamud, Bernard. *The Natural.* New York: Farrar, Straus and Giroux, 1952.

Mandelbaum, Michael. *The Meaning of Sports: Why Americans Watch Baseball, Football, and Basketball and What They See When They Do.* New York: Public Affairs, 2004.

Markovits, Daniel. *The Meritocracy Trap: How America's Foundational Myth Feeds Inequality, Dismantles the Middle Class, and Devours the Elite.* New York: Penguin, 2019.

McCrisken, Trevor B., and Andrew Pepper. *American History and Contemporary Hollywood Film.* Edinburgh: Edinburgh University Press, 2005. http://www.jstor.org/stable/10.3366/j.ctt1r21c6.

Millet, Kate. *Sexual Politics.* Garden City, NY: Doubleday, 1970.

Mittell, Jason. *Genre and Television: From Cop Shows to Cartoons in American Culture.* New York: Routledge, 2004.

Montesquieu. *De l'esprit des lois,* in *Œuvres complètes,* vol. 2, edited by Roger Caillois, 227–995. Paris: Bibliothèque de la Pléiade, 1951.

Montesquieu, Charles Louis de Secondat. *The Spirit of Laws.* Vol. 1 of *The Complete Works of M. de Montesquieu.* London: T. Evans, 1777. https://oll.libertyfund.org/titles/montesquieu-complete-works-vol-1-the-spirit-of-laws.

Mulvey, Laura. "Visual Pleasure and Narrative Cinema." *Screen* 16, no. 3 (Autumn 1975) 6–18. https://doi.org/10.1093/screen/16.3.6.

Nabulsi, Karma, and Stuart White, eds., *Radical Republicanism: Recovering the Tradition's Popular Heritage.* New York: Oxford University Press, 2020.

Nadel, Alan. *Flatlining on the Field of Dreams: Cultural Narratives in the Films of President Reagan's America.* New Brunswick, NJ: Rutgers University Press, 1997.

Nichols, Jack. *Men's Liberation: A New Definition of Masculinity.* New York: Penguin, 1975.

North, Joseph. *Literary Criticism: A Concise Political History.* Cambridge, MA: Harvard University Press, 2017.

Noverr, Douglas A. "The Ballpark: Out of the Shadows and Indistinct Background and into the Heart of the Baseball Film." In *Locales in American Film,* Vol. 4 of *Beyond the Stars: Studies in American Popular Film,* edited by Paul Loukides and Linda K. Fuller, 172–182. Bowling Green, OH: Bowling Green University Popular Press, 1993.

Nystrom, Derek. *Hard Hats, Rednecks, and Macho Men: Class in 1970s American Cinema.* New York: Oxford University Press, 2009.

Oriard, Michael. "Muhammad Ali: The Hero in the Age of Mass Media." In *Muhammad Ali: The People's Champ,* edited by Elliott J. Gorn, 5–23. Urbana: University of Illinois Press, 1995.

Orlick, Terry. *The Cooperative Sports and Games Book: Challenge without Competition.* New York: Pantheon, 1978.

Patterson, Orlando. *Freedom: Freedom in the Making of Western Culture.* New York: Basic, 1991.

Peirce, Charles S. *Collected Papers of Charles Sanders Peirce.* Edited by Charles Hartshorne and Paul Weiss. Cambridge, MA: Belknap Press, 1965.

Pettit, Philip. *Republicanism: A Theory of Freedom and Government.* Oxford: Clarendon Press, 1997.

Piketty, Thomas. *Capital in the Twenty-First Century.* Translated by Arthur Goldhammer. Cambridge, MA: Harvard University Press, 2014.

Pippin, Robert B. *Hollywood Westerns and American Myth: The Importance of Howard Hawks and John Ford for Political Philosophy.* New Haven, CT: Yale University Press, 2012.

Pippin, Robert B. *Philosophy by Other Means: The Arts in Philosophy and Philosophy in the Arts.* Chicago: University of Chicago Press, 2021.

Postel, Charles. *The Populist Vision.* New York: Oxford University Press, 2007.

Powell, Larry, and Tom Garrett, *The Films of John G. Avildsen: "Rocky," "The Karate Kid," and Other Underdogs*. Jefferson, NC: McFarland, 2014.

Prager, Jeffrey. "Moral Integration and Political Inclusion: A Comparison of Durkheim's and Weber's Theories of Democracy." *Social Forces* 59, no. 4 (June 1981): 920. https://doi.org/10.2307/2577974.

Prince, Stephen, ed. *American Cinema of the 1980s: Themes and Variations*. New Brunswick, NJ: Rutgers University Press, 2007.

Prince, Stephen. *A New Pot of Gold: Hollywood under the Electronic Rainbow, 1980–1989*. New York: Scribner's, 2000.

Rabaka, Reiland. *The Négritude Movement: W. E. B. Dubois, Leon Damas, Aimé Césaire, Leopold Senghor, Frantz Fanon*. Lanham, MD: Lexington Books, 2015.

Rancière, Jacques. *La Fable Cinématographique*. Paris: Seuil, 2001.

Rawls, John. *A Theory of Justice*. Cambridge, MA: Belknap Press, 1971.

Rayner, Jonathan. *The Cinema of Michael Mann: Vice and Vindication*. Directors' Cuts. London: Wallflower, 2013.

Reid, Mark A. *Redefining Black Film*. Berkeley: University of California Press, 1993.

Reemtsma, Jan Philipp. *More Than a Champion: The Style of Muhammad Ali*, translated by John E. Woods. New York: Knopf, 1998.

Robbins, Bruce. "Fashion Conscious Phenomenon." Review of *Critique and Postcritique*, eds. Elizabeth S. Anker and Rita Felski. *American Book Review* 38, no. 5 (July/August 2017): 5–6. http://doi.org/10.1353/abr.2017.0078.

Rodríguez-Ruiz, David. "Mann's Biopics and the Methodology of Philosophy: *Ali* and *The Insider*." In *The Philosophy of Michael Mann*, edited by Sanders Steven, Aeon J. Skoble, and Palmer R. Barton, 244–245. Lexington: University Press of Kentucky, 2014. http://www.jstor.org/stable/j.ctt5vkktc.18.

Rogin, Michael. "Blackface, White Noise: The Jewish Jazz Singer Finds His Voice." *Critical Inquiry* 18, no. 3 (1992): 417–453. http://www.jstor.org/stable/1343811.

Roosevelt, Theodore. *The Strenuous Life: Essays and Addresses*. New York: Century, 1900. http://www.bartleby.com/58/1.html.

Rosen, Philip, ed. *Narrative, Apparatus, Ideology: A Film Theory Reader*. New York: Columbia University Press, 1986.

Rosenblatt, Helena. *The Lost History of Liberalism: From Ancient Rome to the Twenty-First Century*. Princeton, NJ: Princeton University Press, 2019.

Rousseau, Jean-Jacques. *A Letter from M. Rousseau of Geneva to M. d'Alembert of Paris, Concerning the Effects of Theatrical Entertainments on the Manners of Mankind*. London: J. Nourse, 1759.

Rushton, Richard. *The Politics of Hollywood Cinema: Popular Film and Contemporary Political Theory*. New York: Palgrave, 2013.

Samuel, Lawrence R. *The American Dream: A Cultural History*. Syracuse, NY: Syracuse University Press, 2012.

Sanders, M. Elizabeth. *Roots of Reform: Farmers, Workers, and the American State, 1877–1917*. Chicago: University of Chicago Press, 1999.

Sarris, Andrew. "Why Sports Movies Don't Work." *Film Comment* 16, no. 6 (Nov./Dec. 1980): 49–53.

Saussy, Haun. *The Ethnography of Rhythm: Orality and Its Technologies*. New York: Fordham University Press, 2016.

Schmidt, James. "The 'Eclipse of Reason' and the End of the Frankfurt School in America." *New German Critique* 100 (Winter 2007): 47–76. http://www.jstor.org/stable/27669187.

Skinner, Quentin. *Liberty before Liberalism*. Cambridge: Cambridge University Press, 1998.

Slater, Phil. *Origin and Significance of the Frankfurt School: A Marxist Perspective*. London: Routledge, 2020.

Smukler, Maya Montañez. *Liberating Hollywood: Women Directors and the Feminist Reform of 1970s American Cinema*. Rutgers University Press, 2018.

Streible, Dan. *Fight Pictures: A History of Boxing and Early Cinema*. Berkeley: University of California Press, 2008.

Swartz, David R. *Moral Minority: The Evangelical Left in an Age of Conservatism*. Philadelphia: University of Pennsylvania Press, 2012.

Synnott, Anthony. *Rethinking Men: Heroes, Villains, and Victims*. Farnham, UK: Ashgate, 2009.

Taft, Chloe E. *From Steel to Slots: Casino Capitalism in the Postindustrial City*. Cambridge, MA: Harvard University Press, 2016.

Taylor, Charles. *Hegel*. Cambridge: Cambridge University Press, 1975.

Taylor, Charles. *A Secular Age*. Cambridge, MA: Harvard University Press, 2007.

Tudor, Deborah V. *Hollywood's Vision of Team Sports: Heroes, Race, and Gender*. New York: Garland, 1997.

Valdivia, Angharad N. "Stereotype of Transgression? Rosie Perez in Hollywood Film." *Sociological Quarterly* 39, no. 3 (1998): 393–408. https://doi.org/10.1111/j.1533-8525.1998.tb00510.x.

Vantornhout, Kris. "Film Analysis of *A League of Their Own*: Myths and Portrayals of Heroines in Sport." Master's thesis, San Jose State University, 1995. https://doi.org/10.31979/etd.vw78-gydx.

Vera, Hernán, and Andrew Gordon, *Screen Saviors: Hollywood Fictions of Whiteness*. Lanham, MD: Rowman and Littlefield, 2003.

Villa, Dana. "Genealogies of Total Domination: Arendt, Adorno, and Auschwitz." *New German Critique* 100 (Winter 2007): 1–45. http://www.jstor.org/stable/27669186.

Webb, Lawrence. *The Cinema of Urban Crisis: Seventies Film and the Reinvention of the City*. Amsterdam: Amsterdam University Press, 2014.

Weber, Max. *On Charisma and Institution Building: Selected Papers*. Edited by S. N. Eisenstadt. Chicago: University of Chicago Press, 1968.

Welsch, Wolfgang. "Sport Viewed Aesthetically, and Even as Art?" In *The Aesthetics of Everyday Life*, edited by Andrew Light and Jonathan M. Smith, 135–149. New York: Columbia University Press, 2005.

White, G. Edward. *The Eastern Establishment and the Western Experience: The West of Frederic Remington, Theodore Roosevelt, and Owen Wister*. New Haven, CT: Yale University Press, 1968.

Wice, Paul B. *Rubin "Hurricane" Carter and the American Justice System*. New Brunswick, NJ: Rutgers University Press, 2000.

Wiedenfeld, Grant. "Multicultural American Heroes: Reading the Obama-Era Biopics of Jackie Robinson and Jesse Owens through the Lens of American Civil Religion." In *Sport, Film and National Culture*, edited by Seán Crosson, 48–63. Milton Park, UK: Routledge, 2020. https://doi.org/10.4324/9780429327018-5.

Wildermuth, Mark E. *Blood in the Moonlight: Michael Mann and Information Age Cinema*. Jefferson, NC: McFarland, 2005.

Wilkerson, Isabel. *Caste: The Origins of Our Discontent*. New York: Random, 2020.

Wollen, Peter. *Signs and Meaning in the Cinema*. Bloomington: Indiana University Press, 1972.

Wood, Robin. *Hollywood from Vietnam to Reagan*, rev. ed. New York: Columbia University Press, 2003.

Wright, Julie Lobalzo. "The All-American Golden Boy: Robert Redford, Blond Hair and Masculinity in Hollywood." *Celebrity Studies* 7, no. 1 (2016): 69–82. https://doi.org/10.1080/19392397.2016.1104895.

Zamora, Daniel, and Michael C. Behrent, eds. *Foucault and Neoliberalism*. Cambridge: Polity Press, 2016.

Index

For the benefit of digital users, indexed terms that span two pages (e.g., 52–53) may, on occasion, appear on only one of those pages.

Figures are indicated by *f* following the page number